W9-ACO-392

Living Psychology

AN EXPERIMENTAL APPROACH

Living
AN
EXPERIMENTAL
APPROACH

Psychology

Gerald L. Hershey ▪ James O. Lugo

Both of Department of Psychology, Fullerton Junior College, Fullerton, California, and Educational and Psychological Associates, Inc.

The Macmillan Company ▪ Collier-Macmillan Limited, London

First Printing

Library of Congress catalog card number: 78–87892

The Macmillan Company

Collier-Macmillan Canada, Ltd., Toronto, Ontario

Printed in the United States of America

For Their Love and Patience We Dedicate This Book to:

Our Wives:	Shirley and	Maria
and		
Our Sons:	Bruce	James
	Dale	Tony
	James	Johnny
And Our Parents		

Preface

More and more society is turning to psychology to answer some of the serious human problems of our day and age. The public already is convinced of the benefits of using psychological findings in solving such diverse problems as mental illness, human factors in space exploration, and student counseling in the schools, as well as in helping persons become more self-actualizing.

As college students enroll in their first psychology class they bring with them many preconceived notions of how modern-day psychology can solve many of man's problems. Certainly one of the goals of an introductory course is to show students that, although psychology as a science and profession can offer possible solutions to some of man's problems, it is still a young and growing science with many areas of human behavior in need of much more research.

Yet we feel that there is much that modern-day psychology has to offer the beginning psychology student that may help him as he develops into a unique individual and a participating citizen in our fast-moving society.

Problem

For a long time we have known that there was a problem: trying to teach an introductory psychology course to students with a wide diversity of backgrounds, motivation, achievement potentials, and interest levels. Over the years it has become clear that a specialized introductory text was needed to take more of these factors into account.

METHODS USED IN DEVELOPING A TEXTBOOK TO HELP SOLVE THE PROBLEM

In an informal survey among many of our introductory psychology students the following comments were made regarding what they want to see included in a psychology textbook; appearing alongside these suggestions is a list of the ways that our text attempts to take into account these factors.

Student Suggestions	Methods Used in Trying to Solve the Problem
"Write a book that is meaningful to my particular major."	Through style of writing and encouraging the student to apply the concepts presented to his own present and future life.
"Write a book that is interesting so that I will *want* to read it."	Through the personal writing style, use of actual student quotes, beginning chapter sections designed to build interest ("Prelude" and "Why Is It Important?").
"Write a book that is personally meaningful so that it helps me with some of my present problems."	"Student's Viewpoint," examples from our own students' experiences; application section, "Living with Yourself."
"Write a book that is not written just for potential psychologists; for many of us, this will be our only exposure to psychology."	Each chapter applies material to living with yourself, others, and society.
"Write a book that may get me so excited about psychology that after the course, I may even want to do additional reading on my own (without a grade!)."	Psychologist cameos introduce student to some of the important and stimulating men in the field today; extensive chapter bibliographies with both paperback and hardcover sections.
"Write a book that may help me with some of my learning, study, and reading problems."	Learning and problem-solving chapters apply research to school situations. Has built-in learning and study aids, e.g., chapter outlines, intermediate and final chapter summaries, on-the-spot vocabulary, and chapter study guides at the beginning of each chapter.
"Write a book that may help me in my future work and family life experiences."	Every chapter has an applied section on living with yourself, others, and society. Book has "living in the world of tomorrow" orientation.
"Write a book that may help me understand my parents and my past better, so that I can live more effectively in the world of tomorrow."	Past, present, and future orientation of text helps student relate his present behavior to his past early experiences.

Results

In more general terms, we asked ourselves such questions as the following: What does modern-day psychology have to offer the student of today as he enrolls in his first (and for many, his last) introductory psychology class?

Does modern-day psychology have any practical answers to offer the student as he faces the problem of (1) living in a society with rapid technological and social changes that often result in personal feelings of alienation and aloneness; (2) living in a shrinking world where nations are becoming more interdependent; and (3) living with himself and his future family as he seeks to define his role as father, worker, and citizen in the community and the world of tomorrow?

The approach of *Living Psychology*, then, is based on an attempt to provide some partial answers to these and other basic questions that many students are asking. To summarize, the *Living Psychology* approach is:

1. A systematic and thorough study of the academic needs and characteristics of our general psychology students. Included among these are studies of the reading and conceptual skills; personal problems of students; immediate and long-range life goals; present conceptions of what psychology is; and motivational techniques that help students become involved in and see meaning in psychological theory and research in relation to their own lives.

2. An emphasis on the uniqueness and dynamic growth potential inherent in every individual.

3. An emphasis on theory and research that has meaningful and practical significance for the student as he prepares for his future roles as a unique, creative, and growing individual; a husband or wife; a parent; a worker; or a citizen in his community, nation, and the world.

4. An attempt to encourage students to use problem-solving models that will aid them as they face stress and conflict in everyday living.

5. An attempt to encourage the student to appreciate better how he developed characteristic ways of behaving (including how he expresses emotions, how he perceives the world, how he solves problems, why certain motives are more important to him than others, and so forth) so that he is aware of his uniqueness.

6. A demonstration of how we learn many of our ways of behaving and—equally important—how human behavior can and does change over time.

7. A demonstration to students that they can learn to relate various theories, concepts, and research findings to live more effectively with themselves, others, and society in the past, present, and future.

8. Hopefully, the stimulation of students' interest in further individual study and reading in some areas of psychology *after* the formal course is over.

9. An attempt, through a personal writing style, to help students see some of the relationships between theories of psychology and their implications for practice in their own lives.

10. An attempt to develop within the student not only a historical perspective about his own and others' behavior (how through learning techniques our behavior is shaped), but also a "future-oriented" perspective to help him realize his role as a responsible and growing citizen in the world of tomorrow.

11. A more positive emphasis throughout the book, focusing on the mentally healthy person as a model to follow for developing into the kind of person needed to cope with the realities of the world in the next fifty years.

12. An applied interdisciplinary emphasis showing the contributions of such fields as anthropology, sociology, psychiatry and medicine, physiology, philosophy, and statistics to a better understanding of human behavior.

13. Whenever possible, an emphasis on human rather than animal studies in terms of helping the student develop a more sound and scientifically based understanding of man's behavior.

For a much more thorough discussion of the underlying assumptions, specific goals of the text, and the text organization, the reader is encouraged to read the Prologue before beginning with Chapter 1.

DISCUSSION OF RESULTS

The results of our problem-solving efforts (this textbook and the specialized features that we have included) are actually the accumulation of many associations with our students, colleagues, and former teachers. We would like, at this time, to give thanks to some of them.

To the many students who have become involved with us and our classes, we owe a great debt of appreciation for helping to give us a better understanding of young people today (and also of ourselves).

To our former teachers who have influenced and inspired us, we can only say "thank you for being so human." We make special mention of the following professors: Erich Fromm, University of Mexico and New York University; Gardner Murphy, The Menninger Clinic; James Bugental, James C. Coleman, John P. Seward, and Waldo Fergason of the University of California at Los Angeles; Henry C. Smith, Donald M. Johnson, and Don Hamacheck of Michigan State University; Ben Thompson and Loraine Shepard of Antioch College; and John Krumboltz, Stanford University.

To those who have taken their time to make critical comments and offer invaluable suggestions as the manuscript developed, we say thank you. Of special mention are the following: Velma Duvall, East Los Angeles College; F. A. Fredenburgh, Miami-Dade Junior College; W. S. Hall, New York; James McCamey, San Diego; and Richard A. Rasor, American River College.

To some of our former students who have helped us with various library and clerical tasks, we offer our appreciation and wish to give them credit at this time: Constance Kirkpatrick, Gary Smith, Paul Harbitz, and Linda Dye. Special thanks are given to Larry Till for his special efforts and sustained interest; also for his help in preparing and outlining the Appendix on physiological psychology.

Special thanks are also due to "Rusty" Davis and William O. Heckman, Fullerton Junior College, for their advice and encouragement.

For their patience, faith, and many fine suggestions, we offer our final note of appreciation to our Psychology Editors from The Macmillan Company: John H. Quigley and Thomas P. McConahay.

Fullerton, California

GERALD L. HERSHEY
JAMES O. LUGO

Contents

Prologue

Sometimes it seems as if life has become a "play" and we are all actors playing a part. The feelings seem to be gone. When you walk down the street, and you meet someone you know, you ask him, "How are you, Jim?" He smiles and says, "Just fine!" And you respond by saying, "I'm just great too!" We all play our parts, and hide our feelings. That's okay because we can't go around griping. But how often are we ourselves these days?

As the preceding statement, made by one of our students, suggests, man may be phony and life hardly worth the effort. Man not only seems to be playing games, but the games appear to be getting him into trouble. Every year more people are killed by crimes of violence. More people commit suicide than ever before. More people are using alcohol as an escape. The use of drugs to keep happy or to relax is becoming an accepted practice. Racial hatred is increasing.

As a result, psychologists and sociologists have been spending more and more time attempting to understand why so many are living lives of unhappiness and pain. One pattern emerging from their studies suggests possible reasons for so much of this human suffering and, more important, offers ways to prevent at least some of it.

Man, it seems, is very similar to other animals in many biological respects: He has to eat, he has to be protected from the elements, and he expresses emotions. At the same time, man differs from the other organisms: He can express feelings and emotions in many different ways with the help of his ability to reason and think.

Now, it seems that something happens to this intelligent expression of feelings and emotions when people live in large groups such as cities and urban centers, bringing about the depersonalization and dehumanization of man. Man somehow forgets that he is human—which, among other things, means that he has the ability to express basic inner feelings and emotions. Man forgets how to cry or how to laugh or how to love. You might say he becomes a machine.

Some social scientists have used the term *alienation* to describe such a state. Erich Fromm (1955), for example, writes: "Alienation as we find it in modern society is almost total; it pervades the relationship of man to his work, to the things he consumes, to his fellows, and to himself." (p. 124)

1

Eric and Mary Josephson (1962) express it this way:

> Confused as to his place in the scheme of a world growing each day closer yet more impersonal, more densely populated yet in face-to-face relations more dehumanized; a world appealing ever more widely for his concern and sympathy with unknown masses of men, yet fundamentally alienating him even from his next door neighbor, today western man has become mechanized, routinized, made comfortable as an object; but in the profound sense displaced and thrown off balance as a subjective creator and power. (p. 10)

The point is that we are also very concerned about the serious results of alienation. We are concerned when we see so many of our students only half alive, responding to only a small fraction of the beauty and excitement in the world, and using only a fraction of their potential. So we have attempted to write a text that has relevance and significance not so much for students who will become psychologists or social scientists, but more for those planning careers in other areas. We hope it will have special significance to all who will be getting married and raising families and to all who will be contributing members of their community, the nation, and the world.

UNDERLYING ASSUMPTIONS

Certain beliefs undergird our approach. We would like to share these with you now.

1. We believe man is not doomed to a life of alienation and suffering even in a time of rapid population increase and technological advances.
2. We believe man has far more potential than he realizes.
3. We believe man can learn how to utilize much of this potential.
4. We believe psychology has much to offer man as he seeks to develop himself.
5. We believe there are certain basic concepts, theories, and research findings (some admittedly tentative) offering ways of relating to oneself and the world that can promote the full growth of the individual.
6. We believe the understanding and application of these concepts, theories, and research findings can profoundly reduce the amount of individual and group suffering we see in the world today.
7. We believe college students have the ability to grasp these basic concepts, theories, and research findings and apply them to themselves.
8. We believe it is even possible to get students excited enough about these ideas to do further reading and study on their own after the course is over, perhaps for the rest of their lives.

GOALS

We would also like to share with you our goals—what specifically this text attempts to do. We want you to understand yourself and others, and to be knowledgeable about certain principles and theories of modern psychology.

Equally important, we want you to learn to think more effectively. And we want to stimulate you too. Let's look at each of these goals in a little more detail.

UNDERSTANDING YOURSELF. It seems to us that a beginning psychology course should cause each student to see himself differently and, as a result, view his own behavior more realistically. We are aware of the dangers involved in "sidewalk psychoanalysis," so we certainly don't pretend that this book will help you solve all your personal problems. If it simply helps you to accept yourself, we will feel that our goal has been achieved.

UNDERSTANDING OTHERS. Those who understand and accept themselves tend to be able to relate more effectively to others. Therefore, one of our goals is to help you view other people in a more objective manner and to enable you to communicate with them more satisfactorily.

UNDERSTANDING PRINCIPLES OF MODERN PSYCHOLOGY. Psychology is now one of the most rapidly developing of the social sciences. Research is conducted in many different areas, from pigeon's playing ping-pong, and the learning behavior of a sow bug, to the selection of the most psychologically qualified astronauts. Over twenty-five journals present reports of such research in psychology. For college students, however, these publications are often too technical; it is difficult to understand just what the researchers have found. Here in this book we summarize the results of numerous research studies in words that make sense to students. We have been selective, so all results reported have direct relevance to you.

UNDERSTANDING SOME THEORIES IN MODERN PSYCHOLOGY. A theory in psychology is a tentative explanation of some aspects or variables of human behavior. Even though there are different theories that are by definition tentative, the authors feel there are some that are more important for beginning students to be exposed to and work with. These will be stated and explained in the text, again in language for the student rather than the professional.

Figure 0–1
This book is based on the principle that the past, the present, and the future compose the inseparable strands of living.

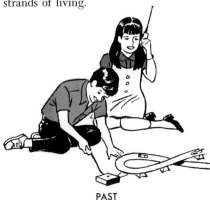

PAST

PRESENT

FUTURE

UNDERSTANDING HOW TO THINK MORE EFFECTIVELY. The authors are convinced that a by-product of the study of psychology is the discovery of approaches to the solving of problems. Problems might range from how to understand another person to how to study for a final exam. We'll introduce you to strategies for tackling various problems that you now face or may face in the future.

STIMULATION FOR FURTHER STUDY. Indirectly, our major goal is to pass on to you some of the real excitement and enthusiasm we feel about modern-day psychology. We want to increase your desire to do further reading and study on your own, for your benefit and mankind's.

ORGANIZATION

While writing this book, we continuously asked ourselves what would be personally meaningful to college students. In fact, this question pervaded our entire thinking, even about how to organize the text. Thus, this book begins with you, the student, as you are. It then moves back to your past. Later it will bring you ahead to the future. Table 0-1 gives you the picture. Look at it now.

Table 0-1
Text Organization

I. Understanding Yourself (Immediate Present)
Chapters
  1. The Healthy Personality
  2. Effective Learning
  3. Effective Thinking and Problem Solving

II. Understanding the Development of Human Behavior (Past to Present)
  4. Childhood and Adolescence
  5. The Why of Behavior
  6. Understanding Emotions
  7. Understanding Perception

III. The Dynamics of Human Behavior
  8. Understanding Personality
  9. Coping with Normal Personality Problems
  10. Understanding the Unhealthy Personality
  11. Diagnosis, Treatment, and Prevention of Unhealthy Personalities

IV. Understanding Your Future (Present to Future)
  12. Challenges of Tomorrow

When we asked which relevant areas of life students would want to have discussed in detail, the following were emphasized:

1. Living with yourself

2. Living with others

3. Living with society

We have tried to relate each chapter of the text to the preceding material, so that you will be able to see the implications of what is personally important to you. We cannot possibly discuss the implications for all problems. We hope that you will be able to apply the general principles presented here to your unique life situation. As a result, it is hoped that you will be able to lead a more productive life as a full participant in the world of today as well as tomorrow.

References

Fromm, E. *The sane society.* New York: Holt, Rinehart & Winston, 1955.
Josephson, E., and Mary (eds.). *Man alone.* New York: Dell, 1962.

Part I Understanding Yourself

In this section the focus will be on you in your immediate present situation as a unique, creative, and growing individual seeking answers to such questions as: Who am I? What are my potentialities? Where am I going? How can I more effectively learn all there is to learn? How can I cope with or more efficiently solve the many problems I face in my daily interactions with myself, others, and society in general?

More specifically, in Chapter 1 you will be introduced to some new and exciting research regarding healthy personalities. From this discussion the authors hope that you will better realize the tremendous potential for growth that we all have. Furthermore, they hope it will offer some goals for you to work toward as you develop and grow during your lifetime. And, finally, it may help you realize that you are not a "totally fixed personality," set into a mold by your parents and society, but that you are a "dynamic, growing personality" in a continual process of growth—that you are and can become a free individual to do with your life what *you* feel is right.

Since most of you are now undergoing drastic changes as a result of learned experiences, especially in school, in Chapter 2 the authors discuss the learning process and how you can make your own growth through learning much more enjoyable and efficient.

In Chapter 3 the authors introduce you to a problem-solving model that should help you approach more effectively and creatively the many daily situations that you face in living with yourself, others, and society in general.

Chapter 1 The Healthy Personality

Chapter Outline

Study Guide

To get the most value from Chapter 1 take the following steps in reading. Practice these steps as you read.

PREVIEW
Before reading the chapter, read the prelude, the chapter heads, cameos, the intermediate summaries, and the final summary. By doing so you will better understand the purposes of the chapter.

CHECK MARKS
As you read the chapter, checkmark parts that you do not understand. After reading the chapter, go back and reread each part checked. Because you will

Figure 1-1
Each chapter has a study guide designed to help you to read with greater comprehension and to prepare more effectively for examinations.

Photo by Bruce Jacobson

know more, you may now be able to comprehend. If not, ask your instructor for help.

NEW WORDS
Check the meaning of new words. (The definition is given in brackets after the word, in each case.)

SUMMARIES
Before reading the intermediate summaries again, look away and think about your own summaries. Write them down. Doing this will improve your retention of the material read.

REVIEW
Reread each of the summaries. The main ideas are found in the topic headings. Rephrase all of these in the form of questions. Test yourself to see if you can answer them satisfactorily.

Prelude

As was noted in the prologue, the authors believe that psychology has much to offer man in helping him solve at least some of the problems brought about by alienation. More specifically, believe psychology has a great deal to offer you in becoming a better person. The discussions with you will therefore begin with an introduction of some new and exciting research that is currently being conducted on some very special people—some who are not alienated and alone—who are, in fact, leading lives of fulfillment.

For too long, most psychologists have stressed the sick, the poorly adjusted, and the mentally ill. This approach has been too one-sided; it has ignored the healthy. The person with a healthy personality enjoys just being alive, takes pleasure in helping others to make their dreams come true, and adds zest and enthusiasm to each human adventure.

In this chapter, the authors will discuss these healthy persons in greater detail. As you read and think, keep these questions in mind: Who are the healthy people? What are they like? How did they develop their healthy personalities? Is it possible for each of us to develop healthier personalities? If so, how can we become our own architects in constructing a better life?

Students' Viewpoints

There is a very good chance that you know some mentally healthy persons. These people tend to stand out from others in special ways. In a study of our college students' descriptions of mentally healthy persons, the statements in the next paragraphs were typical.

One student had this to say:

Basically, I consider her mentally healthy because of her aliveness, optimism, love of life, and general good nature. I like her attitude for living. She puts her heart in everything she does; she is alert and aware of the most minute details; if she fails or falls short, she tries it again or comes up with a new approach. She has an active, sharp mind and an equally sharp sense of humor. Not only does she have a wit but she looks (or tries to look) at most things with a sense of humor. In addition, she's physically healthy, which I feel is an important factor. She is intelligent and willing to learn. She will give most anything a try and yet has enough common sense to know when she shouldn't. She can talk and listen, give and take and with the slightest cue—respond. She's alive!

Another student put it this way:

She is a very likable person; everyone who knows her likes her. She has a very pleasing personality. The reason why I think she is so likeable is because whenever she meets a person she thinks the best of him that she can. She never judges a person by the first meeting. She always has nice things to say about a person, too. I have never heard her say something bad about a person since I've known her. Her general outlook on life is very good. She loves nature and the out-of-doors' life.

WHY IS IT IMPORTANT?

What relevance do these comments have for your life, you might very well be asking at this point. Basically, it is important for you to become familiar with the nature of the mentally healthy for the following very practical reasons:

1. These people tend to enjoy life more.
2. They respond to many more dimensions of life.
3. They have deep and lasting human relations with others.
4. They tend to lead happier, self-fulfilling lives.
5. Their families and children tend to be happier.
6. They perform better in their work—whether it be at school or on the job.

In short, healthy people tend to get much more out of life. You, too, can move in these directions, for the results of *research* (use of the scientific method) indicate that it is possible for people to learn to become healthy persons. Thus, it is significant for all of us to consider the research and *theories* (reasonable, tentative explanations) about these people.

BASIC THEORY AND RESEARCH

Who Are the Mentally Healthy or Self-Actualizing People?

(*Note:* The authors use the terms *mentally healthy* and *self-actualizing* interchangeably.)

Much of the research on mentally healthy persons has focused on very famous, highly productive people. Thomas Jefferson, Walt Whitman, William James, Spinoza, Albert Einstein, and others have been used as examples. You might be saying to yourself that because you are not capable of performing as these people have, this research is of no value to you. However, the research does in fact have direct relevance for you; you do not have to be a genius to become a mentally healthy person.

It should be emphasized at this point that becoming a mentally healthy person is not an either/or matter. That is, one day you are mentally unhealthy and the next day you do something and you suddenly become mentally healthy. The concept of mental health is discussed as a matter of degree, rather than as a black and white dichotomy. The subsequent illustration should give you a visual picture of this continuous relationship from mental health to mental illness.

Figure 1-2
How Psychologists View Mental Health and Illness. The road from mental illness to mental health consists of three over-lapping areas on a continuum (an unbroken line). Therefore, we can speak of degress of health or illness rather than refer to a person's being mentally healthy *or* ill.

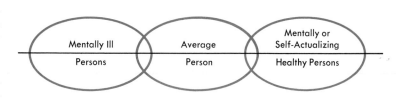

It can be seen that all of us differ in our position along this line. Where would you place yourself? We will further discuss this question in Chapter 10 when we discuss how psychologists define mental illness.

One of the first *psychologists* (one who applies the scientific method to describe and predict behavior) to study mentally healthy persons was Dr. Abraham Maslow (see cameo). Much of Dr. Maslow's research has been focused on extremely mentally healthy persons or, as he calls them: self-actualizing persons (one who is in the process of developing all his abilities and potentials). These people are in fact very rare; however, these unusual men and women can serve as models for us, and the research can provide goals toward which we all can strive.

How Do Psychologists Study Mentally Healthy People?

Now let us look at how Maslow conducted his original research. It should be pointed out that his research differed from traditional research methods in that it was *highly subjective* (having to do with personal thoughts and feelings). Maslow (1956) himself says:

The study to be reported here is unusual in various ways. It was not planned as an ordinary research; it was not a social venture but a private one, motivated by my own curiosity and pointed toward the solution of various personal moral, ethical, and scientific problems. I sought only to convince and to teach myself (as is quite proper in a personal quest) rather than to prove or to demonstrate to others. For this reason, it has no "design."

Finally, I consider the problem of psychological health to be so pressing, that any leads, any suggestions, any bits of data, however moot, are endowed with a certain temporary value. (pp. 160–161)

Maslow selected his *subjects* (persons or animals used in research studies) from among personal friends, public and historical figures who had biographies or autobiographies, and 3,000 college students—only one of whom, incidentally, met the requirements. He then compared the *behavior* (any observable activity) of his subjects to a series of requirements. Among these were lack of tendencies toward mental illness and the full development of talents, capacities, and *potentialities* (what one is capable of doing or learning).

He next selected two groups: people who met these requirements to the fullest and those who did not fulfill these *criteria* (a set of standards used for making a decision). After the two groups were studied, through interview and biography, a list of characteristics of the mentally healthy persons was made.

Intermediate Summary

Extremely mentally healthy persons tend to be happier and to get far more out of life than others. Although psychologists have found very few, they can serve as models to be followed.

What Are Some Characteristics of Mentally Healthy People?

Since Maslow, others have studied the people with the very best mental health (see Table 1-2, p. 24). As a result, many characteristics have appeared. They vary in length from 5 to 20. Fortunately, many overlap. The authors feel that there are essentially seven characteristics that should be of practical importance to you.

An Ability to Accept Oneself, Others, and Nature

Maslow found that the mentally healthy tend to accept themselves. In fact, they like themselves. Putting it another way, they have a positive *self-concept* (how one feels and thinks about oneself); they tend to view themselves as people who are acceptable and able living in a world where they can make a contribution.

Maslow also found that these people tend to accept others. Feeling good about themselves, they can accept the other person even if he is different. In general, mentally healthy persons seem to have the ability to accept people and the world. This ability can often be seen in children, who experience life as it is, and, sometimes, to the embarrassment of parents, tell others how it is!

Maslow (1956) explains it as follows:

They can accept their own human nature with all its shortcomings, with all its discrepancies from the ideal image, without feeling real concern. It would convey the wrong impression to say that they are self-satisfied. What we must say rather is that they can take the frailties and sins, weaknesses and evils of human nature in the same unquestioning spirit that one takes or accepts the characteristics of nature. One does

Figure 1-3
Abraham H. Maslow, Ph.D. (1908), Clinical
Psychologist

Academic Career
B.A., M.A., Ph.D. University of Wisconsin

Professional Experience (in part)
Research assistant in social psychology and later, instructor, University of Wisconsin
Carnegie research fellow, Teachers College, Columbia University
Professor and chairman of psychology department, Brandeis University
President of the American Psychological Association (1967–1968)
Currently associated with the Center for Studies of the Person, La Jolla, California

C A M E O

Areas of Interest
As a major promoter and developer of the humanistic approach to psychology, Dr.
Maslow has applied his interests and efforts in areas of psychodynamics (studying mental
and developmental processes with concentration on the energy force behind them),
motivation theory, and mental health. He supports the self-actualization concept and
is noted for his idea of a hierarchy (arranged in order of importance) of needs. These
needs range from "lower," or basic, ones (hunger, thirst) to the "highest" (self-fulfillment).
Lower needs must be fulfilled before the development of the individual can advance.
To further explain his self-actualization theory, Maslow created his list of fifteen characteristics. These define the truly self-actualized person.

Selected Readings
Maslow, A. H. "Self-actualizing people: a study of psychological health." *Symposium
No. 1 1950. Values in Personality Research* (Werner Wolff, ed.). New York: Grunet
Stratton, 1950.
—. *Motivation and personality.* New York: Harper, 1954.
—. "Personality problems and personality growth." In C. E. Moustakas (ed.), *The self.*
New York: Harper, 1956.
—. *New knowledge in human values.* New York: Harper & Row, 1959.
—. *Toward a psychology of being.* Princeton, N.J.: Van Nostrand Co., 1962.
—. *Religions, values, and peak experiences.* Columbus, Ohio: Ohio State University Press,
1964.
—. *Eupsychian management: a journal.* Homewood, Ill.: Richard D. Irwin, 1965.

15

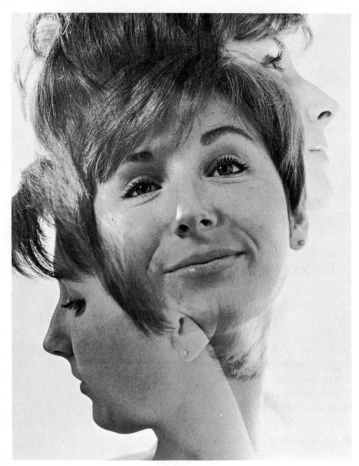

Figure 1-4
Mentally healthy persons tend to accept themselves as they are—even the
different aspects of themselves.

Photo by Don Sakall

not complain about water because it is wet, or about rocks because they are hard, or about trees because they are green. As the child looks out upon the world with wide, uncritical, innocent eyes, simply noting and observing what is the case, without either arguing the matter or demanding that it be otherwise, so does the self-actualizing person look upon human nature in himself and in others. (p. 168)

(*Note:* All detailed references will appear at the end of each chapter.)

(2) More Profound Interpersonal Relations

Another quality of these people, Maslow found, is that they tend to get closer to people. Because they feel good about themselves, they can afford to have deep human relationships with others. It must be noted that Maslow also found that these strong ties were usually to only a few people, for a deep involvement with even one person takes considerable time.

Furthermore, the extremely mentally healthy tend to be kind to and patient

Courtesy of Peace Corps. Photo by Paul Conklin

Figure 1-5
Mentally healthy persons tend to have more profound interpersonal relationships. Peace
Corp volunteer James Portman has a variety of projects underway in Tonacatepque, San
Salvador. Here he cares for ducks he has purchased with his own funds for his 4H club.

More Efficient Perception of Reality and More Comfortable Relations with It

It seems that the truly healthy do not have to fool themselves about the world and the people in it. Again, having a good self-concept, these people do not have to hide behind a mask through which they filter reality.

Their *perceiving* (how one sees the world) the world as it really is and people as they really are means that these people are operating with valid information. The result is that they tend to get more done—they don't "spin their wheels." When a problem arises they can solve it more efficiently because they can make their decisions in terms of how things really are, rather than on how they wish they were.

Maslow (1956) cites a study he conducted that tends to support this observation:

The first form in which this capacity was noticed was as an unusual ability to detect the spurious, the fake, and the dishonest in personality and, in general, to judge people correctly and efficiently. In an informal check experiment with a group of college students, a clear tendency was discerned for the more secure (the more healthy) to judge their professors more accurately than did the less secure students. (p. 165)

Continued Freshness of Appreciation

People like Maslow's subjects also tend to continually find enjoyment and appreciation in just being alive. They tend to respond to many more things in life as if they were doing each for the first time.

Here is how Maslow (1956) describes it:

Self-actualized people have the wonderful capacity to appreciate again and again, freshly and naïvely, the basic goods of life—with awe, pleasure, wonder, and even ecstasy, however stale these experiences may have become to others. Thus, for such people every sunset is as beautiful as the first one, any flower may be of breathtaking loveliness even after he has seen a million flowers. The thousandth baby he sees is just as miraculous a product as the first one he saw. He remains as convinced of his luck in marriage thirty years after his marriage and is as surprised by his wife's beauty when she is sixty as he was forty years before. For such people even the casual workaday, moment-to-moment business of living can be thrilling, exciting, and ecstatic. (p. 177)

Autonomy, Independence of Culture, and Environment

Having a good feeling about oneself generates trusting oneself. So the most healthy among us rely on their own insights about what is right and what is wrong, and about what should be done in a given situation. Thus, they tend to be more *autonomous* (independent in thought or action) relying more on their own standards of behavior and values rather than always overemphasizing what others expect of them or what their *culture* (the ways of living of a group of people) demands.

Maslow (1956) illustrates this point as follows:

> One characteristic of self-actualizing people which to a certain extent crosscuts much of what we have already described is their relative independence of the physical and social environment. . . . This independence of environment means a relative serenity in the face of hard knocks, blows, deprivations, frustrations and the like. These people can maintain a relative serenity and happiness in the midst of circumstances that would drive other people to suicide. They have also been described as "self-contained." (p. 176)

Creativeness

Mentally healthy persons seem to approach anything they do in a creative manner. Those who feel secure about themselves and with others are able to perform a task or solve a problem in new and different ways; they don't have to get in a rut and respond in the same way over and over again, as so many of us find ourselves doing.

Maslow (1956) comments on this as follows:

> This creativeness appears in some of our subjects not in the usual forms of writing books, composing music, or producing artistic objects, but rather may be much more humble. It is as if this special type of creativeness, being an expression of healthy personality, is projected out upon the world or touches whatever activity the person is engaged in. In this sense there can be creative shoemakers or carpenters or clerks. Whatever one does can be done with a certain attitude, a certain spirit which arises out of the nature of the character of the person performing the act. One can even see creatively as the child does. (p. 186)

A Democratic Character Structure

You might say that a by-product of being a mentally healthy person is the development of a democratic character structure (a consistent way of behaving). This always involves an appreciation and respect for the rights of others, a willingness to listen and learn from others, and a reverence for uniqueness and differences in other persons.

Maslow (1956) expresses the point as follows:

> They find it possible to learn from anybody who has something to teach them—no matter what other characteristics he may have. In such a learning relationship they do not try to maintain any outward "dignity" or to maintain status or age prestige or the like. It should even be said that my subjects share a quality that could be called "humility" of a certain type. They are all quite well aware of their own worth, so that there is no humbleness of the cringing or of the designing and calculating type. They are equally aware of how little they know in comparison with what could be known and what is known by others. Because of this it is possible for them without pose to be honestly respectful and even humble before people who can teach them something which they do not know or who have a skill they do not possess. They give this honest respect to a carpenter who is a good carpenter; or for that matter to anybody who is a master of his own tools or his own craft. (pp. 182–183)

Table 1-1
Behaviors Leading to Self-Actualization (Maslow, 1967, pp. 281-284)

WAYS IN WHICH ONE BEGINS TO SELF-ACTUALIZE	EXAMPLES
(1.) Self-actualization processes begin to occur by experiencing fully, vividly, selflessly, with full concentration and total absorption.	(1.) To become totally absorbed in a task; to lose yourself in a job or while interacting with another person or other people.
(2.) One moves toward self actualization by thinking of life as a process of choices, one after another. These choices involve being honest with oneself and others or being dishonest; whether to tell the truth or lie.	(2.) To make choices that seem right to you as a unique person. To be honest in your feelings with yourself and others. Not to be phony.
(3.) When one realizes that he has a unique self to express and he begins to express how he feels about things, he is considered to be moving along the road toward self-actualization.	(3.) To realize that you are a unique person. To listen to yourself, rather than do what others have taught you to do or believe.
(4.) When in doubt, be honest rather than not.	(4.) Be responsible toward **yourself** by being honest in responding to the world. Or, when in doubt, act according to your impulses.
(5.) When one dares to listen to himself, his own self, at each moment in life, and to say calmly, "No, I don't like such and such." To be courageous rather than afraid is another version of the same thing.	(5.) To speak out and say how one feels about a painting or an unusual situation, even if you risk being unpopular.
(6.) Self-actualization is not only an end state, but also the process of actualizing one's potentialities at any time, in any amount.	(6.) Using one's intelligence; working hard to be the best one can in whatever field one wants to go into. It may mean going through a period of time when one works very hard in order to attain a certain goal.
(7.) Peak experiences are transient moments of self-actualization.	(7.) When one becomes one with his environment, another person or an object such as a tree, a sunset, etc.
(8.) Finding out who one is, what he is, what he likes, what he doesn't like, what is good for him and what bad, where he is going and what his mission is—opening oneself up to himself . . . means the exposure of psychopathology. Inadequate ways of relating to oneself, others, and the world in general.	(8.) When we get to know ourselves, there may be things that we see that we don't like; things that get in the way of seeing the world and others as they are. We have to learn to drop these; this may be painful.

We should point out that Maslow's research on mentally healthy persons is also one aspect of a theory of motivation that will be discussed further in Chapter 5.

More recently, Maslow has attempted to make the concept of self-actualization even more understandable. Table 1-1 is a summary of some behaviors that seem to lead to increased self-actualization.

21
The Healthy
Personality

Intermediate Summary

Extremely healthy persons mentally enjoy these characteristics:
Accept other persons as they are
Express intense and warm feeling toward friends they select
See others as they really are
Have the wonderful capacity to enjoy the same things over and over
Maintain relative calmness during very difficult moments
Are creative in everyday activities
Practice democracy by showing respect to others

What Are Some Other Approaches in Studying the Mentally Healthy?

Another psychologist who has done extensive research on mentally healthy persons is Carl Rogers. (See cameo.)

Rogers, however, used a different method from Maslow's. Rogers' research was developed through many years of experience with troubled or emotionally ill individuals. Rogers found that as disturbed persons were allowed to be themselves in a relaxed, free, one-to-one personal interaction, certain things began to happen to them. Perhaps Rogers (1951) can explain this relationship, called Client Centered Therapy (helping others in an accepting atmosphere), more fully:

. . . If the therapy were optimal, then it would mean that the therapist has been able to enter into an intensely personal and subjective relationship with the client— relating not as a scientist to an object of study, not as a physician expecting to diagnose and cure, but as a person to a person. It would mean that the therapist feels this client to be a person of unconditional self-worth: of value no matter what his condition, his behavior, or his feelings.

For the client, this optimal therapy would mean an exploration of increasingly strange and unknown and dangerous feelings in himself, the exploration proving possible only because he is gradually realizing that he is accepted unconditionally. Thus he becomes acquainted with elements of his experience which have in the past been denied to awareness as too threatening, too damaging to the structure of the self. He finds himself experiencing these feelings fully, completely, in the relationship, so that for the moment he is his fear, or his anger, or his tenderness, or his strength. And as he lives these widely varied feelings, in all their degrees of intensity, he discovers that he has experienced himself, that he is all these feelings. He finds his behavior changing in constructive fashion in accordance with his newly experienced self. He approaches the realization that he no longer needs to fear what experience may hold, but can welcome it freely as a part of his changing and developing self. (p. 203)

What Rogers is saying, then, is that after a period of time in a situation of basic trust and honesty between two people, a person changes. The changes allow him to become a more mentally healthy person. Rogers has found certain consistent patterns of behavior among these mentally healthy persons. Let us study some of these patterns.

Willingness to Accept What He Experiences

The healthier person seems to be more aware of his own feelings and attitudes. And he does not try to run away from himself or disguise his real feelings. In addition, he begins to look at the world in a more realistic way. He doesn't respond to life rigidly, with preconceived ideas; rather, he looks at the world as it is. In his relations with others, he is also more realistic.

Trust in Himself

The improving person begins to accept and trust the *impulses* (action without thought) and feelings that he finds emerging. He actually finds he fears himself less and less. He even develops an affection for all of his own feelings.

Self-Reliance

Next develops a greater reliance on one's own feelings and *attitudes* (how one feels and thinks about something) of right and wrong. There is less reliance on what society expects, on what friends and relatives expect:

As Rogers (1961) puts it: "He recognizes that it rests within himself to choose; that the only question that matters is: 'Am I living in a way which is deeply satisfying to me, and which truly expresses me?' This I think is perhaps the most important question for the creative individual." (p. 119)

Willingness to Continue to Grow as a Person

The more healthy people tend to understand the idea that being alive means allowing oneself to grow and to change as a person, rather than reaching some end point and standing there.

As one of Rogers' (1961) patients put it: "I haven't finished the job of integrating and reorganizing myself, but that's only confusing, not discouraging, now that I realize this is a continuing process. . . . It is exciting, sometimes upsetting, but deeply encouraging to feel yourself in action, apparently knowing where you are going even though you don't always consciously know where that is." (p. 122)

OTHER RESEARCH ON THE MENTALLY HEALTHY

Although we have emphasized the research of Maslow and Rogers, it should be pointed out that many other psychologists, psychiatrists, and even philosophers

CAMEO

Photo by Charles Schneider

Figure 1-6
Carl R. Rogers, Ph.D. (1902), Clinical Psychologist

Academic Career
B.A. University of Wisconsin
M.A., Ph.D. Teachers College, Columbia University

Professional Experience (in part)
Director of the Child Guidance Center, Rochester, New York
Established a Counselling Center and Professor, University of Chicago
President, American Psychological Association (1946–1947)
Professor, University of Wisconsin
Currently associated with the Center for Studies of the Person at La Jolla, California

Areas of Interest
   Dr. Rogers has had a strong influence on personality theories through his work in the area of self-actualization. His theories concerning the study of the normal and healthy personality developed from his practical clincial experiences. He later organized these theories in his writings. His major contribution in the practice of psychotherapy is the nondirect approach, wherein the therapist reflects the ideas and opinions of the patient back to the patient without influencing them. Dr. Rogers has devoted his life to helping persons adequately actualize their abilities, talents, and creativities.

Selected Readings
Rogers, Carl. *Client centered therapy: its current practice, implications, and theory.* Boston: Houghton Mifflin, 1951.
—. Dymond, R. F. (ed). *Psychotherapy and personality change.* Chicago: University of Chicago Press, 1954.
—. *On becoming a person: a therapist's view of psychotherapy.* Boston: Houghton Mifflin, 1961.

23

Table 1-2
Some Other Theories of Mental Health (Adapted from Jourard, 1963, pp. 7-11)

NAME OF THEORIST	MAJOR EMPHASIS IN THEORY	CHARACTERISTICS OF MENTALLY HEALTHY
Fromm (1955)	Productive orientation	Able to love self; love others; uses reason to understand the world; can do productive work
Adler (see Ansbacher, 1956)	Social interest and feeling	Lack of competitiveness in relations with others Views fellowmen as worthy
Sullivan (1953)	Accurate perception of people	Ability to view others as they are Effective interpersonal relations
Rank (see Thompson, 1950)	Affirmation of one's will	Courage to be a unique person Courage to express your differences from others Courage to be creative
Tillich (1959)	Courage to be	Knowing one's feelings, opinions, beliefs Willingness to accept consequences of your own behavior
Tournier (1957)	Man as a person	Treat others as persons, not as objects, tools, or instruments
Buber (1955)	I–thou relationships	Ability to live in dialogue with fellowmen

have studied and written about their concepts of the mentally healthy person. For those of you who may wish to study further in this area, Table 1-2 gives you a brief summary of some of the other theories of mental health.

How Do Mentally Healthy Persons Develop?

Among the very important questions that the researchers asked were these: How do these special people develop? What kind of backgrounds tend to produce more mentally healthy persons? Although the research has been quite limited, there do seem to be some trends.

Using the term *adequate personalities* in the same way the authors have used the term *mentally healthy personalities*, Combs and Snygg (1959) offer some ideas for further research.

Adequate personalities, we have seen, have generally positive perceptions of themselves and the world in which they live. They see themselves as people who are liked, wanted, acceptable, and able, living in a world with which they can cope. Such concepts of self do not arise in a vacuum. They are the product of the experiences of the individual in his development. Nor does one have to be an expert to design a kind of program which would be likely to lead to such a characteristic way of seeing self and the world. The kind of experience needed to produce this kind of self-definition is apparent from the definition itself. One needs only to ask:

How shall a child feel liked unless somebody likes him?

How shall a child feel wanted unless somebody wants him?

How shall a child feel accepted unless somebody accepts him?

How shall a child feel able unless somewhere he has success?

In the answers to these questions lie clues to ways in which it may be possible to construct life situations more likely to lead to adequacy.

Positive self-definitions can arise only from positive self-experience. Similarly, a positive view of the world is likely to be found only in those who have found their own experiences with the world to be generally enhancing. (p. 262)

Therefore, it seems that one of the important prerequisites to becoming a mentally healthy person is having early experiences that convey to you a positive feeling about yourself.

Yet many people have anything but positive experiences. Have they therefore "had it?" Are they doomed to remaining less than what they might have become? The answer is "No!" As Rogers and Maslow have suggested, people can become fully healthy in many different ways.

Having warm, close human relations with just one other person seems to help the process along. A relationship of basic trust with another person seems to facilitate the development of some of the other characteristics of the healthy, such as trust in oneself and acceptance of reality.

Too, it seems to help people grow when they are able to be alone with themselves for periods of time. Then a person can allow himself to experience various human feelings. These experiences help him understand more of his *personality* (consistent ways of behaving and thinking).

There is no doubt that still another way in which the mentally healthy people grow is in having success while developing social, intellectual, and vocational competencies. Involved are such factors as hard work, learning how to concentrate, and the willingness to make sustained, long-term efforts at the expense of immediate reward. Success experiences at school, on the job, and interacting with others are thus vital.

Another method involves contact with new ideas, new philosophies, and new personalities. This can occur through reading and through reacting to drama and music. It can also happen directly, as through traveling and meeting new people.

In addition, it seems evident that it is very helpful for people to find ways of expressing their emotions fully. As was mentioned in the prologue, so many people in our society today are *alienated* (lack of ability to feel) from themselves; they are afraid to experience basic human feelings. Involvement in any relationship or activity that allows a person to be himself is helpful. Such things as hobbies, deep relationships with friends, "bull sessions," or even walks in the park alone can facilitate the release of basic emotions.

Achieving independence is another way of becoming more healthy. Of course this occurs gradually as one gains freedom from parental control. However, there are certain ways to develop more independence. Accepting more responsibility, whether it be in the home, on the job, or in school, seems to facilitate the feeling of independence. Freely expressing views, when it is appropriate, strengthens a personality. Questioning some of the values of parents or society also helps.

Becoming independent is a process involving the formation of one's own set of values. Ideally, each independent person is unique; there is no one else quite like him.

Moving in these directions, a person becomes more creative. He does not behave in a standard way in all situations. He becomes more spontaneous in his relations with the world and others. And he can tolerate different situations. Everything no longer needs to be black or white.

Probably one of the most significant by-products of being a mentally healthy person is the ability to behave in democratic ways. This involves respecting the opinions of others and realizing the dignity of the individual regardless of his background. There is also the willingness to work for programs that support the rights of the individual.

Intermediate Summary

These are some of the qualities that extremely healthy persons developed as they were learning to become more healthy:

Warm relationships over long periods of time

Faith in themselves and their abilities

Liking themselves

Note: Anyone can develop these qualities.

What does all of this mean to you? Does it really have any relevance to your life? Let us explore this research on the healthy person.

APPLICATION

Living with Yourself

Increased understanding of yourself is the first major step in achieving a psychologically healthy personality. A person lacking self-understanding is like a ship without a rudder, doomed to go wherever the wind blows or wherever the currents flow. Self-understanding provides us with the means of giving direction to our lives.

Self-understanding consists not only of knowing what we are like, but also of grasping what we are capable of becoming. Of course, no one can know all about himself. In fact, if we were to know all about ourselves, life would become a terrible bore. The words are *discover* and *uncover*. We work to discover more and more about ourselves and to uncover, and then use, our potentialities. Such exploring can be tremendously rewarding and exciting, particularly because of what it suggests of man. Certainly if man were only a product of his environment and heredity, then he would be nothing more than a dressed-up, two-legged rat in a large black box called earth. Man is more than an animal; he has the capacity to interpret what is going on in unique and highly personal ways. It is in these interpretations and subsequent behaviors that our personality is revealed. Therefore, the more involved we can become with many people and in different situations, the more we can learn about ourselves.

Self-understanding requires involvement with other people, because self-understanding begins, grows, and is reaffirmed in our daily contacts with other people. Therefore, understanding other people becomes essential for understanding ourselves.

Living with Others

BASIC TRUST

To begin to understand other people in healthy ways, we must be capable of reasonable basic trust in others. By basic trust we mean that we believe in the honesty and integrity of other persons from the moment that we meet them and until there is sufficient evidence to believe otherwise. People tend to reveal themselves as they really are only in situations in which they feel themselves to be accepted and wanted. This is why psychologists who wish to understand people make such definite efforts to make people feel accepted and wanted. However, the positive results of maintaining trust in others can be seen in everyday life. Children who feel trusted and wanted tend to behave in such ways as to prove to others that they can be trusted and wanted. College students who are allowed to take examinations without supervision tend not to cheat. Several college professors who believe that students are basically honest have permitted their students to determine their own grades, and they found that the vast majority graded themselves in a manner consistent with the professors' opinions.

EMPATHY

Another way of understanding others is through empathy. By *empathy* is meant the ability to see things as others do, to feel the same emotions as others, and to be able to think in the same ways as others in order to try to understand other persons from their point of view. Empathy involves the process of putting oneself in the place of another. However, it does not mean that one must agree with the other person's viewpoint. In learning how to use empathy, one must be careful not to condemn or to criticize negatively because this forces the other person to defend rather than to reveal what he is really like. Here is an example, based on the experiences of one of the authors, of how trust and empathy can be used to help and to understand another person.

Tom was 15 years old and he had flunked every grade since entering school. He had normal intelligence, but unknown to his teachers he suffered from a minor brain dysfunction that prevented him from learning in the same ways as other students. His parents finally took him to a large university medical center where they were informed that Tom could learn only if taught by special techniques. Subsequently, Tom was referred to one of the authors for specialized help.

Try to imagine how Tom felt toward teachers and schoolwork. Consider how you would feel if you were Tom. He was approached with the belief that despite all that had happened, Tom, like all human beings, still wanted to improve and to learn. After several weeks of patient but unsuccessful teaching, he was told this: "Deep down you really want to learn, but you have been hurt so much in the past that you won't let yourself try. We have been working together for several weeks now, and it's clear that you can learn if you will only try. Let's make a deal. You can watch TV all you want or you can sit down and really learn. The choice is yours." After three days of watching television, Tom said "Let's get to work."

Several weeks later Tom was watering the lawn when one of the authors was walking up to his home. Without warning he turned around and soaked him. Tom, with a smile on his face, said "I'm sorry. I didn't see you coming." The first impulse was to discipline Tom, but then the author realized that the dousing was a very small revenge for all that Tom had suffered in the hands of teachers. At the moment of dousing the author was all teachers wrapped up in one. All Tom's hate was concentrated on the author. After he realized that his feelings were understood, a good working relationship was established.

BROTHERLY LOVE

Persons with healthy personalities tend to like and to accept all people. They judge people not on the basis of superficial group characteristics such as socio-economic level, nationality, or political affiliations but rather on a highly individualized basis. Healthy persons psychologically can be friends with the college president or with the janitor because it is the person that matters and not the label in front of his name. Let us illustrate the application of brotherly love.

While tutoring a student at a large university, one of the authors was constantly being interrupted by other faculty members. As a matter of courtesy, the student was introduced to the staff members. However, once the janitor, John, interrupted and the student became very upset until it was explained that the author had great admiration for John as a human being. In fact, when John retired, the psychology department gave him a farewell party just as it did when professors retired. John was far more than a janitor. He was a warm, intelligent, and lovable human being.

LIVING WITH YOUR FAMILY

All of the research seems to indicate that the mentally healthy person tends to experience a good family relationship. It seems clear that the family that helped produce the unusually mentally healthy person is probably very unusual also. As Combs and Snygg suggest, because a positive self-concept is a prerequisite to becoming a mentally healthy person, it is the family that respects the child and treats him with dignity that will tend to produce more of these people. Therefore, the family that can tolerate uniqueness and respect each member will tend to be the family in which each person grows toward self-fulfillment. As mentioned earlier, trust in each other will also allow each the freedom to be what he can become.

Because mentally healthy persons see reality as it is, there is less "game playing" in the families of the mentally healthy. The members tend to get less involved in misunderstandings and conflicts, because they usually are able to see what the problems of the family are and to discuss them freely.

These families not only tend to be quite active but are also usually in a process of growth. They are not rigid or static. They don't seem dead. They are generally the families that will seek new experiences together and remain receptive to new ideas.

These families also tend to allow for the autonomy and inner feelings of the individual member; therefore, they will not usually attempt to force a particular belief or idea on one of the family members. Rather, they will allow that person to explore other ideas and values freely and to find the right ones for himself.

These families also tend to operate with a fundamentally democratic orientation. Problems that arise are openly discussed and all the possible solutions are explored.

Then too, these families tend to have friendly relations with people from many areas of life. That is, their criteria for friendship are not based on race, religion, or money, but on their involvement with others as fellow humans.

In general, these families seem to manage all areas of their life in a much more efficient way—whether it be money matters, internal conflicts, illness, or death. Again, perceiving reality as it is, they do not waste time on piecing together inaccurate information, but seem to be able to get at the root of the problem and deal with it in a realistic way.

In summary, we might say that mentally healthy families are happy families; they are lively, humanly responsive families who care for each other and also have a deep sense of love for their fellow man. Most of all, there is the self-perpetuating situation: Children from healthy families produce healthy children in their own families who in turn raise healthy children in theirs.

LIVING WITH CHILDREN

Childlike

Psychologically healthy persons are often described as being childlike themselves, for, like children, they tend to see the world with innocent and uncritical eyes. When they meet people they have no need to make them fit preconceived patterns based on color of skin, or shape of nose, or occupation. They allow other persons the freedom of becoming and developing themselves solely on the basis of their own private relationship with them.

Consider this analogy: Most parents know that there are many kinds of windows through which to look at and to learn about the world, yet many insist that their children learn about the world only through a certain kind of window. Some parents choose yellow windows; others blue or red. Some parents provide large windows; others but peepholes. Unfortunately, many children grow up with a colored window between themselves and the outside world, a window that distorts what is really there. As such children grow up, their view of the world becomes more and more distorted; misconceptions are added to misconceptions. Parents of psychologically healthy persons insist that their children see the world through large and clear windows. They also expect their offspring to view the world through many kinds of windows, to provide their children with opportunities to understand the views of others when those views are distorted.

Love

Babies and young children seem to have the ability to sense what other persons are feeling. This ability to sense the feelings of others makes the need for intense love on the part of the parents essential for the development of basic trust. A child who senses warmth and love is free to explore and to develop a positive self-concept. The child begins to feel early in life that this is a wonderful and exciting world to live in. Children reared in love are free to develop their individual potential in ever-widening areas of life. Hence, they learn more, feel more, and are more aware of their own potential as growing human beings.

Living with Society

As was discussed earlier, mentally healthy persons tend to relate very well on a one-to-one basis with others. What role do they play in working with several other people in club, community, or large organizations? How do they relate to society in general.

Perhaps the most important characteristic related to these questions is the fact that such people tend to have a basically democratic character structure. That is, they tend to relate well with people regardless of race or socioeconomic grouping. They respect the integrity of the individual in a group. Therefore, they tend to be able to participate in group life with a firm belief in the principles of the democratic tradition—equal representation and discussion of all sides of an issue and a respect for majority rule.

Another facet related here is the fact that these people also tend to be able to be independent of subtle and obvious group pressures for conformity. That is, they tend to rely more on their own sense of right and wrong rather than going along with the hidden persuaders of a mass society. This means that they will stand on principles and will debate and argue for their point of view—always, however, respecting the other points of view.

In summary, we might say that the mentally healthy person can have com-

Figure 1-7

Figure 1-8

Photos by Bruce Jacobson

Parents provide the "windows" through which their children learn about the world. Some parents provide large, clear windows; others distorted and colored windows; and still others may provide only a knothole.

passion for man in whatever group or society he finds him. Put another way, he is *man-oriented* rather than *group-oriented* or *society-oriented*. Therefore, his criteria for evaluating group or societal life are always based on the values related to the idea of what is best for man and his full growth and development.

Frequently, then, the role of mentally healthy persons in group and community life is not a pleasant one. They are often the ones who speak out when they see inequalities in the treatment of their fellow man; it makes no difference whether these be inequalities based on racial origin, wealth, or political orientation. It is no wonder then that such men as Ghandi, Jesus, and Schweitzer are always included in the lists of mentally healthy persons.

LIVING IN SCHOOL

How does our research of the healthy personality relate to you as a student and learner? Do healthy people differ in their ability to understand and explore new areas of knowledge? Are these people more open to new ideas that may change their behavior and help them become more efficient in their lives and work? The answer is Yes!

As we have seen earlier, mentally healthy persons in general can see reality more clearly. This means that in a learning situation they are able to gather in all the available information, whether this be in the form of a lecture by a teacher, readings from a book, or a bull session in the student center. After gathering this information, they put it together in ways that make sense to them. Therefore, these people often do better in school because the information they have is not distorted by inaccurate data.

Another quality of healthy people that relates to education and learning is their ability to appreciate life again and again. Therefore, these people tend to get excited and emotionally involved with learning itself. They frequently are willing to spend time and energy on a project or assignment that has aroused their interest. The result of this is that they tend to find more enjoyment in their studies; and learning itself becomes not a dull, boring process but a stimulating, self-perpetuating event.

Feeling good about themselves and having a sense of autonomy, these people are not overwhelmed by an exposure to new ideas or complicated materials. In fact, they are challenged by what they read and hear and frequently can critically evaluate it in terms of its relevance for them.

That healthy persons are willing to continue to grow means that they can admit to themselves that they don't know everything. They also tend to view learning as a continuous process, one they will engage in all their lives.

LIVING WITH YOUR JOB

Do mentally healthy persons tend to approach their jobs in a different way from other individuals? Do they have more success in the world of work? Do they tend to get more satisfaction out of their jobs? The answer to all three questions is Yes!

There is a tendency for mentally healthy persons to take a different view of their jobs from most people. One of the basic reasons that this occurs relates back to the major characteristic of these people: they like themselves. Having a positive self-concept means that they approach their work in a much more free and optimistic manner. They are not failure oriented, as so many working people are. They are essentially success oriented. They can attempt new jobs or additional responsibilities without being afraid of failure. If they fail or make mistakes they are far more apt to admit this to themselves or to their supervisor.

Another characteristic of these people, which makes them more efficient on the job, is that they have the ability to view reality as it is. The information they get about reality is, therefore, much more valid; consequently, their decisions are based more on fact and they are more valid. These people do not "spin their wheels" or waste time at work by dealing with inaccurate information. So, they tend to be much more efficient and productive.

The fact that these people tend to be more open toward others means that they get along at work with their friends. They also tend to get more satisfaction from the job. Their human relations are more satisfying because they can empathize with their fellow workers.

The creativeness of mentally healthy persons means that they tend to approach their work in a unique and different manner. They tend to be able to relate new ideas or ways of approaching the job so that it doesn't become just a job for the sake of earning money. These people get excitement out of whatever they are doing and their freshness and appreciation for life add to this excitement.

Final Summary

We now know that some persons are extremely healthy psychologically. Some of their characteristics are that they are more accepting of other persons, and they can express warm and intense feelings toward others; they can judge other persons more realistically, and they can maintain relative calm during moments of crisis; in their everyday activities, they are more creative, and they live democracy by relating well with people regardless of race or socioeconomic groupings.

We know too that all persons can become more healthy psychologically. Some of the qualities that we should develop are the ability to maintain warm friendships over long periods of time; to have growing faith in our abilities but, also, to want to continue to learn and to improve; and to develop positive feelings toward ourselves.

If the research on extremely psychologically healthy persons is to be of value, then we must apply it in our everyday lives. We must live it. Self-understanding grows as we relate intensely to more and more people in more and more situations. Living with our families provides us with the opportunity to develop the characteristics of psychological health. Living with others provides us with the opportunities to practice and to further develop these characteristics. In a true sense, all of us are the architects of our own personalities. Just as we build healthy bodies, we can build exciting personalities.

Specific Chapter References

Ansbacher, H. L., and Ansbacher, Rowena R. (eds.) *The individual psychology of Alfred Adler.* New York: Basic Books, 1956.

Buber, M. *Between man and man.* Boston: Beacon Press, 1955.

Combs, A. W. (Chm.). *Perceiving, behaving, becoming.* Yearbook Association Supervision Curriculum Development (Department National Education Association), 1962.

Combs, A. W., and Syngg, D. *Individual behavior.* New York: Harper & Row, 1959.

Fromm, E. *The sane society.* New York: Rinehart, 1955.

Maslow, A. H. *Self-actualization and beyond.* In J. F. T. Bugental (ed.), *Challenges of humanistic psychology.* New York: McGraw-Hill, 1967.

—. *Self-actualizing people: a study of psychological health.* In C. E. Moustakas (ed.). *The self: explorations in personal growth.* New York: Harper & Row, 1956.

Otto, H. A. *Explorations in human potentialities.* Springfield, Ill.: Charles C Thomas, 1966.

Rogers, C. *Client-centered therapy: its current practice, implications, and theory.* Boston: Houghton Mifflin, 1951.

—. *On becoming a person.* Boston: Houghton Mifflin, 1961.

Sullivan, H. S. *The interpersonal theory of psychiatry.* New York: Norton, 1953.

Thompson, Clara. *Psychoanalysis: evolution and development.* New York: Hermitage, 1950.

Tillich, P. *The courage to be.* New Haven: Yale University Press, 1959.

Tournier, P. *The meaning of persons.* New York: Harper & Row, 1957.

Recommended Further Readings

Paperback Books

Allport, G. W. *Becoming: basic considerations for a psychology of personality.* New Haven: Yale University Press, 1955.

Fromm, E. *Man for himself.* New York: Rinehart, 1947.

Gunther, B. *Sense relaxation below your mind.* New York: Collier Books, 1968.

Maslow, A. H. *Toward a psychology of being.* New York: D. Van Nostrand, 1962.

May, R. *Existential psychology.* New York: Random House, 1961.

—. *Man's search for himself.* New York: Norton, 1953.

Severin, F. T. *Humanistic viewpoints in psychology.* New York: McGraw-Hill, 1965.

Hardcover Books

Bonner, H. *On being mindful of man.* Boston: Houghton Mifflin, 1965.

Bradford, L. P., Gibb, J. R., and Benne, K. D. *T-group theory and laboratory method: innovation in re-education.* New York: Wiley, 1964.

Bugental, J. F. T. *Challenges of humanistic psychology.* New York: McGraw-Hill, 1967.

Jahoda, Marie. *Current concepts of positive mental health.* New York: Basic Books, 1958.

Jourard, S. M. *Personal adjustment: an approach through the study of healthy personality.* New York: Macmillan, 1963.

May, R., Angel, E., and Ellenberger, H. F. (eds.). *Existence: a new dimension in psychiatry and psychology.* New York: Basic Books, 1958.

Murphy, G. *Human potentialities.* New York: Basic Books, 1958.

Srole, L., *et al. Mental health in the metropolis, the midtown Manhattan study.* New York: McGraw-Hill, 1962.

Chapter 2 Effective Learning

Chapter Outline

Study Guide

You will find this chapter more difficult to read because we introduce more specific ideas and we start using graphs. To understand specific ideas we recommend that you underline these ideas and read them slowly.

PREVIEW

Before reading the chapter, read the prelude, chapter outline, cameo, the intermediate summaries, and the final summary of Chapter 2. By doing so you will better understand the purposes and ideas of this chapter.

CHECK MARKS
As you read the chapter, check mark parts you do not understand. After reading the chapter, go back and reread each part checked. Because you will know more, you may now be able to comprehend. If not, ask your instructor for help.

NEW WORDS
Check the meaning of new words. (Definitions are given in brackets after each word.)

SUMMARIES
Before reading the intermediate summaries again, look away and think about or write down your own summaries. Doing this will improve retention of the material read.

REVIEW
Reread each of the summaries. The main ideas are found in the topic headings. Rephrase all of these in the form of questions. Test yourself to see if you can answer them satisfactorily.

Prelude

The alienation that we spoke of in the prologue seems to be related to the gap between the vast technological changes and man's ability to *learn* (a change in behavior as a result of experience) to handle these rapid changes. And, as we discussed in Chapter 1, the healthy personality seems to be in a much better position to handle these changes, as a result of his openness to reality and his willingness to experience new ideas.

But what about the average person? Can he learn to cope with these changes? Is it possible to learn how to accept change? How can people be motivated to learn, not just while in school but all their lives? In this chapter we hope to answer some of these questions, all of which relate to the psychology of learning.

Students' Viewpoints

When we talk about learning what kinds of things do you think of? If you are like many students, you will probably think of school and your experiences in school with teachers and learning. And, again, if you are like many students, you will also bring along with your reaction a lot of negative feelings. It seems that students enter school with such excitement and enthusiasm toward learning new ideas and skills; yet, too frequently, this enthusiasm soon leaves, and the student succumbs to resignation or even bitterness.

It is really too bad that many people today leave school with the idea that learning is dull, threatening, and something that should be avoided at all costs.

Photos courtesy of Fullerton Junior College and Autonetics, a division of North American Rockwell Corp.

Figure 2–1

Figure 2–2

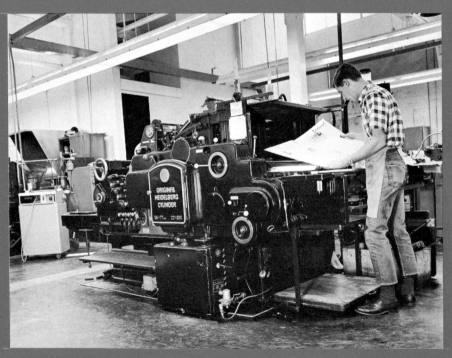

Figure 2-3

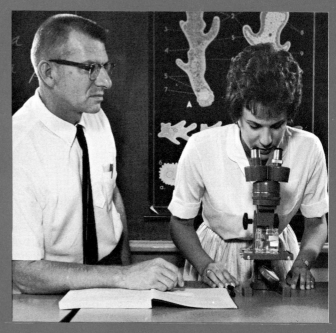

Figure 2-4

Learning involves a great variety of different and complex skills. As a result of the many and rapid changes of a complex technological society, learning and learning how to learn have become cornerstones of modern living.

Learning can be one of the most humanly rewarding and growth-producing experiences. Through learning we continue to grow as people, not only intellectually but in our ability to understand and develop empathy with our fellow man.

WHY IS IT IMPORTANT?

But does learning just take place in school? Is learning merely the three R's? Does learning have anything to do with you personally? For the answer to these questions, would you spend a minute answering another question?

What is there about you as a unique person that is a result of learning? In other words, what kind of things about you were you born with and what kind of things about you did you learn?

As you think about this question, you will soon begin to realize that *you* are one giant bundle of learning! That is, there are many aspects of you that are a direct result of experience with your *environment* (people and objects in your experiences). In fact, it may seem that that's about all you are! However, there is substantial evidence that your genetic characteristics (which include physiological factors) also affect learning. Let's make a list of some factors primarily determined by learning processes:

How you walk (motor skills).

How you talk.

How you feel about yourself (self-concept).

How you express your feelings (emotions).

How you go about solving problems that you face.

How you feel about certain people, ideas, and so on (attitudes).

What you feel is right and wrong (values).

What you want to do with your life (motives).

What kinds of things you are interested in (interests).

How you view the world (perceptions).

How well you write.

How well you read.

How well you swim.

How well you play golf.

As you can see by now, we could continue this list into thousands of different kinds of behavior that you have learned since you were born.

The fact is that learning is personally a most important process for you to know something about. Because the learning process is so much a part of the behavior of each of us, psychologists have been studying it for years. We certainly don't know all there is to know about how people learn, but we have accumulated quite a few principles of learning that have direct relevance to you. We know, for example, that it is possible for you to learn how to study more effectively in school. We know that it is also possible for you to learn how to think and solve problems more effectively. And we know how to help you develop certain skills faster and easier.

What we are going to do, then, in this chapter, is to select out of the research some truths about learning that we think you will find helpful for learning in school and in life. We will call these principles of learning.

The principles involve two considerations. We must consider the principles related to the person, and we must consider the principles independent of the individual. Let's call these the *subjective* and the *objective principles*. The subjective principles of learning are related to internal factors within the person such as heredity, past experiences, and personal views and values. The objective principles are related to external factors outside the person such as study techniques, rewards received for learning, and length and frequency of study periods.

BASIC THEORY AND RESEARCH

Subjective Principles of Learning

THE SELF AND LEARNING

The *self* (what one believes to be true about himself) is learned. It is not ready-made. The self develops as one's inherited potentials meet with the experience of everyday life. The self is constantly changing and growing as one meets new and different experiences.

As the self develops, it becomes the center point around which new experiences gather to be given meaning, acceptance, or rejection. New experiences are learned more effectively if they agree with or enhance our self-concept. On the other hand, if a new experience is painful and insulting, we tend to reject or to forget it even if its acceptance would help us to become better persons. The learning of new ideas that do not fit within our present frame of reference is difficult, but often it is the most important kind of learning.

It is true that psychologists have documented many good ideas about effective learning. Yet no one really understands the learning process completely. With this in mind, let us explore some ideas that may be of value in helping you learn more effectively.

PAST EXPERIENCES AND LEARNING

Persons relate what they see and hear to their own past experiences. What is learned is a combination of the experience itself and the person's previous knowledge about that experience. For example, a research study found that children from poor families tend to see coins as larger than they really are, whereas children from wealthy homes see the same coins as smaller. (Bruner, 1947) Heavy rainfall may be accepted as a blessing by the farmer, as an unfortunate event by the mail carrier, and as an interesting scientific phenomenon by the meteorologist. To learn more effectively a person should be aware of the influence of his limited and selective personal experiences and to maintain an open and flexible attitude, especially when the new learning is opposed to his own views.

INTELLIGENCE AND LEARNING

Although high *intelligence* (learning capacity) helps one to learn, it is not the sole cause of effective learning. Many years ago a psychologist, Terman (1947), studied the lives of 1,500 highly intelligent children. Most of them eventually were very successful, in business, at school, and in their interpersonal relations, but some were failures. The important idea to remember is that the difference in intelligence between most and least successful was only six points on the intelligence tests. This difference was insignificant. Undoubtedly, other factors such as confidence, creativity, leadership, and desire to achieve also helped to determine effective learning.

Intelligence test scores are only estimates of what a person has learned about his world compared to what others of similar backgrounds have learned. It is assumed that all persons tested have had equal opportunities to learn, and that they were all taught the same information. These assumptions can be questioned. For example, a person reared in a city scores higher than a farmer because of the nature of the question asked. (Eells, 1951) The children of migrant laborers usually cannot take full advantage of educational advantages; therefore, their intelligence test scores tend to be lower. (Laird, 1957) Their lower intelligence scores do not mean that they are less capable of learning.

Are intelligence scores open to change? Research findings generally support the idea that intelligence scores do change, because intelligence scores tell what we have learned under our unique life curcumstances while using our present ways of learning. We can improve both our environment and our ways of learning. There is much evidence that intelligence scores can be changed. (Lee, 1951) Children reared in ophanages tend to achieve higher scores once they are moved to a more stimulating and exciting environment. (Skodak, 1936, 1945, 1949)

MOTIVATION AND LEARNING

Common sense tells us that our attention is directed to what is interesting to us. What is most interesting is whatever might help us solve our problems and whatever might add to our enjoyment of life. Psychologists call this process of wanting, *motivation* (motives, then, would include anything within or without the person that creates a desire). The new mother wants to know about infant care. The unhappy person wants to know how to be happier. The main point is that when we are really interested and involved we will learn better.

Look at Figure 2–5. It shows what is called a reversible figure-ground relation. It can be seen as either a vase or as two human facial profiles. It is impossible for most to see the vase and the profiles at the same time. Pretend that the vase represents your personal goals such as finding a job or getting married, and that the profiles represent what you are trying to learn in college. It should be apparent that it is difficult to do justice to both at the same time. Effective learning requires that we give our full attention to what we are trying to learn.

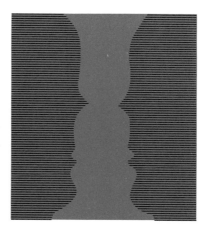

Figure 2–5
Illustration of a reversible figure-ground relationship. Look at the center and the vase. Then look
at the two profiles of human faces. Then try to
see both the vase and the facial profiles at the
same time.

Let us illustrate again the importance of attention for learning. You are sitting in the middle of a room and two people talk to you at the same time. What is going to happen? Will you understand both speakers, or just one, or will you understand nothing? Because we can pay attention to but one thing at one time, we must listen to one only, or take turns listening to one or the other, if we are to learn anything. Do not try to listen to both at the same time. The main idea is that effective learning requires that we pay full attention to what is being presented.

EMOTIONS AND LEARNING

When we are enthusiastic, we tend to learn better. We would expect that our schools would be places of joy and happiness. Instead we find that, for many students, happiness consists of getting away from school. This is understandable because no one wants to remain in painful situations. Possibly this is one of the reasons why school attendance is often required by law.

When a person is under constant threat and finds no escape, his *emotional feelings* (those that accompany thoughts and actions) turn into *anxiety* (unexplainable feelings of fear). Anxiety is actually worse than *fear* (feelings aroused by threat), because fearful persons know exactly why they feel as they do. When we feel anxiety, we cannot specify the exact reasons. An individual under too much anxiety finds that his learning ability is usually reduced. (Farber, 1954) Time after time, we have seen capable students fail examinations when they were undergoing the stress of personal problems such as broken engagements, illness in the family, or financial difficulties. On the other hand, mild stress or anxiety may help learning by making us more alert. (Birch, 1945) For example, when a person nearly trips on the stairs, he becomes more aware of how he walks. A near accident on the road has improved the driving of many persons.

In general, fearful situations impair learning ability. (Maier, 1949). The fearful person tries to hold on to those ideas he already has, instead of trying to learn new ideas. We have seen students cringing in their seats frightened and bewildered. Studies show that animals who have been exposed to continuous failure become fearful, indifferent, and violent. (Wolpe, 1958)

Intermediate Summary

Thus far, we have seen that learning is an important area for you to study because much of your own behavior is a result of learning processes. We have also discussed how such subjective factors as the self-concept, past experiences, intelligence, motivation, and emotions affect learning.

Objective Principles of Learning

Now let us look at some of the objective principles of learning that have come out of years of research by learning psychologists. These objective principles are different from the subjective principles in that they relate to factors outside the person. Some of these objective principles are basic to all learning.

LEARNING AND FORGETTING

How fast we learn and forget depends on many factors. In general, learning is very slow at first, increases rapidly, and then slows down again until we have learned the new ideas and skills. The general learning curve is shown in Figure 2–6.

However, there are enormous differences in learning curves of different individuals. Some persons learn some materials very rapidly, whereas some other person may find the same materials very difficult. Look at the differences in learning rates of students in the same classroom.

The graphs illustrate the improvement in speed reading of three college students. Notice that the beginning speed of reading was the same for all three, but that their individual rates of improvement were all different. It is important to remember, however, that the student with the poorest performance may later surpass students who did better work at first. Increased effort often accounts for

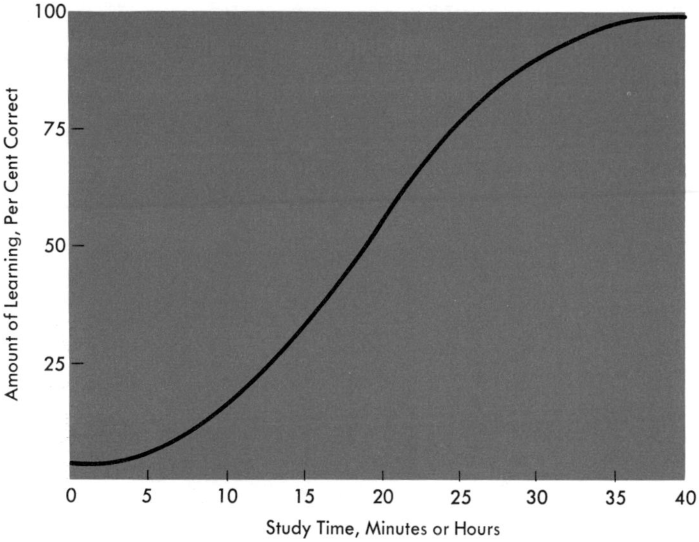

Figure 2-6

General Learning Curve. The general learning curve shows the relationship between study time and the amount of learning. At first learning slows down until all the material assigned has been learned.

After Ebbinghaus, 1885

the dramatic academic improvement of some students. Although no one can predict with certainty the learning rate of one person on a particular test, we know the general trends of his learning rate and we know that learning takes time and patience.

Whenever we learn something, we are faced with the problem of forgetting. After learning has occurred, the rate of forgetting is very rapid. Just how rapid depends on the meaningfulness of the material, its complexity, how often we use it, and our purpose for learning it. The rate of forgetting is more rapid than the rate of learning.

Notice that more than half of the material was forgotten after twenty-four hours when the material learned was not meaningful to the student. In this case, students had to memorize nonsense syllables: lum, rep, bif. For meaningful materials the rates of forgetting are slower. (Katona, 1940)

However, it is important to know that forgotten information is not the same as material that was never studied. Forgotten material is like hidden treasure. It can be uncovered quickly by the process of review. For example, most of us have forgotten how to find a square root even though we learned how to some time ago. A quick review is usually sufficient to relearn how to do square roots. The quick recoverability of forgotten knowledge is an important advantage that the educated man has over the person who has never attended school.

REVIEW

When material is relearned by review it takes far less time and the rate of forgetting is slowed down. With each succeeding review it takes less time to relearn and the rate of forgetting becomes slower and slower as shown. Students with high grades are keenly aware of the tremendous importance of review. It is the only way to hold back rapid forgetting. The student who has systematically

45

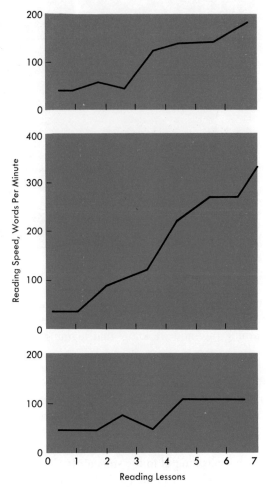

Figure 2-7
Rates of Learning. Rates of learning are different even on the same learning task. The three graphs show the progress of three students in a speed-reading class.

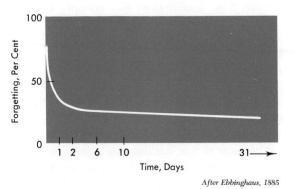

Figure 2-8
General Forgetting Curve. The rate of forgetting is more rapid than the rate of learning. At first the rate of forgetting is very rapid.

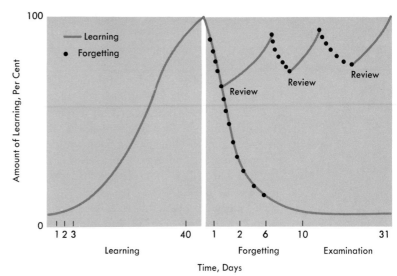

Figure 2-9

The Relationships Between Learning, Forgetting, and Reviewing. After learning, forgetting is very rapid. Only reviewing can slow forgetting. Reviews result in faster and faster relearning and in greater and greater retention. The student who reviews frequently should get higher grades than the student who studies but does not review.

After Ebbinghaus, 1885

reviewed his assignments before an examination has an insurmountable advantage over the student who has studied but who has not reviewed at all. The important idea to remember is this: If you do a daily review of all assignments, including previous assignments, and then make weekly reviews of the materials, it will take less and less time to review and your retention of the materials will get better and better.

Reviewing is important because it is the only way of slowing the forgetting process. There are two ways to review, rereading and recitation. Rereading what we have studied before is not efficient because we will be reviewing many ideas that we still remember. That is a waste of valuable time. It is best for us to spend most of our review time in recitation rather than in rereading. *Recitation* consists of reading the main idea only and then trying to remember as much as we can about the topic. Secondly, we should check the correctness of our answers. If we answer incorrectly or if we cannot remember an answer, then we should reread the material. We can practice recitation by looking at the table of contents, the bold print in the chapter, and the index.

Practicing recitation is vital for taking school examinations. An examination requires that you recognize correct answers for multiple choice tests, and that you reproduce correct answers for essay tests. Taking a test is not the same as reading. Reading provides you with answers. A test requires that you produce answers. The reason for the superiority of recitation is that it duplicates for the student a situation very similar to taking a test. Both test taking and recitation require that you recognize and reproduce correct answers.

THE EFFECT OF SEQUENCE OF EVENTS ON LEARNING

As was defined earlier, learning is any permanent behavior change or modification as a result of experience. In order to understand how learning takes

47

place, psychologists have conducted a number of research studies. Results indicate that sequence or order of events is one of the very important factors in learning, particularly the learning of *habits* (behavior without thinking). (Thorndike, 1911; Hull, 1952)

In his original studies, Ivan Pavlov (1927) found that dogs could be trained to salivate to a variety of *stimuli* (anything that produces thoughts, feelings, or actions), such as a tone, a bell, or a touch on the paw. How did he do this? He found, through extensive studies, that if you repeatedly rang a bell and then presented food to a hungry dog, soon just the ringing of the bell alone was enough to produce salivation. Again, in a series of other experiments, Pavlov and others (Dollard and Miller, 1950) found that a certain sequence of events seemed to produce the most effective learning.

The major point in this research boils down to this: Events that occur repeatedly together or are associated together tend to be connected in such a way that in the future the happening of one event (or stimulus) will increase the chances of a certain type of response or behavior to occur.

Let us look at an example with humans. Why do many children cry the first time they enter a barber shop? As babies they received many painful injections from the family doctor. The injections made them cry and the doctor was dressed in white. The sequence of needle–pain–crying and the color white was established at an early age. Consequently, the sight of a man in a white suit, such as the barber, automatically brings out a crying response. Some barbers, knowing this, make it a point not to wear white clothing in their shops.

REWARDS AND LEARNING

Rewards are important for effective learning because of the simple fact that we learn better when we want to. Rewards may consist of food and water, love or praise, or material objects such as money, awards, and honors. B. F. Skinner (see cameo) has done considerable research on the role of rewards in learning. Much of our discussion is based on his original research.

Rewards are effective for learning only if the rewards are important to the person. Praise received from a loving parent or a respected teacher can be an effective reward. The art student will value comments from the art instructor more highly than he would from the football coach. To the starving person a baked potato is far more valuable than a new car or a date with a movie star.

Even appropriate rewards are effective only if given at the proper time. The ideal time to give or to receive a reward is immediately *after* the right answer or a response has been given. Figure 2–12 indicates that the greatest amount of learning occurs when the reward comes immediately after the correct response and that the amount of learning decreases sharply as the time between the response and the reward increases.

There are many examples of this type of learning in life. A two-year-old who touches a hot stove learns very quickly that pain is relieved by his taking his hands off the stove. Unfortunately, many persons are unaware of the crucial importance of providing the proper sequence of learning. For example, a mother

Figure 2-10

B. F. Skinner, Ph.D. (1904) Experimental Psychologist

Academic Career

B.A., Hamilton College, Clinton, New York

M.A., Ph.D. Harvard University

Professional Experience (in part)

Instructor University of Minnesota, 1936–1939

Professor and chairman of psychology department, Indiana University

Professor at Harvard University.

Areas of Interest

Dr. Skinner is recognized as the leading American proponent of behavioral psychology. In explaining more what a person *is not,* Skinner contends that man has neither a free will nor the capacity for natural action. Man's behavior is a result of constant contingencies (chance happenings) of events that are functionally related in a universe wherein everything is assumed to be ordered. Skinner has a nontheoretical approach to the psychology of learning. Rather than test theories of learning he contends that efforts should be concentrated "to obtain data showing orderly changes characteristic of the learning process" (1950, p. 215). Organisms will perform actions that will lessen or completely stop unadaptive states. Part of these actions are innate but many are learned. It is the consequences that control behavior and this is said to be learned. This concept was termed *operant behavior* by Skinner (1938).

Selected Readings

Holland, J. G., and Skinner, B. F. *Analysis of behavior.* New York: McGraw-Hill, 1961.

Skinner, B. F. *The behavior of organisms.* New York: Appleton-Century-Crofts, 1938.

—. *Verbal behavior.* New York: Appleton-Century-Crofts, 1957.

—. *The science of human behavior.* New York: Macmillan, 1953.

—. *Walden two.* New York: Macmillan, 1948.

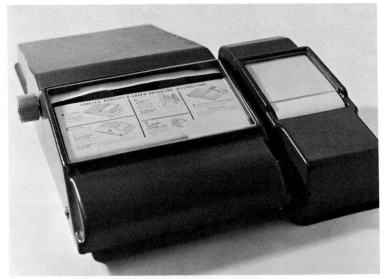

Figure 2-11
Teaching Machine. A teaching machine incorporates important learning principles: step-by-step learning, immediate rewards, and feedback. The lesson is presented step by step in small parts. Questions are asked about each step and the answers are written down. The student checks his answers immediately. If right, he continues to the next step; if wrong, he restudies the same step.

Photo by Ron Sakall

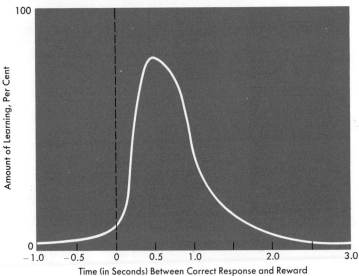

Figure 2-12
Relationship Between Learning and Timing of Reward. Learning is more effective if the reward (or punishment) is given after the response has occurred. Learning is greatest when the time interval between the response and reward is very short.

After Perin, 1943

tells her disobedient child that his father will spank him when he returns home. Or a teacher tells a student to see her after class for the answer to his question. Neither is using sound principles of learning, for the time between the thing to be learned or the punishment in these cases is too great. There is an interesting story of a college student who wished to teach his dog to bark for food. The student waited until the dog was hungry (motivation) and then offered him food (reward). Just before giving the dog the food he said "Bark for your food." The dog just looked. The student imitated barking but to no avail. The sequence was repeated day after day for a week. Finally, to the student's dismay, the dog refused to eat unless the student barked first! The mistake was giving the reward *before* the correct response. For effective learning, the correct behavior must occur first, before the reward is given, and the reward must then be given at once.

SEQUENCE OF REWARD LEARNING TO LONG-RANGE LEARNING

After a person has learned a skill efficiently, we want him to retain the skill for a long time without the need for constant reteaching. A mother wants her child to become independent of her training, and a teacher wants his students to work on their own. How can this important objective of long-range learning be achieved? The essential steps are (Skinner, 1938):

CONTINUOUS REWARDS. Begin the training by providing the proper reward after the person has produced the proper response. For example, when the child starts to read for the first time, tell him what a good boy he is *every time* he starts to read in order to establish a new habit.

INTERMITTENT REWARDS. After the child has started to form the habit, praise him every other day. Studies indicate that learning under intermittent rewards lasts longer than learning under continuous rewards.

VARIABLE REWARDS. After the child's habit is well established, praise him irregularly so that he never knows when he is going to be rewarded. In life, rewards are given occasionally, not every time. Research indicates that learning under variable rewards lasts longer than learning under continuous rewards.

No REWARD. In order to develop persistent and possibly life-long habits, the dependency on external rewards must be gradually removed. If the first three steps are followed, then rewards are no longer necessary because the learned behavior is now self-rewarding. Self-rewarding behavior feels good and the child too "wants to keep it up." He has now developed a habit and it becomes an automatic part of his way of living.

GENERALIZATION AND DISCRIMINATION

Fortunately for us, all learning is generalized. By *generalization* we mean that once we have learned a bit of information or a particular skill we have, in reality, learned whole classes of similar information or skills. If we learned to read the word *cat* in small manuscript writing, we do not have to relearn the word CAT when written in a large bold print. If we learned to drive in a stick-shift Ford, our skills are generalized so that we can now drive most stick-shift automobiles. The fact of generalization helps us to learn even what we have never studied if it is similar enough to what we have actually learned.

Although generalization helps us to learn large amounts of information at one time, generalization can lead to trouble. A young child loves all men to a degree because all men resemble father. However, calling all men Daddy can be embarrassing to mother. The skills of driving an automobile may not be generalized to a diesel truck. To avoid such problems we must be aware of the process of discrimination.

Discrimination is common to all learning. By the process of *discrimination* we learn that different responses have to be used in situations that are similar. The light changes, but red means stop and green means go. A certain siren sound means it's time to go home, but another siren sound may mean to move your car to one side of the road and to stop.

Figure 2-13
Discrimination Learning. Modern learning requires efficient discrimination learning. This machine is used to study individual reaction time to colored lights such as red, green, and amber. The time between the presentation of the light and the response is called "reaction time" and is recorded on the timer.

Courtesy of C. H. Stoelting Co. Photo by Ron Sakall

In order to apply discrimination learning, certain behaviors should be rewarded and others not rewarded. After numerous repetitions, persons learn to respond correctly to different but similar situations.

Intermediate Summary

Objective Principles of Learning
1. People differ in their rate of learning.
2. Forgetting is more rapid than learning.
3. Review is essential to retain what has been learned.
4. Learning is more effective when followed by appropriate rewards.
5. Habits are better formed when the sequence of continuous, intermittent, and variable reward schedules are followed.
6. When the preceding schedules are followed, the behavior can become self-rewarding.
7. Generalization permits the learning of large amounts of information.
8. Discrimination permits appropriate usage of information learned through generalization.

Special Learning Techniques

We have discussed the essential principles of learning. Before going on, we should know that there are special learning techniques that help us to apply the learning principles more effectively.

PLANNING THE SEQUENCE OF LEARNING

In general, when we have to learn a large amount of information such as complex directions or a long poem, it is best to distribute our total learning time into separate periods. In other words, learning section by section is a better technique than trying to learn all at the same time. We call this technique *distributed practice*.

Learning to solve a problem or learning an entire sequence at one time with no rest or interruptions we call *massed practice*.

In most learning situations, we should read over the assigned task first and then decide whether to use distributed or massed practice. If the assignment is lengthy or complex, it is generally best to use distributed practice to learn the assignment. However, students should experiment with both procedures to find out which is best for them.

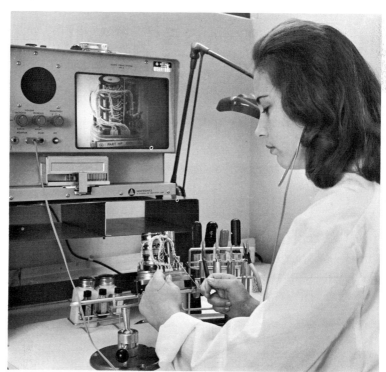

Figure 2-14
Learning Made Easier. Learning is easier when the materials are presented step-by-step and when there is immediate feedback. Electronic assembling is taught through an audiovisual system. The screen shows step-by-step views of circuit progress.

Courtesy of Autonetics, a division of North American Rockwell Corp.

FEEDBACK

Persons learn better when they are informed as to the correctness or incorrectness of their responses. This process is called *feedback*. There is much evidence that we learn better when we are constantly informed as to how we are doing and shown ways to improve. (Goldstein and Rittenhouse, 1954) In one experiment (Greenspoon and Foreman, 1956) persons were asked to draw three-inch lines while blindfolded. Those who were informed immediately on how they were doing showed the best learning. Persons who were not informed about how they were doing showed very poor performance.

Learning is usually better when there is constant feedback. Children are very dependent on others for feedback while they are learning. However, adults have the advantage in that they are more capable of making their own judgments regarding their learning performances. Nevertheless, adults also learn better when they are constantly being informed about their errors and ways of improving their performance.

OVERLEARNING

Overlearning occurs when we have learned correct responses but we continue to practice the correct response. This technique is useful when correct knowledge is important, such as on a new job or in taking an examination. We want to be sure that we will know what to do even though we will be anxious. Figure 2–15 demonstrates the higher retention of learning materials when overlearning is practiced. Students who practiced overlearning remembered a greater number of correct answers during the examination. Overlearning does take extra time, but it can provide a strong influence on grade-point averages.

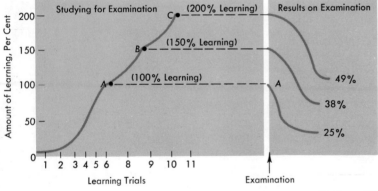

Figure 2–15
Relationship Between Amount of Study and Results on Examinations. All students memorized twelve nouns until they could recite them all correctly. Group B studied 55% more than group A and group C studied 100% more than group A. The examination was given one day afterward.

After Krueger, 1929

Special Learning Techniques
1. Massed learning is the continuous study of an assignment until mastered.
2. Distributed learning is the study of an assignment interrupted by other activities.
3. For complex assignments distributed learning is superior.
4. Learning is superior when one receives continuous feedback regarding his progress.
5. Overlearning assures a higher level of performance.

APPLICATION

Living with Yourself

UNDERSTANDING YOURSELF

All of us want to learn to become the best that we can become. The human potential to learn is apparently limitless and the desire to improve and to learn is present at all times.[*] What we need to develop are goals and the means to achieve these goals. Finding and accepting goals are highly personal processes. The more we understand about ourselves the more likely we are to find acceptable goals in life.

Because we are products of our own learning, no one knows us better than ourselves. Certainly we should evaluate what others say to us, but the final decision is ours. Psychologists more and more have come to agree that what we feel and hear, what we touch and taste, and what we see are important only to the degree that these external events are important to us. Let's try to illustrate this point through the experience of one of the authors.

This writer was hired to install a reading improvement program in a large high school. Because of a misunderstanding, the counselors had assigned only the students with top academic grades to the reading classes. A few weeks later the superintendent informed the author that he wanted the top students removed from the reading classes and replaced with students with low reading-test scores and lower grade averages. It was explained that the top academic students needed to stay in the program because they saw themselves as inadequate

---

[*] According to Herbert A. Otto, Director, of The Human Potentialities Research Project, University of Utah, "The recognition that healthy man is operating at 10 to 15 percent of his potential is both the major challenge and the major promise of this age." (Otto, 1966)

readers despite their high reading scores, the opinion of the counselor and teacher, or the feelings of the superintendent. This writer explained that the individual's knowledge of his own ability and attitudes is more important than that of any outsider because the individual's opinions about himself determine how he will act. The superintendent replied that he had never thought of understanding students from their viewpoint. He agreed, and the students were permitted to remain in the reading class. Frankly, the reading improvement shown by these students was beyond the authors' fondest expectations.

What we are in our own eyes has been determined largely by our interpretation of our own experiences. Unfortunately, most of the experiences that compose what one calls "me" have been forgotten. Although we have forgotten our past experiences, the consequences of these experiences still influence our present and future learning and thinking. Therefore, it is important for us to *review* our own past history in order to understand ourselves better.

One way to review our past experiences is to think about them as we try to solve present and future problems. Our past experiences compose a huge reservoir of previous learning waiting to be used. As we tap the reservoir, we will make the forgotten information useful again.

Another technique to help students solve a present problem by understanding their past experiences is to have the student write down the events that led up to the problem. While doing this exercise, many students find the solution to the problem. Psychologists who help people with their personal problems report that often persons talk for an hour, pay their fee, and walk out happily although the psychologist didn't say a word. The psychologist just listened while the patient reviewed the history of his problem and found his own solution.

Other techniques for learning more about yourself include discussions with families and friends, preparing autobiographies, and testing yourself in real situations that require skill and learning such as in school, on the job, and meeting new people in new situations.

Even in new circumstances the more we know about our strengths and talents, as well as our weaknesses, the better able we will be to judge our capacities correctly and solve any problems. The know-how that we bring into solving a problem depends on knowing about our reservoir of past experiences. The more we have learned in the past, the greater our storehouse of previous experiences.

Living with Others

Think about the happiest moments of your life. Although happy experiences are different, there will be one common element: Happy experiences were shared with friends or loved ones. When we hear a funny story, we want to share the humor. When we are sad or depressed, talking to others makes us feel better.

AVOID LABELS

If we really wish to understand others, we must avoid the use of labels. Labels classify persons into categories on the basis of racial and religious membership or in terms of behavior that seems odd or strange. They block understanding. We must try to understand the why of each person's behavior. We must realize that other persons have *learned* to be the way they are, just as we have *learned* to be the way we are.

If a person is not friendly, we would do well to believe that in the past he was not rewarded properly for trying to be friendly. Maybe he was hurt so many times for trying to be friendly that he finally learned to be cold and indifferent to others.

If a student is flunking college and isn't trying to pass, can we really believe that his previous efforts at study were successful? The answer is No! He may have tried hard in the past, without success, without rewards. He learned that by not studying hard he would be treated the same as if he had studied hard.

Some people find satisfaction in failing or in not being friendly. They have become experts at flunking even though they are intelligent and could succeed. To understand why, we must learn about the past experiences that made them as they are now.

PEOPLE DO CHANGE

People can and do change. They learn to find new ways of coping with their situation. The authors have seen many students change from sullen, indifferent persons into dynamic, studious, and dedicated students. Typical student remarks are these: "I never realized the importance of education." "I needed time to adjust." "I just can't believe that I used to be so indifferent." The main point is that people can and do learn to change their behavior.

SOME STEPS IN HELPING OTHERS TO CHANGE

Uncritical Acceptance

Persons learn better when they feel wanted and accepted. Because there is no need to defend one's self, energy and attention can be directed toward new learning. When one of the authors was working with severe problem children or adults, he spent hours and even days reassuring the person first before beginning to teach him new skills. Remember that no one learns well when he is being attacked and belittled.

Removal of Negative Conditions

As you remember, events that have occurred together in the past tend to occur together again. If a student has been failed by teachers repeatedly, he tends to dislike all teachers. This is understandable. However, at this point the student also dislikes nearly everything about the school—books, cafeteria, food, buildings. He automatically applies the principle of generalization, which explains why certain behaviors become more and more common. If a person has been disappointed in his relations with the opposite sex, that person tends to avoid nearly all situations involving the opposite sex. Hostile feelings are already built in when that person goes out on a date, even though he has never met the other person.

If we are to help such persons to change, we must teach them to *discriminate* (tell the difference) between the past and the present and to avoid the use of labels when talking about others. For example, when students say that all teachers are unfair, ask them to name the unfair teachers and why they were unfair. Help them to realize that all teachers are not the same. Urge them to talk with the teachers about *why* they received their grades. Most teachers are eager to talk with their students. If your date is aloof and untrusting, teach her with your kind and considerate behavior that *all* persons are not elusive. By so doing, the original negative attitudes can be weakened and the person can be prepared for adopting new, positive attitudes.

Introduction of Proper Rewards

We are now ready to introduce proper rewards. What is a proper reward depends on the particular situation and the particular person. In a factory, a smile from the boss may be sufficient reward. In school, a suitable reward may be an afterschool conference with the instructor. For a tough juvenile delinquent, the reward may be a ticket to a drag strip. Rewards are ways of telling another person that we are pleased with his new behavior.

LIVING WITH YOUR FAMILY

A major part of our self-concept was learned in the family situation. Our attitudes toward others—how we talk and walk, our values in life, and how we express feelings such as love and hostility—were formed there. In a true sense, the more we know about our families, the more we know about ourselves. The following account illustrates this point.

A mother of three children had asked for a divorce because her husband was extremely suspicious. As a marriage counselor, one of the authors spoke with her husband about this suspiciousness. He said he was aware of this but that he just couldn't help it. After weeks of counseling, the husband explained that he had found the reason for his suspiciousness. The previous day he had supper with his parents and noticed that his mother would taste everything his father was about to eat. He asked his father, "How come mother had onion soup? I know she hates onions." His father replied that his wife had to taste everything before he could eat it.

Later that evening his mother said that she was going to the store. His father asked her to check the mileage on the car. When the son asked why, his father explained that he always checked on where his wife went by counting the number of miles on the car. The amazing point was that this young man had never been aware of all this. Now that he understood the foolish basis for his extreme suspiciousness, he was able to change this behavior.

Although our self-concept is determined largely in the family setting, there is no perfect match between us and our families. Conflicts of ideas and values are inevitable because important parts of our self-concept are formed outside of the family. Schools, churches, news media, and friends are constantly providing us with rich sources of new ideas.

The new ideas that we bring into our homes often disagree with those held by our families. Conflicts can be resolved, because what the family believes was learned also. The fact that we can learn and then relearn is what makes life a challenge. We grow and improve as we are forced to consider both sides of arguments and to make decisions. It is when there are no decisions to make that we stop learning and growing.

It is to our advantage to benefit from the experiences of our families and, in a sense, to stand on their shoulders as we attempt to construct better lives for ourselves and our children.

Living with Society

LIVING IN SCHOOL

What does our discussion of the principles of learning have to do with school and education? It is probably apparent by now that most of the principles that we have discussed earlier in this chapter can help you become more effective in your learning activities in school if you *want* to apply them. The trouble is that many students *know* what they should do to improve their learning in school but they often don't do anything about it until it affects them directly.

An example of this occurred to one of the authors when he was placed on academic probation during his second year of college; it wasn't until then that he really wanted to do something about his poor grades. So he talked with one of his professors and together they attempted to analyze where the difficulties were.

Part of the difficulties were found to be within himself; for example, his past experiences with learning in high school had encouraged the practice of waiting until the night before an exam to study. In high school, at least, this behavior was rewarded by his achieving above-average grades.

Another area that seemed to need some change was in the area of reading. After taking some reading tests in the counseling center, he found that his reading level could be improved considerably. He enrolled in a remedial reading course for a semester and found that it helped to improve this skill considerably.

As they discussed his problems, another factor emerged, having to do with his emotional reaction to tests. It seemed that in most classes there were two exams: a midterm and a final. Usually the midterm and the final exam each counted 50 per cent of the course grade. He soon realized that he was being put under tremendous emotional strain during those two testing periods. Frequently, the experience was so painful that he would attempt to escape by not preparing properly for the examinations: "If I don't know it by now, I'll never know it, so why study!" was one of his favorite comments. The results were disastrous!

Perhaps the most important result of this experience was that it helped him to look at himself more objectively and to understand himself better. In fact, it was soon apparent that the field of study he had chosen was not exactly what he really wanted to do with his life, but more an idea of his parents. As a result, he was able to look around at other possible career fields and after another semester changed his major to psychology.

After the general problem area was explored, the professor offered some specific advice to help him solve some of his study problems. As he looks back now he can see that this advice was based on very sound principles of learning. Perhaps some of these principles could also help you with your problems.

Learning Takes Time

One of the things that the student finally became aware of was that effective learning takes considerable time and energy. Earlier in this chapter we discussed the importance of distributed practice for learning complex materials. Generally this holds true for school learning. For example, he worked out a study schedule to allocate time for various subjects.

A study schedule can be a great help in terms of spreading out your study time so that you don't have to cram the night before a test. Table 2-1 illustrates a simple type of study schedule.

Table 2-1
Study Schedule

	MON	TUES	WED	TH	FRI	SAT	SUN
7 A. M.							
8 A. M.							
9 A. M.							
10 A. M. etc.							

As he used the study schedule, he found that he actually didn't have enough time available to meet the reading and study requirements of his courses. There were two possibilities: either to cut down on his part-time jobs or to cut down on his units. Because he had to earn his own way and his budget was very limited already, he decided to drop two classes. This brought his total units down to twelve. This, of course, meant that he would have to go to summer session or spend an extra semester in school. For many students, this seems very advisable; in fact, in several colleges, students who have to work long hours, or who have verbal-reading problems can enroll in a five- to eight-year program rather than in the four-year plan.

Another outcome of working with a study schedule was the discovery that there were certain hours in the day when he accomplished more while studying. He soon realized that in his schedule he should attempt to make maximum use of these periods of time, particularly for subjects that were more difficult for him. You might think about when you seem to study most effectively before you work on your own schedule.

As he worked with his schedule, he found a remarkable thing. He could allow free time for coffee breaks, dates, and bull sessions and he actually could relax and enjoy these periods of time. Whereas, before, he would feel guilty for not spending every minute studying, because he was so far behind anyway.

Another side effect of working with a study schedule is that you feel that you are doing your best and are able to develop some control over your own behavior. This helps give you additional self-confidence in your ability to handle other frustrating situations when they occur.

It should be pointed out that it is not possible to follow a study schedule perfectly. There are times when situations arise that interfere with study plans and schedules may have to be revised. However, having a study schedule does serve as a starting point for effective use of your time and energies.

It's All Right to Forget

One thing that used to bother the authors was the fact that they didn't remember everything they learned. They often felt stupid when they tried to recall ideas from some of the books they had read or lectures they had heard. When they found out that everyone forgets things that he no longer uses or needs, they were relieved.

As is mentioned earlier in this chapter, the pattern of school learning requires that we recall material on examinations sometimes several weeks after we have spent time studying it or discussing it in class. We know that periodic review helps to keep material from fading away. Another advantage of the study schedule is that you can include periodic review sessions.

Learning for Its Own Sake Can Be Rewarding

It took us a long time to realize that learning can be self-rewarding. In elementary and high school it often seemed that one did well on exams in order to be rewarded by the teacher or one's parents. In college, frequently one never gets to know the teacher that well, so one has to develop his own self-rewarding system in learning and mastering new ideas and materials.

Teachers and Subjects You Will Not Like or Not Want to Accept

It has been these authors' experience as well as that of many of their students that in their school backgrounds there were certain teachers with whom they had difficulty in relating. No matter how much they tried they often felt hostility or apathy. To be able to accept this fact may help in being able to mobilize your energies to learn in spite of the teacher! There are many possible reasons for having difficulties in relating to certain teachers: previous negative experiences with a subject matter area; a teacher who uses methods similar to a former teacher with whom you may have had a bad experience; unconscious hostility you may have toward adult authority figures; or simply realization that the teacher himself dislikes teaching and/or people in general and takes out his hostilities on the students.

You Can't Study in a "Nuthouse"

Another revelation to the authors in trying to improve their learning habits was the fact that one really can't concentrate on studying in a place where there are many distractions. It seems to help if you have a particular place where you go to study and concentrate. Frequently this is a desk in the corner of your bedroom, but it can be a corner of the college library. The important point is that you literally condition yourself to do nothing but study in this area, and when you take a break you leave the area. It is also important that you select an area that is free from noise, has good lighting and ventilation, and is comfortable. The authors have found that many of their students' poor grades and learning difficulties could be related merely to the fact that they did not have a place of study at home. Some ingenious students have used closets, or blocked off a corner of their garage with masonite or plasterboard to get a place with some peace and quiet.

Make Material Meaningful to Learn Effectively

As was mentioned earlier, when material makes sense to you, you tend to learn it much more easily and much more effectively and you also tend to forget it less rapidly. This principle of learning can be applied by reorganizing your lecture notes and outlining chapters in the books you are using. By going over lecture notes and jotting down and organizing the ideas in some way that you find meaningful, you will remember it much better, particularly on exams. Another technique students have found very helpful is to jot down notes in the right-hand margins of their textbooks and to review these. Sometimes outlining the major points from each section of the text chapters helps in terms of seeing the overall organization of ideas.

You Can Learn Things Outside the Classroom

A final item is that you can learn many things outside the classroom itself. You might think of college as a cluster of resources of which you can make much or little use. Students can have many exciting hours browsing through their college library shelves, or reading a chapter or a few pages from a book or magazine. There are many stimulating seminars and discussions sponsored by college clubs.

Some of the artist-lecture series that some colleges offer can introduce you to new artists and ideas. Working with international students on campus can provide good human contacts as well as exchanges of ideas between people of different cultures.

At your school you probably have a large number of similar resources; ones that will help you grow into a more self-actualizing person. Why not explore them and get involved in those you find interesting. Indirectly, this will facilitate a more positive attitude toward the school and toward learning in general. Instead of a place to dread or to get away from, school may become something you can't stay away from.

LIVING WITH THE JOB

Learning involved in a job or career field follows the same basic principles as learning in school. However, there are basic differences between school and job learning. Learning in school involves constant exposure to new ideas at different levels of complexity. On the other hand, learning on the job usually consists of repeating the same or similar patterns of behavior. You can see that once a job is learned such objective principles as forgetting, the need for review and recitation, and overlearning are not as important as certain subjective factors in learning.

Jobs can be looked at from many different points of view. In relation to the discussion here, in some jobs the subjective elements (such as the self, motivation, emotions, intelligence) play a major role in the successful learning and maintaining of that job. Think for a moment about a salesman's job; in most cases the actual skills involved in writing an order play a lesser role than his eagerness to sell a particular item to a customer. On the other hand, other jobs require more basic skill learning (auto mechanic, draftsman, dental assistant, or X-ray technician) and the subjective factors, although important to a point, play a lesser role. Where would the jobs of a teacher, a nurse, or a secretary fit in relation to this distinction?

Today probably one of the most important human questions about the world of work is whether, with the extent of automation and mass production, the identity and satisfaction that the individual worker once felt in his role as an employee can or should be maintained. There is increasing evidence that work no longer seems to offer the individual the human rewards that it used to offer. With many routine jobs being done more effectively by computers, and new jobs being created that merely require a person to watch for a red light or listen for a buzzer, what can the individual worker do to retain his feeling that a job is in fact worthwhile or necessary?

Many former students of the authors have expressed their concern about the loss of feeling of importance on the job. It seems that one answer lies in a change in the way we view work and leisure time. It seems inevitable that you will have to use leisure time in ways that will allow you to continue to grow and learn. Some of the authors' students have continued their education in night classes. Others have developed hobbies through which they can express their individuality and creativity. Some students do volunteer work in mental hospitals. The point is that you can do things off the job that may help alleviate some of the built-in routine that many jobs today require.

Final Summary

Learning is perhaps the most basic of all human experiences. It includes intellectual, emotional, and physical learning. The principles through which old behavior is modified and new behavior is acquired are divided into three areas: (1) subjective principles, (2) objective principles, and (3) special learning techniques.

The subjective principles are concerned with what the individual brings to the learning situation and includes self-concept, past experiences, intelligence, motivation, and emotions.

The objective principles deal with factors relevant to learning situations and include rates of learning and forgetting, reviewing, rewards, reward schedules, self-rewards, generalization, and discrimination.

Special learning techniques are used to increase learning efficiency and include massed and distributed learning, feedback, and overlearning.

Specific Chapter References

Birch, H. G. The role of motivational factors in insightful problem-solving. *Journal of Comparative Psychology*, 1945, 38, 295–317.

Bruner, J. S., and Goodman, C. C. Value and need as organizing factors in perception. *Journal of Abnormal and Social Psychology*. 1947, 13, 33–44.

Dollard, J., and Miller, N. E. *Personality and psychotherapy*. New York: McGraw-Hill, 1950.

Ebbinghaus, H. *Memory* (trans. H. A. Ruger and C. E. Bussenenius). New York: Teachers College, 1913.

Eells, K., Davis, A., Havighurst, R. J., Herrick, V. E., and Tyler, R. W. *Intelligence and cultural differences: a study of cultural learning and problem-solving*. Chicago: University of Chicago Press, 1951.

Farber, I. E. Anxiety as a drive state. In M. R. Jones (ed.), *Nebraska symposium on motivation*. Lincoln: University of Nebraska Press, 1954.

Goldstein, M., and Rittenhouse, C. H. Knowledge of results in the acquisition and transfer of a gunnery skill. *Journal of Experimental Psychology*, 1954, 48, 187–196.

Greenspoon, J., and Foreman, S. Effect of delay of knowledge of results on learning a motor task. *Journal of Experimental Psychology*, 1956, 51, 226–228.

Hull, C. L. *Essentials of behavior*. New Haven: Yale University Press, 1952.

Katona, G. *Organizing and memorizing*. New York: Columbia University Press, 1940.

Kreuger, W. C. F. The effect of overlearning on retention. *Journal of Experimental Psychology*, 1929, 12, 71–78.

Laird, D. S. The performance of two groups of 11-year-old boys on the Wechsler intelligence scale for children. *Journal of Educational Research*, 1957, 51, 101–107.

Lee, E. S. Negro intelligence and selective migration: a Philadelphia test of the Klineberg hypothesis. *American Social Review*, 1951, 16, 227–233.

Maier, N. R. F. *Frustration: a study of behavior without a goal.* New York: McGraw-Hill, 1949.

Otto, H. A. *Explorations in human potentialities.* Springfield, Illinois, Charles C Thomas, 1966.

Pavlov, I. P. *Conditioned reflexes.* G. V. Anrep (trans. and ed.). London: Oxford University Press, 1927.

Perin, C. The effect of delayed reinforcement upon the differentiation of bar responses in white rats. *Journal of Experimental Psychology*, 1943, 32, 95–109.

Skinner, B. F. *The behavior of organisms.* New York: Appleton-Century-Crofts, 1938.

Skodak, M. Children in foster homes: a study of mental development. *University of Iowa Study of Child Welfare*, 1936, 16, No. 1.

Skodak, M., and Skeels, H. M. A follow-up study of children in adoptive homes. *Journal of Genetic Psychology*, 1945, 66, 21–58.

—. A final follow-up study of one hundred adopted children. *Journal of Genetic Psychology*, 1949, 75, 85–125.

Terman, L. M., and Oden, M. H. *The gifted child grows up.* Stanford, Calif.: Stanford University Press, 1947.

Thorndike, E. L. *Animal intelligence.* New York: Macmillan, 1911.

Wolpe, J. *Psychotherapy by reciprocal inhibition.* Stanford University Press, 1958.

Recommended Further Readings

Paperback Books

Borger, R., and Seaborne, A. E. *Psychology of learning.* New York: Pelican, Penguin, 1968.

Braun, J. R. (ed.). *Contemporary research in learning.* Princeton, N.J.: Van Nostrand, 1963.

Ellis, H. *The transfer of learning.* New York: Macmillan, 1965.

Harris, I. *Emotional blocks to learning.* New York: Free Press, 1961.

Harris, T. L., and Schwahn, W. E. *Selected readings on the learning process.* New York: Oxford University Press, 1961.

Mednick, S. A. *Learning.* Englewood Cliffs, N.J.: Prentice-Hall, 1964.

Smith, W. I., and Moore, J. W. *Conditioning and instrumental learning.* New York: McGraw-Hill, 1966.

Hardcover Books

Bugelski, B. *The psychology of learning.* New York: Holt, 1956.

Deese, J., and Hulse, S. H. *The psychology of learning.* New York: McGraw-Hill, 1967.

Hall, J. F. *The psychology of learning.* New York: Lippincott, 1966.

Hebb, D. O. *The organization of behavior.* New York: Wiley, 1949.

Hilgard, E. R., and Bower, G. H. *Theories of learning.* (3rd ed.) New York: Appleton-Century-Crofts, 1966.

Klausmeier, H. J., and Goodwin, W. *Learning and human abilities: educational psychology* (2nd ed.). New York: Harper & Row, 1966.

Mowrer, O. H. *Learning theory and behavior.* New York: Wiley, 1960.

Travers, R. M. W. *Essentials of learning; an overview for students of education* (2nd ed.). New York: Macmillan, 1967.

Chapter 3 Effective Thinking and Problem Solving

Chapter Outline

Study Guide

Information from the previous chapters is woven into this chapter. It is important to review previous assignments in order to set the stage for the current assignment.

REVIEW
Review Chapters 1 and 2 by reading the intermediate and final summaries. Restudy what is not clear.

PREVIEW

Read the prelude, chapter outline, topic headings, cameo, and summaries of Chapter 3. Turn major topic headings into questions. Proceed to answer these questions and to learn more about effective thinking and problem solving.

READING

Read the chapter straight through. Adjust your speed of reading to the difficulty level of the passages; and check mark topics not understood as you read. After major topics and summaries, stop and review by glancing at the topic headings, turning them into questions, and jotting down or saying to yourself all you remember. When you draw blanks, reread the selections. Reread checkmarked topics.

REVIEW

Review by practicing forced recall. Glance at each topic in the chapter outline, turn each topic into a question, close the book, and repeat all you remember. Repeat the same procedure with all topic headings in the chapter. Reread only what you have forgotten.

Prelude

We have seen that much of our behavior is learned and how it is affected by both subjective (inner) factors and objective (outside) factors.

A unique thing about being human is our ability to use learning principles more effectively than animals. We can do so because man is capable of thinking before he acts. Because he can think about learning, man can imagine what the consequences of his actions will be before the actions occur. We call this process *thinking*.

Thinking (attempts at solving a problem; usually referring to ideas that precede an action) involves a wide variety of processes, from very vague daydreams to more specifically directed thinking about how to solve problems that we face. Like the learning process, the thinking process is not something we are born with. We learn how to think.

Students' Viewpoints

In talking with their students, the authors realize that they are continually faced with problems and often have confused thoughts about themselves and others. Here are a few statements by some students writing about their problems:

(1) I would like to know more about jealousy and how it affects peoples' lives. I would like to know what causes a person to become continuously jealous and how he might control it. Because a person is jealous, does it cause him to be possessive also?

Photos courtesy of the Peace Corps and Autonetics, a division of North American Rockwell Corp.

Figure 3-1

Figure 3-2

Thinking occurs when we try to solve problems, whether in a chemistry laboratory or in classrooms in disadvantaged parts of the world, or when efforts are made to convince others of the values of birth control and family planning.

Figure 3-3

The only person I am jealous of is my boyfriend. I think it might be because of a fear of losing him and a lack of trust. About two years ago I trusted him completely and he hurt me very much. I realize what happened was just part of a boy growing up, and I completely forgive him now, but I am now very jealous and afraid of trusting him.

(2) First of all, my biggest problem right now is my mother. I'm really not too sure if she's the problem, or if I am. We just don't seem to get along too well at all any more. We used to get along fine; but it seems like the older I get, the more we argue

69

about. And it's sort of strange too. You see, we are so terribly much alike it isn't even funny. We agree on taste in clothes, how to do things around the house, opinions on certain people, and I guess everything in general. Now it is the little things that set us both off. Not the big things that anyone would think. This is my biggest complaint. When I do things that she should really get mad at, she just says don't do it again. But then when it is something that is stupid she blows her top. I have been told that it is because no house is big enough for two women. I don't know about that but I wonder if I should continue living at home or move out. This bothers me a great deal and I wish someone could answer this for me.

(3) I would say that my utmost major problem would be that I cannot decide what is to become of my future. I cannot seem to get it straightened out in my mind what I truly want to be. I am wasting my time taking classes which are no good to me. I have already wasted away two years of my life in a junior college and have nothing to show for my efforts. I am right now deciding if I should change my major again but wonder if I really should, because I haven't really taken any classes in this newly elected major so I cannot really judge it.

Perhaps you have experienced similar problems. Perhaps you have shared some of their confused thoughts and feelings about how to approach the solving of such personally important problems.

WHY IS IS IMPORTANT?

One of the most frequent causes of emotional suffering is the failure to understand how to go about solving problems. Psychologists have studied how people go about solving problems of all kinds. They have also studied the strategies people use in thinking about problems. They have developed some useful techniques for helping people become more effective in thinking and *problem solving* (methods or techniques used in solving a problem).

It is important for you to know that there are ways for you to learn to think about and approach some of the problems you face. Much of the time and energy you now use in ineffective problem solving could be used for more productive and creative pursuits. Through learning more about how to think and solve problems more effectively, you will be able to resolve some of the conflicts that are troubling you and hindering deep and warm human relationships with others.

BASIC THEORY AND RESEARCH

Thinking, then, like learning, can be affected by both subjective (within the person) and objective (outside the person) factors. Let us look at some of these.

THE SELF AND THINKING

How one, feels about himself affects not only the content of his thinking but the way he thinks. A person who has a positive self-concept tends to spend more time thinking about his good qualities and his success experiences, whereas a person with an essentially negative self-concept spends more time thinking of his failures in life and his inadequacies as a person. (Combs and Snygg, 1959; Barron, 1968)

There is also evidence that how one feels about himself is related to how effectively he thinks. People who do not like themselves tend to have difficulty in solving problems effectively, whereas people who feel good about themselves tend to be much more effective in problem solving. (Combs and Snygg, 1959, pp. 208–209; Barron, 1968, pp. 48–49)

Figure 3-4

Barriers to Goals May Be External or Internal. You desire a date with a particular girl. A barrier may exist within yourself (you feel that she may say no) or the barrier may involve her going steady with another man (external barrier).

People who feel inadequate tend to think more rigidly; they tend to think in terms of black and white or good and bad, rather than in shades of gray. (Rokeach, 1960)

People who feel good about themselves also are able to tolerate complex or ambiguous situations. People who do not feel good about themselves cannot tolerate ambiguity; they have a need for an immediate answer to a problem. (Gough, 1957); Rokeach, 1960)

People who feel comfortable about themselves can bring new and unique ideas into their thoughts about a problem situation. They are much more creative and far more apt to come up with original ideas. (Combs and Snygg, 1959, p. 209)

PAST EXPERIENCES AND THINKING

Most people who have been reared in environments where they have been encouraged to think about the solving of problems or to think about the consequences of their behavior will be far more effective in their lives than those who have never had this opportunity. Many parents never allow their children to think things through to the solution of a problem nor give them time to think about the consequences of their behavior. Instead these parents give their children pat answers or tell them what to do. They do their children's thinking for them. Consequently the children develop inadequate or ineffective ways of thinking during childhood. If as a child you were rewarded for ineffective or inadequate ways of thinking about the world and your interactions with it, there is a good chance that ineffective thinking will persist. Examples of inadequate ways of thinking include rigid thinking, magical thinking, drawing the wrong conclusions from experiences, social pressure, and the inability to use *symbols* (a word or sign that represents an object or an idea) correctly.

Examples of Inadequate Thinking

RIGID THINKING. This kind of a thinking pattern occurs when the solution to a problem is thought about in an either-or manner. Statements such as "You either can do it my way or not at all" and "There are only two possible solutions to this question" reflect such a pattern. People who come from backgrounds where everything is evaluated in terms of right or wrong, black or white, good or bad are prone to rigid thinking. As a result they fail to evaluate the many alternatives present in any complex problem.

MAGICAL THINKING. Many people come from backgrounds where thinking occurred in an almost magical or mystical way. The reasons for a certain difficulty were attributed to the position of the stars or to the phases of the moon. The fact that a person is continually plagued with problems results from his being born on a certain day or at a particular hour. There are those who have been led to believe that only certain people can help you solve a problem, those gifted with certain "magic" powers.

DRAWING WRONG CONCLUSIONS. Some people have never had the opportunity to think long enough about a situation to reach accurate conclusions. Consequently, their analysis of a situation is incomplete; they do not collect the necessary information. Some parents demand of children that they make their decisions immediately. They indirectly teach the child not to tolerate an indecisive moment or ambiguous situation. Thus, the child never gets any practice in finding out what the factors are in making a decision.

SOCIAL PRESSURE. Some families encourage their children to think like everyone else or to accept what they are told and what they are given to read without question. After their early years, those so trained tend to accept ideas automatically from their peer group and from political or religious groups. These are the people who fall victims to advertising campaigns, unscrupulous salesmen, sometimes even to racketeers and "con" men.

INABILITY TO USE SYMBOLS. People who are familiar with and can manipulate symbols are likely to think more effectively. One of the reasons that school is such a necessary part of everyone's experience is that in school we learn how to use words and to think about ideas and concepts. Students often feel that they are learning little from school because they forget many of the specific facts they are exposed to. However, a more important goal of education involves the learning of tools and techniques (these would include the use of symbols such as words and concepts) through which one can learn to think more effectively in order to solve problems in later life.

As was said earlier in the discussion of learning, having a high intelligence may help one think more effectively because intelligent people tend to have more information available. However, intelligence is not the sole cause of effective thinking. There is certainly a point below which very little effective thinking can occur; above that, however, other factors such as the self, past experiences with thinking, motivation, and personality, seem to be more important. Very little study has been done relating intelligence to effective thinking, but several studies relating creativity and intelligence conclude that there is a very low relationship between the two. (Barron, 1961, p. 10) In other words, a person with average intelligence may have as much creativity as one with high intelligence.

MOTIVATION AND THINKING

There is evidence to suggest that motives affect the nature of our thoughts. (Rhine, 1957; Heilbrun, 1959; Katchmar *et al.*, 1958) People who are hungry, for example, tend to spend more time daydreaming about food. (Keys *et al.*, 1950; Guetzkow and Bowman, 1946.) Men in the armed forces overseas spend much time thinking about their wives and families and girlfriends.

Men who have a high need for achievement and success tend to have many more fantasies about getting promoted or winning in athletic competition than men who do not have such strong needs to try for the top. (McClelland *et al.*, 1953; French and Thomas, 1958)

People who have developed a need to express hatred toward a particular group will tend to think of them in very rigid terms (that is, as good or bad, right or wrong). They also tend to remember, as well as exaggerate, the elements in an event or picture that fit the need to show hostility toward a minority group. (Lindzey, 1950; Adorno *et al.*, 1950, p. 971; Suchman *et al.*, 1958, p. 59; Allport and Postman, 1958)

EMOTIONS AND THINKING

Our emotions affect the nature of our thinking and the ways we think; conversely, our thinking can affect our emotions. (Lefford, 1946; Mohsin, 1954; Cowen, 1952) Recall the last time you were really angry. Did you stop to think of the consequences before you acted, or did you say and do some things that you were sorry about later? Were you careful to analyze the situation to determine why you were angry? Did you try to think of alternative ways to remedy the situation?

Sometimes our thoughts can affect our emotions. Think for a moment of the saddest experiences you have had in your life. How did you feel? Now think of one of the pleasurable things that have happened to you. How did you feel then?

A dramatic example of how emotions affect our thinking is illustrated by the classroom demonstration that one of the authors has used. One day he came into the room and gave a surprise quiz, something he had never done before. The students were quite surprised. Some were hostile. One half of the class was given a quiz that was impossible to answer correctly. For example, the answers to the questions were not in the textbook. The other half of the class received a quiz so simple that the questions could be answered by a person who had not been listening in class or reading the text. The teacher then collected the papers and told the class that the test would count heavily on their midterm grades. He then asked the class to complete some sentences such as these: I feel _____. Teachers are _____. School is _____. Examinations are _____. As you might expect, the students who had the easy quiz gave fairly neutral responses. The students given the difficult quiz completed the statements with comments such as the following: I feel guilty. Teachers are unfair. Examinations are a pain. School is frustrating.

Sometimes our emotions can affect how critically we think. For example, think about your first boyfriend or girlfriend. No one (especially your parents) could get you to think about certain faults in him or her. He or she was perfect. Not until your first argument or after you broke up could you think objectively about some of the faults of the person.

Historically, emotional responses have been used to get people to act without thinking very carefully about the consequences of their behavior. Think of how many Germans were swayed by Adolph Hitler's emotional appeals about German superiority over other races. Think of the lynch mobs and vigilante committees that hung Negroes in the South a few years ago. Think of the emotional appeals of hate groups that talk about their superiority over other races.

Intermediate Summary

The following are important subjective factors involved in thinking and problem solving: how and what you think about yourself, the effects of your previous experiences, the effects of your intelligence, the effects of your motives, and the effects of your emotions. Inadequate thinking is often the result of one or more of the following factors: rigid thinking, magical thinking, drawing wrong conclusions, social pressure, and the inability to use symbols.

Objective Principles of Thinking

WHAT IS THINKING?

As was mentioned earlier, complex thinking is one of the characteristics of man that separates him from other animals. Thinking involves the ability to span time—to operate in the past, present, and future, symbolically. Putting it another way, thinking can be looked at as a way of using what we have learned to solve

Photo courtesy of Harvard University

Figure 3-5
Jerome Bruner, Ph.D. (1915)
Experimental psychologist

Academic Career
B.A., Duke University
M.A., Ph.D. Harvard University

Professional Experience (in part)
Associate professor, Harvard University
Senior field representative, Princeton University
Chairman the National Academy of Sciences (1959)
Currently Professor at Harvard University

CAMEO

Areas of Interest
   Dr. Bruner is involved in general experimental psychology work with major emphasis in the area of cognitive processes (how we imagine, remember, perceive, reason, and judge). He has also been involved in research on opinions and attitudes.

Selected Readings
Blake, R. R., and Ramsey, G. V. (eds). *Perception, and approach to personality.* New York: Ronald Press, 1951, 121–247.
Bruner, J. S., Goodnow, J. J., and Austin, G. A. *A study of thinking.* New York: Wiley, 1956.
—. *On knowing: essays for the left hand.* New York: Atheneum, 1967.
—. *The process of education.* Cambridge, Mass.: Harvard University Press, 1960.
—. *Toward a theory of instruction.* Cambridge: Harvard University Press, 1966.
Smith, M. B., Bruner, J. S., and White, R. W. *Opinions and personality.* New York: Wiley, 1956.

75

problems. So thinking and learning and problem solving are all closely related.

As already mentioned, thinking can vary from the vague and fleeting thoughts we have when we are relaxing, to the highly directed thinking that we engage in when we are trying to study or solve a problem. Human thinking is a very difficult activity for psychologists to study because it is highly subjective.

Psychologists have studied types of thinking (Murphy, 1947; Rapaport, 1951), strategies of thinking and problem solving (Bruner, *et al.*, 1956; Woodworth and Schlosberg, 1954), how thinking takes place (Dashiell, 1937; Hebb, 1949, 1966; Osgood, 1953; Podell, 1958), and the nature of creative thinking (Anderson, 1959; Barron, 1968; Kneller, 1965). The most meaningful parts of the research for students are some of the techniques involved in effective thinking and problem solving as well as the discussion of some of the techniques of creative thinking.

Techniques of Effective Thinking and Problem Solving

Perhaps one of the best methods developed for effective thinking and problem solving is the scientific method. Most of you have been engaging in "midget scientific studies" all of your lives. Essentially, the scientific method employs the same steps that most of you use in thinking about and solving everyday problems:

1. Defining the problem
2. Planning a method of attack
3. Carrying out the plan
4. Evaluating the results

With certain problems you may actually go through these four steps very quickly. With attempts to solve major problems—ones that could have important consequences—you may take several days, even weeks, to go through these four steps.

DEFINING THE PROBLEM

One of the things a scientist does is to go about searching for answers to problems. He gets his ideas from what other researchers have done, from reading books on theory, and from his own hunches and observations. Once he selects a problem to study he must define all its variables or factors.

Unlike the scientists, most people do not go around looking for problems to solve. However, life often presents them with the necessity of making decisions about problems. These decisions may be involved with processes within the person, such as a conflict in values between what parents taught and what the person feels is right. Or these decisions may be involved with processes outside the person—wanting to date a particular person but finding out that the person is going steady.

How do you go about defining a problem? Actually, the sources you use in defining your problems are similar to those of the scientist. A difference is that you use the results of the experiments you have been running throughout your life (past experiences) plus your own "theories" about people and the world. Mentally healthy persons tend to be such good problem solvers because they can evaluate and define problems more effectively. Their theories about people and the world are more often based on reality. There are certain common difficulties people have in defining their problems objectively. These are as follows: (1) faulty assumptions, (2) rigid mental attitude, (3) emotions, and (4) oversimplification. (Coleman, 1960, pp. 378–381)

Faulty Assumptions

An assumption is a kind of frame through which you see the world; or, as was mentioned earlier, it is like the color of the window you look through when you view the world. If your assumption is that the world and people in it are generally bad and not to be trusted, then when you attempt to define a particular problem it will be like looking through black or dully colored glass.

Rigid Mental Attitude

A person who has a rigid mental attitude is one who refuses to consider alternatives in solving a problem. "There is a wrong way and a right way to solve this problem (or, to fix this car, or to deal with this situation)." "Now, you do it my way." "Accept my advice or forget it!" How many times have you heard people say such things! Often society is responsible for teaching us only certain ways of dealing with problems. Our past experiences reinforce these ways, and often we remain unaware that there are other ways.

Emotions

Our emotions affect the manner in which we try to solve problems. Frequently the situation we are in is highly emotionally loaded; this in turn may block our attempts to be objective. Sometimes it is best to let our emotions cool down before we attempt to solve a problem.

Oversimplification

People have a tendency to reduce complex problems to a simpler level. This is sometimes desirable; however, in doing so frequently or always, people may leave out some of the basic factors involved in the problem. Political speeches are oftentimes examples of this tendency to oversimplify causes of very complex national and international problems. You may have heard people make such comments as the following in discussing rather complex issues: "Eliminate welfare and those people will get to work." Or, "There would be no more unrest or riots on college campuses if all those who were involved were kicked out or charged a stiff tuition."

PLANNING THE METHOD OF ATTACK

Once the problem has been carefully analyzed, the scientist (or you) is ready to decide how to go about attempting to solve the problem or answer the research question. He does this by making a prediction of the outcome of the research (a hypothesis). He then decides on one of the many research methods that he has been trained to use in psychology: the experiment, the survey, the interview, the observation, or the testing method. (For a further discussion of research methods see the Student Workbook.)

When you go about planning to solve a problem you will tend to use methods that you have learned from past experience. Some of these methods may be quite effective, but frequently some of your problem-solving methods will not be successful.

Most problems can be visualized in terms of a barrier between you and the desire to attain a particular goal. Figure 3-6 illustrates the basic factors involved in a problem situation.

There are a number of strategies employed in solving problems. Which of

Courtesy of Autonetics, a division of North American Rockwell Corp.

Figure 3-6
Once a person feels safe and wanted, he is ready to learn and to think more effectively. A positive self-concept makes us more open and willing to accept new experiences.

these is the most effective will depend on your analysis of the problem situation, your past experiences in solving problems, and also on your ability to withstand stress and frustration. Which of these do you tend to use most frequently?

STRATEGIES USED IN SOLVING PROBLEMS

Retreating

Sometimes, depending on the nature of the barrier, it is wise to retreat from the solving of a problem if after analysis it appears to be insoluble. Our success-oriented society may frown on this type of behavior and call it failure, yet at times it may be wise to retreat in order to build up new skills and self-confidence, and develop new attitudes. For example, a number of our students who drop out of college and then return a year or so later complete their college work successfully.

Attacking

To attack is perhaps one of the most humanly impulsive things to do when we are confronted with a barrier or block to the attainment of a goal. However, it may not be the most desirable. It is a good strategy when we know we have what it takes to accomplish our goal. For example, the authors have seen students overcome major obstacles by a tremendous mobilization of their energy and efforts. One of the authors' students after a prolonged illness returned and successfully completed his course work through tremendous efforts and determination.

Going Around the Barrier

Sometimes it is wise to discover new pathways to achieving a desired goal. A student may find that he is not succeeding in a particular college. He, therefore, investigates similar programs in other schools and transfers to another college. Other students may find the means to their goals outside of college. For example, a student who wants to become a businessman may find real life experiences in the world of business just as valuable as classroom experiences.

Seeking Expert Opinion

During your lifetime there is a good chance that you will be confronted with a problem that requires some expert help to solve. This is becoming more necessary because of the rapid development of specialized knowledge. Often a lawyer, doctor, dentist, auto mechanic, plumber, family counselor, teacher, psychologist, or psychiatrist has worked so long with certain solutions to problems and has employed so many strategies that not seeking his help is foolhardy.

Changing the Goal

After analyzing a problem, we may see that the attainment of a particular goal is beyond our capabilities as a result of factors within ourselves or because of the nature of the barriers. We may then see that an alternate, but attainable, goal may also give us the same satisfactions. Many students who are failing in one major may find success and satisfaction in a related field.

Changing Yourself

After the analysis of the problem we may find that the barrier lies within ourselves, so that the solution may involve a changing of ourselves in some way. Changing might involve such things as the practice of certain skills to qualify for a particular job, the loss of weight to become an airline stewardess, or attaching less value to money so that one can go into a lower paying but more satisfying occupation.

Crying, Worrying, and Whining

This is probably the most ineffective method for solving problems, yet it is the most frequently used. It probably accounts for much of the misery and human suffering that we see around us today. It results essentially from previous learning as children when these methods payed off in "instant problem solving" by mama or papa. Although ineffective, this method helps us to temporarily "let off steam" so that we may seek better ways of solving our problems at a later time.

Is the Price Too High?

When faced with a barrier to a desired goal we should be concerned with the amount of effort, time, and money involved in achieving the goal. Sometimes we may decide that the price is simply too high to pay for the attainment of that goal. For example, a capable student may decide to drop out of college because the price of getting a college degree is too great. This frequently happens to married students with children when they are offered a high-paying job as well as the opportunity of being able to spend more time with their families.

CARRYING OUT THE PLAN

After one has decided the plan of attack in solving a problem he must then follow through by actually carrying out the plan. Frequently, this is one of the most difficult parts of solving problems because it means actually doing something about what is bothering you or blocking your progress toward a specific goal. Many people go through an elaborate plan of what they are going to do about some problem, but they never seem to put it into action. You probably know people who keep talking about how they are going to do this and that with their lives, but who never carry out these plans. This is the cause of many difficulties; they know they have a problem and know what to do, but they refuse to follow through.

EVALUATING THE RESULTS

After one has actually taken some action in the solution of a problem he then must evaluate the results. Often the results can immediately be seen in terms of the attainment of the desired goal or the reduction of tension. But sometimes solving problems takes time and one cannot expect immediate results, especially when one is involved in a long-term project such as getting an education.

Again, many people tend to leave out this step and never seem to learn from their problem-solving efforts. That is, they continually use ineffective methods for solving problems and continually fail to gain any satisfaction; yet they persist in this behavior mainly because they have not evaluated the results of their behavior.

Research indicates that people who are involved in the attainment of long-term goals find much satisfaction in the successful accomplishment of intermediate goals or subgoals. These provide the necessary feelings of success or reinforcement important in motivating a person to continue the efforts necessary for achieving long-range goals.

Intermediate Summary

The four basic steps involved in effective thinking and problem solving are (1) defining the problem, (2) planning a method of attack, (3) carrying out the plan, and (4) evaluating the results. People often have difficulties in attempting to define a problem because of faulty assumptions, a rigid mental attitude, emotional reactions, or oversimplification.

The following strategies are the most frequently used in planning a method of attack: retreating, attacking, going around the barrier, seeking expert opinion, changing the goal, changing yourself, and crying, worrying, and whining.

Creative Thinking

Psychologists have studied creative thinking and found that it seems to lead to more effective and satisfying ways to solve problems. (Anderson, 1959; Barron, 1968; Ghiselin, 1952; Moustakas, 1967)

In discussing creativity, it is convenient to follow Maslow's distinction between "special talent creativity," which requires special skills and training, as well as unusual inborn capacities and "self-actualizing creativity," which is related much more to psychological health in the kind of society in which we live. (Maslow, in Anderson, 1959, p. 83)

Too often we have stressed special talent creativity—the Newtons, Flemings, daVincis, Shakespeares—and ignored self-actualizing creativity as seen in persons around us—the newsboys, the clerks, the mechanics, teachers, and students. All of us are creative in different ways and in varying degrees. The key question is how can we become more creative so that we can develop hidden talents and resources.

The products of creative thinking are not always the great masterpieces by

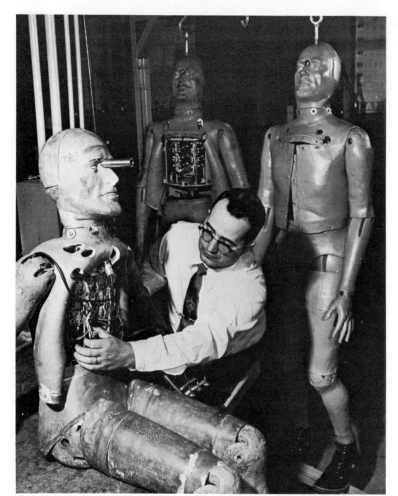

Creativity. Creativity can be expressed in many different ways. Special-talent creativity can be seen in the design and construction of human robots. The more individualized self-actualizing creativities can be seen in painting and crafts.

Figure 3–7

Picasso or Van Gogh or the great inventions by Edison or Einstein. Creativity may refer to everyday experiences such as making up a funny story, putting a wheel on a wagon for the first time, arranging living room furniture in a different style, even using a new recipe for apple pie. Somehow, it is fun to create, to explore, to discover, and to put things together in different ways.

HOW CAN CREATIVE THINKING BE DEVELOPED?

Chapter 1 mentioned several important characteristics that help us to become more creative. As you may remember, some of the characteristics of self-actualizing persons are: (1) openness to new experiences—that is, rejecting the idea that we know all the answers; (2) lack of fear of the unknown—in fact, often self-actualizing persons are more attracted to the unknown than

Figure 3-8

*Photos courtesy of Fullerton Junior College and
Autonetics, a division of North American Rockwell Corp.*

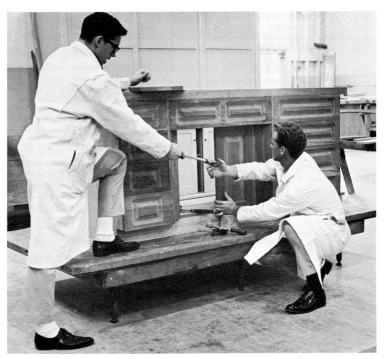

Figure 3-9

as these: People are basically evil; people are not to be trusted; and people are out to get you. No matter how he may have tried to conceal these thoughts, they were conveyed to others, sometimes in subtle ways (tone of voice, facial expressions, muscle tension) or sometimes in obvious ways (verbal attacks, physical attacks, sarcasm).

The point is that how we think about other people and the world in general cannot be separated from how we behave toward others and what we do with our lives.

YOUR OWN WORLD OF THINKING

What can you learn from Bob's experience? First, you might begin with a project to determine what your inner world of thoughts consists of. There are many ways of doing this: talking freely and honestly with a close friend in a relaxed atmosphere; talking with a teacher or counselor about your ideas and thoughts; or keeping a "Thinking Diary" (jotting down the kinds of things you spend a lot of time thinking about or wondering about, especially when you are alone in the day, driving to and from school, or while lying in bed at night before you go to sleep).

By taking a look at your own inner world of thoughts you may find some amazing things. Maybe you, like Bob, tend to dwell on negative past experiences, or perhaps you are more concerned with pleasant experiences, or concerned about the future and what you will do with your own life. In so doing, you will become more aware of how these thoughts affect your daily life and interactions with people.

PROBLEM SOLVING

One kind of thinking that all of us engage in a good part of our lives is the kind involved in the solving of problems. Some of these problems exist within the self and others involve the person and his environment. In this section the focus is on problems within the person. Many of the students that we have talked with have had problems involving such things as: their *real self* (what a person believes about himself) versus their *ideal self* (what a person would like to become).

Problems with the Self

How one feels about oneself is a most important determiner of whether one is a mentally healthy or self-actualizing person or not. Thus, the self-concept plays a major role not only in our way of thinking but in how effectively we solve problems.

One of the recurrent problems that students bring to teachers is that of the self-concept. George was an average student who had been told by his parents since he was small that he would go to college and become a doctor. George had been told this so long that he began to picture himself as a surgeon living in a large house and driving an expensive car (his ideal self). Yet when George came to the authors, he was failing most of his classes. As they talked, his real feelings about himself were expressed (his real self). George really did not view himself as a student; in fact, he hated school and his studies. He was flunking not because he wasn't intelligent, but because he wasn't spending any time studying. He spent most of his time surfing or skiing.

Basically, then, George had a problem that involved what he was and how he really felt (his real self) versus what he (and his parents) thought he *should* be (his ideal self). Through becoming more aware of this conflict and being able to talk freely to his parents about it, he soon resolved the problem by selecting a nonpreference major that allowed him to take courses in many areas. He could then select what he really wanted rather than what his parents thought he should have.

Using the problem-solving model discussed earlier, analyze the steps that George went through in solving his problem. What strategies did he use? You may want to do the same for the cases that follow.

Value Problems

Other problems students frequently face are those involving value conflicts.

Mary was brought up in a highly religious home. Part of the values of her religion included no drinking or smoking. Mary, now a college student, went to parties where students drank beer. Mary was considered by others not really a part of the group because she refused to participate. Mary came to see one of the authors and in discussing the situation, she expressed a real desire to experiment with new ways of behaving; yet her previous training in the home and in the church made the decision a difficult one. We suggested that she make a list of the possible consequences of her two choices: to drink or not to drink. The next day she came in with two long lists of consequences. If she drank, the consequences might include guilt feelings; discovery by her parents and possible rejection; legal problems (because she was under age); and the possibility that she might form a bad habit.

The consequences of not drinking included: the loss of some friends; not being invited to parties; and being considered a "square."

She finally decided that the consequences would be much greater if she drank, so she decided not to give in to her impulses. The last time the author saw her she was involved with a different group of friends.

Problems with Emotions

Another problem many of us face within ourselves has to do with conflicting emotional reactions. All of us have experienced combinations or alternations of the following emotions: love and hate; curiosity and disgust; enjoyment and pain; being joyous and yet sad.

As you learn to relate to members of the opposite sex, the conflict in feelings between love and hate seems to be a very common problem as demonstrated by the following account.

Georgia had been going steady with Bill for more than two years. During this time they had become very close. Georgia came to one of the authors in tears one day because as she said: "I'm being torn up inside. I love Bill but he does things to hurt me and I want to get back at him."

She explained how often she really hated Bill, and yet she cared for him so much. By talking about it she soon began to realize that the problem was not so much with Bill as with herself. She was really angry with Bill because she wished she could date other fellows once in a while, but Bill would have nothing to do with it. She finally developed enough courage to tell Bill to stop seeing her so she could date other fellows.

Now, being freed from obligations to Bill she was able to explore relationships with other young men without feelings of guilt.

Living with Others

To live happily with those we love is probably the greatest joy in life. We want to share with our loved ones our good fortunes in the same way that we want them to share their good fortunes with us. But we love each other for better and for worse. Conflicts, disagreements, and, at times, feelings of hatred arise. These are normal and healthy. They occur in any human relationship. However, it is also normal and healthy to try to resolve problems and deal with feelings.

Let's discuss a problem a young couple had, applying what we have learned so far about problem solving.

A young lady student came to see one of the authors about a year after her marriage to a former student of his. She was terribly unhappy because she felt her husband no longer loved her and the baby.

The first step was to *define the problem* accurately. Was the problem really that her husband no longer loved her? Because persons are capable of empathy, especially when they love each other, the author asked her how and when her husband began to change his feelings and behavior toward her. She explained that they were married when she finished high school and he was a sophomore in college. When the baby was born she had had to quit her job. Her husband dropped out of college and took a higher paying job, which he disliked. He enrolled in evening college but dropped out because he couldn't keep up.

About this time, she began to notice that his behavior was changing. He didn't play with the baby anymore. He came home late at night. He withdrew into a shell; he would come out only to speak harshly to her.

Finally, she understood the problem and said, "My poor husband! Now I can see why he's acting the way he is. He sees no future for himself. I have a nice home, a nice baby, and I'm in college. How could I have been so insensitive to his feelings and needs. I've been thinking only of myself! How can I help him is the real problem?"

The next step was *planning a method of attack.* The author suggested that she talk to her husband about going back to college, but she said she knew from experience that this would only make him angry. "What if I told him that I was tired of going to college and that I wanted to work for a while?"

she asked. I told her that would be a fine idea because he loved her too much to ask her to drop out of college so that he could return.

The next step was to *carry out the plan,* whereby her husband could get back to college and still feel that he was not hurting his wife or his baby. The plan did work. She went back to work so that her husband could finish his education.

She made a sacrifice willingly because she knew that her husband had done the same for her. The results were that they loved each other more than ever before.

Living with Society

Many times we find that our problems and goals are related to other persons. That is, if we are to solve our problems and achieve our goals, we must work with and cooperate with others in mutually beneficial efforts.

THINKING AND PROBLEM SOLVING

The first major step is to apply what we have learned about thinking and problem-solving techniques and how their proper application increases effective thinking when we are working with others. Let us review some of these techniques in the manner used by one of the authors in training teachers to teach remedial reading in a high school.

During the first session the teachers were praised for their excellence in their profession and for their reputation for helping students. They were praised for volunteering to learn something new and difficult like remedial reading. Why was this done? Teachers are human beings and in a new situation they feel threatened and inadequate. People who feel threatened are not open to new learning. They feel uncomfortable and seek immediate answers to complex problems. However, when people feel important and accepted, they are ready to learn even if the work is hard and extensive.

They were made to understand that mistakes and failures were expected as a result of the newness of the situation; the mistakes and failures were not their fault. They were, however, expected to ask for help in order to improve their teaching (seeking expert opinion).

The first day of class the author found himself eager to take over the teaching himself. He walked into the classrooms. He saw the teachers making mistakes, but he walked away. He had to. Otherwise, the teachers would feel that he did not really trust them. A person who feels untrustworthy cannot do his best work. That afternoon all the teachers came to see the writer with many questions.

At times they would make mistakes of which they were not aware. This problem was handled in either of two ways: The teacher was invited to the office. The teacher was first praised sincerely for his good work and then suggestions for improvement were offered. At other times, a lecture on a specific reading method was presented to the group instead of to the particular person who needed the additional training. The important lesson is to help others to maintain a positive self-concept through sincere praise and constructive ideas.

The preceding example is illustrative of the effective uses of the thinking and problem-solving model presented in this chapter when working with other people. Perhaps you have been in situations where your employer or teacher has employed similar techniques effectively in order to achieve good working relationships with others.

THE THINKING MODEL

Defining the Problem

Once persons feel safe and wanted, the problem can be introduced and defined in detail. The problem was to introduce a remedial reading program into a high school. The objectives were to train teachers to teach remedial reading and to improve the reading skills of the students. The author was the reading expert, but the teachers knew their students far better than he did. Therefore, they needed to think together about the best possible solutions.

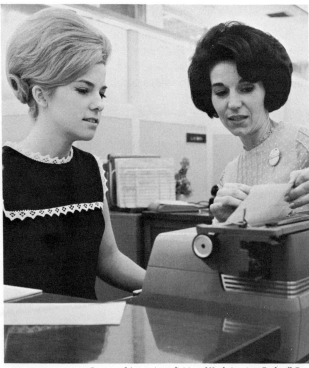

Figure 3-10
We learn and think better when we are first praised for our efforts. Here a former student continues to learn in the world of work.

Courtesy of Autonetics, a division of North American Rockwell Corp.

Planning a Method of Attack

They discussed the students' reading problems, they studied their school records and they gave them many tests. They then formed a total picture of their reading difficulties.

Once the problem has been defined in detail, alternative solutions are likely to become more apparent. At this point, creative thinking is most appropriate. What new ways are there to teach word-attack skills, study skills, and vocabulary building? They did not want to use old methods because these students had learned to read poorly using old methods. Finally, they decided to use a combination of teaching methods never used before: audiotutorial programs using the tape decks of the foreign language department, college-level reading exercises for special students, and techniques borrowed from the field of visual training.

Carrying Out the Plan

Carrying out the plan of action is often the most difficult part of problem solving, yet it can also be the most exciting. Would the plan really work? What changes, if any, must be made? What unforeseen obstacles would arise? Even the best plans may need to be modified when put into action. In this case the authors, working with the teachers, selected the materials, trained the teachers, had practice trials, and organized the classrooms.

Evaluating the Results

Will this plan of action be successful? Will the students really improve their reading skills? They had to evaluate the results. They gave the students reading tests before and after the reading course. They found that nearly all had made tremendous progress. The school administration was so pleased that they decided that all students with reading problems should take our reading course. Of course,

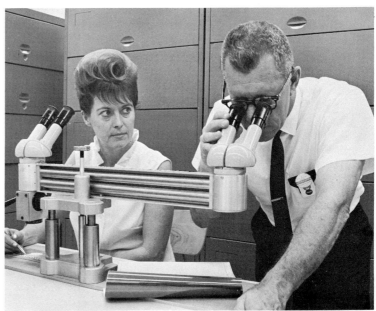

Figure 3-11
We learn and think better when we feel that others trust us and want to help us. Here the instructor checks the work of a trainee with a dual-training microscope. Assembling microelectronic circuitry requires new methods and special techniques.

Courtesy of Autonetics, a division of North American Rockwell Corp.

if they had not been successful, they would have tried other methods of teaching remedial reading.

Naturally, not all problems are so complex. In cases of emergencies, which require immediate action, we have to take short cuts. For example, while crossing the campus, one of the authors met a student nearly in tears. She was about to drop out of college because she had to work full time. She told him how much she loved going to college, but what could she do?

The solution was really simple, but for her it was difficult because she lacked sufficient information to solve the problem. The author informed her that as a registered day student she could transfer her classes to the evening college and continue to study while she worked during the day.

The point to remember is that during moments of crisis we often do not think very well. We should not hesitate to ask for help and information from others during such emergencies.

Final Summary

Thinking and effective problem solving are necessary for effective living. Our thinking always involves subjective and objective factors. Important subjective principles of thinking include:

- How one feels about himself affects both the content of his thoughts, and how effectively he thinks.
- People learn how to think as a result of past experiences.
- Poor thinking can result from a failure to recognize the complexities of problems.
- Magical kinds of thinking can interfere with effective problem solving.
- Failure to analyze problems sufficiently can lead to the drawing of wrong conclusions.
- Strong social pressures can lead to ineffective thinking and problem solving.
- Adequate language mastery aids effective thinking.
- Intelligence is not the most important factor in effective thinking.
- One's motives and emotions affect the content and the way he thinks.

Important objective principles of thinking include the following:

- In solving a problem effectively, there are four steps: (1) defining the problem, (2) planning a method of attack, (3) carrying out the plan, and (4) evaluating the results.
- Research on effective creative thinking suggests the following as important factors: hard work; youth; individuality; and the realization that immediate answers are not always the best and that there may be many solutions to one problem.

Adorno, T. W., Frenkel-Brunswik, Else, Levinson, D. J., and Sanford, R. N. *The authoritarian personality.* New York: Harper, 1950.

Allport, G. W. and Postman, L. J. The basic psychology of humor. In E. E. Maccoby, et al. (eds.), *Readings in social psychology* (3rd ed.). New York: Holt, Rinehart and Winston, 1958.

Anderson, H. (ed.) *Creativity and its cultivation.* New York: Harper & Row, 1959.

Barron, F. Creative vision and expression in writing and painting. In Institute of Personality Assessment and Research, *The Creative Person.* University of California and University Extension, Liberal Arts Dept., 1961, pp. 1–19.

—. *Creativity and personal freedom.* Princeton, N.J.: D. Van Nostrand, 1968.

Bruner, J., Goodnow, J., and Austin, G. *A study of thinking.* New York: Wiley Science Editions, 1956.

Coleman, J. C. *Personality dynamics and effective behavior.* Chicago: Scott, Foresman and Co., 1960.

Combs, A. W., and Syngg, D. *Individual behavior: a perceptual approach to behavior.* New York: Harper, 1959.

Cowen, E. L. Stress reduction and problem-solving rigidity. *Journal of Consulting Psychology,* 1952, 16, 425–428.

Dashiell, J. R. *Fundamentals of general psychology.* Boston: Houghton Mifflin, 1937.

French, Elizabeth G., and Thomas, F. H. The relation of achievement motivation to problem-solving effectiveness. *Journal of Abnormal and Social Psychology,* 1958, 56, 45–48.

Gardner, R., Holzman, P. S., Klein, G. S., Linton, Harriet, and Spence, D. P. Cognitive control: a study of individual consistencies in cognitive behavior. *Psychological Issues,* 1959, 1, No. 4 (Whole No. 4).

Ghiselin, B. *The creative process.* New York: Mentor Books (New American Library of World Literature, Inc.), 1952.

Gough, H. G. Imagination—undeveloped resource. In *Proceedings of the 1st Conference on Research Development in Personnel Management.* Los Angeles: University of California Institute of Industrial Relations, 1957. Pp. 4–10.

Guetzkow, H. S., and Bowman, P. H. *Men and hunger.* Elgin, Ill.: Brethren Publishing House, 1946.

Hebb, D. O. *The organization of behavior.* New York: Wiley, 1949.

—. *A textbook of psychology.* (2nd ed.) Philadelphia: Saunders, 1966.

Heilbrun, A. B., Jr. The effects of various shock stress conditions upon a complex perceptual-motor task. *Journal of Personality,* 1959, 27, 285–299.

Katchmar, L. T., Ross, S., and Andrews, T. G. Effects of stress and anxiety on performance of a complex verbal-coding task. *Journal of Experimental Psychology,* 1958, 55, 559–564.

Keys, A., Brozek, J., Henschel, A., Mickelson, O., and Taylor, H. L. *The biology of human starvation.* Minneapolis: University of Minnesota Press, 1950.

Kneller, G. F. *The art and science of creativity.* New York: Holt, Rinehart and Winston, 1965.

Lefford, A., The influence of emotional subject matter on logical reasoning. *Journal of Genetic Psychology,* 1946, 34, 127–151.

Lindzey, G. Differences between the high and low in prejudice and their implications for a theory of prejudice. *Journal of Personality*, 1950, 19, 16–40.

McClelland, D., *et al. The achievement motive*. New York: Appleton-Century-Crofts, 1953.

Mohsin, S. M. Effect of frustration on problem-solving behavior. *Journal of Abnormal and Social Psychology*, 1954, 49, 152–155.

Moustakas, C. *Creativity and conformity*. Princeton, N.J.: D. Van Nostrand Co., 1967.

Murphy, G. *Personality: a biosocial approach to origins and structures*. New York: Harper and Row, 1947.

Osgood, C. E. *Method and theory in experimental psychology*. New York: Oxford University Press, 1953.

Podell, Harriet A. Two processes of concept formation. *Psychological Monographs*, 72, No. 15 (Whole No. 468), 1958.

Rapaport, D. Toward a theory of thinking. In D. Rapaport, (ed.) *Organization and pathology of thought*. New York: Columbia University Press, 1951.

Rhine, R. J. The effect in problem solving of success or failure as a function of cue specificity. *Journal of Experimental Psychology*, 1957, 53, 121–125.

Rokeach, M. *The open and closed mind*. New York: Basic Books, 1960.

Suchman, E. A., *et al. Desegregation: some propositions and research suggestions*. New York: Anti-Defamation League of B'nai B'rith, 1958.

Woodworth, R. S., and Schlosberg, H. *Experimental psychology*. (rev. ed.) New York: Holt, Rinehart and Winston, 1954.

Recommended Further Readings

Paperback Books

Barron, F., *Creativity and personal freedom*. Princeton, N.J.: Van Nostrand, 1968.

Bruner, J. S., Goodnow, Jacqueline J., and Austin, G. A. *A study of thinking*. New York: Macmillan, 1967.

Carroll, J. B. *Language and thought*. Englewood Cliffs, N.J.: Prentice-Hall, 1964.

Duncan, C. P. (ed.) *Thinking: current experimental studies*. Philadelphia: Lippincott, 1967.

Humphrey, G. *Thinking: an introduction of its experimental psychology*. New York: Wiley Science Editions, 1951.

Manis, M. *Cognitive processes*. Belmont, Calif.: Wadsworth, 1966.

Ray, W. S. *The experimental psychology of original thinking*. New York: Macmillan, 1967.

Singer, J. L. *Daydreaming: an introduction to the experimental study of inner experience*. New York: Random House, 1966.

Hardcover Books

Almy, Millie. *Young children's thinking, studies of some aspects of Piaget's theory*. New York: Columbia University Teachers College Press, 1966.

Anderson, R. C., and D. P. Ausubel (eds.) *Readings in the psychology of cognition*. New York: Holt, Rinehart and Winston, 1965.

Barron, F. *Creativity and psychological health*. Princeton, N.J.: Van Nostrand, 1963.

Berlyne, D. E. *Structure and direction in thinking*. New York: Wiley, 1965.

Bruner, J., Goodnow, Jacqueline, and Austin, G. *A study of thinking*. New York: Wiley, 1962.

Smith, P. *Creativity: an examination of the creative process.* New York: Hastings House, 1959.

Stein, M. I., and Heinze, Shirley J. *Creativity and the individual.* Glencoe, Ill.: Free Press, 1960.

Wallach, M., and Kogan, N. *Modes of thinking in young children.* New York: Holt, Rinehart and Winston, 1965.

Part II Understanding the Development of Human Behavior

In Part I we explored several important areas of behavior that are of particular concern to you now. We discussed some new research about mentally healthy people. This research has revealed many positive goals that you, as a unique and creative individual, may want to work toward.

We then discussed some learning principles and how they affect you as a person and how they can be used to grow in learning about yourself, the world, and others. How you think and solve problems that face you was the next section. There we tried to help you explore your own world of thought and action in relation to situations you face now and in the future.

We hope that this material helped you look at yourself and others in a new light. We hope that in some ways you have already begun to think about ways to become more self-actualizing. We hope that by understanding how much learning influences your behavior, you will become more and more effective in learning about yourself and others and in school. We hope that you will be more effective too in solving the problems that you face every day. And, we hope that you may even become more creative in your thinking and in your ways of relating to the world in general.

In Part II we go back to "the good old days," when you were a baby. Why? Because we want you to now look at the development of your behavior, to answer the question of how you became the person you are. How did your personality develop as a result of early and middle childhood experiences? How did you develop during adolescence?

In Chapter 5, we hope to help you understand how and why certain motives play an important part in your life; why you may seem to need to succeed in everything you do, or why certain needs are stronger than others.

In Chapter 6, we explore how your emotional reactions were developed. Why do you get angry in certain situations? Why are you afraid of certain things? How did you learn to love?

And, finally, in Chapter 7, we discuss how you learned to view the world as you do, why you tend to select certain things in the world instead of others, and why everyone doesn't always see the world in the same way.

Chapter 4 Childhood and Adolescence

Chapter Outline

Study Guide

Reading, in a sense, is like meeting a person for the first time. The reader brings with him experiences, feelings, and hopes that interact with those expressed in the book. Just as friendships fail to develop because of a lack of common interests, a reader may "reject" a book for the same reasons. Because readers without children may not be interested in children, they should make special efforts to read this chapter with extra care.

REVIEW

Review the first three chapters by reading quickly all summaries. If any topic is not clear, restudy it now.

PREVIEW

Read the prelude, chapter outline, headings, cameo, and summaries now. Turn some of the headings into questions. Proceed to answer these questions in order to learn more about human development.

READING

Read the chapter straight through. Adjust your speed of reading to the difficulty of the passages. Check mark topics not understood. After major topics and summaries, stop and review by glancing at the topic headings, turning them into questions, and jotting down or saying to yourself all you remember. When you draw blanks, reread the selections. Reread check marked topics.

REVIEW

Review by practicing forced recall. Glance at each topic in the chapter outline, close the book, and repeat all you remember. Reread only what you have forgotten.

Prelude

In the first three chapters we were concerned with you, as a grown-up, unique person. We focused our attention on you as a potentially mentally healthy person, on how you think and solve problems. Now, we plan to go back to the beginning of your development. We will be concerned with you and your development through early and middle childhood and into adolescence and how your development relates to your children, who will be living in the world of tomorrow.

Students' Viewpoints

How far back does your memory go? We did a study with college students and found that the earliest average event remembered was when a student was nearly 4 years old. (Lugo and Canon, 1964) As you can see, many of us have forgotten much of what happened during these important years of our development.

Nearly all experts on human development agree that the first five years are the most important years of our lives because it is during these years that the foundations for our later personality are formed. (Hunt, 1961; Bloom, 1964) However, as adults we have amnesia about these formative years. That is, we have forgotten how we were reared as children: This means that there are three to four years of our lives that are practically blank to us. Try to think of your earliest experiences as a child.

WHY IS IT IMPORTANT

At times, all of us have said to ourselves, "I could have done a much better job *then* if I knew what I know *now*."

A Threshold of Hope for Newborn *

For a short while we joined the baby watchers in the hospital's maternity ward. Standing on the outside looking in—forbidden to touch, to contaminate.

For a few days, these babies will live a sameness with their contemporaries, until they are slipped into their respective social slots, with different opportunities, different homes, different neighborhoods and different ideologies shaping their futures and personalities.

Picked at random, five babies who look so alike in their cribs today will have different lives in years to come. What can they look forward to as they begin to sense reality?

Cathy will never know her natural parents but chances are she will find a good home before she is 2 months old. More than 50% of adoptive fathers eligible to choose her for their own will be college graduates. The majority will be in their early 30s, the mothers in their late 20s. Approximately 34% of these prospective parents will be in a $10,000 to $14,000 income bracket, 14% will be above that figure. Cathy's chances of being adopted are better than the average child born out of wedlock. Our society classifies her as "ideally adoptable." Why? Her parents and both sets of grandparents are college educated. In addition, she's charming, she's a WASP—White, Anglo-Saxon, Protestant.

Antonio's mother left her home in Guatemala a year ago, married an American and bore him a son in this country. Antonio can look forward to a bilingual childhood. His mother cannot speak English. Only time will tell whether Antonio will choose to dismiss his Spanish heritage or draw on it and turn it into an asset.

Kerri is the child of working parents involved in education and youth projects. Both are college educated, both are anxious to give their first-born every opportunity to develop a healthy mind and body. Kerri can anticipate good care, a good education and above all a realistic outlook on life. She will be shown how to cope with her limitations. She will be taught to hold her head high with good reason—because she'll be proud she is a Negro.

Jeffrey is the second boy born to an attractive housewife in Baldwin Park. His father is a stockroom clerk. The family lives in an average home, has the average kind of problems. Jeffrey can anticipate an average education, a life free of hangups except for those he can create himself. He is a healthy, good-looking Caucasian whose parents believe in the fundamental right to equal opportunity for all.

Little *Jane* is 25 days old. At birth she was tossed into a trash can in an alley behind a market. Miraculously, she survived suffocation in her garbage crib.

Figure 4-1
Antonio. A bilingual childhood. Will it be used to his advantage?

Figure 4-2
Kerri. A little girl with much to live for—a good home, love, and hope.

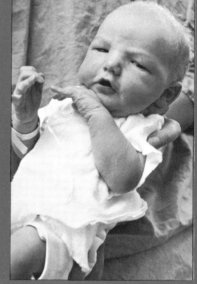

Figure 4-3
Jeffrey. A healthy, average boy from a normal family. Will he be free of hangups?

Figure 4-4
Jane. Born in anonymity, her crib was a trash can. Her life can only improve.

Figure 4-5
Cathy. The ideally adoptable child. The prospects of finding a home for her are far better than average.

Courtesy of the Los Angeles Times

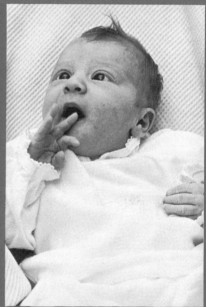

These are just a few of the thousands of infants who, newborn, will be finishing their first year and beginning another. Never again will they share total ignorance of what it means to have or not, to hurt or be hurt, to be accepted or rejected.

And, like their parents, they're unaware as to what the future will hold.

Evelyn de Wolfe, 1969
° Courtesy, *Los Angeles Times*

We often reminisce about what could have been but never was because we lacked sufficient information and proper guidance at the time.

Most of us will have the opportunity to relive our lives through our children. This opportunity to rear our children to be better and happier than we were and to build a better world for them to live in is a privilege given to most of us. A purpose of this chapter is to help you to rear your children with these goals in mind.

As we learn more about how to rear our children, we also will learn more about ourselves and how we came to be as we are today. Jersild (1968), a well-known child psychologist, says:

So, in a sense, we come as strangers when we seek to enter the world of a child or try to re-enter the world of our own childhood. But we do not come as complete strangers. We cannot read the child's mind but we can go far in judging the nature of his strivings, thoughts, and feelings as compared with our own. In the sphere of emotion, for example, the feelings expressed by a child when he is only a few weeks old are made of the same raw material as our own. Furthermore, the child each of us once was still resides in us. Even if we try to abandon him by turning our minds to other things he will never abandon us. He is an essential part of my existence as I write, and of your existence as you read. And nothing comes closer to the essence of life than our own existence. For this reason it is a rewarding task to endeavor to understand the children we know in the light of the children we once were. (p. 4)

BASIC RESEARCH AND THEORY

Have you ever thought what the world would be like in the year 2000? You probably have. All of us should because this is the world that our children will live in. In other words, we must rear and educate our children not for the world of the past, nor the present, but for the world of tomorrow. Part of our job as parents or parents-to-be is to try to think of what the world will be like twenty years from now and to prepare our children to live in it. What trends of living do we see now that may develop into important characteristics of the world of tomorrow?

Trends in the Future

MOBILITY

We are becoming more and more mobile. We move geographically more than ever before. Even back in 1940 one out of 10 school-aged children had moved. (Wattenberg, 1966) In the year 1959, more than 21 million Americans moved. Americans are a people on the move in an effort to find even better ways of life for themselves and their children.

How does mobility affect children? One study found that the more frequently a child moved, the lower were his school achievement scores. (Wattenberg, 1966) Those who moved often had difficulty both making new friends and understanding teachers.

Such difficulties are understandable when we realize that these children were not educated for mobility. The authors believe that if children are reared for the mobility required of them to live in the world of the future they will find stability in mobility.

The authors believe that parents can help their children to find the stability in mobility required for good adjustment in the world of the future in the following ways:

1. Encourage the child to associate with other children and adults from different social, economic, religious, and ethnic backgrounds. It is very difficult to dislike others who are our friends.

2. Prepare the child when moving to a new neighborhood by showing your own excitement about the pending activities. Show maps and pictures of the new place and the surrounding area.

SWITCH FROM BRAWN TO BRAIN POWER

The technological world of today requires that we become better educated. Back in 1900, few Americans went beyond the eighth grade; today most Americans finish high school; and the need for higher education, college, is apparent to all of us. (Slocum, 1966)

The need for better education is apparent also in the increasing demands for preschool education. Nursery school programs and Operation Headstart programs are indicative of the growing concern for preschool education. (Smart and Smart, 1966)

We want our children to share in the great American dream of abundance and a better life. The educational ladder has become the only way to achieve the great American dream. The educational ladder is becoming longer, but we believe parents today are willing to help their children to climb higher, educationally, than ever before.

EQUALITY OF THE SEXES

Today's world asks that we treat each other as equal, regardless of race, creed, or national origin. The world of tomorrow will add "equal regardless of sex."

Photo by Charles Gibbs

Figure 4-6
The technogical world of today requires better education than ever before for all
people regardless of one's sex. The world of tomorrow will demand even better education for our children.

In other words, young people of today are growing up in a world where they
will be treated more as individuals and less as members of a particular sex,
race, or creed.

The American family is a democratic one in which women live and work as
members of a team to make families happy and prosperous. When necessary,
women work to earn money and husbands help with chores at home. In today's
world it is not unmanly to change the baby's diaper or to help dry the dishes.
It is not unfeminine to help paint the house or to obtain an education equal to
one's husband's.

All these changes in the ways that men and women behave make child rearing
more difficult. For example, if this book were being written in 1900, the authors
could simply list ten masculine behaviors for men and ten feminine behaviors
for women and inform parents to teach their children to act either in the
masculine or the feminine way. However, for the world of tomorrow we would
have to teach not only the ten masculine traits to a boy but also combinations
of the masculine with feminine traits. In the world of tomorrow the child may
have to perform jobs now restricted to the opposite sex. Do you know in how

Figure 4-7A

Courtesy of Autonetics, a division of North American Rockwell Corp.

Learning begins early and never ends. Young people today are growing up in a world where they are treated more as individuals regardless of sex, race, creed, or age. Our children must be prepared to live in such a democratic society.

Figure 4-7B

Photo by Ron Sakall

many different ways ten traits can combine with ten different traits? The answer is 1,028. The change in sex roles is making child rearing more difficult and requires that we treat each child with more emphasis on the individual and less on whether the child is male or female. According to Thorpe (1962):

Men and women cannot be considered exclusively "male" or "female" in any of their behavioral or personality characteristics. Strength, protectiveness and provision, physical courage and endurance are among the qualities usually associated with manhood; tenderness, care of the young, gentleness in speech, and well-ordered management are among those identified with women. But these traits are more correctly universal characteristics of human personality and can be expected in various combinations in the well-adjusted man or woman. (p. 287)

A CHANGING WORLD

We are living in a dynamic world. The world has changed more in the past fifty years than in the past 500 years. Change is all around us and we must learn new ideas, techniques, and processes.

We see the changes in mass communication, transportation, education, and medicine. We see it even in the clothes we wear and the food we eat. One of the most significant results of all these technological advances in recent years is the change in the nature of education and employment. As Sofokidis and Sullivan (1964) point out:

The fastest growth of the labor force is that of technical and professional jobs requiring 16 or more years of schooling. Technical and semiprofessional jobs requiring one, two, or three years beyond high school are the second fastest growing category in the labor force. During the past decade jobs filled by high school graduates rose 30 percent while jobs for those with no secondary school decreased 25 percent. (p. 13)

A SMALLER WORLD

Mass communication and easy travel have made contact with the world at large an everyday fact. We could say that a young person today sees and learns more about the world in one year than our ancestors did in a lifetime. In the year 2000, our world will have become more like one large community. Our children will need to learn more foreign languages and world history, and to be able to adjust to different cultures easily and rapidly.

Two educators, Saylor and Alexander (1965) conclude:

Travel to and in foreign countries is increasing yearly, business is conducted on an international scope. Common Market arrangements have a profound effect on trade among nations, awareness of the importance of developments in other countries grows, exchange of students is extensive, and a network of television stations may bring a common program simultaneously to all the people of a continent and, already realized, of the world. Are American children being properly schooled to live in this new, closely knit world of interdependent peoples of many nationalities? (p. 112)

Goals for Child-Rearing

The person of tomorrow the authors call the self-actualizing person. They believe that this kind of person will be able to live effectively in the world of tomorrow. Let us review the essential characteristics of the self-actualizing person.

1. They see reality more clearly.
2. They have deeper and more profound interpersonal relations.
3. They are more open to and accepting of new experiences.
4. They trust and believe in themselves.
5. They are more creative in everyday activities.
6. They find it possible to learn from anyone who has something to teach them.

The authors believe that all these characteristics of self-actualizing people can be generalized into two major ones: (1) self-actualizers can love and be loved and (2) they can both learn and work effectively. If a person feels wanted and loved he is at his best; he can use all his personal resources. He has no need to hide, to deny, or to distort what he feels. Feeling good about himself, he is now open to all experiences and can learn more effectively.

Early Childhood

DEVELOPING NECESSARY COMPETENCIES FOR SELF-ACTUALIZATION

The foundations for an adequate self-concept begin at the moment of birth and continue for a lifetime. In early childhood we are concerned with providing the infant with certain kinds of positive experiences so that he can develop psychologically, socially, and biologically to the fullest extent possible.

THE CAPACITY TO LOVE AND TO BE LOVED

The capacity to love and to be loved underlies all human development. Furthermore, love is the characteristic most essential to the development of healthy self-actualization.

Bowlby (1956) studied the scientific literature dealing with the early lack of love and concluded:

Prolonged breaks during the first three years of life leave children who appear emotionally withdrawn and isolated. They fail to develop loving ties with other children or with adults. It is true that they are sometimes sociable in a superficial sense, but if this is scrutinized we find that there are no feelings. Parents and teachers complain that nothing you say or do has any effect on the child. It appears to be of no essential consequence to these lost souls whether they are in favor or not. Since they seem unable to make genuine emotional relations, the conditions of a given relationship at a given moment lack all significances for them.

Harry F. Harlow, Ph.D. (1905) Experimental Psychologist   C A M E O

Academic Career
B.A., Ph.D., Stanford University

Professional Experience
Director, Primate (animal) Laboratory, University of Wisconsin
Director, Wisconsin Regional Primate Research Center
Chairman, Psychology Department, University of Wisconsin

Areas of Interest
   Learning theory and infant development are primary interests for research by Dr. Harlow, as well as the study of *primates* (the highest developed mammals including man, apes, monkeys, and so on). A major concept he coined and contributed to psychology is the idea of a *learning set*. The concept resulted from his studies with monkeys who were given over two hundred problems in discrimination and then later were found to have gained the ability to solve a problem in one trial only. The monkey in effect had learned to learn. Affectional responses in the infant monkey was another major study of Harlow's, wherein he investigated the role of contact comfort. By using a substitute dummy mother made of terrycloth, in contact with an orphaned monkey, Harlow discovered that contact with the soft cloth "mother" rather than a mother made of wire was more important in the development of responses of affection (clinging). By having both the wire mother and the cloth mother give milk to the infant monkeys the discovery that contact was more important was shown.

Selected Readings
Harlow, H. F. Primate learning. In C. P. Stone (ed.) *Comparative psychology* (3rd ed.). Englewood Cliffs, N.J.: Prentice-Hall, 1951. Pp. 183–238.
Harlow, H. F. Learning set and error factor theory. In S. Koch (ed.) *Psychology: a study of a science*. Vol. 2. New York: McGraw-Hill, 1959. Pp. 492–537.
Harlow, H. F., and Zimmermann, R. Affectional responses in the infant monkey. *Science*, 1959, 130, 421–432.
Harlow, H. F., and Harlow, M. F. Social deprivation in monkeys. *Science*, 1959, 130, 421–432.

   Here, in brief, are some of the typical features of children who had grossly disturbed relations with their mothers in their early years: superficial relationships; no real feelings; no capacity to care for people or to make true friends; an inaccessibility exasperating to those trying to help them; a curious lack of concern; deceit and evasion; and a lack of concentration at school. (Bowlby, 1966)

STAGES OF INFANT LOVE

Intense Love
   During the first few months of life an infant needs to be held very closely, played with, and talked to. The infant needs to feel that he is still a part of his mother.
   Constant gentle handling is vital to the infant's normal development. There

is evidence that living organisms need constant gentle handling just the way they need proper food and fresh air. (Dennis, 1957; Levine, 1960)

Harlow (1958, 1962) found that some infant monkeys who received no love (contact comfort) actually died. Those infants who did live were not normal. They were frightened and nervous as they grew up. As adults these monkeys refused to take care of their infants. It seems that even lower animals who receive no love during infancy are incapable of giving love to their young.

Spitz (1945) studied what happened to motherless human infants. His study has been criticized as not being truly scientific. However, his study has had profound effects on pediatric care. Today the medical profession takes great care to provide all babies with love, either by their own mother or through mother substitutes. Today most hospitals place the newborn with their mothers as soon as possible. If mother is ill, a nurse is assigned to cuddle the baby.

The investigation by Spitz was carried out in two institutions. In one institution, called the Nursery, the mothers were in jail but were allowed to come to the Nursery to take care of their babies. The food, housing, and medical care were adequate. The second institution, called the Foundling home, was far superior. The Foundling Home was located among gardens outside the city. Each infant had a specially prepared diet and was checked each day by a team of medical doctors. These infants had excellent physical care. However, the eighty-eight infants were taken care of by ten nurses who had little time to cuddle them.

The contrast in the development of the infants in the two institutions was astonishing. The infants in the Nursery developed normally. The infants in the Foundling Home had a downward trend. They never learned to speak, to walk, or to feed themselves. By the end of two years, 37 per cent had died. Those who survived were human wrecks.

The authors believe that the central factor in the infant's development is the tender loving relationship with the mother or a mother substitute. Try to imagine that you are an infant. The first thing you discover is that the world is a cold and harsh place to live in. There in discomfort, hungry and wet you lie, and no one comes to help. One may begin to believe that this is the way the world is—cold and painful. One may determine that he is responsible for the pain and that other persons do not really care. Many an infant may grow up distrustful of himself and others, constantly anxious, trying not very successfully to handle all of life's problems by himself.

Supportive Love

The intense love of the first few months should give way gradually to supportive love. The second stage of infant love requires that the parents realize that the infant is now beginning to develop as an individual. During the fifth and sixth month of life the baby begins to note the difference between "I" and "not I." Before this time the baby believed the world to be an extension of himself. He now wants to explore the world. He begins to recognize strangers as being different from his parents. In other words, the self-concept is now beginning to take shape. The infant is developing a will of his own. He now wants to pay attention to the exciting world about him. He begins to ignore mother and the games she wants to play because he has his own interests. (Thomas, 1963)

Intense love, if continued too long, may crush the beginnings of the infant's efforts to be himself. Supportive love requires that the parent give love and protection and still recognize and respect the baby's needs as an individual.

Parental Love

By the end of the first year, parental love is the kind of love needed by the infant. This kind of love is possibly the most difficult kind. Parents may want to continue the intense and supportive love, but these kinds of love will not allow the infant to grow and to learn. Parental love consists of caring for the child and wanting the best for him, but with the growing realization that the infant's life is his own. A truly loving parent is one whose love does not smother; one who guides and teaches the child skills that he will need to achieve gradual independence from the parents. Figure 4-8 shows the three stages of infant love.

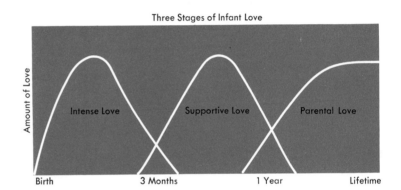

Figure 4-8
Three Stages of Infant Love

Intermediate Summary

The foundation for an adequate self-concept begins at birth. The capacity to love and to be loved underlies all human development. The three stages of infant love are intense love, supportive love, and parental love.

THE CAPACITY TO LEARN

Sensory-Motor Learning

The second major task during early childhood is to develop fully the infant's potential to learn effectively. Developing the capacity to learn in children is a step-by-step process just as developing the capacity to love. Each step, of course, depends on the preceding step. The first stage in the development of the capacity to learn is called the *sensory-motor* (because the infant uses only his senses and physical movements to learn). An infant has five ways to learn about the world around him: he can see, smell, feel, hear, and taste. These are the five ways for information to enter the human system. As early as possible the five channels should be made effective transmitters of the world of knowledge.

The program recommended by Doman and Delacato (1965) is given subsequently. It does not promise to make your child smarter, but it does encourage and stimulate a greater use of his potential.

First Month

MOBILITY. If the child is ever to have a playpen, give it to him now. Cover the floor of the playpen with a plastic mat and turn the little one loose on his tummy. Do not restrain him with tight clothes and heavy blankets. Dress the child in a light shirt and diaper so that he can move around as much as possible.

Encourage him to roll over and as soon as he does turn him back over on his tummy (praising him of course for his mighty feat). It is at this time that he will begin his very first crawling movements. Do not put him on the carpet because the friction will prevent movement and discourage him.

SEEING. Babies receive their very first training for reading readiness when the doctor shines a light in his eyes to test the contraction of the pupils. It is not a gentle test, but babies' eyes do not need gentleness, they need stimulation, exercise, and use.

When it is dark outside, turn on the lights in the baby's room. You might keep a reasonable amount of light on all night. It won't disturb his sleep, and it will help his eyes exercise when he wakes up.

Just looking around won't provide contraction of the pupils, so you can turn off the light for a few seconds and on again several times in the evening. For these newborn eyes hungry for visual experience, that's a more thrilling experience than fireworks.

HEARING. When the doctor claps two objects together to test his "startle reflex" that is the beginning of his training for speaking. You can continue to stimulate this training by cooing, singing, laughing, talking to him. Let him hear lots and lots of music—especially with a strong not too fast beat. Vary the beat, and make it good music.

FEELING. Cuddle baby's bare skin against yours. Let him learn through the powerful instrument of love what it feels like to feel. After you bathe him, gently rub his skin with soft nubby towels. Tickle, squeeze, and gently pinch him. Put "feeling" objects into his hands—pieces of velvet, an old silk purse, a dry sponge. Things that are too big for his mouth, but small enough for two inquisitive hands. And at this stage don't bother with toys. That little stuffed duck may be the cutest thing in the world, but it means nothing to the baby who has never seen a duck, except perhaps for a good "feeling" object.

TASTING AND SMELLING. Tasting and smelling are by far the most enjoyable experiences of the one-month-old infant. He delights in this stimulation during feeding, especially breast-feeding when he is exposed to the sweet aroma of his mother's milk.

Keep him near the kitchen when you are preparing meals so he can smell the good smells of Mom's home cooking. And don't be afraid to take him outside on a warm day and let him smell the wonderful scent of fresh-cut grass.

Second Month

MOBILITY. During the second month infants usually show signs of holding up their head and rolling from their belly to their back. If placed on a linoleum floor, he will be able to pivot part of a circle. It is at this time that he is close to this first important movement—the act of moving forward.

When he does start crawling along the floor, Mom must put him back in the middle when he reaches a wall, or he will become frustrated in his new adventure.

SEEING. If possible move the child's crib once a week. Putting it in different spots in his room will give him something different to look at. You will know how he feels if you have ever been sick and restricted to lying flat on your back.

NEVER place the side of his crib against the wall. That position forces a child to look in only one direction, which ever is the most interesting. His eyes will learn to turn in only one direction. To supplement change of direction, you can place the baby with his head at different ends of the crib from day to day. And if you bottle feed your baby, hold him in one arm one time, and in the other arm the next, as though he were being breast-fed.

Hang a mobile in the baby's room. Get four or five (or make them) and change every few days. If there is no warm gentle breeze, blow it yourself when you are in the room. Make his furniture brightly colored. Pastels are for weary, nervous adults who need soothing, not for babies who need stimulation.

In line with the mobiles, you can cut out large shapes, squares, circles, etc. from brightly colored paper. These you can pin on the wall, or hold before the child. They can also be incorporated into a homemade mobile.

HEARING. By the time the little one is two months old any mother can distinguish two different cries. One is for pain or discomfort, and the other is just because he can cry. This crying is his first step toward language—he has used two different sounds to communicate two different needs.

You can make your own vocal sounds to stimulate him. Make soothing rhythmic sounds when rocking; happy, laughing, splashy sounds for bathing; delicious sounds for feeding, etc. Let him know that sounds are related to meaning.

Three to Six Months and Later

MOBILITY. During these months baby actually starts crawling at this time. And unfortunately, this is the time when mothers put their child in a playpen. But if anything, they should get rid of it. The ideal crawling space is a piece of linoleum on top of carpet, so it is both warm and smooth. In baby's room keep the temperature up and remove threats of floor lamps, small table, ash trays, doors that open inward and uncovered electrical outlets.

When baby wants to creep remove the linoleum. He now needs friction to creep. His feet should be kept bare so they have a chance to feel what it is like to be feet.

Above all remember that this is the year to slow down. You want to encourage and stimulate neurological growth, but there is one thing you should not do. DO NOT MAKE BABY STAND UP AND WALK BEFORE HE IS READY. A playpen at this time will give him no alternative. When he is ready, and he will know, he will stand up all by himself.

SEEING AND HEARING. In this time the child is starting to combine skills. At age one he knows the meaning of many words before he can speak them. Use this advancement to stimulate both language and the eyes. Tell him to "look at Daddy." Help him to focus far and near (good exercise for reading readiness). This helps him to coordinate sound with sight, and words with things.

Never say "shhhhh. We have a baby." Don't stop other children in the family from making noise, or keep the TV down. Babies like to hear noise and activity. If you have a singing bird put him in the baby's room. Let the baby crawl and creep in the dining room during meals so he can hear the tinkle and clatter, and the hubbub of voices that accompanies meals.

When he speaks to you in nonsensical sounds, wait till he is finished and speak back to him just as seriously in either words or sounds. When he does start talking with real words, don't respond with baby talk. Include a little talk over his head so he has something to strive for.

These methods do not guarantee that your child will be a genius, or even get smarter. But they do promise a happy childhood, and a home that is full of noise, activity, and many memories of the infant as he grows and explores this most fascinating and exciting world that he has been thrust into.

Preschool Learning

Sensory-motor experiences continue as the main channel of learning until about age two. At age two the child can start using language as a tool for learning. The beginnings of thinking can be observed in that the child can think about objects and events that are no longer immediately present. In other words, the child is now able to learn more rapidly and to learn more complex relationships. (Flavell, 1963)

There are many things that the family can do together that are fun and will help the child get ready for school learning. Here are some of the ways that parents can prepare their child at home for the exciting experiences of learning.

Playful Experiences

AGES 2 TO 4. After much study, experts have come to agree that play is important to the child's development. (Johnson and Medinnus, 1965) Play is the way a child learns what no one can really teach him. Through play he explores the world at his leisure. He experiments, manipulates, and pretends in order to orient himself to space, time, things, animals, and people. Through play he can be father and mother, policeman, Tarzan, an astronaut, anyone or anything he wishes. Through play the child learns how to live in our world. He can practice in the safety of playful experiments the skills that he must later use in the outside world. Play, we can say, is the child's main job.

The child's play experiences should be encouraged and respected. The child wants to develop his inner resources and his ability to cope with the world. He wants desperately to learn an endless number of things: how to mop the floor; what happens when a cat's tail is pulled or when pots and pans are piled high; the sound a hammer makes when it strikes wood, glass, or, for that matter, his little brother's head. No one can do this for him and, equally important, he learns what he can do and not do.

Preparation for School

AGES 4 TO 5. Four is said to be the age of expansion. The child at that age is very interested in adult activities. In some ways he is very much a member of the family, yet in other ways he has already begun to leave the home setting. He is interested in playing with persons his own age.

During this period the parent should try to prepare the child for school learning. Some of the specific ways the parent can help the child are listed subsequently. Remember what the child can do in cooperation today he can do alone tomorrow. With assistance, a child can do more than he can by himself.

Visual Helps

1. Put objects on a table. Take away one object. Tell which one is gone.
2. Look at a picture for ten seconds. Take it away. Tell about it or answer questions about it.
3. Have a child draw a picture and tell about it.
4. Go through magazines and cut out all objects of one kind; that is, cars, hats, shoes. Paste them on separate papers.
5. Build things with blocks or tinker toys. Tell about things.
6. Use coloring books, keeping within the line.
7. Find letters or words in newspaper headlines. Paste in a scrapbook all those starting with A, B, C, and so on.
8. Make up stories about a picture book.
9. Match real-life objects with pictures (for example, see a bird and go home and find it in a bird book).
10. Work picture puzzles.
11. Put objects on a table. Take them all away. Name as many as possible.

Auditory Helps

1. Speak distinctly to the child. Correct his speech mistakes by pointing to the object and giving the correct pronunciation slowly.
2. Read poems to the child. Ask which words sound alike.
3. Play rhyming games. For example, "I see something in the room that rhymes with boat." (coat)
4. Give names to unknown objects, thus increasing vocabulary.
5. Make a scrapbook of pictures of objects beginning with consonant letters: s, c, l, m, and so on.
6. Listen to story records and repeat the story.
7. Sing rhyming jingles and simple songs that rhyme.

Memory and Comprehension Helps

1. Read most of a story and ask the child to finish it. See if it comes out as he thinks it should.
2. Develop interest in collecting things—trains, animals, and so on—and have a place for his collections.

3. Foster and encourage interest in the out-of-doors by walks and trips to the woods.

4. Take a child on short trips (shopping, to the bakery, and the like).

5. After a trip have some activity that will tell about the trip: drawing a picture, building something, telling father, dictating a letter to grandmother.

6. Read a story to the child and ask specific questions about it.

7. Play "Grandmother's Trunk," a memory game; say "I am packing Grandmother's trunk and in it I am going to put a (coat)." Next player repeats your article and adds one, and so on.

8. Give him opportunity to act out things: trains, animals, and so forth.

Intermediate Summary

The second major task during early childhood is to develop fully the infant's potential to learn effectively. The stages of learning include sensory-motor, language learning, play experience, and preparation for school learning.

Later Childhood (Ages 6 to 12)

LOVE

We have just finished discussing what kinds of important things happen to children during early infancy that will affect their ability to cope with some of the drastic changes that will occur in the world of tomorrow. We saw how motherly love plays a crucial role in the development of a child's self-concept. We also saw how the lack of love, sensory stimulation, and physical contact can lead to intense insecurity and even sickness or death.

Let's say that your child has gotten through this period all right and that he has begun to develop a healthy or positive self-concept. Now, what are some other important experiences that will help to prepare your child for the world of tomorrow?

During the period of later childhood (approximately ages 6 to 12) there are many important experiences that will have a great impact on the child's personality development. For one thing, his experiences related to love will shift from the unconditional form of mother love to the conditional type of father love. Another significant change involves the expansion of the self-concept through more and more interaction with other people outside the immediate family, a process called *socialization* (learning social behavior). In addition, the child begins to learn, think, and solve problems at a more complex level. This occurs principally during his schooling.

Development of Fatherly Love

The infant is first exposed to the warmth and tenderness of motherly love, which is unconditional in nature (that is, I am loved for what I am). As he grows older, he soon learns a new kind of love, called *fatherly love*. This kind of love is quite different; Fromm (1956) describes it as conditional love. Its principle is "I love you because you fulfill my expectations, because you do your duty, because you are like me." (p. 36)

So, the purpose of fatherly love is to help guide the child with certain underlying principles. Fromm feels that it should be a patient and tolerant type of love with the major goal of helping the child increase his own sense of competence. The ultimate goal is to help the person become his own authority. In a sense you might say that the major function of motherly and fatherly love is to help each person become mature enough to be his own mother and father. As Fromm (1956) puts it:

. . . The mature person has become free from the outside mother and father figures, and has built them up inside.

In this development from mother-centered to father-centered attachment, and their eventual synthesis, lies the basis for mental health and the achievement of maturity. In the failure of this development lies the basic cause for neurosis. (p. 37)

SOCIALIZATION

As the child grows older, the influence on the growing self-concept shifts from the immediate family to society and the world outside. Because the self-concept develops as a result of experiences with other people, it is no wonder that a portion of our self-concept reflects the people we interact within our environment. You might look on the child's environment as not a single culture but a series of subcultures: the family, the community, the school, the church, the state, the nation, and the world.

Socialization Through the Neighborhood and Community

The growing child emerges from the family and moves into the world usually as a result of human interactions with playmates in the neighborhood or friends of the family. Because the core of the self-concept is formed during the day-to-day family interaction, it is no surprise that the child carries with him feelings about himself as he relates to other people.

One consequence of a healthy or positive self-concept is that it develops a sense of trust toward other people. Or, putting it in the terms of the learning principles we discussed earlier, the child generalizes his ways of relating what he has learned in the home to other people he comes in contact with. For example, if his experiences in the home have led him to believe that he is an unworthy person (negative self-concept) then he will react to people defensively or very cautiously.

Some recent research with monkeys seems to indicate how important these early play and friendship experiences are for later development. Harlow (1962), for example, found that monkeys deprived of experiences with other monkeys in early life not only have difficulty in mating, but tend to make poor mothers.

Socialization and Developing Values

A by-product of interactions with others in the neighborhood and community is the development of a set of *values*. Values are learned essentially by the process of reinforcement that was discussed earlier. That is, if when a person behaves in a particular way his behavior is rewarded (with a smile, a gift, or being accepted in a play group, for example), then that behavior tends to be repeated. Gradually, then, a person learns to value certain ideas or ways of relating to the world.

This is just the reason why the development of a positive self-concept will tend to predispose you toward a particular set of values, which will include respect and love for others as opposed to hostility and lack of trust in others. That is, a person who feels good about himself and has a sense of being loved will be less likely to accept negative values about other persons.

Socialization and Developing Sex Roles

Another important thing that happens to children during this period is the development of the various roles we play. Have you ever watched children playing house? Notice how each child plays his role as mother or father, usually in an exaggerated manner. It is through such experiences in play and daily peer-group (people of similar ages) interaction that children learn their appropriate sex roles. Society insists that boys and girls behave differently. Boys and girls are treated differently by their parents, playmates, and teachers. However, the accepted position is that children learn their appropriate sex roles primarily from the family. One study (Sears, 1946) found that male children reared in families where the father was absent were slower in the development of male role traits than in families where the father was present. Whenever the father or the mother is absent because of divorce or death, the remaining partner should seek the assistance of other appropriate sex models, such as an uncle for the male child or an aunt for the female child, as substitutes for the missing parent. Frequently, adults volunteer their services for children who lack one parent through the local branch of Big Brothers and Big Sisters of America.

LEARNING TO LEARN, THINK, AND SOLVE PROBLEMS DURING LATER CHILDHOOD

Another important development during this period of later childhood is in the area of effective learning, thinking, and problem solving. It is during this period that children are most ready to explore and manipulate objects and to discover symbols in their world. The school plays a major role in helping children develop this interest, particularly through verbal and numerical manipulations: reading, writing, and arithmetic.

Ideally, school should be an intensely exciting experience for children. It should help youngsters to get excited about reading and to be able to express ideas in both written and oral forms. It should encourage students to think effectively about problem solving. It should indirectly help them to feel better about themselves by allowing them to have success experiences in learning and thinking situations. Think back to your own experiences in elementary school. Did these things happen to you?

Indirectly the school conveys to the child a system of values about learning, human relations, and democratic ideals. It should convey values of worth and self-realization through learning. It should help the child accept individual differences not only in learning ability, but in the areas of personality and ethnic backgrounds. It should develop and encourage democratic ways of group problem solving and decision making.

Intermediate Summary

During middle childhood there is a continued growth in the abilities to love and learn. The stages of love include a shift from motherly to fatherly love, and from the immediate family to society and the world outside. Learning now occurs through verbal and numerical manipulations required for reading, writing, and arithmetic.

SUGGESTIONS FOR HELPING CHILDREN DURING LATER CHILDHOOD TO DEVELOP COMPETENCIES FOR LIVING IN THE WORLD OF TOMORROW

Having outlined some of the important changes that occur during this period of the child's life, we now want to discuss what you as a potential parent can do to help children develop effectively so that they will be able to live productively in the world of tomorrow.

Learning to Work and to Study for Future Goals

Most learning during the first six years is reinforced by the parents. A parent is usually nearby, ready to reward and to encourage learning, step by step.

In school and in society there is usually a large group and only one teacher, or leader, or employer. As a result, good work is often overlooked until the finished product is turned in for evaluation. Even then good work may not be recognized, for in large groups there are usually one or two persons who may do a better job, and it is they who receive the high grades or the honors.

Developing Efficient Work Habits

How are we to produce hard-working youngsters without constantly providing them with rewards? One answer is to apply the reinforcement schedules explained in Chapter 2. The sequence is as follows:

TOTAL REINFORCEMENT SCHEDULE. This is the beginning schedule in which we reward the child every time for correct behavior. Once his behavior starts to become dependable, we switch to the variable reinforcement schedule.

VARIABLE REINFORCEMENT SCHEDULE. We now reward the child for correct behavior every second or third time. Typically, the child will not protest because by this time he feels good about just doing the correct thing. The beginning basketball player needs to be told by the coach how well he is doing. As he improves he has less need to be praised because he senses that he is doing better. Each time he makes a basket he feels good.

LITTLE OR NO REINFORCEMENT SCHEDULE. Once the child has established a good habit, he will need little if any reinforcement. He knows, for example, that he is a good speller, so he has a reputation to maintain. He knows he is good; he has little need to be told. Sometimes a smile or a pat on the head is all he needs.

Developing More Independence

Children need to develop independence so that eventually they can cope with life on their own. To do this they must practice getting involved with life's problems in order to learn the competencies required to fulfill the ever-increasing demands placed on them. It is important to remember that children learn responsibility by being given rich and varied opportunities to practice responsibility.

The key idea regarding the development of greater independence is to provide children with ever-increasing areas of responsibility in accordance with the individual child's competencies to handle the situation. Some children are ready to assume responsibility before others in particular situations but not in others.

Most parents want to overprotect their children. However, adults can teach, guide, and advise—but they must let go so that their children can grow. Parental love remains the most difficult kind of love because parents want their children to be with them always, yet recognize that true love involves preparing their children to live without them.

Helping Children Through Crucial Problems

All of us sooner or later face problems that are too difficult for us to solve by ourselves. We need help, temporarily, from others. Such situations are common even during childhood, because there are so many problems that children are facing for the first time. Children will fail enough times in life without their parents' facilitating more failure. Remember that an adequate self-concept develops through success and not failure.

The key idea for helping children over hurdles is to provide them with temporary crutches and aids until they can produce the correct responses. At this point we remove the crutches because the children know what to do. However, children will often drop the crutches themselves immediately after achieving success.

For example, suppose a child cannot spell the word *hat* when it is being taught in the usual way. The teacher writes the word and pronounces *hat* emphasizing the short *a* sound. This child, if he is not to fail, may need some spelling crutches such as reviews of initial and final consonant sounds, flash cards with the words printed on them, or a training technique combining sight, sound, and motor learning. The point is that once he can spell correctly the crutches can be removed and he will remain a good speller.

This idea, used intensively in remedial work with children and adults, is known as the "crutch first, independence later" principle. Why wait, however, until children have met tremendous failure before using it? The authors recommend that the principle be used to *prevent* failure.

Intermediate Summary

Important objectives during later childhood include developing efficient work habits by use of reinforcement schedules; developing greater independence by providing ever-increasing areas of responsibility in accordance with children's competencies; and helping children through crucial problems by use of the "crutch first, independence later" principle.

Adolescence

As just discussed, the period of middle childhood is a time when a variety of important developments occur in the individual. Adolescence, too, is a period during which significant changes are taking place. Adolescents are attempting to develop in the area of mature and brotherly love; their self-concepts are becoming more defined ("Who am I?" or the search for identity); they are experimenting with more mature social roles (son, daughter, boyfriend, girlfriend, student, and citizen); they are developing more complex interpersonal techniques with other people, particularly their peer group; they are becoming more competent in the areas of learning to learn, think, and solve problems more effectively; they are developing their own value system; they are beginning to think about career possibilities and further education; and they are beginning to become more a part of the community and society of which they are a part. All of these changes might be viewed as occurring in three major areas: (1) within the person, (2) between the person and other people, (3) between the person and the society within which he interacts.

DEVELOPMENT WITHIN THE PERSON

Search for Identity and the Self-Concept
By the time of adolescence, the person's self-concept is almost fully developed. However, frequently the ideas one has about himself are based on what others

(parents, friends, relatives, teachers, and so on) think he is or should be. From
these experiences with others the person develops what is frequently referred
to as an *ideal self* (the part of the self-concept based on the expectations of other
people important to him).

This ideal self frequently is challenged during adolescence because it is during
this time that the person develops more independence and autonomy so that
his *real self* (that part of the self-concept that is based on what the person feels
about himself) can develop more fully. This real self, then, develops as the
adolescent has more experience in the world in general. This is why it is often
during adolescence that such intense conflicts develop between parents and their
children. It is in this conflict between the real and ideal self that the person
is able to develop further toward self-actualization.

Love of Self and Others (Brotherly Love)

It is during adolescence, as the person begins to understand himself more, that
he truly begins to learn to love himself as a unique, unfolding person. Thus, as
in the definition of love by Fromm, the person truly begins to know and care
for himself, to assume responsibility, and to respect himself as an individual.

Figure 4-9   *Photo by Charles Gibbs*
Brotherly love is love for all human beings. Differences in talents, religion, and knowledge are trivial compared to the important similarities common to all humans.

With the development of self-love, the adolescent begins to develop brotherly
love. At first these two ideas may sound contradictory. Fromm (1956) clarifies
the point as follows:

If it is a virture to love my neighbor as a human being, it must be a virtue—and not a vice—to love myself, since I am a human being too. The love for my own self is inseparably connected with the love for any other being. (p. 49)

The most fundamental kind of love, which underlies all types of love, is brotherly love. By this I mean the sense of responsibility, care, respect, knowledge of any other human being, the wish to further his life. This is the kind of love the Bible speaks of when it says: love thy neighbor as thy self. Brotherly love is love for all human beings; it is characterized by its very lack of exclusiveness. If I have developed the capacity for love, then I cannot help loving my brothers. In brotherly love there is the experience of union with all men, of human solidarity, of human atonement. Brotherly love is based on the experience that we all are one. That differences in talents, intelligence, knowledge are negligible in comparison with the identity of the human core common to all men. (p. 47)

Development of Independence and Autonomy

During adolescence there is a shift from dependency on the home and parents for a sense of security, to reliance more on one's self and friends. There are wide individual differences in the way families handle these changes. In some families

---

Erich Fromm, Ph.D (1922) Psychologist and Psychoanalyst C A M E O

Academic Career
Ph.D, University of Heidelberg
Berlin Psychoanalytic Institute

Professional Experience
Chicago Psychoanalytic Institute
National University of Mexico
New York University

Areas of Interest
Fromm has dedicated his life's work to explaining and finding ways of making man's existence more meaningful. He believes that man feels very much alone and alienated from himself. Therefore, his works are directed toward finding the basic internal psychological needs of man, the social, economic, and political conditions of man's social environment, and the kinds of personalities that have resulted as man has been forced to compromise between his inner needs and the requirements of society.

His efforts to resolve man's dilemma have made child psychology, social psychology, sociology, anthropology, religion, history, philosophy, and political systems areas of interest. Although man has not succeeded in constructing a society that meets his basic needs, Fromm believes that it is possible to create a society that will put man back in the saddle where he belongs.

Selected Readings
Fromm, Erich. *Escape from freedom.* New York: Farrar and Rinehart, 1961.
—. *Man for himself.* New York: Rinehart, 1947.
—. *The sane society.* New York: Rinehart, 1955.
—. *The art of loving.* New York: Bantam Books, 1956.
—. *The heart of man.* New York: Harper and Row, 1964.
—. *The revolution of hope.* New York: Bantam Books, 1968.

this is a period of real conflict and tension. We have actually seen parents order their own children out of the house for wanting too much independence too fast.

On the other hand, some adolescents are so dependent on their parents for a sense of security that it takes encouragement from the family to get the person to become more self-reliant and independent.

Changes in Values

Partly as a result of the conflict between the ideal self and the real self, and the development of autonomy, adolescents begin to question values learned from the family, church, and community. As a result they often discard or alter old values; more frequently they develop new values, ones that make sense to them. Parents often perceive this as very threatening, and this is why the peer group is so important to the adolescent; with peers he often shares his new-found ideas about values.

CHANGES THAT OCCUR BETWEEN THE ADOLESCENT AND OTHER PERSONS

Parent Interactions

Many parents find it difficult to accept some of the changes that occur within the adolescent. Changes in the ideal self (which is often based on what parents think) are often perceived as a threat to all their efforts to rear what they think is a nearly perfect son or daughter.

Adolescents frequently assert their independence in such various ways as dress, length and style of hair, explorations in drinking alcohol and using drugs, or sexual behavior. Parents find it difficult to accept many of these assertions of autonomy and react by restricting the behavior of their children instead of attempting to channel their drives into more productive areas: a part-time job, certain privileges at home that the younger members of the family don't enjoy, or recognition for independent work in school or in the community.

Peer Group Interactions

Adolescence is a time for developing interpersonal techniques more fully, for learning to relate to and accept other people as they are. An important part of this is learning brotherly love.

The importance and influence of the peer group will partly depend on the degree of independence that is allowed by the parents, and how fully the real self has matured. Frequently, adolescents who have not had the chances to fully develop their autonomy or real selves will rely quite heavily on their peer group for support. Hence, we often get a high degree of conformity during this period.

Development of Sexual Roles

Adolescence marks the period when the roles of males and females begin to make a difference. Part of this is heightened by the important outward physical changes that are occurring. Combined with the physical changes (breast development, facial hair, muscular development, and so on) are the internal glandular changes that often produce highly emotional reactions in both male and female adolescents.

Through the sex roles developed during middle childhood and the help of the peer group, the adolescent begins to learn how boys and girls are supposed to react in various situations. Through dating, the adolescent begins to learn his role and ways of relating to the opposite sex.

Intermediate Summary

The psychological development of the adolescent may be viewed as occurring in three major areas. The first development takes place within the person and involves the search for identity and further development of the self-concept. The second development is between the person and other people, which essentially involves brotherly love, parent interactions, peer-group interactions, and the development of sex roles.

INTERACTIONS IN THE SCHOOL COMMUNITY AND SOCIETY

One of the most complete studies on the adolescent period was reported in *The Adolescent Society* by Coleman (1961). One of his major findings is summarized by him as follows:

Our adolescents today are cut off, probably more than ever before, from the adult society. They are still oriented toward fulfilling their parents' desires, but they look very much to their peers for approval as well. Consequently, our society has within its midst a set of small teen-age societies, which focus teen-age interests and attitudes on things far removed from adult responsibilities, and which may develop standards that lead away from those goals established by the larger society. (p. 9)

Thus, adolescents are often forced in our society to form their own world, and not much interaction in the "real community" is possible.

What kind of values does this adolescent society encourage? One description of the current youth scene describes the most prevalent values as irreverent, humanistic, experiencing, spontaneous, and tolerant.

1. One of the fundamental characteristics of the hang-loose ethic is that it is irreverent. It repudiates, or at least questions, such cornerstones of conventional society as Christianity, "my country right or wrong," the sanctity of marriage and premarital chastity, civil obedience, the accumulation of wealth, the right and even competence of parents, the schools, and the government to head and make decisions for everyone—in sum, the Establishment.

2. Another basic aspect of the hang-loose ethic is a diffuse and pervasive humanism which puts great store upon the value of human beings and human life. Adherents don't necessarily proclaim but they do claim that people are precious and that their full development is perhaps the most worthwhile of all things.

3. Another basic aspect of the hang-loose ethic is the pursuit of experience both as a thing in itself and as a means of learning and growing. The idea is that a great variety and depth of experience is beneficial and not at all harmful as long as you can handle

Figure 4-10

Young Americans are becoming more involved in efforts to improve man's condition. The first shows a VISTA volunteer, herself one of ten children of a poor family of Mexican ancestry, helping the Choctaw Indians in Idabel, Oklahoma. The second picture shows a Peace Corps teacher in the far-off town of Lobatsi.

it. This entails a heightened attention to the present ongoing moment and far less concern with the past or future. It also involves a mistrust of dogmas and principles which tend to obscure the richness of life. For this reason, they also often reject the catagorizing and generalizing which is so rampant in our educational system.

4. As part and parcel of the importance placed on directly experiencing oneself and the world, we find that spontaneity, the ability to groove with whatever is currently happening, is a highly valued personal trait.

5. Another facet of the hang-loose ethic is an untutored and unpretentious tolerance. Do whatever you want to as long as you don't step on other people while doing it. (Simmons and Winograd, 1966, pp. 12–15)

Despite the difficulties youth has in finding avenues of entering the community, there are hopeful signs. Many of the national and international volunteer programs offer youth an opportunity to express their concern for the conditions in the world (for example, the Peace Corps; see Fig. 4-11).

One of the most popular domestic programs is called VISTA (see Fig. 4-10). VISTA (Volunteers in Service to America) is a federal program of full-time service to combat poverty in the United States. VISTAs live with the people they serve, receiving only sufficient financial support to cover essentials. There are presently over 4,000 VISTAs in the field and in training.

At certain community colleges programs are now being developed for social service programs in which young people have experiences in helping other people. The emphasis in education on effective thinking and problem solving and away from rote memory is also encouraging. The development of inexpensive world travel facilities for the young makes possible an exploration of the cultures and ideas of their fellowmen.

Figure 4-11

Photo courtesy of Peace Corps

School and Learning During Adolescence

Learning ability reaches its highest level during adolescence. The adolescent can now use truly abstract thinking to learn and to solve his problems. He has the ability to do scientific investigation—that is, he is capable of gathering data, forming hypotheses, testing hypotheses, and arriving at tentative conclusions. (Inhelder and Piaget, 1958) He can do so in the classroom, at home, and on the job.

The objectives of school learning during adolescence are to learn how to earn a living and how to become a good citizen in a democratic society.

Earning a Living

Recent research indicates that persons have a great many different abilities and not just varying amounts of general ability. (Guilford, 1967) This means that each adolescent needs to explore his own abilities to see how he would fit into various vocations and professions. Furthermore, most jobs provide in-service education and training because it is possible to improve our abilities and to learn the specific skills required for earning a living.

School learning provides a good testing ground for discovering and improving abilities. A scientific approach to learning about our abilities would be as follows:

1. *Investigation.* The student gathers all the information he can about different vocational opportunities. What are the requirements for employment? Where are the jobs located? What are the chances for advancements? How does one apply for a job?

2. *Hypothesis.* Once a student has decided upon a tentative vocational choice, he should plan the sequences for meeting the job requirements. He should discuss his plans with his counselor, teachers, family, and friends.

3. *Testing the Hypothesis.* The student should read more about his vocational choice. He should become acquainted with persons working in his field. During vacations or week-ends, he should find work in the general area of his vocational choice.

4. *Conclusions.* Having done an "informal experiment" the student arrives at tentative conclusions. On this basis he may accept the original hypothesis or he seeks new ones.

The cultivation of the individual's potentialities, the self-fulfillment of the learner, is a stated ideal and goal of our society's educational system. Recent studies have contributed much insight into the great variety of ways and rates of learning.

The most exciting insight that has come from creativity research is that different kinds of children learn best when given a chance to learn in ways best suited to their motivation and abilities. Whenever teachers change their ways of teaching in significant ways, different groups of learners become the "stars." This idea has far-reaching implications for educating a larger number of people to a higher level and for achieving a higher level of human dignity and mental health in our society. (Torrance, 1960)

Intellectually, the adolescent can cope not only with present social problems but also with problems never experienced before. He can diagnose and solve problems by thinking about them. He can imagine what the consequences of certain actions would be in this or that situation without ever actually performing the actions. In so doing, young people can eliminate inadequate solutions and zero in on solutions that may be worth trying out in real life.

The ability to deal with the world through words and ideas instead of through real objects and persons is essential for learning to live in a complex technological society. In primitive societies, teachers can show their students all there is to learn. In our society we teach through words, pictures, and images, all of which only represent the real world. (Bruner, 1968)

Young people can learn to become good citizens through free and frequent discussion and by practicing good citizenship in the miniature worlds called *home* and *school*. (White House Conference, 1929)

The following Bill of Rights for young people well represents ideas that can be put into action by parents, teachers, and adults in order to produce good citizens.

Youth's Bill of Rights

(A PETITION DIRECTED TO PARENTS, TEACHERS, AND OTHER MISCELLANEOUS ADULTS)

1. Stand by us, not over us. Give us the feeling that we are not alone in the world, that we can always count on you when we are in trouble.

2. Make us feel that we are loved and wanted. We want to love you, not as a duty but because you love us.

3. Train us by being affectionately firm. You really will achieve more with us through patient teaching than punishment or preaching. Say "No" when you feel you have to, but explain your rules, don't merely impose them.

4. Bring us up so that we will not always need you. Teach us how to take on responsibility and become independent of YOU. We will learn this faster and better if you will let us question you, your ideas and standards.

5. Don't act shocked when we do things we shouldn't. It is going to take us time to learn how to grow into life properly.

6. Try to be as consistent as possible. If you are mixed up about what you want from us, why shouldn't we be mixed up, too, in what we give you?

7. Don't try to make us feel inferior. We doubt ourselves enough without your confirming it. Predicting failure for us won't help us succeed.

8. Say "Nice work" when we do something really well. Don't hold back the praise when we deserve it. That's the way to spur us on.

9. Show respect for our wishes even if you disagree with them. Respect for you will flow naturally from your respect for us.

10. Give direct answers to direct questions. But don't give us more than we ask or

can understand. When YOU don't know, say so, but find someone for us who does know.

11. Show interest in what we're doing. Even though by your standards our activities may not be important or interesting, don't reduce them in our eyes by your indifference.

12. Treat us as if we are normal, even when our conduct seems peculiar to you. All of God's children have problems. That doesn't mean we're all problem children.

13. Sometimes all of us run into serious emotional difficulties. Should that happen, obtain for us professional counseling. It isn't always easy for boys and girls to understand themselves or know just what they want. That's why there are specialists in personal adjustments and vocational selection.

14. Teach us by example. "What you are speaks louder than your words."

15. Treat each one of us as a person in his own right. Children are people, not carbon copies of grownups. Treat all children in your care fairly; that is, as of equal value to you. That is how we will learn to respect the rights of other people and to treat them fairly.

16. Don't keep us young too long. We want a chance to prove what we can do as soon as we are ready to give proof. Don't hold us back by love which over-protects and paralyzes.

17. We need fun and companionship. Help us share our interests and happy feelings with groups of friends. Give us time to be with them and make them welcome when they come to visit.

18. Make us feel that our home belongs to us. We are AT LEAST as important as the furniture. Don't protect "things" at our expense by making us feel like intruding bulls in a china shop.

19. Don't laugh at us when we use the word "love". The need to love and be loved starts early (and never ends). Getting romantic is merely setting to soft music the eternal desire to belong to someone and have someone belong to us.

20. Treat us as junior partners in the firm. Democracy starts at home. If you want us to be worthy successors to you, take us into your confidence, and let us help you in managing *our* school, and *our* community.

21. Make yourself an adult fit for a child to live with. Prove to us "it ain't so" that parents are the worst persons in the world to have children, or that teachers are precisely the people least suited to teach. Show that home and school are not simply places where children learn how to get along with disagreeable adults.

22. Prepare us to lead *our* lives, *not* yours. Find out what *we* can do or *we* want to be before you force us beyond our capacity or make us become what *you* want us to become.

23. Give us the right to a major voice in our own lives. Decisions that will affect our whole future should be made *with* us, not *for* us. We have a right to our kind of future.

24. Let us make our own mistakes. To make wise decisions takes experience. That means we have to try ourselves out and find out for ourselves. We can only learn from our own actions—not yours.

25. Permit us the failings of average children, just as we permit you the failings of average parents. Let us both break the rules sometimes. We can grow only at our own rate, which means in easy stages. We want to become the best we can become, but we would not be human if we were perfect. (White House Conference on Children and Youth, 1929)

Intermediate Summary

Important aspects of learning during adolescence include learning to live in the community and society, using abstract thinking and the scientific method to solve problems, deciding on a vocation, and becoming a good citizen.

APPLICATION

Living with Yourself

We have discussed some of the more important changes that occur in the human as he develops from infancy into adulthood. What does all this have to do with you? How does this help you live with yourself better?

When we discuss this material in class, one of the frequent reactions of students is hostility toward parents. Why didn't my parents think of some of these ideas when I was a child? Didn't my parents realize how they were affecting my self-concept when they used to treat me that way? I never received much real love when I was a child! My parents never prepared me to live in the world of tomorrow! We also remember thinking some of these same thoughts in my psychology classes.

All right! Maybe your parents were not perfect. Neither were ours. The most important question you can ask yourself is this: Now that I understand, what can I do to grow in certain areas so that I can become more self-actualizing? And, what can I do as a parent to help my children to live better in the world of tomorrow?

TAKING A LOOK AT YOURSELF AS AN ADULT

One of the first things that may help you in growing toward more self-actualization is to realize that you are no longer a child, but an adult. As an adult you are now an equal not only with your parents but also with other adults. As a child you were smaller, not only physically, but intellectually as well. Now, you can relate to others as an adult. You have certain built-in advantages: You have the ability of abstract thought to judge the adequacies of your own behavior; in a sense you can be your own mother and father (unconditional and conditional love). Thus, you can give yourself rewards for accomplishments; you are capable of making your own decisions and of taking chances; you are probably better educated than many adults in the world around you; and you have a much better chance of rearing your own children in ways that will help them grow more healthy in the world of tomorrow.

DOING SOMETHING ABOUT POSSIBLE GAPS IN YOUR OWN CHILDHOOD DEVELOPMENT

As an adult, you are more aware of yourself. You are better able to cope with and handle the world around you. You can begin to make specific plans for change and improvement in certain areas of your behavior. Let's look at a series of problems faced by students and see how they attempted to improve.

Lack of Love

"They never loved me for me! They only loved me for the praise I brought to them." These are the exact words used by Bill as he described his relationship with his parents. Bill was a champion swimmer who had been trained to swim from an early age. His parents used Bill and his ability to gain status and prestige in their small community. It took Bill a long time to face the realization that his parents had loved him, not so much for himself, but as an object that brought them recognition.

At first he was angry and felt that he had been deprived and used by his parents. He felt he couldn't trust other people anymore. Gradually, he realized that instead of blaming them and feeling like a cripple, he had to do something himself to develop his feelings of love for himself and others. He began by placing trust in a few of his friends in very simple ways such as loaning them money, his car, a coat, or tie; gradually he began to trust them in other more important ways by telling them about his own feelings. Soon, he began to relate better with other adults, particularly with his teachers. His dating activities began to be more meaningful and he started going steady. However, the clearest sign of his self-understanding occurred during one of the last meetings the authors had with Bill. He said that he felt he could now fully forgive his parents, that he finally understood why they treated him as they did. He said, "I think now, for the first time in my life, that I can really say that I love my parents and mean it."

Lack of Independence and Problem-Solving Experiences

Many parents are afraid to let their children grow up. That is, many parents have learned to feel security in the knowledge that someone needs them and depends on them. Other parents build their entire lives around this dependency of their children. The thought of losing this is a real threat to the security of these parents. So, they do everything possible to raise a child who is not allowed to grow in independence or the solving of problems on their own.

You may know people like this; some of them are so affected by being dependent on their parents that they never leave home. Others marry a mother or father substitute to rule their lives for them. Still others are used by insensitive and aggressive persons to their own advantage.

To change a pattern like this is not simple. Sometimes the person may require counseling from a professional person such as a school counselor, minister, or teacher. Sometimes the person has to be gradually given more independence in small ways (for example, a part-time job or completing some small job or assignment in school on his own). Probably one of the best ways to help a person grow in independence is by telling him that we have faith in him to act in responsible and independent ways. Frequently, just this is enough to start him behaving more independently.

Lack of Effective Interpersonal Techniques

Think about the opportunities in your own family for developing effective interpersonal techniques. Were there many different opportunities for you to try out some of these? Or were these opportunities extremely limited?

Some students have been reared almost in total social isolation. Their parents have had very few friends and few relatives ever visited the home. Frequently, they wouldn't allow their children to get too friendly with neighbors or the neighbor's children.

Students from homes like this often feel most inadequate when expected to interact with others in the school and community. Again, there is no magic formula to help a person learn more effective ways to relate to others, but knowing that it can be done is the first step. Knowing that there are others who feel and have felt this way before helps one realize that he is not alone.

One technique that we have found helpful is to get students involved in some group activity in which they are interested, such as volunteer work, clubs, church groups, student government activities, or being a member of an athletic team.

For some students who are very withdrawn socially, a one-to-one relationship seems to work best. That is, by having one good relationship with another person and learning how to relate to that person, the individual will feel more comfortable when he interacts with other people.

Lack of Development of a Value System

A very important part of our personality that develops during childhood is concern for values, for the kinds of things that we think are right or wrong. Sometimes these are learned informally by observing parents' behavior toward others and the world in general. Sometimes values are learned in more formal ways, through the church or education.

The authors have had frequent discussions with students about conflict in values, conflict between what their parents or what the church has taught them, and how they feel now. Some students are very angry with their parents for making them believe in these values so strongly that they feel extremely guilty when they violate or question them. Of course, parents themselves often make it difficult for their children to question even these values.

The authors often have their students write papers on the topic: What to Me Are the Most Important and Unimportant Things in Life? Just the act of organizing their thoughts seems to help them understand better their own feelings and beliefs as contrasted with those of their parents. They have also often asked students to write out their problems before they come to see them.

A considerable number of parents fail to offer any model for the formation of values in their children. Frequently, they are so inconsistent in the ways they relate to the world and others that the child is confused. He doesn't know *what* is important to the parent. Students with problems in this area sometimes find it meaningful to read books presenting ideas or points of view in philosophy or religion. Bull sessions with friends and teachers are also often helpful. But probably experiences with other people in the world are the best when it comes to deciding what is right and wrong.

Living with Others

The first step in understanding others is self-understanding. The more we know about ourselves the easier it is to change what we do not like about ourselves. Changing what we don't like about ourselves reduces the possibilities of attributing to others what we don't like about ourselves. For example, the student who cheats often believes that others cheat. The selfish student feels that others are selfish also. This kind of behavior is called *projection* (the process of attributing to others what is true of ourselves and not true of them). Projection interferes with living effectively with others.

The second step in understanding others is to realize that others *learned* to be as they are, too, and that they can change *their* behavior just as we can change *ours*. Here is an example. When one of the authors was working as a school psychologist, a teacher referred a boy to him who was too aggressive in class, too difficult to control. A few days later he discussed the boy's past history with the teacher. The boy's parents did not want him. As a young child he had cried for hours "banging his head until it was bloody." Still his parents did not care. He was removed from his home by legal action and taken to an institution for children who had no parents. Thus, he had never known love or tenderness. He had never known what it is like to have motherly or fatherly love. In fact, the only social role he knew was the role of the "rebel" or the "tough guy." Underneath he was really begging for love. And the question was: would he ever be able to trust anyone sufficiently to allow his need for love to be openly expressed? The author told the teacher that once the student knew that she really cared for him, he would change his behavior. The teacher's attitude toward this boy changed from anger to deep understanding. She became eager to help and not to punish him. Soon the boy did change his behavior toward her!

Because changing behavior is often a difficult task, it is far more efficient to prevent the formation of bad attitudes and undesirable behavior early in life. For example, to successfully rehabilitate a criminal is a major job. Studies indicate that signs of delinquency that can lead to adult criminal behavior can be seen as early as the eighth year of life. Therefore, the ideal time to develop healthy behavior is during childhood.

Another example of the importance of early prevention was a student with very high intelligence who could not do passing schoolwork. Despite all efforts no-one could get him to study. His childhood experiences told why. His father was a lawyer, while his mother had had little formal education. However, the mother had achieved financial success as well as respect from others by operating a boarding home. The father, it turned out, was not a successful lawyer. The student had, thus, learned in childhood that a good education did not result in success, nor in respect from others. He had seen proof of this all his life, so all arguments for better education fell on deaf ears. He dropped out of school and took a job as a box boy in a grocery store. The main point is that an ounce of prevention during childhood is worth far more than a pound of treatment later in life.

UNDERSTANDING PARENTS

No parent can be perfect, nor can any parent expect a perfect match between his or her personality and that of his child. Therefore, conflict must be expected. The effort must be to minimize the amount of conflict and to maximize the amount of understanding. Adolescents tend to be more mature when parents have cared for, guided, and shown affection toward them during the early years. College students who feel close to their parents, when compared to those who do not, see themselves as more worthwhile, make friends with the opposite sex more easily, and have healthier attitudes toward life. It is clear that the time to reduce conflicts between young persons and their parents is during childhood.

When conflicts arise, they are usually the result of differences about what is proper behavior. Because we are living in a fast-changing and shrinking world, it will be wise for young persons today to keep in mind that their world is as different from that of their parents as it will be from the world in which their children will grow up. The best that both parents—those of an older generation—and young persons—those of the new—can do is to relax, to be themselves, and to respect differences in opinion. However, as long as a young person is living at home, he should practice exchanging ideas freely with his parents. Then, as he moves out into the world, he will be better equipped to deal with the many others who think differently. Moreover, some day the scene at home will be repeated with the roles reversed. Your children will be in your shoes, and you'll be wearing the parental ones. We hope that you will not be incurably and completely old-fashioned!

Here is a letter written by a student to her parents. (Lane, 1964) It represents the views of many of the authors' students.

Dear Parents:

This is a letter to all parents throughout the world pertaining to parts of the "Youth's Bill of Rights." This is written to try and promote better communication between two generations held together by the bonds of childbirth and torn so widely apart by impatience. I am expressing the things that I and my brothers and sisters ask of you and the same things we shall give to you in return. If you and I could build a strong relationship formed on these "rights," I could do the same for my children and in time the world would become a better place.

"Make us feel that we are loved and wanted." The most basic need we have is to be loved and to love in return. A forming adult needs love and complete acceptance to continue growing. He needs an adult figure to guide him along the many streets of life. In time, when he has developed fully, he can make these decisions without the clouded vision of youth. And yet, in spite of this need, I have seen too many of my generation destroyed because the only tie left with their parents is the duty of loving them. Too often it is forgotten that a little love goes farther than anything in the world. Love comes in many phases, degrees, and for many reasons; there is no reason it should become a duty except that it is made so.

"Train us by being affectionately firm . . . . " Part of love is the need for discipline, kind but firm. Many times the anger at the deed covers over the child's desire only for your discipline. Discipline, when given correctly, must be because you care and are concerned with our welfare, this we understand and want. The key rule here is to explain the reason for denying something. If you would take the time to explain to us why you feel our decision is wrong, you may be surprised with the results. A child's mind is instinctively open to learning and a well-explained rule may point out to him things he could not see, but can accept. Sometimes you don't realize we will disregard your objections because we can't see what's ahead of us and haven't been given a rightful chance to understand it.

"Don't try to make us feel inferior." To us this is so important, for we get tired of living in the shadow of your life. The world has changed too drastically for us to accomplish the same things you did. You have worked hard to give us a better home, education, and life. Why do you try to deny it to us now? The phrase, "When I was your age . . . ," becomes tiresome and degrading. If you will give us a chance we will show our appreciation to you. We are inspired by the pride you feel for us and your acceptance generates our pride in you.

"Show respect for our feelings. . . ." It is humanly impossible for two people to be born exactly alike, so it is therefore impossible for people to feel the same as someone else. As a person we have the right and need for an opinion of our own. We accumulated our opinions from the interaction of things and people in our environment, an environment you can't completely share. On this basis we deserve the respect you would show anyone. It can be harmful to our character to force your opinions on us, we need to make our own. Although we may be wrong, if you treat us fairly when our feelings are incorrect, we may soon come to understand and accept the right way because you first respected us.

"Treat us as if we were normal . . . ." We are normal and don't ever think some of your actions don't look peculiar to us. Try to remember that we are young, maturing adults trying to push our way into maturity. Each new thing we discover in life must be dealt with specially and tried on many different ways before it fits. For this reason we go through many different phases which may be odd and irritating to you. Please help us find our way, don't confuse the situation by making us feel like specimens in a science lab. Try and think of what you felt like at our age.

"Make us feel that our home belongs to us." We so desperately need a place to come where we can be ourselves and still be accepted. A home is not a showplace but a place where a *family* should come to be together and help each other. So often our homes become a hotel where five people, linked by so much, come to eat and sleep. For this reason too many of us must tour outside our homes, perhaps to gangs, for the necessary understanding and acceptance.

"Give us the right to a major voice in our own lives." The moment we were created in your womb we became an entirely different person, unique in our feelings and needs. Along with this personality came the controlling factor of our lives. Although we must answer to you and so many others, we must first to ourselves and God. If you will consider us as you yourselves want to be considered perhaps you will understand. Don't do things for us but try and do them with us. We know our own capacities and desires, and we don't want to fail in our eyes or yours. You can easily create a bar between us by placing us in a situation where it is too difficult to succeed. You will find that we perform much better if we are allowed to decide our future with your complete acceptance; we may later find you were right but we have a lifetime, and what is a year compared to our future.

"Permit us the failings of average children." We are all human and must make mistakes at times. We are small images of you with more idealistic views, things that happen to you can happen to anyone, including us. If you accept and understand our failings, we can more readily accept yours and others. As disappointed as you become in us, we too become in you—a little tolerance goes a long way.

"Stand by us . . . ." Every point I have brought out and all the others are ways of saying the same things, stand by us in everything we do. If you can do this our chances of becoming good people are unquestionable. Juvenile delinquents are born from non-acceptant parents. The child's need for a parental figure can be filled in many ways and his young mind often leads to the acceptance of the wrong person. If you stand beside us we won't feel we must prove ourselves to you and therefore will want to do the right things.

The Children of the World:

I wrote my paper in this manner to try and dramatize my own feelings and those I have found in my friends. Although I completely advocate this Bill of Rights to parents, I feel someone should write one for adults. The business of living is not a one person deal and therefore faults fall on both parties. . . . If all of us could learn to follow these rules pertaining to everyone we deal with, wars would be nonexistent.

I want to leave you with one last thought from all the children of all ages to all parents and parents to be. Remember, we were given life by you and through your love, we didn't ask for it. But now that we're here let us both work to make it a life we're thankful for.

Living with Society

How will your understanding of your own development from birth to the present help you in living with society? It should make it easier for you to understand your current behavior in the community. It should help you to rear your children better.

UNDERSTANDING YOURSELF AND YOUR ROLE IN SOCIETY

Did your parents rear you to live in the society of today? There is a good chance that they did not even if they intended to. The reason is found partly in the rapid changes in technology and partly in the events that have taken place in the world during the last twenty-five years. Such events and so much change your parents could not possibly have forseen. A partial list of some of these drastic developments would include the development of the atomic bomb and nuclear energy; World War II; developments in air and space travel; the development of the United Nations; research in the behavioral and social sciences; development of television on a world wide scale; developments in computers and automation; and the independence and freedom of smaller colonial nations. It would have been very difficult for your parents to have predicted most of these changes. There is a good chance, then, that your adjustment in entering society as an adult may be more difficult than for the generations before you. Are you, though, doomed to a miserable life as a misfit in our society? Not necessarily! Some effort on your part can ease the difficulty. You can attempt to fill in gaps in your own background, to develop yourself enough to live and work productively in this fast-moving society.

Thinking about the following suggestions. Study them and then follow through in your own lives in meeting the demands of our society:

1. Work to develop yourself into a truly self-actualizing person.
2. Realize that you must be prepared for drastic changes in the world.
3. Continue learning all your life so that you will remain ready for change.
4. Expose yourself readily to the ideas and cultures of peoples all over the world.
5. Develop fully the capacity to love others.

HELPING YOUR CHILDREN TO LIVE IN THE SOCIETY OF TOMORROW

The authors hope you have become more aware of how to help your children develop more fully so that they can live a better life in their world. Here are some reminders:

1. Help each child to develop a positive self-concept.
2. Help each child to be prepared for a great deal of change in his world.
3. Help each child to develop his capacity for brotherly love.
4. Help each child to learn to think more effectively.
5. Help each child to solve problems creatively and to think ahead about the consequences of his behavior.
6. Help each child to satisfy his more basic needs effectively so that he can be free to satisfy higher level needs.
7. Help your child to learn how to learn and to keep on learning all of his life.

Final Summary

Most of us will have the opportunity to relive our lives through our children. Parents should try to rear their children for the world of the future. Based on the trends we see now, the characteristics found in the self-actualizing person appear to offer the best guidelines for helping children live productively in the world of tomorrow. Essentially, parents should help their children to develop the abilities involved in learning to love and work creatively.

In early childhood, infant love has essentially three stages: intense love, supportive love, and parental love. The capacity to learn is developed through the stimulation of the senses and the various physical movements. Children can develop preschool learning experiences through play and the practice of certain sensory experiences.

Later childhood (ages 6 to 12) represents a period when the individual shifts from the unconditional type of motherly love to the conditional type of fatherly love. Through the process of socialization, the child begins to develop interests in the neighborhood and community. As a result his self-concept expands and he begins to develop values and sex roles. In school, the child develops his ability to use symbols and to solve problems more effectively. In addition, the child grows in his ability (1) to work efficiently toward long-term goals, (2) to become more independent, and (3) to solve crucial problems.

Adolescence involves changes in the development of brotherly love, a redefinition of the self-concept, and further development of independence and changes in values. Interactions between the parent and the adolescent often reflect a conflict between what the parent thinks the adolescent should be and what the adolescent himself feels he is. The adolescent is now exploring further sex roles with friends and members of the opposite sex.

As the adolescent tries to develop interactions with the community and society, it is often difficult for him to find ways of achieving these experiences. Thus, adolescents are often forced to develop their own society with norms and values different from the larger society. Through school learning, the adolescent further develops his ability for abstract thought, he develops interests in certain jobs or careers, and he develops techniques for participating as a citizen in a democratic society.

Much of what we are saying in this chapter is best summarized in the Bill of Rights.

Chapter References

Bloom, B. S. *Stability and change in human characteristics.* New York: Wiley, 1964.

Bowlby, J. *Child care and the growth of love.* New York: Penguin Press, 1956.

—. *Maternal care and mental health.* New York: Schocken Books, 1966.

Bruner, J. S. *Toward a theory of instruction.* New York: Norton, 1968.

Coleman, J. S. *The adolescent society.* Glencoe, Ill.: Free Press, 1961.

Dennis, W., and Najarian, P. Infant development under environmental handicap. *Psychological Monographs*, 1957, 71, No. 7.

Doman, G., and Delacato, C. Training your baby to be a genius. Dayton, Ohio: *McCall's Magazine*, March, 1965, Vol. 92, No. 6, pp. 65 and 169–172.

Flavell, J. H. *The developmental psychology of Jean Piaget.* Princeton, N.J.: Van Nostrand, 1963.

Fromm, E. *The art of loving.* New York: Bantam Books, 1956.

Guilford, J. P. *The nature of human intelligence.* New York: McGraw-Hill, 1967.

Harlow, H. F. The nature of love. *American Psychologist,* 1958, 12, 673–685.

Harlow, H. F., and Harlow, M. K. Social deprivation in monkeys. *Scientific American,* 1962(b), 207, No. 5, 136–146.

Hunt, J. McV. *Intelligence and experience.* New York: Ronald Press, 1961.

Inhelder, B., and Piaget, J. *The growth of logical thinking from childhood to adolescence.* New York: Basic Books, 1958.

Johnson, R. C., and Medinnus, G. R. *Child psychology.* New York: Wiley, 1965.

Lane, T. A letter to parents pertaining to the Youth's Bill of Rights. Unpublished term paper, Fullerton Junior College, 1964.

Levine, S. Stimulation in infancy. *Scientific American,* May, 1960, 1–8.

Lugo, J. O., and Canon, R. A survey of the earliest childhood memories of Fullerton Junior College students. Unpublished study, Fullerton Junior College, Calif., 1964.

Saylor, J. G., and Alexander, W. M. *Curriculum planning for modern schools.* New York: Holt, Rinehart and Winston, 1965.

Sears, R. R., Pintler, M. H., and Sears, P. S. Effect of father separation on pre-school children's doll play aggression. *Child Development,* 1946. XVII, 219–243.

Simmons, J. I., and Winograd, B. *It's happening.* Santa Barbara, Calif.: Marc-Laird Publications, 1966.

Slocum, W. L. *Occupational careers.* Chicago: Aldine, 1966.

Smart, M. S., and Smart, R. C. *Children development and relationships.* New York: Macmillan, 1967.

Sofokidis, L. H., and Sullivan, E. A new look at school dropouts. *Health, Education, and Welfare Indicators,* April, 1964, p. 13.

Spitz, R. A. Hospitalism: an inquiry into the genesis of psychiatric conditions in early childhood. *Psychoanalytic Study of the Child,* 1945, 1, 53–74.

Thomas, A., Birch, S. C., Hertzig, M., and Korn, S. *Behavioral individuality in early childhood.* New York: New York University Press, 1963.

Thorpe, L. P., and Johnson, V. *Child psychology and development.* New York: Ronald Press, 1962.

Torrance, E. P. *Assessing the creative thinking abilities of children.* Minneapolis: Bureau of Educational Research, 1960.

Wattenberg, W. W. Mobile children need help. In M. Haimowitz and N. Haimowitz *In human development.* New York: Thomas Crowell, 1966.

White House Conference on Children and Youth, 1929.

Recommended Further Readings

Paperback Books

Almy, Millie, *et al. Young children's thinking.* New York: Columbia University, 1966.

Berelson, B., and Steiner, G. A. *Human behavior: shorter edition.* New York: Harcourt, Brace and World, 1967.

Dennis, W. *Readings in child psychology.* (2nd ed.) Englewood Cliffs, N.J.: Prentice-Hall, 1963.

Elkin, F. *The child and society.* New York: Random House, 1960.

Erikson, E. H. *Childhood and society.* (2nd ed.) New York: Norton, 1963.

Erikson, E. H. (ed.). *The challenge of youth.* Garden City, N.Y.: Anchor, 1963.

Evans, E. D. (ed.). *Children: readings in behavior and development.* New York: Holt, Rinehart and Winston, 1968.

Frank, Mary, and Frank, L. K. *Your adolescent at home and in school.* New York: Signet, 1956.

Frank, L. K. *On the importance of infancy.* New York: Random House, 1966.

Friedenberg, E. Z. *The dignity of youth and other atavisms.* Boston: Beacon Press, 1965.

Gordon, I. J. *Human development.* Chicago: Scott, Foresman, 1965.

Ilg, Frances L., and Ames, Louise B. *Child behavior.* New York: Dell, 1955.

Isaacs, Susan. *Intellectual growth in young children.* New York: Schocken Books, 1966.

McNeil, E. B. *The concept of human development.* Belmont, Calif.: Wadsworth, 1966.

Mussen, P. H. *The psychological development of the child.* Englewood Cliffs, N.J.: Prentice-Hall, 1963.

Muuss, R. E. *Theories of adolescence.* New York: Random House, 1962.

Opie, Iona, and Opie, C. *The lore and language of schoolchildren.* Oxford: The Clarendon Press, 1959.

Peck, R. F., *et. al. The psychology of character development.* New York: Wiley, 1960.

Piaget, J. *Play, dreams and imitation in childhood.* New York: Norton, 1962.

Rosenblith, Judy F., and Allinsmith, W. *The causes of behavior II: readings in child development and educational psychology.* (2nd ed.) Boston: Allyn and Bacon, 1966.

Seidman, J. M. *The child.* New York: Holt, Rinehart and Winston, 1958.

Stendler, Celia B. *Readings in child behavior and development.* New York: Harcourt, Brace and World, 1964.

White, R. S. *Lives in progress.* (2nd ed.) New York: Holt, Rinehart and Winston, 1966.

Whiting, J. W. M., and Child, I. L. *Child training and personality: a cross-cultural study.* New Haven: Yale University Press, 1953.

Hardcover Books

Baller, W. R., and Charles, D. C. *The psychology of human growth and development.* (2nd ed.) New York: Holt, Rinehart and Winston, 1968.

Bernard, H. W. *Human development in western culture.* Boston: Allyn and Bacon, 1962.

Breckenridge, Marian E., and Vincent, E. L. *Child development.* Philadelphia: Saunders, 1960.

Carmichael, L. (ed.). *Manual of child psychology.* (2nd ed.) New York: Wiley, 1954.

Crow, L. D., and Crow, Alice. *Child development and adjustment.* New York: Macmillan, 1962.

Dinkmeyer, D. C. *Child development.* Englewood Cliffs, N.J.: Prentice-Hall, 1965.

Gardner, D. B. *Development in early childhood: the preschool years.* New York: Harper and Row, 1964.

Garrison, K. C. *Psychology of adolescence.* (5th ed.) Englewood Cliffs, N.J.: Prentice-Hall, 1956.

Garrison, K. C., Kingston, A. J., and Bernard, H. W. *The psychology of childhood.* New York: Scribner's, 1967.

Hoffman, Lois, W., and Hoffman, M. L. (eds.) *Review of child development research.* New York: Russell Sage Foundation, 1966.

Hurlock, Elizabeth B. *Child development.* (4th ed.) New York: McGraw-Hill, 1964.

Hutt, M. L., and Gibby, R. G. *The child.* Boston: Allyn and Bacon, 1959.

Jersild, A. T. *The psychology of adolescence.* (2nd ed.) New York: Macmillan, 1963.

Johnson, R. C., and Medinnus, G. R. *Child psychology: behavior and development.* New York: Wiley, 1965.

Maier, H. W. *Three theories of child development.* New York: Harper & Row, 1965.

McCandless, B. R. *Children and adolescents; behavior and development.* New York: Holt, Rinehart and Winston, 1961.

Seidman, J. (ed.). *The child—a book of readings.* New York: Holt, Rinehart and Winston, 1960.

Stone, L. J., and Church, J. *Childhood and adolescence.* New York: Random House, 1968.

Stott, L. H. *Child development.* New York: Holt, Rinehart and Winston, 1967.

Thompson, G. G. *Child psychology; growth trends in psychological adjustment.* (2nd ed.) Boston: Houghton Mifflin, 1962.

Thorpe, L. P., and Johnson, Virginia. *Child psychology and development.* New York: Ronald Press, 1962.

Watson, R. I. *Psychology of the child.* New York: Wiley, 1959.

Chapter 5 The Why of Behavior

Chapter Outline

Study Guide

Motivation is a topic that most people feel they understand. Therefore, they feel justified in reading into the textbook their own ideas and opinions. Remember, however, that examinations are based primarily on the theory and research presented in the text.

REVIEW
Review the last chapter by reading the summaries. Restudy what is not clear.

Motivation helps us to understand behavior. For what different reasons do students attend college? Are different needs met by different activities?

Figure 5-1

Figure 5-2

PREVIEW
Read the prelude, chapter outline, headings, and summaries. Turn major headings into questions. Proceed to answer these questions and to learn more about emotions.

READING
Read the chapter straight through. Adjust your speed of reading to the difficulty level of the passages. Check mark topics not understood. After major topics and summaries, stop and review by glancing at topic headings, turning them into questions, and jotting down or saying to yourself all you remember. Reread check marked topics.

REVIEW
Review by practicing forced recall. Glance at each topic in the chapter outline, turn each topic into a question, close the book, and repeat all you remember. Repeat the same procedure for all topic headings in the chapter. Reread only what you have forgotten.

Prelude

We have seen how much of what we are today depends on what happened during our early years. We have noted that it is possible to help children develop attitudes and behaviors that can help make them healthy self-actualizing persons. Certainly there can be no greater architectural achievement than to enable young people to be courageous, open to new experiences, constructive, and defenders of justice and human dignity.

Students' Viewpoints

Have you ever asked yourself these questions: Why am I in college? Do I really want to be here or am I just conforming to group pressure? What do I really want in life? If I had all the money I needed, what would I really want to do? The authors remember a student who drew a picture that showed a college student carrying a sizeable number of books but wearing a swim suit and riding a skate board! When they asked him what this meant, he said that he was really not aware of what he had in mind as he drew it. However, he admitted he was debating whether to stay in college or to drop out and "play around" for a few years.

As you can see from this story, motivation is complex because motives are often in conflict. We want a good education, but we also want to marry and start a family. We want a job that we enjoy, but we also want a secure one. So we have to decide which is more important for us now and for the future.

Certainly we don't want to be like the proverbial donkey who, when given a choice of two piles of hay, died of starvation because he couldn't make up his mind which one to go to.

WHY IS IT IMPORTANT?

Knowing about motivation is central to the understanding of behavior. Why does a person engage in an activity at a particular time? There could be limitless answers to this question and it is possible that no one, not even the person himself, knows the real purpose. But we must try to understand the purposes behind behavior. Otherwise we are faced with the almost unbearable condition of not knowing why we or others behave as we do. Such a condition goes against common sense and scientific knowledge.

All behavior has a purpose. The purpose may be due to the effect of body chemistry, such as the need for water and food, or the need to fulfill social expectations such as going to school and finding a job. In most cases there is no simple reason for what happened. The problem of motivation is one of bewildering complexity, but one that we must try to understand.

Our legal system, for example, has long taken into account that the motivation for a crime is as significant as the crime itself. Our courts, before deciding on the severity of punishment, inquire into the reasons behind the crime. During the Korean War an entire company of American soldiers was found guilty of running away from the enemy. The company commander had repeatedly shouted, "Attack, advance," yet all the soldiers had ignored his commands. Were all these men cowards? Of course not! It turned out that not one soldier understood English. They were American soldiers from Puerto Rico, where Spanish is spoken. The Army, therefore, changed the verdict to innocent. The significant point is that our legal system considers the understanding of the motivation producing an unlawful behavior to be very important if justice is to be served properly.

BASIC THEORY AND RESEARCH

Man has been concerned for centuries with the question of why people behave as they do. During the years, many theories have been put forth regarding man and his basic motives. Some of these were very simple explanations: they attributed most of man's behavior to one major factor or drive. Others were more complex, suggesting the interaction of several factors. In general, these theories of motivation came from three areas of human thought: religion, philosophy, and science.

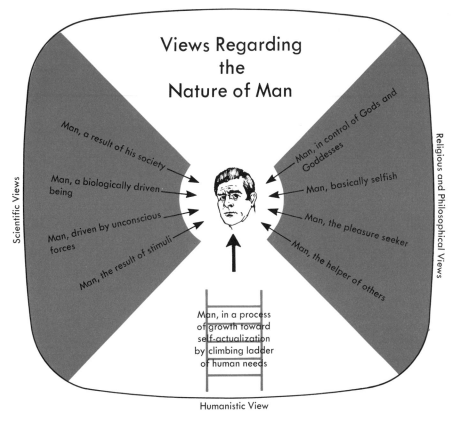

Figure 5-3
Views Regarding the Nature of Man

Fatalistic Views of Man's Basic Motives

One of the early religious theories to account for man's behavior was a theory called *fatalism* (that all of man's behavior is predetermined). This theory suggested that man really doesn't have much to say about his own behavior because it is already planned by an outside force or power. This power often took the form of a diety or god who had all of man's future preplanned. The elaborate system of gods and goddesses during the Greek and Roman period is a good example of this theory. In Table 5-1, you can see how certain forms of behavior or areas of nature were attributed to a certain god or goddess. (Hamilton, 1940; Graves, 1955) Little or no control over his own behavior is left to man in this system.

Table 5-1

Areas of Human Behavior Controlled by Gods and Goddesses

NAME	AREA OF BEHAVIOR OR NATURE
Gods	
Zeus	Lord of the sky; rain god; cloud gatherer
Poseidon	Ruler of the sea; storm and calm
Hades	Ruler of the dead; ruler of underworld; god of wealth (precious metals)
Phoebus Apollo	Master musician; archer god; the healer; god of light; god of truth
Hermes	Graceful and swift; guide of the dead; Zeus's messenger
Ares	God of war
Hephaestus	God of fire
Eros	God of love
Goddesses	
Pallas Athena	Battle goddess; goddess of the city
Artemis	Lady of wild things; huntsman-in-chief
Aphrodite	Goddess of love and beauty; laughter-loving goddess
Hestia	Goddess of the hearth (symbol of the home)
Hebe	Goddess of youth
Eileithyia	Goddess of childbirth

Philosophical Views of Man's Nature

RATIONALISM

After several hundred years the fatalistic viewpoint began to decline somewhat and another point of view, called *rationalism* (that man is in control of his behavior because he has the power to reason, think, and decide for himself), emerged. This point of view is just the opposite of fatalism. It says that man has intelligence and the capacity for rational thought. So, the question of why man behaves the way he does lies *within* man and is not in the responsibility of an outside force.

From this theory of man there came several subtheories—all of which say that man is in control of his own behavior, but that the directions of his behavior differ considerably.

EGOISM

In the fifteenth century, an Italian nobleman by the name of Machiavelli wrote the following:

It is customary for those who wish to gain favour of a prince to endeavour to do so by offering him gifts of those things which they hold most precious, or in which they know him to take especial delight. (p. 31)

I must not omit an important subject, and mention of a mistake which princes can with difficulty avoid, if they are not very prudent, or if they do not make a good choice. And this is with regard to flatterers, of which courts are full, because men take pleasure in their own things and deceive themselves about them that they run the risk of becoming contemptible. Because there is no other way of guarding one's self against flattery than by letting men understand that they will not offend you by speaking the truth; but when every one can tell you the truth, you lose their respect. (p. 116)

A man who wishes to make a profession of goodness in everything must necessarily come to grief among so many who are not good. Therefore, it is necessary . . . to learn how not to be good, and to use this knowledge and not use it, according to the necessity of the case. (p. 130)

This point of view, then, suggests that man is essentially out for his own good—even at the expense of others. It is interesting to note that such people as Mussolini, Hitler, Lenin, and Stalin used Machiavelli's writings as their inspiration during the twentieth century. (Gauss, 1952, p. 8)

ALTRUISM

Other writers have suggested that man, rather than being rather selfish and egoistic, is in fact driven by a basic tendency to help others. One of the earliest proponents of this theory was Auguste Comte. One writer explains his position as follows:

If there was any one purpose pre-eminent over others in Comte's philosophy, it was to devise means for improving relations among men. He did not agree with Bentham that the actions of individuals are motivated exclusively by self-interest. He avowed, on the contrary, that men are influenced by nobler impulses of altruism, or feelings for others, as well as by instincts of selfishness. The great object of all social teaching should be to promote the supremacy of altruism (a word invented by Comte) over egoism. (Burns, 1963, p. 654)

HEDONISM

The hedonist point of view suggests that man is driven by a basic desire for pleasure. In 1789, Jeremy Bentham published his famous book *Principles of Morals and Legislation*. In it he put forth his theory of hedonism, which one writer describes as follows:

Bentham's Utilitarianism derives its name from his cardinal teaching that the supreme test to which every belief and institution should be made to conform is the test of utility or usefulness. This test he defined as contributing to the greatest happiness of the greatest number. . . . Not only did he maintain that the interest of the community is simply the sum of the interests of the several members who compose it, but he was quite frank in admitting that the motives of individuals are purely selfish. The mainspring of human action is the desire to secure pleasure and to avoid pain. (Burns, 1963, p. 652)

Scientific Views Regarding Man's Nature

SOCIOLOGICAL VIEW

Largely as a result of research by social scientists, the why of man's behavior can be partly attributed to his interactions in a given society or culture. Thus, man's motives are seen as a reflection of certain values and customs of the particular society in which he is reared. For example, in our society one motive learned by many children early in life is the need to achieve or to do well at all things they attempt. In certain other societies this motive, rather than being encouraged, is actually punished. (Atkinson, 1958)

BIOLOGICAL VIEW

Another important view that has contributed to our understanding of man's behavior has come from research done by biologists, physiologists, and psychologists. This point of view suggests that our behavior is also largely a result of the functioning of our own bodies. We behave in certain predictable ways when we are hungry, when we're thirsty, and even when we don't have enough air or haven't had enough sleep. There have been many studies conducted on how the physiology of the body affects our motives. (Morgan, 1965)

PSYCHOANALYTIC VIEW

Sigmund Freud, the great Viennese doctor, was one of the first to question the rationality of man. He suggested that man does not always know why he behaves the way he does, that maybe man does things that he really can't explain. He suggested that all of us are driven by *unconscious motives* (behavior that the person engages in without fully being able to explain why).

He found, for example, that many of his patients would act aggressively toward another person because they were driven by a tendency to hurt or destroy themselves. (Freud, 1954) More of Freud's theory and contributions will be discussed later, in the chapter on personality.

BEHAVIORISTIC VIEW

In describing his view of man, John Watson wrote:

Behaviorism, on the contrary, holds that the subject matter of human psychology is the behavior of the human being. Behaviorism claims that consciousness is neither a definite nor a usable concept. The behaviorist, who has been trained always as an experimentalist, holds, further, that belief in the existence of consciousness goes back to the ancient days of superstition and magic.

The great mass of the people even today has not yet progressed very far away from savagery—it wants to believe in magic. The savage believes that incantations can bring rain, good crops, good hunting, that an unfriendly voodoo doctor can bring disaster to a person or to a whole tribe; that an enemy who has obtained a nail paring or a lock of your hair can cast a harmful spell over you and control your actions. . . . The extent to which most of us are shot through with a savage background is almost unbelievable. Few of us escape it. (1958, p. 2)

Thus, Watson began a school of thought called behaviorism because it focused only on the observable behavior of man, rejecting any inferences about hidden drives or motives within the person. Basically, Watson said that man is like a modern-day computer, that man's behavior is essentially the result of input (that is, stimuli fed into man through his sense organs—eyes, ears, nose, and others). If we study man long enough we will be able both to predict and to control his behavior (his responses or output) with a high degree of accuracy.

This point of view has recently been modified by Dr. B. F. Skinner. Skinner still retains the point of view that much of man's behavior is determined by his learning a sequence of rewarded responses. In 1948, Dr. Skinner wrote a novel *Walden II,* in which he developed a model society based on state-controlled stimuli that are programmed into man from birth. At one point in the book Skinner says:

Now that we know how positive reinforcement works and how negative doesn't, we can be more deliberate and hence more successful in our cultural design. We can achieve a sort of control under which the controlled, though they are following a code much more scrupulously than was ever the case under the old system, nevertheless feel free. They are doing what they want to do, not what they are forced to do. That's the source of the tremendous power of positive reinforcement—there is no restraint and no revolt. By a careful cultural design we control not the final behavior but the inclination to behave—the motives, the desires, the wishes. The curious thing is that in that case the question of freedom never arises. (p. 218)

Intermediate Summary

Motivation studies attempt to answer the question of the "why" of behavior. Understanding motivation is very difficult even though all behavior has a purpose. Major theories of motivation have come from three areas of human thought: religion, philosophy, and science. Religious and philosophical viewpoints include fatalism, rationalism, egoism, altruism, and hedonism. The scientific viewpoints include the sociological, biological, psychoanalytic, and the behavioristic.

Scientific Views Regarding Man's Future

Which of the previous points of view is correct? Is man's behavior merely the result of his society? Is man merely an animal driven by a series of biological drives? Is man really only half aware of his own behavior? Or is man just a big machine into which certain data are fed and out of which a programmed sequence of behavior flows?

As you probably guessed by now, man's behavior is a result of all of these forces and no one of them is completely responsible for all of our behavior.

Think of your own behavior today from the time you woke up. How much of it was a result of these four influences: the social, the unconscious, the biological, and the result of learning?

In recent years there has emerged a new theory of motivation that actually incorporates some of these other points of view in a single theory. It is a unique theory of motivation because it suggests that man is neither a bundle of learned stimuli (response connections) nor a being driven unconsciously by all kinds of drives, of which many are evil. It suggests instead that man is in a process of continual growth toward something very beautiful and good. This point of view is called by many names, we shall refer to it as the humanistic viewpoint.

Humanistic View Regarding Man's Nature

In Chapter 1 you were briefly introduced to Abraham Maslow and his research regarding self-actualizing persons. As part of his research on these unique people, Maslow has developed a theory of human motivation that integrates most of the basic motives psychologists have been studying for many years. Still tentative, this theory changes many of the traditional ways that psychologists and people in general view human beings. In fact, Maslow (1962) had some mixed feelings about presenting his theory before it had been studied more carefully:

There is now emerging over the horizon a new conception of human sickness and of human health, a psychology that I find so thrilling and so full of wonderful possibilities that I yield to the temptation to present it publicly even before it is checked and confirmed, and before it can be called reliable scientific knowledge. (p. 3)

Maslow begins his theory of human motives by a series of assumptions about the human being.

1. We have, each of us, an essential biologically based inner nature, which is to some degree "natural," intrinsic, given, and, in a certain limited sense, unchangeable, or, at least, unchanging.
2. Each person's inner nature is in part unique to himself and in part species-wide.
3. It is possible to study this inner nature scientifically and to discover what it is like (not *invent—discover*).
4. This inner nature, as much as we know of it so far, seems not to be intrinsically evil, but rather either neutral or positively "good." What we call evil behavior appears most often to be a secondary reaction to frustration of this intrinsic nature.
5. Since this inner nature is good or neutral rather than bad, it is best to bring it out and to encourage it rather than to suppress it. If it is permitted to guide our life, we grow healthy, fruitful, and happy.

6. If this essential core of the person is denied or suppressed, he gets sick sometimes in obvious ways, sometimes in subtle ways, sometimes immediately, sometimes later.

7. This inner nature is not strong and overpowering and unmistakable like the instincts of animals. It is weak and delicate and subtle and easily overcome by habit, cultural pressure, and wrong attitudes toward it.

8. Even though weak, it rarely disappears in the normal person—perhaps not even in the sick person. Even though denied, it persists underground forever pressing for actualization.

9. Somehow, these conclusions must all be articulated with the necessity of discipline, deprivation, frustration, pain, and tragedy. To the extent that these experiences reveal and foster and fulfill our inner nature, to that extent they are desirable experiences. (Pp. 3–4)

In other words, Maslow views the person as having an inner nature that is constantly unfolding and growing. Erich Fromm, in a seminar one of these authors attended, expresses the same idea in a slightly different way. He said that you might look at man in the same way that you look at a seed. A seed is very unimpressive to look at; in fact some are so small that you need a microscope to see them. Yet, within this seed there lies a tremendous amount of potential for growth. If you were to take a seed, let's say a flower seed, and throw it into an open field and kick some dirt over it and water it, it would probably sprout within a week or two. And, if you watched the progress of the plant for a period of weeks, you would observe it develop buds and eventually produce a flower. Then, if you were to examine the plant closely, you would probably see that it had a small flower with dull-colored petals, and leaves that were small and underdeveloped. Maybe you would see insects eating away at it. In general, you might say that this plant was stunted—it had not developed into what it might have been.

Now, if you were to take another seed of the same kind, plant it at just the right depth in soil prepared in a particular way and then give it the right amount of water, light, and nutrients, you would in time see a beautiful plant with full green leaves and flowers of a brilliant hue. You would see a plant that had developed close to its full potential.

Fromm said that we are all much like that first plant, rather stunted. So many of us live and die without realizing the tremendous potential we each possess.

How can we grow to allow this inner nature to develop, or to allow our own self to blossom as beautifully as that flower? Maslow says that growth has to occur in a certain sequence or certain order, so that we may achieve the end result he calls self-actualization.

In order to help you visualize his theory you might think of how you climb a ladder—that is, one step at a time. Well, this is how Maslow views man developing this inner nature through self-actualization—that is, it is like climbing up the rungs of a ladder one at a time.

Maslow (1943) feels that there are certain basic needs that must be met before man can become concerned with the satisfaction of other needs. Figure 5-4 is an overall picture of Maslow's theory of the stepladder, or hierarchy, of needs.

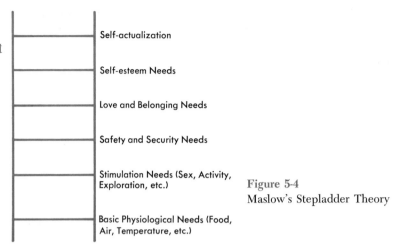

Self-actualization

Self-esteem Needs

Love and Belonging Needs

Safety and Security Needs

Stimulation Needs (Sex, Activity,
Exploration, etc.)

Basic Physiological Needs (Food,
Air, Temperature, etc.)

Figure 5-4
Maslow's Stepladder Theory

In summary, then, Maslow is saying that we all have these six basic needs. However, a person must have one set of these met to a minimum or relative degree before he can become concerned with the satisfaction of the next set. Maslow is also saying that certain people may live their entire lives on one rung of the ladder. At this moment there are thousands of people in the world who will live and die on its bottom rung, people who barely have enough food to keep themselves and their families alive.

Others in the world never get past the third rung of the ladder; among them are the people living in countries where their safety is continually threatened by a dictator or those in control in a police state.

Then there are the persons who spend their entire lives searching for love and desiring to belong—those who as children never felt they were loved or accepted; those who never experienced motherly or fatherly love.

Or, as frequently happens in the Western world, those who are hung on the rung of status and prestige; those whose whole life revolves around material possessions: the big car, the big jewels, the big title. How many people do you know like this?

Where are you on this stepladder? If you are like many of our students you probably have enough to eat, you probably have sufficient stimulation, and you probably feel safe and secure. But you probably feel that you don't belong completely, that you need more love and intimate human contact. You also probably sense that you could use more feelings of success and self-worth. As you develop in your relations with others and have success experiences in school and/or on the job, these needs will probably be met to a degree where you can reach the top rung of the ladder.

Achieving the top rung of self-actualization means the opportunity to begin developing the inner nature or the potential we each have within us. As we mentioned in Chapter 1, (p. 18) this can take the form of being one's self and being humanly responsive to the world at home, at work, or with friends. It means being open and allowing yourself the freedom to be and to feel. As Fromm (1957) puts it, "... to be alive and respond ... this could be the response to another person or to a flower or to a sunset ... this response might be being sad or it might be being joyful ...."

WHERE ARE YOUNG PEOPLE ON THE HIERARCHY OF MOTIVATION?

As we can see from Maslow's hierarchy of motivation, the motives for our behavior change gradually as we grow older. Obviously the psychological needs of a two-year-old are quite different from a ten-year-old. They live in different worlds and face significantly different problems.

A recent study by Lugo and Meyers (1964), in which forty-two school psychologists participated, revealed the following about the problems faced by young persons as they grow up.

Elementary School

1. Academic achievement (greatest problem)
2. Learning difficulties (second greatest problem)
3. Acting out (doing things without thinking)
4. Frustration
5. Overly ambitious parents
6. Paying attention
7. Immaturity
8. Identification (sex roles)
9. Who am I?

Junior High School

1. Social inferiority (greatest problem)
2. Academic achievement (second greatest problem)
3. School phobia (severe fright about school)
4. Behavior problem
5. Lack of parental control
6. Becoming mature
7. Who am I?

High School

1. Social problems (greatest problem)
2. Social status (second greatest problem)
3. Career decision
4. Emotional behavior
5. Value system
6. Rebellion
7. Academic achievement
8. Independence from family
9. Dropout
10. Who am I?

Figure 5-5

Photo courtesy of VISTA

As we can see from this study, young people are concerned principally with (1) belonging and love needs and (2) esteem needs—the need for achievement, reputation, and prestige. We can sense the beginnings of the need for self-actualization, which is the need to become what one is capable of becoming, and the growing need for satisfying sex relations.

FEELINGS OF BELONGING AND LOVE

The need to feel that one belongs in some group and that someone belongs to him begins early in life and never stops. During adolescence one learns that important rewards depend more and more on group approval. Young people in school join many organizations in order to become part of some meaningful group. As soon as they feel wanted and loved by others, their need to belong becomes less strong and they become more concerned with personal achievement, reputation, and prestige.

Figure 5-6

Photo courtesy of Fullerton Junior College

Where are these persons on the stepladder of motivational needs? Is it possible for this poor mother with child to concern herself with self-actualization? The man with her is a lawyer from VISTA. Are students on the way toward greater self-actualization? Students must meet other needs before they can become fully self-actualizing.

FEELINGS OF SELF-ESTEEM

Self-esteem refers to the need for mastery over our problems, for the feeling that we are "the captains of our own ships." Persons at this level want to feel that they are wanted and important. Wealth becomes less important than a sense of personal worth. We become more concerned with our dignity as an individual and less with group membership. A person with self-esteem is less likely to cheat on a test, to turn in a poor term paper, or to lie to friends for personal gains. He's too proud of himself as a person to lower his self-esteem in order to obtain group approval. Of course, a person at this level of motivation rarely has occasion to cheat or to lie because he has developed the skills to do a good job.

SEX SATISFACTIONS

Young people are concerned about finding socially acceptable means for the release of sexual tensions. The Kinsey study (1948) of thousands of males and females found that 60 per cent of females at age 22 had experienced sexual orgasm and that 80 per cent of males had experienced orgasm by 15 years of age and 98 per cent by 18 years of age. Although biological forces are important in determining sex behavior, cultural factors determine the kinds and frequency of sexual behavior permitted. (Mead, 1944)

Our society officially condones sexual intercourse only in marriage. This means that the sex drive, a low-level motive, is not satisfied for many years. Therefore, sex remains an important motive for many young people.

Sex activities remain high for the adolescent because (1) society tries to block sex activities but offers nothing in return, (2) our environment is highly stimulating sexually, (3) as a result of the high rate of geographic mobility, many young people do not develop long-term friendships that can lead to mutual respect, and (4) the availability of contraceptive devices has lowered the risk of pregnancy and permitted females greater sexual freedom. Therefore, studies show that sexual motivation during adolescence is high and that outlets are constantly being sought, especially by males, who have a stronger drive than females. (Stone and Church, 1968, pp. 484–485)

THE BEGINNINGS OF SELF-ACTUALIZATION

We believe that young people are eager to engage in self-actualizing activities —that is, to improve themselves and the world—but that nearly all their time is spent on meeting the more basic needs of security and self-esteem as measured by those around them. Young people, when given the opportunity, are eager to explore and to experiment. The beginnings of self-actualization in young people can be seen in their creation of new art, music, clothing, and even speech patterns. We believe that if the school would allow greater time for self-expression by students that self-actualizing activities would be common.

Intermediate Summary

A new theory of motivation, the humanistic theory, views motivation as the continual growth toward self-actualization. It is assumed that motives are arranged in the form of a hierarchy in which the basic needs must be met before the higher needs can be satisfied. One study has suggested that young people are concerned about achieving satisfying sex relationships, feelings of belonging and love, and esteem needs.

Principles of Motivation

Thus far, we have looked at some theories of motives and we have discussed certain specific motives such as desire to belong, achievement, and sex. What we would like to do now is summarize for you certain principles derived from research. These principles will illustrate how motives operate in real life.

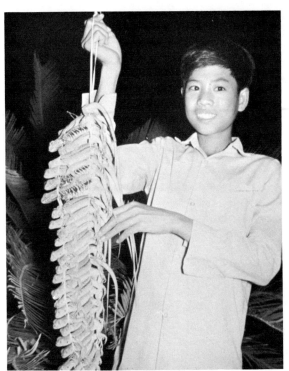

Figure 5-7
There are many ways of satisfying the same need. Here a boy from southwest Asia holds up lizards that will provide food for his table.

Photo by Dennis Hartling

MANY OF OUR MOTIVES ARE LEARNED

As you may have already discovered, most of our motives and the manner in which we satisfy them are learned. That is, we are not born with a need to achieve or a need to be successful in school or on a job. Even certain of our physiological needs (food, water, air), though built in, are affected by learning. We do not all satisfy our need for food in the same way—think of the types of foods eaten in other countries as compared to what we eat in our own society. In Italy, for example, wine is considered the basic liquid, not water.

How are motives learned, then? As you recall from the chapter on learning, behavior that is rewarded tends to be repeated by the person, whereas behavior that is not rewarded will gradually stop (see p. 48). Thus, certain people reared in families that encourage their children to do well at everything they attempt will tend to have children with a high need for achievement. You can now begin to understand why certain motives are encouraged in certain societies and discouraged in certain others.

The number and complexity of these learned needs is illustrated by a scheme of twenty-eight social needs developed by Murray in 1938. Some of these included are the following:

159

Table 5-2
Many Motives Are Learned

Social Need	Definition
Need Acquisition	To gain possessions and property
Need Conservance	To collect, repair, clean and preserve things
Need Order	To arrange, organize, put away objects
Need Retention	To retain possession of things
Need Exhibition	To attract attention to one's person
Need Dominance	To influence or control others
Need Affiliation	To form friendships and associations
Need Play	To relax, amuse oneself, seek diversion and entertainment (pp. 80–83)

MOTIVES CAN CHANGE

As you climb the stepladder of needs, as certain basic needs are satisfied, other needs become more important. A good example of this would be found in the people of the newly developing and independent nations of the world. Many of them have almost solved the problems of housing and food in their countries. Now, they are increasingly concerned with the satisfaction of higher needs such as developing self-esteem through education and recognition by other peoples of the world.

Ways Motives Change

How to help people to change their motives is a question psychologists have been trying to answer for a long time. For example, psychologists who work with delinquents or criminals are particularly concerned with the changing of those motives that produce antisocial behavior.

Psychotherapy

One technique that essentially tries to change motives is called *psychotherapy* (the psychological methods used in helping people with emotional problems). Although there are several types of psychotherapy (they will be discussed in detail in Chapter 11), generally this method is used to change motives that are so well established that the person, alone, cannot alter his behavior.

Dramatic Event or Experiences

Sometimes, as a result of some sudden, personal event or experience, a person may dramatically change some of his basic motives. A death in the family has often changed a person who has had a rather carefree or irresponsible set of motives to one who is very dedicated, committed to others and the world.

Marriage for many people often brings about an abrupt change in motives and the way they behave. Often our motives toward the meaning of education and school change markedly after marriage; even our grades reflect this change in motives.

Men returning home after experiences during a war seem to be almost different persons. Their goals and motives have shifted considerably.

A long series of experiences can also change your basic motives. A friend of the authors who became a policeman in a large city came to visit them several years after they had graduated from college. They didn't really know him anymore because he had changed in his ideas about people. Before, he was quite tolerant and understanding of others (in fact, he went into police work as a result of a need to help unfortunate people). Now, he didn't trust other people. In fact, he talked about people as if they were all stupid and lazy. His basic motive now was to punish people for their ignorance.

Trust or Faith in Another Person

Sometimes, a good, trusting experience with another human has an effect on a person's underlying motives, for example, the first encounter with a great teacher in college who loves and respects his students. One of the authors remembers such an experience in one of his classes which stimulated him to think, for the first time, about teaching as a career. Maybe you have had similar experiences with a teacher, friend, or relative.

Education

We would like to think that education has some effect on the changing of motives. One recent study, however, suggests that college students change their motives and values more as a result of interaction with other students through informal bull sessions. (Gottlieb and Hodgkins, 1963)

You are probably a different person in terms of your basic motives as a result of your experiences in school. You probably have been influenced by the school in your motives relating to learning, working with other people, and career possibilities.

Social Pressure

Many of your motives can be changed by the informal and formal pressure exerted by groups in society. Think for a moment how many of your motives are related to what other people think you should desire or strive for. Also, think about how, when you have moved into another group or have moved to another part of the country, you changed some of your motives so that you would feel more accepted by others.

MOTIVES ARE NOT ALWAYS CONSCIOUS

We all like to think of ourselves as having complete rational control over our own behavior. We like to think that we know exactly why we do certain things or say certain things to certain people. Yet, the fact is that we do not always have complete control over all our behavior. There are many times that we say or do something that puzzles us. You have probably asked yourself these questions: Why did I do that? Why did I say that? There is a good possibility that you were acting on motives of which you were unaware.

Why do we have motives of which we are not fully aware? Are we trying to fool ourselves? In a sense, yes, we are. That is, motives that pose a threat to our self-concept are often hidden from our conscious awareness on purpose so that we won't feel uncomfortable. We call this process *repression* (the non-purposeful or automatic act of forgetting some unpleasant feeling or thought that may cause a person to feel uncomfortable or guilty about the self-concept).

Psychologists have been able to demonstrate repression in laboratory experiments by using hypnosis. One famous experiment, for example, shows how an unconscious motive affects what we say:

The subject was brought into a state of profound hypnosis, during which he was instructed that after awakening he would (1) notice Dr. D. searching vainly through his pockets for a package of cigarettes; (2) that he then would proffer his own pack, and (3) that Dr. D. absent-mindedly would forget to return the cigarettes whereupon the subject would feel very eager to recover them because he had no others. He was further told that (4) he would be too courteous to ask for the cigarettes either directly or indirectly but that (5) he would engage in a conversation that would cover any topic except cigarettes although at the time his desire for the return of the cigarettes would be on his mind constantly.

When he was awakened the subject saw that Dr. D. was looking for cigarettes. He thereupon courteously offered his own and at the same time became involved in a conversation during which Dr. D., after lighting the cigarette absent-mindedly placed the pack in his own pocket. The subject noted this with a quick glance, felt of his own pockets in a somewhat furtive manner as if to see whether or not he had another pack, and showed by his facial expression that he had no others. He then began chatting casually, wandering from one topic to another, always mentioning in some indirect but relevant fashion the word "smoking." For example, he talked about a boat on the bay at New Haven, commenting on the fact that the sight of water always made him thirsty, as did smoking. He then told a story about how the dromedary got one hump and the camel two. When the question of travel was raised he immediately pictured the pleasure he would derive from crossing the Sahara Desert rocking back and forth comfortably on a camel. Next he told a tale of Syrian folklore in which again a camel played a role. When he was asked to tell something interesting about patients he told of taking a patient to see a marathon dance which the latter enjoyed immensely while he himself was reminded by the antics of the dancers of a circus where one would see elephants, hippopotami and camels. Asked what he would like to do, he commented on the pleasant weather and said there was nothing more glorious than paddling in a canoe or floating at ease on the water, smoking. (Erickson, 1939, pp. 339–340)

When do we know if our motives or those of another person are possibly unconscious? Jourard (1963) lists three general signs of unconscious motivation as follows:

(1) When the person acts in ways that produce consequences he denies intending to produce; (2) when he manifests many expressive signs of emotional tensions, feelings, and so on, without acknowledging to the observer he feels any of these things; and (3)

when there are obvious inconsistencies in behavior at different times, e.g., kindness and brutality, intelligent and stupid behavior. (p. 50)

In addition to these general signs of unconscious motivation, Jourard (1963) lists six more subtle indicators that may be evidence of the operation of unconscious motives:

1. Dream-content which seems bizarre and incomprehensible to the dreamer.
2. Fantasy-content which surprises and shocks the day-dreamer.
3. Errors and slips in speech, writing, and gestures.
4. Body postures and evidence of bodily tensions.
5. The forgetting of intentions, names, and so on.
6. Accidents of all kinds. (p. 50)

In our society, aggression and sex seem to be two of the motives that are most frequently repressed. Direct expression of aggressive or sexual behavior is highly regulated in our society, yet people have these motives and have a need to express them. Some observers of American culture have attributed the popularity of movies, plays, and novels dealing with sexual themes to the repression of the sexual motive. Other observers feel that our society has built-in institutions for encouraging more acceptable forms of aggressiveness: prize fights, wrestling matches, football, and sadistic television programs, for example.

MOTIVES ARISE FROM WITHIN AND WITHOUT

All of us are aware of how we feel when we want something. We feel motivated from within when we are hungry or thirsty. Animal behavior depends almost completely on motivation from within; that is, on the physiological level. However, even animals are motivated somewhat from without. For example, a chicken, when given a large pile of food, will eat until he finishes it, apparently completely satisfied. However, if the first pile of food were to be replaced with a new pile of similar food, the chicken would eat more. (Katz, 1937, pp. 160–162)

Human behavior depends more on motivation from without than is the case for animals, because man, through language and images, can pretend that he has what others have or that he too can do what others are doing. If you see a picture of Hawaii with its lovely beaches, you can imagine that you are there. In a few minutes you find yourself wishing or planning a trip to Hawaii. Or a young man walking through the park sees a couple embracing. When he gets home, he calls his girlfriend because he now wants to be with her. His motivation is now from within, but originally it came from without.

The principle that motives can arise also from without helps us to understand why we can learn to develop new motivation and why we can unintentionally engage in behavior not planned ahead of time. Unplanned-for behavior often occurs when we go to new and different places as on vacation. At times unexpected and undesirable behavior occurs under such circumstances. The conduct of soldiers overseas is not typical of their behavior when home. The young girl from a small town who goes to live in a large city may find herself motivated to engage in new and different behavior.

THE UNDERLYING UNITY OF MOTIVATION

One Motive May Be Seen in Different Kinds of Behaviors

Whenever we study the endless varieties of human behavior, we find the same basic motivations underneath. This means that as we try to understand why people do what they do, we must often search for the hidden or disguised motives. For example, the obese college student who never seems to stop eating may feel terribly lonely and unwanted. Instead of seeking new friendships and joining school activities, the student eats on and on. Another person who feels unloved may demonstrate this unsatisfied need by never saying no, by never standing up for his rights. He already feels so inadequate that he cannot afford to antagonize the few friends that he does have. Girls often reveal the same basic need by engaging in frequent and indiscriminate sexual behavior. It is not that they have a high sex drive but that they feel very lonely, unwanted, and unloved.

Different Motives May Combine

Often different motives combine to form the basis for certain behaviors. Such combinations may produce extremely powerful behavior.

A student may go to college to satisfy his parents, to make more money in the future, to increase feelings of being worthwhile, to find outlets for loneliness and sex drives, and to find a suitable marriage partner. Such a powerful combination of motives may keep a student in college even though there is a desire to satisfy immediate needs such as a new car or early marriage.

On the other hand, two or more motives may combine in such a way as to produce no behavior. A girl desires to marry and to raise a family in order to feel self-esteem and to fulfill her role as a female. She meets a young man and agrees to marry him at a certain date. As the day of the wedding approaches, the young woman becomes more and more fearful of the pending "sexual assault." She has been reared in the belief that sex is dirty. The day before the wedding she changes her mind. The two motives, the desire to get married and her fear of sex, have canceled each other out.

We Are Not Always Tied to the Hierarchy of Needs

College students, upon studying the hierarchy of motivations that leads to self-actualization, become concerned because it takes such a long time to meet the basic needs. They ask, "Must we wait until we are 40- or 50-years old to become self-actualizing?"

We feel that the answer is, "No." Self-actualization can be seen in the behavior of many young people. A student who tutors a failing student and asks nothing in return is practicing self-actualizing. A young man who does shopping for an elderly couple who can no longer drive to the store is self-actualizing. Young people who protest social injustices show the autonomy typical of self-actualization.

In fact, any person who is seeking to improve, to build, to go beyond what has been done, or demonstrates that he cares for the welfare of others, is practicing self-actualization. The same is true for each person involved in hobbies, games, music, or art. While doing these things we are developing our potential as unique human beings.

We Can't Always Find Deep Reasons for Our Behavior

In reading over the ideas presented in this chapter you may have gotten the impression that there is a reason for all behavior, even though some of them may be hidden from view. We also may have started you off on your own "sidewalk psychoanalysis" kick, so that you are now going around analyzing all your own motives and those of your friends and relatives.

We hope that you have, instead, some better understanding of your own motives and those of others, and we certainly want to stress one very important point: you will never understand all your behavior. None of us can find deep reasons for every aspect of our behavior. For one thing, sometimes we do things on the spur of the moment because we feel like it. And sometimes we do something because it is enjoyable. There isn't anything complex about it.

Why do some children like to run around trees or play Ring Around the Rosy? Now, you probably could develop—and maybe some psychologists have—a ring-around-the-rosy theory of motivation to account for the underlying need for this type of behavior. But, is this necessary? Maybe children do this merely for its own sake—maybe it's just plain fun.

Why do you sometimes feel like taking a walk in the woods or in a park? Again, we could develop all sorts of hypotheses regarding certain unconscious motives. But maybe you feel like this because you are a sensitive human who enjoys the smell of grass and flowers and the sound of birds.

It's all right, even healthy, to let yourself express your motives. It's okay to act impulsively and spontaneously once in awhile. Life would be very dull indeed and would get very tedious if we had to explain to ourselves or others why we behaved in a particular way after each experience.

Intermediate Summary

Research has provided certain principles of motivation that illustrate how motives operate in real life: motives can change, motives are not always conscious, motives arise from within and without, one motive can be expressed in different ways, several motives may combine to produce very highly motivated behavior, humans are not always tied to the hierarchy of needs, and important reasons cannot always be found to explain all behaviors.

APPLICATION

Living with Yourself

We have just seen how motives develop as a result of both internal and external factors. We have also seen how certain motives are more basic than others. And we have considered a rather new theory of motivation that suggests that man is in a process of continual growth toward self-actualization. We hope that you now have a better understanding of why you and others do what you do. Specifically, we hope you can now (1) understand and accept some of your own basic motives; (2) understand how to change some of your motives, those you may not feel comfortable about or are causing you difficulties; and (3) understand how you can begin to gain more satisfaction of the lower needs on the stepladder so that you can climb to the top of the ladder and grow toward more self-actualization.

UNDERSTANDING AND ACCEPTING YOUR OWN MOTIVES

Notice that we talk not only about understanding but about accepting your motives. We know that a person may understand why he does a certain thing, yet may not accept it as a part of his personality. He may, in fact, feel guilty about it. We do not mean to suggest that you must accept all your motives. You may want to change some of them (see next section). But you must first understand and accept your motives as they affect you now before you can develop the strength to change any of them.

UNDERSTANDING WHERE YOU ARE ON THE STEPLADDER

Through understanding why you behave the way you do, you should develop additional compassion for your fellow man. If you learn that certain members of a minority group seem to be concerned with the accumulation of material goods, or are driven by a high need for achievement, you can now develop possible hypotheses about the reasons for their behavior. You don't need to call them stupid or decide that they must have been born that way. If you can figure out why your parents have a need for status through community or church involvement, you can accept it as their need. Maybe you can help them to develop themselves toward self-actualization.

Next, let's look at your own place on the motivational stepladder. Which rung are you on right now? You probably have most of your basic physiological needs met to a relatively adequate degree (unless, of course, you are a working student on your own, and then there may be times when money for your food budget is low).

If you are typical of college students in our current culture, you probably have not had full satisfaction of the stimulation needs, particularly sex. As was mentioned before, our society does not provide avenues for the expression of this need until one is married. Most young people, however, are able to substitute other behavior for the temporary satisfaction of this need: dating, fantasy, creative efforts, friendships, or even athletic competition.

How about the next step on the ladder: safety and security? Many of you may feel quite insecure at times as a result of many conflicts: autonomy versus dependence on your family; sexual freedom versus learned religious and social values; wanting to gain approval in some job in society versus the comfort and protection of home; or asserting yourself with others versus unconditional acceptance and love at home.

Love and belonging are probably two of the needs that most students and many adults feel are not fully satisfied. Part of this is to be expected because you are breaking away from the home. As you find out who you are you'll be better able to relate to others on a close and personal level.

Self-esteem is also a need that is difficult for students to gain in our society. Recognition even in school is often reserved only for the athletically inclined. Even in college somtimes students are discriminated against in many subtle ways, by insensitive teachers, administrators, or secretaries. It should be pointed out that many of your specific needs may not seem to be related to the stepladder needs. That is, oftentimes the deprivation of a need may take many individual and unique forms; one kind of behavior may relate to several different needs.

ACCEPTANCE OF MOTIVE DEPRIVATION

Once you have examined your own need deprivation, what can you do about it? Are you to remain frustrated all your life? Part of the answer lies in accepting the knowledge that at this time in your life you are not able to gain complete satisfaction of all of your needs on the stepladder. You will have to learn to live with feelings of insecurity, with the feeling of not being fully loved, and with some feelings of inadequacy and lack of self-esteem.

The ability to tolerate only partial satisfaction of many of your needs is called *frustration tolerance*. Some people cannot tolerate frustration of their needs. They must have something or someone *now!* They must do something *now!*

One of the characteristics of mentally healthy persons is their ability to withstand immediate need gratification for satisfication later on in life (maybe even years). That is, they would like to feel more secure and feel more self-esteem, but they tolerate these feelings so that they can experience more security and self-esteem later.

Many students face this kind of dilemma. Two, for example, wanted to drop out of school so they could move away from home (more independence) and get an apartment and job (self-esteem). After talking to the authors, they decided that they could tolerate these unfulfilled needs now so that when they became dental assistants they could satisfy these needs more fully by having a skilled job that would allow them to get a better car, bigger apartment, and possibly a more attractive husband later on!

EXPERIMENT WITH WAYS OF SATISFYING
THE STEPLADDER MOTIVES

Maybe you have developed a certain style of satisfying certain motives on the stepladder that are creating problems for you. Essentially, the series of motives on the stepladder represent all the basic needs that all humans everywhere have. Individual differences in behavior occur as a result of different ways of satisfying needs learned by people through family and cultural reinforcement.

The point to be made here was brought out clearly in a discussion with one of the authors' students. Mary felt that something was wrong with her because she had to be with other people all the time. Alone for very long, she became quite anxious, depressed, and scared. She was losing a lot of good friends; they got tired of her hanging around all the time or of answering her calls on the phone two or three times a day or at night.

You might say that Mary had learned to handle her feelings of insecurity and inadequacy by the method of being around others all the time. The youngest in her family of seven, she was alone because her brothers and sisters were married or away at college. She tried to compensate for missing them with her friends, and it was creating problems.

There was no simple, quick solution to Mary's problem. The authors discussed things she could do that might offer additional satisfaction of the need to belong and to feel self-esteem. She joined the art club (she had a talent for painting landscapes). She entered some of her watercolors in an art show. She won a prize! Moreover, she experimented with things to do while she was alone. She found she could enjoy writing letters to friends to whom she felt close. She got satisfaction from sewing and listening to records. When she talked to some friends about her feelings, she was relieved to find that some of them had the same feelings, at least, once in a while, when they were alone.

The main point is that your motives are not fixed but can change. They can change during psychotherapy, as a result of a dramatic event, through trust in another human, education, and social pressure. It is up to you to develop your own methods of carrying out motive change within yourself.

Living with Others

People do countless things. They build bridges, compose music, climb mountains, kill one another, and die for each other. A key tool for understanding the behavior of others is to know why people do what they do—their purposes or motives.

To understand others better, try to place them on the stepladder of motivation. For example, if we try to understand the why's of a young child's behavior, we would expect the following motives to be present: physiological needs, stimulation, security, love, and then exploratory behavior.

UNDERSTANDING OTHER STUDENTS

If we are trying to understand the motivation of another college student, we would expect behavior directed toward belonging and self-esteem. A typical college student, if he feels secure and loved, will be seeking to obtain what other college students have—passing grades, social status, and a career to study for. If a college student feels he belongs and has what others have, he is free to engage in efforts toward satisfying the need for self-esteem. That is, the college student is no longer simply interested in having or doing what others have or do. He wants to do a superior job. An ordinary term paper will no longer satisfy him. He wants to be proud of himself as an individual. He works at self-esteem.

A student with self-esteem is less concerned with what others are doing and more concerned with how he is doing and what he is doing. There is far more concern with the goodness and quality of his own activities. He is also far more sensitive to personal criticism. If a teacher unfairly grades his paper, he will argue the point instead of accepting the unfair grade to remain in the good graces of the instructor. A student with self-esteem will say, "Flunk me, fire me from the job, but don't insult me as a person!"

On the other hand, a student who is still concerned chiefly with being loved and wanted will often accept personal insults and degradation from others, especially from those he considers to be his superiors. A young man who desperately seeks sex satisfaction will often become a slave to the girl he desires. Or, a student will do whatever his teachers asks and never disagree in efforts to obtain a higher grade. The class clown is seeking approval from others because he has failed to do so in socially acceptable ways.

UNDERSTANDING YOUR PARENTS

Most parents of college students can be placed at the security, belonging, and self-esteem levels of motivation. Many long for self-actualizing activities, but their sense of love and duty toward their children and present jobs often blocks their efforts. Concerned with supporting their children, they feel they cannot leave their present jobs, which provide financial security. Many join clubs and organizations in order to maintain social status. Self-esteem can be seen in their efforts to keep nice homes, and buy new cars, and win promotions. Many hope that when their children finish college, they will finally have the time and money to engage in new activities. They expect these new endeavors will be exciting and challenging. Through them, they hope to attain new levels of achievement. There are some, of course, who don't want to wait. As one mother said, "I came to college as a part-time student because I refuse to wait until my children finish college. I want to be more than a mother and a wife NOW. I feel that I have talents and potentials which I want to develop NOW. I feel guilty that I'm not being the perfect self-sacrificing mother and wife, but I am human too." The truth is that as college teachers, the authors find more and more parents, especially mothers, expressing such views.

However, most parents the authors have in class wait until their children have finished college. There was a 50-year-old gentleman in one of our classes, a mature man who had worked for years as an engineer. He had come back to college, taking classes during the evenings and even on his lunch hour! He wanted to become a minister, even though his family and friends thought it a silly idea. Now, he has graduated with a degree in the social sciences, and he has been accepted by a school of theology. He and others have had to postpone self-actualization for quite a while.

Living with Society

As we look around at our society, we find that more and more persons are satisfying all the needs on the stepladder, but few reach the top rung—self-actualization. Many persons feel secure, possess many fine material things, have prestige, and feel that they have achieved a sense of personal worth. They appear to be well rounded and satisfied. Is this all they should strive for? Some say, "Yes." They have achieved all that society values and considers to be important. Therefore, they join more clubs, buy more cars, and build bigger homes. They are like contented cows—they have stopped growing and have ceased to learn. Human nature seems to be such that we function better and more happily when we are active, seeking, exploring, and experimenting. In one sense, we should avoid becoming completely satisfied. Whatever the case, we have a choice to make when we reach the top of the stepladder of needs. We can stay on the top and behave like cheerful robots or we can step off and up from the ladder onto the level of self-actualization. There we can continue to grow and to learn and on a highly individualized, exciting, and personal level!

The authors find it difficult to explain the contented cow idea to college students. Many believe that the very wealthy and successful have achieved the highest level of human existence. For years, one of them tutored the children of very wealthy families in their homes. He was forced to conclude that many of the parents were unhappy even though they possessed fine homes, expensive cars, yachts, and airplanes. For example, one teen-ager asked his tutor to talk to his millionaire father because he had denied him his wish to work at a gasoline station during the summer vacation. The father explained that this was impossible; the family was going to tour the Pacific Ocean again in their own boat! The teen-ager did not want to go on the ocean cruise. He wanted to work at a gasoline station. He wanted to be like other boys his own age, to do what they were doing, to grow and to learn. His parents, like contented cows, were interested in repeating the same actions, again and again.

One of the more important things you can learn from the discussions on motivation is that all people want essentially the same things. However, people learn to achieve the same goals in a variety of ways. To better understand others you have to study the particular and various ways they use to satisfy the same motives.

Final Summary

Motivation includes the study of why people do what they do. Even though all behavior is purposive it is often very difficult to relate specific motives to specific behaviors. The three major theories of motivation have come from three areas of human thought: religion, philosophy, and science. Religious and philosophical viewpoints include fatalism, rationalism, egoism, altruism, and hedonism. The scientific viewpoints include the sociological, biological, psychoanalytic, and the behavioristic.

A new theory of motivation, the humanistic, views motivation as the continual growth toward self-actualization. The theory assumes that all motives are arranged in the form of a hierarchy in which the basic needs must be met before the higher needs. The motivational needs of young people in our society seem to be satisfying sex relationships, feelings of belonging and love, and self-esteem.

Research has provided us with certain principles of motivation that illustrate how motives operate in real life: Motives can change, motives are not always conscious, one motive can be expressed in different ways, several motives may combine to produce very highly motivated behavior, humans are not always tied to the hierarchy of needs, and important reasons cannot always be found to explain all behaviors.

Specific Chapter References

Atkinson, J. W. *Motives in fantasy, action, and society.* Princeton: D. Van Nostrand Co., 1958.

Burns, E. M. *Western civilizations: their history and their culture.* New York: Norton, 1963.

Erickson, M. H. Experimental demonstrations of the psychophathology of everyday life. *Psychoanalytic Quarterly,* 1939, 8, 338–353.

Freud, S. *Psychopathology of everyday life.* (2nd ed.). London: Ernest Benn, 1954.

Fromm, E. Man for himself. Unpublished radio interview, WKAR Michigan State University Radio, East Lansing, Michigan, 1957.

Gauss, C. Introduction to the Mentor edition. In N. Machiavelli, *The prince.* New York: Mentor Books, 1952.

Gottlieb, D., and Hodgkins, B. College student subcultures: their structure and characteristics in relation to student attitude change. *The School Review,* 71, 1963.

Graves, R. *The Greek myths.* New York: George Braziller, 1955.

Hamilton, Edith, *Mythology.* New York: Mentor Books, 1940.

Jourard, S. M. *Personal adjustment: an approach through the study of healthy personality.* New York: Macmillan, 1963.

Katz, D. *Animals and men: studies in comparative psychology.* New York: Longmans, Green, 1937.

Kinsey, A., Pomeroy, W., and Martin, C. *Sexual behavior in the human male.* Philadelphia, Saunders, 1948.

Lugo, J. O., and Meyers, Bernice. School psychologists look at student personality problems. Unpublished study, Fullerton Junior College, Calif., 1964.

Machiavelli, N. *The prince.* New York: Mentor Books, 1952.

Maslow, A. H. A theory of human motivation. *Psychological Review,* 1943, 50, 370–396.

——. *Toward a psychology of being.* Princeton: D. Van Nostrand, 1962.

Mead, Margaret. *Male and female.* New York: William Morrow, 1944.

Morgan, C. *Physiological psychology* (3rd ed.). New York: McGraw-Hill, 1965.

Murray, H. A. (ed). *Explorations in personality: a clinical experimental study of fifty men of college age.* London: Oxford University Press, 1938.

Skinner, B. F. *Walden two.* New York: Macmillan, 1948.

Stone, J. L., and Church, J. *Childhood and adolescence: a psychology of the growing person.* New York: Random House, 1968.

Watson, J. B. *Behaviorism.* Chicago: University of Chicago Press, 1958.

Recommended Further Readings

Paperback Books

Abrahamson, M. *Interpersonal accommodation.* Princeton, N.J.: Van Nostrand.

Alpern, M., Lawrence, M., and Walsh, D. *Sensory processes.* Belmont, Calif.: Wadsworth, 1967.

Argyle, M. *The psychology of interpersonal behavior.* Baltimore: Penguin Books, 1967.

Bindra, D., and Steward, Jane (eds.). *Motivation.* Baltimore: Penguin Books, 1966.

Birch, D., and Veroff, J. *Motivation: a study of action.* Belmont, Calif.: Wadsworth, 1966.

Blum, G. S. *Psychodynamics: the science of unconscious mental forces.* Belmont, Calif.: Wadsworth, 1966.

Butter, C. M. *Neuropsychology: the study of brain and behavior.* Belmont, Calif.: Brooks-Cole, 1968.

Cicala, G. A. (ed.). *Animal drives.* Princeton, N.J.: Van Nostrand, 1965.

Dyal, J. A. *Readings in psychology: understanding human behavior.* New York: McGraw-Hill, 1962.

Fitts, P. M., and Posner, M. I. *Human performance.* Belmont, Calif.: Brooks-Cole, 1967.

Fuller, J. L. *Motivation.* New York: Random House, 1962.

Hebb, D. O. *Organization of behavior.* New York: Wiley, 1949.

Jourard, S. M. *The transparent self.* Princeton, N.J.: Van Nostrand, 1964.

Murray, E. J. *Motivation and emotion.* Englewood Cliffs, N.J.: Prentice-Hall, 1964.

Overton, R. K. *Thought and action.* New York: Random House, 1959.

Packard, V. *The hidden persuaders.* New York: Pocket Books, 1957.

Teevan, R. C., and Birney, R. C. *Theories of motivation in learning.* Princeton, N.J.: Van Nostrand, 1964.

Teevan, R. C., and Smith, B. D. *Motivation.* New York: McGraw-Hill, 1967.

Teitelbaum, P. *Physiological psychology.* Englewood Cliffs, N.J.: Prentice-Hall, 1967.

Hardcover Books

Altman, J. *Organic foundations of animal behavior.* New York: Holt, Rinehart and Winston, 1966.

Berelson, B., and Steiner, G. A. *Human behavior.* New York: Harcourt, Brace and World, 1964.

Brown, J. S. *The motivation of human behavior.* New York: McGraw-Hill, 1961.

Combs, A. W., and Snygg, D. *Individual behavior.* New York: Harper and Row, 1959.

Cooper, J. B., and McGaugh, J. L. *Integrating principles of social psychology.* Cambridge, Mass.: Schenkman, 1963.

Hebb, D. O. *A textbook of psychology.* Philadelphia: Saunders, 1966.

Heider, F. *The psychology of interpersonal relations.* New York: Wiley, 1958.

Hinde, R. A. *Animal behavior: a synthesis of ethology and comparative psychology.* New York: McGraw-Hill, 1966.

Hoagland, H. (ed.). *Hormones, brain, function, and behavior.* New York: Academic Press, 1957.

Landauer, T. K. *Readings in physiological psychology: the bodily basis of behavior.* New York: McGraw-Hill, 1967.

Leukel, F. *Introduction to physiological psychology.* St. Louis, Mo.: C. V. Mosby, 1968.

Maslow, A. H. *Motivation and personality.* New York: Harper, 1954.

McClelland, D. C. *Studies in motivation.* New York: Appleton-Century-Crofts, 1955.

Rethlingshafer, Dorothy. *Motivation as related to personality.* New York: McGraw-Hill, 1963.

Skinner, B. F. *Science and human behavior.* New York: Macmillan, 1953.

Zimbardo, P. G. *The cognitive control of motivation.* Glenview, Ill.: Scott, Foresman, 1968.

Chapter 6 Understanding Emotions

Chapter Outline

Study Guide

Reading about emotions tends to elicit emotional responses. In this chapter the reader should be careful not to allow intense emotions to interfere with learning. However, heightened emotional involvement with the reading materials can produce more efficient and lasting learning.

REVIEW

Review the last chapter by reading the summaries. Restudy what is not clear.

Emotions like the air around us accompany whatever we do. What would your emotions be like if you were taking part in the two situations shown?

Figure 6-1

Courtesy of Charles Gibbs

Figure 6-2

Courtesy of Dennis Hartling

PREVIEW

Read the prelude, chapter outline, headings, cameos, and summaries. Turn major headings to questions. Proceed to answer these questions and to learn more about emotions.

READING

Read the chapter through. Adjust your speed of reading to the difficulty level of the passages. Check mark topics not understood, and after major topics and summaries, stop and review by glancing at topic headings, turning them into questions, and jotting down or saying to yourself all you remember. When you draw blanks, reread the selections. Reread check marked topics.

REVIEW

Review by practicing forced recall. Glance at each topic in the chapter outline, turn each topic into a question, close the book, and repeat all you remember. Repeat the same procedure using all topic headings in the chapter. Reread only what you have forgotten.

Prelude

Some people believe that the best way to understand others is to observe their behavior. Others believe that the best way is to know how and why people think the way they do. This chapter will present the viewpoint that knowing how people feel can help us to understand them, as well as ourselves, better.

Emotions are like the air around us. They accompany whatever we do, learn, or think. At times emotions are stormy and overwhelming. At other times they are subtle and we are hardly aware that they are there.

The unified nature of man is again evident when we attempt to distinguish between motives and emotions. Our motives are often justified by the statement, "I enjoy doing what I do" or, "I don't feel like going there." In other words, we do things over and over because we "feel good" as we engage in those activities. Nevertheless reason and a sense of responsibility can make us do what is not pleasant at the moment, such as studying for an examination or working overtime to pay overdue bills.

Man is not governed solely by his emotions. His reason, logic, code of ethics, and early life experiences determine to a far greater degree what he will do and what he wants to do. However, we tend to do our best work when we enjoy our experiences. We learn better when we have zest and enthusiasm. We feel more alive when we are open and accepting about our emotions.

Students' Viewpoints

Mrs. Pridy was very infirm and her husband had died only a year previously, when she was 80. She lived with a daughter and grandchildren. "I sit here for hours and hours sometimes thinking about it. I get depressed and I start crying. We was always together. I can remember even his laughing. They say what is to be will be. I never thought he'd. . . . But we've all got to go." (Townsend, 1962, pp. 332–333)

I wake slowly and without enthusiasm, spinning out each moment as long as possible. . . . For myself, though, I am content enough alone, although at times the need for emotional contact with another human being becomes hard to bear, and I feel sick with fear that my body will never again sing to the touch of a man's hand. As a rule I feel sexless, unexcited, and unexciting. (Anonymous streetwalker, 1962, p. 426)

My earliest childhood experience that I can remember is the time I got to help my mother bake a cake. It was sure fun, but I'm certain my mother didn't appreciate my taking a spoon and making designs and faces on the walls when she went outside.

My family and I went to the mountains for the weekend. We were going to stay in a friend's cabin. We did stay there a little while until my sister found a bat in the bathroom; my mother found lizards in the kitchen and I found a family of snakes in the living room. Needless to say, we left in a hurry!

I recall being lost in the theater. I went to buy some candy, thinking I could find my way back. I was there with my mother; when I tried to find my way back in the dark, I wandered around without finding my mother. I became very frightened, and felt I would never find my mother again. It was a feeling of being absolutely lost and alone. An usher found me wandering around and brought me back to my mother. What a happy moment!
(Anonymous students' memories of early emotional events)

As you see from these quotes, our past and present emotions have the potential to make our lives fun and exciting *or* to hold us captive, literally taking over our entire behavior.

WHY IS IT IMPORTANT?

We know that our emotions play an important part in making our relations with other people pleasant and joyful, or sad and painful. We also know that our emotions can bring us to heights of sensitivity to nature and empathy with others, as is the case with extremely mentally healthy persons. (Barron, 1968) We also know that our emotions can even affect our physical health. (Alexander, 1950)

What we respond to emotionally is learned. For example, we learn what to get angry at. We learn what situations produce stress or anxiety for us. We learn what kinds of situations leave us with a sense of guilt. We learn what experiences help us to feel joyful and pleasant.

Because emotional responses and expressions are learned, we can learn how to change emotional patterns that are self-defeating or harmful to ones helpful to our growth toward self-actualization. We can also learn how to develop ways to become more emotionally expressive. One of the goals of psychology classes is to help students express emotions more easily. This is related to the idea mentioned in the prologue: in our society people often experience a feeling of alienation or lack of ability to express emotions. And, it sometimes appears that many of us have almost forgotten how to cry or laugh or express genuine feelings for ourselves and others.

The authors hope that this chapter on emotions will help you become a more emotionally mature person and help you better understand the reasons behind some of your emotional reactions to certain people or situations. And we hope that you will be able to get ideas about ways you can change emotional patterns that are giving you trouble in living with yourself or others.

BASIC THEORY AND RESEARCH

Development of Emotions

The capacity to feel and express emotions is present from the moment of birth. A baby cries when startled or hurt. His little heart begins to pound rapidly and he reacts with the usual behaviors of anger and rage. Later, if we cuddle and caress him lovingly, the baby will smile and, often, just fall asleep.

Babies that receive no stimulation seem to lose the ability to feel and to express emotions. In the study by Spitz (1945), the babies who received no love resembled "zombies." When cuddled or cooed to, these poor little babies failed to respond in any way. The study by Bowlby (1966), suggested that babies of this kind are unable to feel real emotions as adults. They can pretend emotions, in the same way that actors do, but underneath the gestures and the words there are no true human feelings.

Emotions and Learning

Each of us, therefore, arrives in this world with a basic capacity to feel a wide range of emotions. What happens to our emotional capacity after birth depends on our learning experiences. For example, we can explain why a person becomes fearful at the sight of a bear even though he has never seen one before: As a child he was severly bitten by a dog, and the principle of conditioning explained in Chapter 2 (see pp. 47–48) tells us that the sight of the dog in the future will elicit a fear response. The principle of generalization (see pp. 51–52) tells us that he will now tend to fear dogs in general. The step from a large dog to a bear is understandable from our knowledge of these two learning principles.

Emotional reactions can also be learned through the gestures and actions of persons who are close to us. Members of different social classes learn unsimilar ways of responding emotionally. (Himmelweit, 1963) For example, a member of a middle-class family in our socioeconomic strata is not expected to demonstrate intensely hostile feelings except in rare situations or in a quiet whisper. A member of a lower-class family is usually freer to express hostility more openly. (Sears, Maccoby, and Levin, 1957)

Psychologists use the term *identification* (to imitate the behavior of others) to explain the similarity in emotions and behaviors between persons who are closely related. For example, a boy tends to think and behave much in the same ways as his father. The college freshman rapidly identifies with his college, its traditions, and emotional tone. The coed learns expected ways of dressing, relating to young men, and even, at times, of walking!

Introduction to Positive and Negative Aspects of Emotions

We have just seen that the manner in which we express our emotions is a result of learning within the family and society. Our emotions have a lot to do with how much pleasure and enjoyment we get out of life. However, our emotions can also have negative effects. That is, sometimes our emotions can cause problems for us. The same emotion in one situation may have positive effects and in another have negative effects.

Let's look at some examples. You are driving your car on a rainy day and while applying the brakes, you temporarily lose control of the car. This produces a strong fear reaction, because you almost hit the car passing alongside you. As a result of this fear reaction, in the future you are far more cautious in driving on rainy days. This fear response, then, had a positive effect on your future behavior.

A child falls into a swimming pool and is rescued by his screaming mother. As a result of this incident the child is desperately afraid of water; when he grows up he avoids going near water or even riding in a boat. In fact, he even refuses to learn to swim. Thus, this fear has resulted in a negative effect, which produces an irrational fear response whenever the person gets near a swimming pool, the ocean, or a lake.

What are we trying to say? Essentially, then, emotion can serve a useful purpose in one situation (positive effect) and in other situations may serve as a hindrance (negative effect). Let's look at some of the more common positive effects of emotions.

POSITIVE EFFECTS OF EMOTIONS

Emotions Increase Our Ability to Communicate with Others

We do not merely communicate with others through the use of words. We also use various emotional reactions in the form of tone of voice, gestures, and the tenseness or relaxation of various muscles of our body.

As a child you may remember times when your parents said one thing, but really meant another. It seems that children can tell more than adults when someone is lying to them or when there is a discrepancy between what people say and what people really mean.

Mentally ill people often cannot connect their emotional responses with other forms of their behavior; that is, they may say one thing but their tone of voice really is telling you something else. (Gordon, 1963)

You have probably interacted with people like this. Good examples are found in the roles that people have to play: the salesgirl who has to wear a smile even though she may not feel like smiling; the school counselor who says: "O yes, I'm so glad to help you with your problem," when he'd rather be doing something else; or the boy who dates a girl for some reason other than because he likes her as a person.

Emotions Help to Mobilize the Person for Action

When our emotions are aroused, many things happen within our body that we have very little control over. (Gardner, 1963) Various physiological reactions in the nervous system, especially emotional reactions such as fear and anger, help prepare the person to react faster and for a longer period of time in emotional situations. (See Table 6-1)

Table 6-1
Some Reactions to Emotional Stress

OBJECTIVE (PHYSIOLOGICAL)	SUBJECTIVE (FEELINGS)
1. Increased heart beat	1. Pounding heart
2. More blood near skin surface	2. Flushed facial feelings
3. Stomach movements	3. "Funny" stomach feelings
4. Increased adrenalin and sugar in blood	4. Feeling stronger and more energetic
5. Increase muscle tension	5. Tight, tense feelings
6. Decrease in saliva secretion	6. Dry mouth

All of us know how we feel during moments of intense emotions such as love, fear, or anger. These subjective feelings and their physiological counterparts are to a large degree common to all human beings. The intensity and duration of emotional reactions depend on the individual and the circumstances.

Emotional Responses Are Pleasant in Themselves

Many emotional responses feel good to the person. Feelings of love, tenderness, and warmth toward other people give one a sense of well-being. Emotions in-

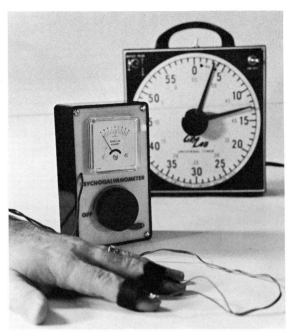

Figure 6-3
When our emotions are aroused, there are bodily reactions over which we have little or no control. Bodily reactions to emotional states include changes in skin resistance to electrical impulses. These changes are measured by the psychogalvanometer.

Photo by Ron Sakall

volved in one's anticipation of some good news he is momentarily expecting feel good. Emotional responses involved in happy or joyful experiences in life are also enhancing to the person. Emotional responses found in humor or laughter tend to help the person feel good about being alive.

Emotional Responses Break the Monotony of Life

Think of how you would feel if you were depressed all of the time or if you felt happy all of the time. All of us experience mood changes in our daily lives, partly as a result of physiological changes in our bodies, but also as a result of our experiences in our environment. Some days we feel very good about life and other people; other days we feel depressed or want to be alone. People vary in these feelings. Those who continually feel depressed usually get very tired of the mood and often seek help to find out what is wrong.

Self-actualizing persons often seek new experiences or challenges in life because they enjoy the emotional experiences associated with them. Young people in general are looking for new emotional experiences: golf, skiing, car racing, swimming, and the excitement and challenge of new ideas. Moustakas (1961, pp. 22–23) relates the following personal experience:

On an especially cold, blustering day, the noisy violence of a raging wind kept me indoors. After almost two days of internment, I began to feel dull and insensible to the children's play and other events going on around me. Everything seemed colorless and toneless. I was on the verge of despair, in the shadows of life, and felt trapped by the violent storm outside. . . . The more I thought about my situation, the more restless I became. A growing inner feeling surged within me. I decided to face the wind. I had

181

never been in a blizzard before—by choice—but in that moment I decided to enter the turbulence outside.

It was cold, yet I was warmed by a tremendous surge of emotion. I felt radiant and alive as I continued my journey. As the wind met me and moved me, I became aware of the whole atmosphere. It was like a powerful dynamo, electrified with clear, ringing sounds which extolled the universal virtues of nature. . . . It was a moment of inspiration and an inner victory over superstition and fear. For the first time in my life I truly understood the meaning of a blizzard from my own direct experience. . . . I felt an expansive and limitless energy. I returned home. Everything took on a shining light and a spark of beauty. . . . Out of the tumultuous experience, I found new joy in life, new energy, uniqueness and beauty. I conquered my lethargy and discovered a lively affinity with everything I touched. Everything which had been dull and commonplace took on a living splendor.

All of us have experienced such moments either by ourselves or with others. These are the moments when we joyously discover our deeper emotions, talents, and potentials.

Emotions Tend to Facilitate Effective Learning

What kind of things do you tend to remember from your classes? Do you remember the list of names and dates you memorized for a test? Probably not. The fact is you probably will tend to remember things that got you aroused or emotionally involved in the class. The teacher you liked very much, the lecture where you got angry and disagreed with what the teacher was saying, the lab class in which you did an original research project. There is considerable evidence to suggest that more effective learning takes place when there is some emotional involvement and concern. (Gilbert, 1938; Cameron, 1966)

Studies on effective teaching have baffled researchers for years because they were trying to come up with a list of common characteristics of effective teachers. They found some effective teachers who made their students love them. They found others who made the students very angry. It wasn't what the teacher did that counted, but whether he evoked an involvement or emotional reaction among his students.

POSITIVE ASPECTS OF SOME SELECTED EMOTIONS

Love, Affection, and Tenderness

The ability to adequately express the emotional responses involved in love, affection, and tenderness are basic to healthy growth and development as a child and as an adult. (Lipton, 1965) You remember the consequence of the lack of infant love, from reading Chapter 4. A person who has not experienced the emotions of love early in life has a difficult time relating to others later in life.

Through emotional reactions of love for self and others, the person is better able to grow toward self-actualization and mental health. In addition, the person is better able to feel a sense of relatedness to others in the world. Indeed, one psychologist has gone so far as to say: "A person who is unrelated to anyone or anything is an insane person." (Fromm, 1960) That is, we as humans cannot tolerate complete aloneness (physical and/or psychological) (Bexton, Heron, Scott, 1954); it is through the expression of emotional feelings of love and tenderness that we meet this basic need.

Sense of Well-Being, Joy, or Zest for Life
Even though psychologists have not systematically studied the quality of joy, happiness, or well-being, you have all experienced this feeling at certain times. Often it occurs when we are actively engaged in the challenges involved in our daily life and work. Frequently it can be observed in younger children as they go about their play activities in an enthusiastic manner. One psychologist feels that it arises *when* a person encounters situations that are going to *stretch* his resources and muscles. Thus, a person who is actively engaged in writing, taking an automobile apart, conversing with someone, or playing tennis will experience and manifest a type of feeling that might be called zest.

Maslow (1956) studied this feeling of zest that occurs in self-actualizing persons. He uses the term *peak experiences* to define moments of great ecstasy and joy. Practically everyone has peak experiences, but they occur more often among self-actualizing persons. They tend to help the person regain a sense of relatedness to life and the world and to encourage further involvement with the world. Expressions such as "It's wonderful to be alive" or "Words cannot express my feeling" are common during these experiences.

Sense of Humor or Laughter
The ability to see the humor in situations and to be able to laugh even at ourselves seems to be a sign of mental health. Jourard (1963, p. 102) points out the importance of laughter as follows:

One psychologist regarded laughter as one of the purest examples of behavior that is characteristically human. That is, laughter is a response to situations which can be made only by persons who have transcended their animal heritage as well as the conformity-producing pressures of society. Laughter is a sort of defiance of necessity, a kind of proclamation of one's independence or of one's ability to transcend the limits of otherwise mundane or grim circumstances.

Of course, there are rough norms extant in society by means of which one can judge the appropriateness or inappropriateness of laughter. Indeed, schizophrenics will often laugh in situations where a more intact person might weep or become angry. But a good sense of humor, the ability to find something ludicrous in situations, is not only a social asset: it is an indication that a person is able to do more than just struggle to exist. (p. 102)

Maslow (1956) lists a sense of humor as one of the characteristics of self-actualizing persons he has studied. He summarizes his finding as follows:

Characteristically what they consider humor is more closely allied to philosophy than to anything else. It may also be called the humor of the real because it consists in large part in poking fun at human beings in general when they are foolish, or forget their place in the universe, or try to be big when they are actually small. This can take the form of poking fun at themselves but this is not done in any masochistic or clown-like way. Lincoln's humor can serve as a suitable example. Probably Lincoln never made a joke which hurt anybody else. . . . (Maslow, pp. 184–185)

TECHNIQUES FOR DEVELOPMENT OF MORE POSITIVE EMOTIONAL RESPONSES

Perhaps you would like to develop your emotional reactions more so that you can experience some of the positive aspects. There are no magic formulas to follow, but research and the authors' experiences with students may offer you some ideas to try.

Accepting Your Emotions As Part of Being Human

Now that you have a more thorough understanding of the positive aspects of emotions, you may be more prone to accept the idea that it's all right to feel or to express emotions. Many segments of our society suggest that to express emotions is a sign of weakness and "You've got to be tough and hard to get along in this competitive world." This is one reason why so many people do not accept or, in fact, try to deny their emotions.

Accepting your emotions means trying to relax and letting your feelings come forth. Knowing that your emotional responses help you to live a more rich life may help. However, actually setting up situations that will enable you to feel free to "let yourself go" may also help. For example:

1. Try listening to some mood music. Close your eyes as the music begins and let your feeling flow with it.

2. Take a walk alone in a park and think about certain people or yourself; or concentrate on a flower or tree.

3. Get together with a close friend and try an "honesty session." Each of you express how you really feel about certain issues, about people, and yourselves, or each other.

4. When you feel in a reflective mood, sit down and write out the way you feel.

5. Read literature (novels and autobiographies) and attend plays and movies. This sometimes helps a person to freely express his feelings through empathy and identification with the characters portrayed.

You can probably think of many other ways to help develop your emotional reactions, and you probably have developed many already by yourself.

Of course, the free expression of emotions can sometimes get you into trouble because being too honest sometimes poses a threat to people. However, by more freely allowing yourself to experience and express your emotions you will find a new and exciting relationship to life and people in general.

Developing Positive Feelings About Yourself

People who feel good about themselves (positive self-concept) are not afraid of their emotional responses. That is, they tend to trust themselves and their emotions. Essentially what we are saying is that self-actualizing persons can afford to be themselves; therefore their emotions and their behavior go together. So, any ways that help you feel better about yourself and indirectly help you experience the more positive emotions and responses will help you to integrate your emotions and behavior into a meaningful whole.

Increasing Your Thinking and Problem-Solving Abilities
Many people cannot experience some of the more positive emotions because they are continually unable to face reality. That is, they are burdened by problems that keep them fearful and frustrated; this in turn leads to feelings of inadequacy, anxiety, and hostility.

By increasing their abilities to think and solve problems more effectively, people can turn their emotional energies to more positive areas. Here again are the four steps in going about solving a problem:

1. Define the problem.
2. Plan the method of attack.
3. Carry out the plan.
4. Evaluate the results.

Intermediate Summary

Emotions form the great unwritten language that can lead to better communication and understanding. Positive emotions such as love, joy, and humor can be developed through continuous practice. Some techniques for emotional development are setting up situations in which they can be expressed, developing positive self-feelings, and learning more effective problem-solving methods.

NEGATIVE ASPECTS OF EMOTIONS
We have just discussed why the mature expression of emotions is essential to the fully functioning or self-actualizing person. A person who denies his emotions becomes stunted and warped in his total growth. Why, if the expression of emotion is so healthy, do most persons tend to deny and to suppress their emotions? Let us discuss some of the reasons.

WHY WE TEND TO DENY OUR EMOTIONS

Western Civilization
Western civilization (our history, culture, and religions) has taught us as well as our ancestors that the ideal man is logical and rational and that the primitive, childish man is emotional and irrational. Therefore, we should be logical, rational,

and try not to reveal our true feelings. For example, the other day while one of the authors was waiting in a doctor's office, he saw the doctor's wife give a cookie to a little girl. The little girl took one bite and put the cookie aside. When the doctor's wife returned she asked the little girl if she liked the cookie. The girl said, "No." Her mother, flushed with anger, said, "You tell her that you liked the cookie." The little girl dutifully acceded to the demand. The doctor's wife smiled and said, "Thank you." There, was a little girl being trained to preserve this tradition. The author couldn't help but feel sad. Was the price too great?

Motion Pictures and Television

Motion pictures and television tend to support the image of the logical and rational man even in absurd situations. The hero is surrounded by hundreds of enemies intent on killing him; his death seems unavoidable. But not one bit of appropriate emotion is shown. No perspiration! No trembling or quickened heartbeat! Even his voice is calm and soothing! Real life experiences tell us that human beings in great danger do not behave like our heroes in the movies or on television. For example, pilots returning from combat report the following symptoms: a sense of unreality, trembling, frequent urination, confusion, stomach sickness, cold sweat, and general weakness. (Shaffer, 1947) We can see that human beings under severe stress undergo profound and diversified emotional changes.

On-the-Job Experiences

Remember the first job you had? Do you remember the joy and thrill!? You would arrive early and leave late, never caring about overtime wages. Then one day the boss called you and said, "You're fired." The shock wave lasted for days, possibly weeks. Finally you said to yourself, "Never will I let myself become so emotionally involved in a job again. This way, if I'm fired again, it will not hurt so deeply."

Psychologists call this process in which we deny and refuse to show our emotions in situations where these emotions may be short-lived or not respected by others, *emotional insulation.*

Love Relationships

Emotional insulation can be seen in romantic relationships. Do you remember your first date? You felt at least ten feet tall, so strong that no obstacle was too great, the image of your "first great love" was nailed to your eyes so that it could not disappear. Then the realities and frailties of human behavior became dramatically apparent.

The love and tenderness of family cannot so easily be transplanted to a stranger. Most college students, tend not to reveal their true emotions, especially when they really love someone. In fact, many times they are colder and more indifferent to those they really care for during predating and early dating behavior. As we can see, emotional insulation is a protective device against hurt.

The danger of too much emotional insulation is that it takes away the joy and excitement of human relationships. It can turn one emotionally into an iceberg, a cold and unfeeling person. Naturally it is very difficult to hurt an iceberg, but isn't the price for this kind of protection really too great?

School Experiences

By the time students reach college, large numbers of them seem to have emotionally insulated themselves from their schoolwork. (Walters, 1961) Previous failures, despite sincere efforts, have led many to use this protective covering. By so doing, a lower-than-expected grade does not hurt as much.

One of the authors worked for a time in a psychology reading clinic where there were cases of very severely emotionally insulated students. Even the slightest effort was too risky for those poor students. To try to succeed and to learn was to become, once more, emotionally involved. They simply couldn't take the chance! For the vast majority, it was a year before school subjects could be taught to them.

We tell our college classes to be aware of emotional insulation. We ask them to trust us and to try hard once again. Without some emotional involvement they practically guarantee school failure, which, in turn, will strongly reinforce emotional insulation. A vicious circle is then established. Failure leads to hurt. Hurt leads to emotional insulation. Emotional insulation leads to further failure and more failure intensifies the insulation!

EMOTIONS THAT TEND TO BE MORE NEGATIVE

Just as there are emotions whose expression generally leads to greater happiness and efficiency, there are other emotions whose expression generally leads to misery and inefficiency. Among the more negative emotions are fearfulness, anger, guilt, and anxiety.

There are two reasons why certain emotions can become negative. First, the open expression of unpleasant emotion is typically not socially acceptable. Therefore, we tend to keep within ourselves unpleasant emotions that really need to be expressed if we are to remain healthy psychologically.

Unpleasant emotions are like "mud" in our system. We can build a dam and hold back the unpleasant emotions and pretend that they do not exist. The key word is *pretend*. To pretend does not make them disappear, because it is well known that unexpressed emotions often underlie mental problems. (Rogers, 1961) The torrent of emotions released during psychotherapy for the mentally ill is called *catharsis*. The complete unawareness of the existence of unexpressed emotions is called *repression*. The denial of emotions that we still feel is called *suppression*. The chapter on mental illness will discuss repression in greater detail.

Fearfulness

Fear is what we feel when we are faced with real or imagined danger. There are profound changes in our body during fear. The physiological responses to fear prepare us to fight or to flee from the danger. Our heartbeat increases rapidly to pump more blood to our muscles, sugar is released by the liver to give more energy and to quicken our thinking process, the pupils of our eyes increase in size, oxygen intake is increased through rapid breathing, platelets are released to aid coagulation of the blood in case we are cut or bruised. And there are additional bodily changes. (Ax, 1953)

All of these physiological changes prepare us for fighting or other emergency actions. Our body resembles a tightly wound spring ready to be tripped into instant action. However, in our society today, rarely will such emergency action be needed. Our advanced and cooperative society has installed safety measures to protect us from situations requiring dramatic physical actions. Therefore, the need to "trip the spring" is rare, and the intense physiological reaction just makes us feel deeply hurt and frustrated.

Think of the last time you were fearful and felt your body reacting in the way just described. Was it an earthquake, a dental appointment, proposing to your girl friend, applying for a job, or fear of losing a job? It would seem that what we fear most frequently is not physical danger but loss of face—ego-deflating situations wherein we may be insulted. In such situations, however, it would be entirely inappropriate to "attack" the person insulting or evaluating our behavior.

The negative aspects of fear can be summarized as follows:

1. The constant physical turmoil may be a causative factor in physical illnesses.

2. The reactions to fear are psychological as well as physical. If a person is constantly unable to remove the cause of his fear and discomfort, he may develop some undesirable symptoms of mental illness.

3. The fear originally produced by a specific situation or object may with the passage of time generalize into other similar situations or objects. For example, fear of teachers may generalize to employers and to others in higher positions. The fear when attributed to innocent persons is uncalled for and may hinder effective interpersonal relations.

4. The original fear may become greater with the passage of time until the fear becomes actual terror and paralyzes the person. For example, if a person nearly drowns, he, with good reason, becomes afraid of water. If he never tries to swim again, his fear of water will become greater and greater with the passage of time. Psychologists call such a growth of fear *incubation*. The way to avoid incubation is to go back to the feared situation and to successfully cope with it. A pilot who crashes should fly a plane again as soon as possible.

The person who falls victim to all four of these negative aspects of fear is a person governed by fears. He cannot take many chances. He must develop a way of living that is safe, cautious, timid, and dull. He is really possessed by fear.

On the other hand, a psychologically healthy person accepts and respects real dangers, both physical and psychological. The fears we really need to fear are those that prevent us from learning and growing. In order to do this we must be able to learn in the face of fear. To run when we are uncomfortable or insecure means to avoid learning the very skills that will enable us to overcome the fear.

Hostility

Hostility is what we feel when the pathways to what we desire are blocked or when we believe that we have been unjustifiably insulted or hurt. In a society such as ours, hostility is quite common because we are often frustrated by obstacles, requirements, and waiting periods. Competition often assures us of being unjustifiably downgraded because there is nearly always one in the group who runs faster, dances better, spells or reads better.

The psychological and physiological responses of hostility are similar to those of fear except that the urge to fight or to destroy is far stronger. To attack or to destroy is almost always condemned in our society. On the other hand, to keep our hostile feelings locked up inside is not healthy physically or psychologically.

The expression of hostility toward social and personal injustices is generally positive. Anger directed toward an unfair grade by a teacher or unfair treatment by an employer is psychologically healthy. Anger toward a parent who deliberately lies and misleads is justifiable. Anger toward a wife or husband who was too gullible or very inconsiderate is fair and should be expressed. In other words, justifiable hostility, which enables us to improve our lives and society, is constructive. Negative hostility is that which prevents us from responding to reality and improving or changing the situation that produced the hostility.

The constructive expression of hostility should be directed at the behavior or situation and not at the persons involved. Attacks on other persons lead almost inevitably to retaliation against us or to alienation from us. Constructive expressions of hostility should help us or other persons to increase their understanding so that the problem will not occur again.

The negative expression of hostility is directed outward to belittle and to destroy others, or turned inward to "punish" ourselves through failure, illness, or guilt feelings. These kinds of expressions of hostility are self-destructive and prevent us from improving and from responding to the world as it really is. They hold us back when we should be learning and improving.

Guilt

Guilt is what we feel when we have failed to do what is expected of us. Feelings of guilt originate during childhood when we cannot avoid all the taboos placed on us by our parents and by society. A child who fails to live up to the rules typically learns rapidly how to feel guilty about his violations. If the parents are very strict, even thought about taboos brings guilt feelings.

Guilt feelings can be positive if such feelings help us to improve and to learn. Guilt feelings about irresponsible and avoidable misdeeds are healthy feelings if they prevent further misdeeds. For example, if a student begins to cheat instead of studying, the growth of guilt feelings may put a stop to the cheating.

Guilt feelings, however, are often negative. It is nearly impossible to avoid all the taboos and expectations placed on us by society. Continuous failure to obtain high grades can produce the additional burden of guilt. Sex activities, real or imagined, can be a constant source of guilt for very conscientious or religious persons and can lead to impotence or frigidity.

What should concern us are unnecessary guilt feelings, which not only prevent us from doing our best work but lead to misery, depression, and self-hate. Unnecessary guilt can be very destructive and inhibiting to the individual.

Anxiety

Anxiety feels the same as fear with the added apprehension that we don't know where the danger lies. In fear we know what we fear; in anxiety the source is unknown or unrecognized. It is the inability to spot the cause of our anxiety that makes anxiety so troublesome in our lives.

Anxiety, like other generally negative emotions, has positive elements. Low levels of anxiety make us more alert and aware of what is going on. A slip in the snow or a probation notice tends to make us aware of what may happen unless we start doing something quickly. Low and moderate levels of anxiety generally produce higher scores on complex learning tasks and problem solving than high levels of anxiety or no anxiety at all. (Farber, 1954) In other words, some anxiety mobilizes us psychologically and physically for effective action.

Anxiety experienced in the areas of illness, old age, and death are normal. Whenever we venture into unknown situations, it is normal to experience some anxiety. And whenever we have too many problems at one time, we should expect to experience some anxiety. On the other hand, not to venture out and to avoid new experiences also bring anxiety because we feel guilty about not having taken a chance. For example, a student developed anxiety because he flunked out of college. Yet he might have developed greater anxiety if he had not attended college at all. To avoid all anxiety is to stop living a normal life.

Negative Aspects of Anxiety

No matter what the cause, anxiety is so unpleasant that we try to get rid of it as soon as possible or to remove it from conscious awareness through the use of repression. Repression is the process by which unbearably disturbing thoughts and feelings are pushed down into the unconscious. The repressed thoughts and feelings, however, are always pushing toward consciousness and come back in disguised forms and substitutions. For example, unexplainable hatred and anger toward an innocent teacher may be the result of unexpressed hostility toward parents. Teachers are more acceptable targets than parents, who are supposed to be respected and loved unconditionally.

Although anxiety may lead to constructive changes in behavior, it can be responsible for negative emotional symptoms that can cripple a person's growth. Anxiety may be the central problem in many emotional and physical ills. (Frazier and Carr, 1964) It is important for us to know that many strange and seemingly unaccountable forms of behavior are the result of a disguised and unconscious release of repressed emotions. The student who cannot and will not learn, although he has the intelligence, is often the victim of overwhelming anxiety. The school rebel, the smart aleck, and the delinquent are often anxious persons. One does not have to tremble to be anxious. Disguised behaviors are ways of trembling!

DEVELOPING COMPETENCIES FOR LIVING
WITH NEGATIVE EMOTIONS

Because emotions generally considered to be negative are a part of living, and are constructive at times, we should develop competencies for living effectively with them.

LEARNING IN FACE OF FEAR AND ANXIETY. It is almost too human to want to run away from threatening situations. If we are unprepared for a test, an illness is a most welcome relief. Cutting class feels good. But the "happy" moment of relief leads to a vicious cycle of anxiety, avoidance, more anxiety, and still more avoidance. We must learn in the face of fear if we are ever to learn the necessary competencies to master threatening situations in the future.

CATHARSIS BEFORE REMEDIAL ACTION. High levels of emotional feeling generally lower our ability to learn and think effectively. Therefore, it is wise to have an emotion-releasing period before deciding on a course of action.

STRATEGIC WITHDRAWAL. There are times when the best way to reduce mounting anxiety is to withdraw temporarily from situations that are overwhelming. We can return to them when we have increased our competencies in dealing with them. This way the odds for winning are better, and the higher probability of success can change our emotion from anxiety to the sweet anticipation of victory.

AVOIDANCE OF INCUBATION. Lifelong crippling fears can be avoided if we return to the dangerous situation well prepared to succeed. The longer the period between the terrifying moment and the successful return to the original scene, the more intense the fear or anxiety.

FINDING IMMEDIATE CONSTRUCTIVE RELEASE. At times the immediate release of pent-up feelings can get us into trouble. Some people find escape and release by watching monster pictures (their troubles seem small compared to the poor fellow being chased by the monster), viewing thrillers on television, or reading murder stories. Others find release in higher-level activities such as sports, hobbies, dancing, and music. Use of a diary, or writing to a close friend, or verbalizing the situation and feelings to a trusted friend often leads to a satisfying release.

Once we have released the negative emotions, not only can we think more effectively about ways to avoid such situations, but we learn to accept the inevitability of negative emotions. After all, we cannot always be successful, and not all people will find us lovable, kind, and intelligent.

Intermediate Summary

Society often encourages the suppression of emotions. Emotional insulation on the job, in human relations, and while learning interferes with effective living.

Unexpressed emotions such as hostility, anxiety, and guilt are like mud in our systems. To pretend that they do not exist does not make them disappear. Some strategies for living effectively with negative emotions are (1) learning in face of fear and anxiety, (2) catharsis before remedial action, (3) strategic withdrawal, (4) avoidance of incubation, and (5) finding constructive release.

Integrating Principles of Emotions

Now that we have looked at some of the positive and negative aspects of emotions we would like to summarize in the form of a series of principles what psychologists know generally about emotions. This will allow us to integrate our knowledge of emotions.

1. Our emotions develop from generalized forms of activity when we are children and are developed into specific emotional responses through the learning process.

2. Some emotional responses have positive aspects; that is, they are facilitating for the individual in his growth toward self-actualization. Examples of the more facilitating emotions include love and tenderness, zest and joy, and humor or laughter.

3. Some emotional responses have negative effects; that is, they often result in severe emotional consequences for the individual and hinder his growth toward self-actualization. Examples of emotions usually having negative effects include fear, anxiety, and guilt.

4. Our emotions are really an integral part of our motives, our learning abilities, and our thought processes; however, they are discussed separately so that we can better understand how they interrelate within the human personality.

5. Our emotions range from vague, ill-defined feelings of uneasiness to highly specific fear responses of panic where the entire physiology of our body is involved.

6. Many of our emotional reactions function automatically through that part of our nervous system over which we exercise little conscious control.

7. Emotional reactions are both interrelated and closely related to our environment and to other people in our environment.

Emotional reactions usually don't occur in a vacuum. They usually result as a reaction to situations and persons we are interacting with. As a result, our emotional reactions are not separate and isolated but may occur together or may overlap. You have probably experienced mixed emotions such as love and hate for another person at the same time. Or maybe you have seen a person crying as a result of hearing some good news. When we talk of different emotions such as love, fear, and hostility, we must remember that they are always integrated within a real life setting and that they often get mixed together in our reactions.

8. Sometimes emotional reactions are triggered by unconscious factors (conflicts). Probably each of us has certain areas of our behavior where we are very emotionally sensitive. That is, we may find ourselves in certain situations that seem to trigger an emotional response for no apparent reason. As we discussed earlier (p. 162) certain situations or events may be automatically forgotten because they were so painful (repression); even though we have repressed the event, it still may unconsciously affect our behavior.

Many fears are examples of this. You may have seen or heard of a person in a near state of panic when caught in an elevator or other closed place. Perhaps you have seen someone who is afraid of animals run for shelter when a small dog comes down the street.

9. All of us have an over-all general pattern of emotional and mood variations. Have you noticed that there are certain days when you feel very happy and life is good; and on certain other days, you wonder whether life is worth it all? Why you feel this way is very complex. It results from an interaction of situations in your environment and your body chemistry. But probably one of the most important factors that accounts for these changes in emotions has to do with your own individual pattern of mood swings. The body's glandular chemistry, which partially accounts for these changes, will not be discussed, but studies indicate that they do vary among different people and that they tend to be recurring over long periods of time. (Selye, 1950; Funkenstein, King, and Droletter, 1957).

10. The society or culture within which you live has a great effect on the development of certain emotional responses and the way in which they are expressed. Shibutani (1961) puts it this way:

Consider, for example, the circumstances under which people become embarrassed. Men in military service are not particularly disturbed about using profanity among their comrades, but the inadvertent use of the same words elsewhere may lead to paralyzing embarrassment. Nudity would be the source of some embarrassment in a classroom, but one thinks nothing of it in a gymnasium shower room. Food taboos also provide illustrations. Most Americans refuse to eat snake meat, horse meat, eel, octopus, and many other items that scientists certify as dietetically nourishing.

Sociologists and anthropologists have studied how certain emotional patterns vary in different cultures. (Kluckhohn, Murray, and Schneider, 1954) For example, absence of overt aggression is an outstanding feature in Saulteaux society; however, a Kwoma child can beat his smaller brother without fear of retaliation. In fact, his parents praise him for this behavior rather than punish him for it.

11. Man has the power to get emotionally involved about future events. Through his ability to symbolize and think, he can anticipate future events and can recall previous experiences. This ability is both a blessing and a curse; through this process, for example, man can relive beautiful experiences he had as a child and become emotionally involved. Or, he can anticipate his homecoming after being away in the military service.

On the other hand, many people continue to get depressed or to feel guilty about past wrong doings, or they anticipate future failures or catastrophes— which often never happen. Thus, many emotional problems (frequently these are physical complaints, in the form of headaches, stomach pains, and the like) develop as a result of this continual worry.

12. Because emotional responses are the result of learning they can be changed. We know that we can help people to change emotional responses that seem to be getting them in trouble. Sometimes this is merely a matter of time and maturity, as in the case of the child who enters kindergarten and leaves the safe protection of mommy and home. It may take him a week or two to get used to being with other children. Soon, however, his original fear gives way to joy and pleasure as he plays with the other children.

Sometimes our emotional responses are so powerful and affect our lives so much that they require long-term treatment by trained persons such as psychiatrists or clinical psychologists. Specific methods for changing emotional responses will be discussed in the applied section of this chapter and also in Chapter 10.

Intermediate Summary

The following integrating principles of emotions help us to understand our emotions better:

- Specific emotional responses in specific situations are learned and developed from the generalized emotional states of early childhood.
- Emotions range from vague ill-defined feelings over which we exercise little control to emotions that are consciously directed.
- Emotions are an integral part of all human activities and can be positive or negative depending on the emotion, the situation, and the individual.
- All of us have an over-all general pattern of emotional variation.
- Society helps to determine when and how emotions are to be expressed.
- We have the ability to become emotionally involved about future events and to change our ways of expressing emotions.

APPLICATION

Living with Yourself

Now that we have discussed some of the ways in which emotions develop and how they may effect our behavior in both positive and negative ways, let's see how this all relates to you as a unique, alive, growing, and feeling individual.

One of the first things that might help you to live with yourself better is to think about your own emotional life—or, putting it another way, take an emotional inventory of yourself as you are now.

One way to do this might be to keep an "emotional diary" of your own behavior for a period of a few days or a week or two. That is, at the end of every day, you might write down your emotional reactions through various periods of the day. You could make a list of the positive emotions (love, affection, tenderness, joy, zest, humor, and laughter) and negative emotions (fearfulness, hostility, guilt, and anxiety) that you experienced during the day. Then you might try to recall the event, situation, or person that tended to produce the various emotional responses. Perhaps you cannot put your finger on one event or person, or perhaps you aren't sure why you were angry or hostile; in that case, put down "unknown" for the cause.

After a week or two, you will be able to analyze some of the patterns in your emotional life. You can ask yourself such questions as:

1. What percentage of my daily life is used in the expression of negative emotional expression? What percentage in positive expression?
2. Are my emotional reactions appropriate to the situation? Was I justified in feeling angry, for example, in the situation that produced this response?
3. How many of my emotional responses are caused by unknown or possibly unconscious factors?
4. How frequently do I change my emotional responses? Do I tend to have very wide variations in my mood swings?
5. Do I tend to use one or two kinds of emotional responses consistently, or is there variety in my emotional responses?

WHY ARE YOU THIS WAY?

Let's say that you have conducted such an inventory and that you have answered the preceding five questions. Your next step is to try to determine why you have established these trends.

Our specific emotional patterns are mostly learned as a result of interactions in the family. To help you understand the reasons for some of your own emotional behavior, you might conduct a Family Emotional Inventory. You can do this by trying to think about your own family background and about how emotional reactions were handled.

You can begin by making a list of the positive and negative emotions. Then you can ask yourself questions such as these:

1. What were the typical ways in which the positive and negative emotions were handled in my family?
2. Which, if any, of the positive and negative emotions tended to dominate my family interactions?
3. Who in my family used more of the positive emotions?

4. Who in my family used more of the negative emotions?
5. What kinds of effective ways of dealing with the more negative emotions did I learn in my family?
6. What kinds of ineffective ways of dealing with the more negative emotions did I learn in my family?
7. How does my own present emotional inventory relate to my family emotional inventory?

DOING SOMETHING ABOUT YOUR EMOTIONAL BEHAVIOR

Now that you better understand at least some aspects of your present emotional behavior and why you have developed these patterns, it is up to you to decide if there are emotional patterns that are interfering with your effectiveness in life, especially in your interactions with other people.

You have been offered a number of suggestions for developing ways to handle the more negative emotions (see pp. 191–192), and have also been given some ideas for developing some of the more positive emotions (see pp. 184–185). Of course, these ideas may not suit you personally, so it is up to you to experiment with yourself in a variety of situations to find ways to help you channel your emotional potential constructively.

A lot of what is being said goes back to development toward self-actualization (see pp. 14–21). It appears that self-actualizing persons are best able to make constructive use of their emotional potential. As one writer puts it:

Healthy personality is manifested by the freedom to experience feeling and also by the capacity to control their expression. A healthy personality will experience anxiety, fear, anger, guilt, tenderness, tears, affection, zest, laughter, boredom, and depression whenever life situations induce such feelings. Since he will have efficient contact with reality, the probability is high that his emotional responses to situations will be appropriate; and since he has the capacity to suppress behavior when it is called for, he will reveal his feelings appropriately and withhold expression when the situation calls for it. (Jourard, 1963, p. 115)

Living with Others

Although people behave in routine ways in everyday situations, their behavior may change radically in different situations. For example, the reaction of visitors to mental hospitals is typically, "Why they behave just like everybody else! How is it they are labeled mentally ill?" The answer is that nearly all patients have learned routine ways of behaving in the hospital. However, the mental patient, if faced with the normal stresses of daily living, will readily reveal inappropriate reactions and emotional responses that, in turn, reveal the nature of his mental problem. Emotional responses, therefore, provide important keys toward helping us to understand others better.

DISPLACED NEGATIVE EMOTIONS

A child asks his father, who is busy with his own work, for help. An expected emotional response would be to respond positively to the child's sincere request for help. However, the father may respond with an outburst of anger. Afterward, the father feels better (catharsis), he apologizes (guilt feelings), and offers to help the child.

The child was the victim of displaced emotions. During the day, aggressive feelings had developed on the job but the father was afraid to release his feelings on his friends or his boss. He chose a less dominant figure, his child, on which to release the aggressive emotions.

All of us have been subjected to displaced emotions, especially by others who are close to us. It is far safer to displace emotions on those whom we love because they are likely to forgive us. In fact, if a child can express anger and resentment to his parent, it is usually a sign that he feels loved and wanted by his parents. A loving wife will often accept displaced emotional outbursts from her husband because she knows that catharsis is important for her husband's mental health.

Exaggerated Displaced Negative Emotions

The danger of displaced emotions is that the process may become too frequent and exaggerated. The recipient of the unearned hostility may reach a point where the pressure is too great. For example, in analyzing the basic problem in a divorce case, the authors realized that the wife was the victim of enormous displaced anger and hostility. She had reached a breaking point and couldn't take anymore. The answer was to remove the causes of the husband's hostility. They finally convinced him to close down a highly frustrating business. In so doing, they broke up a vicious cycle and saved a marriage.

DISPLACED POSITIVE EMOTIONS

Happiness and joy are just as contagious as anger and hostility. A person who has zest and enthusiasm accentuates the positive and the good. A teacher who is fully happy and warm radiates these emotions to the students. A successful husband tends to feel that his wife and children are successful also.

Whatever we can do to make others feel important, loved, and wanted is soon returned to us by changes in their behavior toward us. An employer who lets his workers know that they are doing a good job soon finds that they are doing an even better job. Parents who are happy and dignified tend to have children who are happy and dignified. In other words, emotional tones in social situations, whether positive or negative, depend partly on what kinds of emotions we express during the interaction.

EMOTIONAL INSULATION

Too often an escape from unpleasant life situations is achieved through denial of emotions in circumstances similar to those that have caused pain in the past. College students often bring up the problem of emotional insulation regarding their boy and girl friends. This is understandable because emotions during love experiences are intense and prolonged. There is some truth in the statement that "love makes one go all the way." Yes, our hearts are included, and who wants their hearts and dreams broken repeatedly. The way to help others to overcome emotional insulation is to provide unconditional love and care for a prolonged period of time. Depending on their past negative experiences, it may take months or even a year. The person who has been hurt must be given reassurance that it will not happen again. Therefore, he tends to test the other person's sincerity by intentional insults and lack of reciprocal love and care. Once a person feels that he can trust again, he will have overcome the emotional insulation.

Prevention is, of course, far better than treatment. It is a very fortunate person who can find another person with the love and patience to help him to overcome emotional insulation. We have seen numerous persons who were not helped in schools, clinics, and mental hospitals because no one on the staff had the time to spare to give what was needed—consistent and unconditional acceptance and care.

Living with Society

What we have learned about our own emotional competence in living with those who are close to us serves as the basis for emotional competencies for living with society. In other words, society is the large real-life laboratory in which we can test how well we have learned emotional competencies.

EMOTIONAL ASPECTS OF YOUR CAREER OR JOB

Perhaps one of the most important spheres of life where our learned emotional competencies and/or incompetencies affect us is in the world of work. For it is here, in the day-to-day and year-to-year interactions with others on the job that the real effect of our emotions shows.

You probably know people who literally hate their jobs and yet are caught in a situation where they cannot change them because of family and financial obligations. Probably one of the major causes of worker dissatisfaction is that the job does not satisfy the learned emotional patterns of the worker.

You might say that every job or career has a different set of emotional requirements. Certain jobs may require you to deal with mostly the negative emotions (as a policeman, a criminal lawyer, or a judge); whereas other jobs may require you to deal with more of the positive emotions (as a teacher, minister, social worker, or missionary).

Certain jobs may require more emotional repression (as an engineer, a counselor, or a principal); whereas other jobs require mostly emotional release and expression (as an actor, an artist, or a salesman).

Certain jobs may also require a constancy of emotional expression—that is, there is very little change in emotional behavior required (as an engineer, an assembly-line worker, or a bookkeeper); whereas in other jobs one might be expected to show a high degree of emotional change (as a doctor or nurse who in one case may be required to tell a father that he has a newborn baby or in another case may have to tell someone he has cancer).

You might try to relate some of your emotional patterns to the job or career that you are planning to enter. Through conducting your own emotional inventory you should be in a better position to select a job to suit your emotional needs.

EMOTIONS AND UNDERSTANDING SOCIAL ROLES

The fact that our world is growing smaller socially, psychologically, and economically practically assures us that we will need to interact more with other groups who are different from the one to which we are accustomed. We must be prepared to learn new social roles as we move up or down socially, economically, and educationally and as we interact with different ethnic, religious, and racial groups.

An important part of learning a new social role is to understand the emotional tone. In some groups, if you are to be truly accepted, you must show your emotions not merely by saying, "I'm happy to see you again," but also by physical embrace and warm, prolonged handshakes. Other groups resent any physical contact as evidence of emotional expression. Even standing too close as you speak to them usually brings forth physical retreat.

Certain social organizations and religious groups have solemn rituals that require appropriate emotional expression. In these cases, we pretend to feel as they do. Pretending, in such circumstances, is a sign of respect and not hypocrisy. As we begin to understand the significance of the rituals we learn to really feel as they do. For example, at a baseball game it is understood that we can express emotions for or against a team, but at a bullfight we are all expected to cheer the matador because he symbolizes life whereas the bull symbolizes death. An American who cheers the bull will not be showing appropriate emotions in certain parts of the world.

EMOTIONS AND UNDERSTANDING YOUR FELLOWMAN

It has been said that emotions are one of the few universal languages that man has left to communicate with others regardless of race, color, creed, or language. That is, a smile is understood in any language; an angry or fearful look is universal among most people all over the world.

Thus, our emotional responses can also be looked at as one way that may help us bridge the tremendous gaps of human understanding that separate man throughout the world. Knowing that different groups of people learn to express the same emotions in different ways can reduce the mystery and prejudice that surround certain ethnic and minority groups. Instead of calling them stupid or ignorant, we can understand that this is the way in which they have learned to express a particular emotion.

The authors remember a lesson learned by many young married couples in their university apartments. One Sunday a taxi drove up and an Indian student emerged to visit a married friend whom he had not seen for several years. In

Figure 6-4

Emotions and Occupations. Different jobs require certain kinds of emotions. What kind of emotions do you believe that jobs pictured would require? Consider your emotional makeup and decide which of these jobs might suit you best. The first photograph shows a research engineer in the cockpit of a new flight simulator. The second shows a draftsman, and the third points out the close tolerance required in the fabrication of complex multilayer circuitry.

front of the apartment, both men embraced each other for several minutes and openly cried. For days after that, rumors were spread among the apartments about the homosexual student living nearby! It wasn't until weeks later at a large picnic that the Indian student casually mentioned how in his country friendship is expressed to one of the same sex by a hug and a kiss instead of shaking hands!

Final Summary

Emotions form the great unwritten language that can lead to better communication and understanding. Positive emotions such as love, joy, and humor can aid us to become more self-actualizing. Greater expression of positive emotions can be developed by setting up situations in which they can be exercised, by increasing positive self-feelings, and by learning more effective ways of solving problems.

Although society encourages suppression of emotions, emotional insulation

Courtesy of Fullerton Junior College

Figure 6-5

Figure 6-6

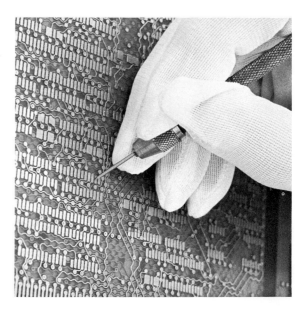

Courtesy of Autonetics, a division of North American Rockwell Corp.

interferes with effective living. Unexpressed negative emotions such as hostility, anxiety, and guilt are like mud in our systems. Some strategies for living with emotions are (1) learning in the face of fear and anxiety, (2) catharsis before remedial action, (3) strategic withdrawal, (4) avoidance of incubation, and (5) finding constructive release.

There are integrating principles of emotions that help us to understand our behavior better. (1) Specific emotional responses in specific situations are learned and develop from the generalized emotional states of early childhood. (2) Emotions range from vague ill-defined feelings over which we have little or no control to emotions that are consciously and clearly directed by us. (3) Emotions are an integral part of all human activities and can be positive or negative depending on the emotion, the situation, and the individual. (4) All of us have an over-all general pattern of emotional variation. (5) Society helps to determine when and how emotions are to be expressed. (6) We have the ability to become emotionally involved about future events. (7) We can change our ways of expressing emotions.

Specific Chapter References

Alexander, F. *Psychosomatic medicine.* New York: Norton, 1950.

Anonymous Streetwalker. In E. Josephson and M. Josephson (eds.) *Man alone.* New York: Dell, 1962.

Ax, A. F. The physiological differentiation between fear and anger in humans. *Psychosomatic Medicine,* 1953, 15, 433–442.

Barron, F. *Creativity and personal freedom.* Princeton, N.J.: Van Nostrand, 1968.

Bexton, W. H., Heron, W., and Scott, T. H. Effects of decreased variation in the sensory environment. *Canadian Journal of Psychology,* 1954, 8, 70–76.

Bowlby, J. *Maternal care and mental health.* New York: Schocken Books, 1966.

Cameron, C. L. *Early memories as recorded by seventh, ninth, and eleventh grade boys and girls.* New York: Teachers College, Columbia University, 1966. Doctor of education project report.

Farber, I. E. Anxiety as a drive state. In M. R. Jones (ed.), *Nebraska Symposium on Motivation.* Lincoln, Neb.: University of Nebraska Press, 1954, pp. 1–46.

Frazier, S. H., and Carr, A. C. *Introduction to psychopathology.* New York: Macmillan, 1964.

Fromm, E. Seminar on psychoanalytic theory. Michigan State University, 1960.

Funkenstein, D. H., King, S. H., and Drolette, M. E. *Mastery of stress.* Cambridge, Mass.: Harvard University Press, 1957.

Gardner, E. *Fundamentals of neurology* (3rd ed.). Philadelphia, Saunders, 1963.

Gilbert, G. M. The new status of experimental studies on the relationship of feeling to memory. *Psychological Bulletin,* 1938, 35, 26–35.

Gordon, J. E. *Personality and behavior.* New York: Macmillan, 1963.

Himmelweit, H. Socio-economic background and personality. In E. P. Hollander and R. G. Hunt (eds.), *Current perspectives in social psychology.* New York: Oxford University Press, 1963, pp. 132–143.

Jourard, S. M. *Personal adjustment.* New York: Macmillan, 1963.

Kluckhohn, C., Murray, H. A., and Schneider, D. M. *Personality: in nature, society, and culture.* New York: Knopf, 1954.

Lipton, E. L., Steinschneider, A., and Richmond, J. H., Swaddling, a child care practice. *Pediatrics,* 1965, 35, 521–567.

Maslow, A. H. Self-actualizing people: a study of psychological health. In C. E. Moustakas (ed.), *The Self.* New York: Harper and Row, 1956.

Moustakas, C. E. The sense of self. *Journal of Humanistic Psychology,* 1961, 1, 22–34.

Rogers, C. *On becoming a person.* Boston: Houghton-Mifflin, 1961.

Sears, R. R., Maccoby, E. E., and Levin, H. *Patterns of child learning.* Evanston, Ill.: Row, Peterson, 1957.

Selye, H. *The stress of life.* New York: McGraw-Hill, 1950.

Shibutani, T. *Society and personality.* Englewood Cliffs, N.J.: Prentice-Hall, 1961.

Spitz, R. A. Hospitalism: inquiry into the genesis of psychiatric conditions in early childhood. *Psychoanalytic Study of the Child.* 1945, 1, 53–74.

Townsend, P. Isolation, loneliness, and the hold on life. In E. Josephson and M. Josephson (eds.), *Man alone.* New York: Dell, 1962.

Walters, P. A. Student apathy. In G. B. Blaine, Jr., C. C. McArthur, *et al.* (eds.), *Emotional problems, of the student.* New York: Appleton-Century-Crofts, 1961. Pp. 170–191.

Recommended Further Readings

Paperback Books

Adler, A. *Understanding human nature.* Greenwich, Conn.: Premier Books, 1954.

Blaine, G., Jr., and McArthur, C. C. (eds.). *Emotional problems of the student.* Garden City, N.Y.: Doubleday, 1961.

Candland, D. K. *Emotion: bodily change.* Princeton, N.J.: Van Nostrand, 1962.

Fromme, A. *The ability to love.* New York: Pocket Cardinal, 1963.

Gellhorn, E. (ed.). *Biological foundations of emotion.* Glenview, Ill.: Scott, Foresman, 1968.

Goffman, E. *The presentation of self in everyday life.* Garden City, N.Y.: Doubleday Anchor Books, 1959.

Goldstein, M. J., and Palmer, J. O. *The experience of anxiety.* New York: Oxford University Press, 1963.

Harris, I. D. *Emotional blocks to learning.* New York: Free Press, 1961.

Menninger, K. A. *Love against hate.* New York: Harvest Book, 1942.

Miller, D. R., Swanson, G. E., *et al. Inner conflicts and defense.* New York: Schocken Books, 1960.

Montagu, A. *Man in process.* New York: Mentor Book, 1961.

Overstreet, B. W. *Understanding fear.* New York: Collier Books, 1951.

Plutchik, R. *The emotions: facts, theories, and a new model.* New York: Random House, 1962.

Redl, F., and Wineman, D. *Children who hate.* New York: Collier Books, 1951.

Singer, J. E., and Whaley, F. L. (eds.). *Patterns of psychological research.* Boston: Allyn and Bacon, 1966.

Slaughter, F. G. *Your body and your mind.* New York: Signet Key Books, 1947.

Terhune, W. B. *Emotional problems and what you can do about them.* New York: William Morrow, 1955.

Hardcover Books

Bennis, W. G., Schein, E. H., Steele, F. I., and Berlew, D. E. (eds.). *Interpersonal dynamics: essays and readings on human interaction* (rev. ed.) Homewood, Ill.: Dorsey Press, 1968.

Bernard, H. W. *Toward better personal adjustment* (2nd ed.) New York: McGraw-Hill, 1957.

Davitz, J. R. *The communication of emotional meaning*. New York: McGraw-Hill, 1964.

Dunbar, F. *Emotions and bodily changes*. New York: Columbia University Press, 1954.

Frank, L. K. *Feelings and emotions: Doubleday papers in psychology*. New York: Random House, 1954.

Glass, D. C. *Neurophysiology and emotion*. New York: Rockefeller University Press and Russell Sage Foundation, 1967.

Lindgren, H. C. *Psychology of personal development*. New York: American Book, 1964.

Overstreet, H. A. *The mature mind*. New York: Norton, 1949.

Saul, L. J. *Emotional maturity*. Philadelphia: Lippincott, 1947.

Selye, H. *The stress of life*. New York: McGraw-Hill, 1956.

Young, P. T. *Motivation and emotion: a survey of the determinants of human and animal activity*. New York: Wiley, 1961.

Chapter 7 Understanding Perception

Chapter Outline

Study Guide

The study of perception is a fascinating topic. It will provide you with many fresh insights and ideas about how you sense and interpret the world around you. However, this study will require increased efforts on your part because of the increased amount of information presented.

REVIEW
Read the Contents for Chapters 1–6.

Prelude

Perception is the attempt to explain how we observe the world around us. We can define *perception* as the process of gathering information. Learning is the process by which we store and classify information, much as a library or a computer does. Thinking is the process by which we use the stored information to solve our problems. For example, before we can solve a mathematics problem we must first learn numbers and signs. But to learn the meaning of numbers and signs, we must be able to observe numbers and such signs as plus or minus.

It seems, at first, that perception is a simple process and that all that is required is to look, listen, feel, taste, and smell. This chapter, however, will attempt to show that perception is a highly personal process, and that it involves our past experiences, emotions, motivations, and conscious and unconscious processes. The outside world offers the same picture to all of us, but what is seen in the picture depends also on the individual. Looked at in this way, perception is the foundation of our present and future knowledge.

Students' Viewpoints

One day in an early morning class, without warning, we all got up and took a silent walk around the campus. Ten minutes later we returned. Not a word had been said during the entire walk. Paper was passed out and students were asked to tell what they saw on their walk; this is what some of them had seen:

As we were walking along the science building, I noticed the jasmine and was trying to smell it but without success. I noticed how the grass had just been cut and watered and two buds on one magnolia tree . . .

Going out the door I saw courtesy when the boys held the door open for the girls. Walking down the stairs I saw people with questioning looks on their faces. Entering the quad I saw happy people sitting together and alone. I saw sunlight gleaming down through the trees with birds flying and singing making truly a peaceful, restful scene. I saw some sleeping in the shade, some sitting on benches, and some going to other classes.

Most of all I saw other people. I saw Cassandra go and sit down on one of the benches, and then later she got up and was walking with Dr. Hershey. I saw John. He was smoking; most of the other guys were also. He had on a yellow shirt and he stood out among the other kids. A lot of the kids were looking at us and a few were talking to the kids that are in this class. I realized that we were going to take a walk around the campus almost as soon as we began. I wondered why you were making us walk around the school.

On the class's little stroll, I saw the campus's quad, and realized the excellent care it must receive. The trees so strong and sturdy. The grass so short and sweet. The sidewalks and their spotless appearance. Plus, how much warmer and fresh outside than inside the classroom. Is it possible to take another little journey again sometime?

Perhaps you have had an experience like this, for it is a common one: You are driving to school one day and while stopped at a corner you witness a serious auto accident. You, along with several other witnesses, are asked to appear in court in one month. As you listen to the testimony of the other witnesses, you wonder if you have lost your memory; it seems that almost every witness is telling a different story!

During the first week of classes, students frequently are asked to sit in small groups, introduce themselves, and talk together for fifteen or twenty minutes. Then they write a first impression of one of the persons in their group whom they have never met before. Here is a set of first impressions written by four different students about the same individual.

My first impression of her is that she has a nice and pleasing personality. She seemed as though she would be a good and easy person to talk with. She also had a good sense of humor. She also possessed an enthusiastic attitude toward life and school.

My first impression of her centers around her gift of gab. No matter what topic was introduced for discussion she took it right over; this wouldn't be bad but she moved right on into perfectly unrelated subjects, giving no one else a chance. She seems terribly immature. Also, I think I detected a slight uppishness in her manner.

She seemed to be more like the out-door and adventurous type of girl. However, she talked of never living in another part of the globe, except where she is now residing. She talked of traveling, yet she acted as if she wouldn't leave Southern California for anything. I felt as though she might have been afraid to do so.

She loves to talk, seems to be easy to get to know, friendly, happy.

These examples all illustrate what is perhaps one of the most important principles in understanding the uniqueness of individual behavior: that it is not so much what is in our environment that makes us behave the way we do, but how we perceive what is out there that affects our behavior. No two people view reality in exactly the same way.

WHY IS IT IMPORTANT?

"Now," you may say to yourself, "this sounds so simple, everyone already knows that!" Perhaps they do, but think about the implications of that principle. This simple fact of human perception is directly related to some of our most serious human problems. Closer to home, it is probably related to many of our personal problems.

Think about the last time you had a misunderstanding with your boyfriend or girlfriend. Or, think about the last disagreement you had with your parents. There is a good chance that a part of the problem was the result of the way you, or your girlfriend, or boyfriend, or your parents perceived the situation.

Let's give a more specific example: A student was thinking seriously of moving away from home because her parents (from her point of view) were being unreasonable. They refused to let her call her boyfriend during the week and they allowed her to stay out only until midnight on a Friday or Saturday date. When she came home, both her parents were awake and they began to give her the "third degree" about what she had been doing. One night when she refused to give them a full account, her father called her a slut. Her mother kept asking her if she and her date had petted very much.

Now, from the girl's view, her parents behavior was totally unfair and uncalled for (particularly because she and the young man had not been intimate; they both felt they should reserve sexual intercourse for marriage). However, it was pointed out to her that if she could understand how her parents perceived the situation and why, it would be helpful. She was asked about her parents' dating experiences when they were younger. She didn't know, so it was suggested she casually discuss the subject with each of her parents sometime.

In a day or two she came rushing back very excited. She said she had talked with her parents about their dating experiences and found that both of them had complete freedom on dates. In fact, *their* parents hadn't seemed concerned. Her dad had even told her that he had been to some wild parties. And, at the end of their talk they said to her: "We know what happens to young people when they are left completely free; we don't intend to let this happen to you!"

The student was very pleased because now she felt she knew why her parents didn't trust her. In a sense, they were seeing themselves in her and her boyfriend. Even though the immediate problem wasn't solved, she could now tolerate her parents' perceptions. She knew they were not just trying to be mean to her. She could see that they were viewing the situation partly in terms of the guilt feelings they had both retained from past experiences.

Now, this same lack of understanding as a result of differences in perception is involved in communication problems not only between parents and their children, but between boyfriend and girlfriend, husband and wife, white-skinned people and black-skinned people, members of one religion and another, and between the people of one nation and another. We hope that you can now see more clearly why we feel that this chapter is one of the most important in your growth in understanding. First, we'll deal with why you perceive the world the way you do; secondly, with the fact that other people may not view reality in the same way as you; and thirdly, we'll try to help you improve your perception of the world, to see it in a more realistic way. At the end, we hope you'll see more of reality and, especially, perceive your fellow human beings more nearly as they are.

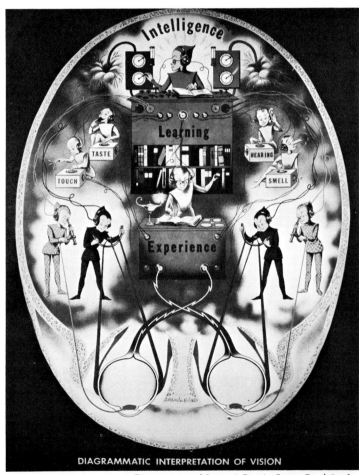

Figure 7–1
Diagrammatic Interpretation of Vision. The eyes as well as the other senses feed information into the brain. How this information is interpreted and how well and quickly it is used depend on the breadth of your experience and the efficiency of your memory.

DIAGRAMMATIC INTERPRETATION OF VISION

Diagram courtesy of Optometric Extension Program Foundation, Inc.

BASIC THEORY AND RESEARCH

General Factors Influencing Perception

Let us consider some general factors that influence the development and the operation of perception. At birth we are all at about the same stage of development. The brain, the storehouse for our future knowledge, is empty and we begin the process of exploring the world for information. At first, the most important sense for learning is taste, because it is at that time the best developed of all our senses. So the infant learns by mouthing objects. Soon he adds to his knowledge by feeling and manipulating objects.

In about the third month of life, vision begins to play an important role in obtaining information. One's eyes can now work together to see the world better. One is now attracted to many new and exciting objects.

Vision rapidly becomes the most efficient way for obtaining information. Once we know what an apple feels and tastes like, the sight of an apple is sufficient for us to remember the feel and the taste. We don't need further exploration. This is why we stress visual perception in this chapter, although we recognize the importance of hearing, smelling, tasting, and feeling.

It is well to remember that vision is not merely a mechanical process like photography; it is rather a complex psychological and physiological process. It is not the eyes alone that see. In a true sense the brain sees also. The eyes report what is out there, but the brain interprets, accepts, or rejects the incoming data. Vision, remember, is our interpretation of what our eyes report. In a summary of research in visual perception, Vernon (1957) pointed out that the individual carries with him into each perceptual situation ". . . his characteristic sensory abilities, intelligence, interest and temperamental qualities."

Of course, the bigger, bolder, and brighter the objects, the greater the influence of their external forces on our visual perception. It is when the external objects are vague and less prominent that the internal forces within the individual tend to modify what the eyes report. In the next section those external factors influencing visual perception will be discussed. Later, the most important internal factors will be explained.

Objective Factors in Perception

MOTION

The ability to see motion develops very early in life. Our eyes are constantly taking photographs of the world, but when our eyes move, the photographs are not seen because they become blurred in the same way as are pictures taken with a camera that is moved around. Our eyes really provide us with a series of still shots that seem to be in motion.

Psychologists explain motion as the result of the very brief time, $\frac{1}{16}$ of one second, between two photographs. For example, if a line is flashed on a screen and a second later a second line is flashed in a different place, we see just two lines. If the time between exposures of the two lines is $\frac{1}{16}$ of one second or less, we see one line moving back and forth. This movement, known as the *phi phenomena* is used to explain the movements in motion pictures and lights moving on the marquees of theaters. (Wertheimer, 1912)

Motion, therefore, depends on the very rapid exposure of an object in different positions in space.

VISUAL ORGANIZATION

Even the simplest experiences are organized into two parts called *figure* and *ground*. If we look at a scene, certain parts stand out clearly. We call what we see clearly the *figure*. The rest blends into an indefinite background called the *ground*. For example, in Figure 7–2, you can see the vase as a figure with the rest of the background or you can see two facial profiles as figures. For further evidence have two friends talk to you at the same time. Can you understand both of them at the same time or only one at a time? You will find that you can listen to one only or you can alternate between conversations, but not both at the same time.

Adults who have suddenly recovered from total blindness show figure–ground organization. When shown a lump of sugar on a table, they say that something (figure) is on something (ground). To recognize the lump of sugar on the table they first must touch the objects. After continuous experiences of touching and seeing, just the sight of a familiar object will be enough for them to name the object and to remember what the object feels and tastes like. (Hebb, 1949)

Figure 7–2
Reversible Figure and Ground

VISUAL GROUPING

Another visual experience, common to all of us, is visual grouping. Look at the series of dots in (a) of Figure 7–3. All we say is "I see many dots." It would be different to say at a glance, "I see twenty dots." However, if the dots were

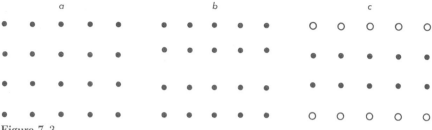

Figure 7-3
Visual Grouping

to be rearranged as in (b) we could say, "I see two rows of dots." The dots are now arranged into two horizontal rows because they are closer together. The process whereby objects join to form a new group because of closer spatial relationships is known as the *law of proximity*. Can you think of any other example? Musical notes in certain proximities in time produce beautiful melodies. On the other hand, the same musical notes if timed in different ways can be called noise.

Similarity

The dots and circles in (c) can, at a glance, be separated into two groups because of the dissimilarities of the dots and the circles. In other words, objects that look alike tend to be placed together more readily than dissimilar objects when all the objects are equally spaced.

Closure

Look at Figure 7–4, and see how you tend to fill in the gaps to form complete circles and rectangles. The tendency to make incomplete objects complete is called closure. A partially drawn figure of a familiar object usually provides sufficient information for you to recognize the object by filling in the missing parts.

Figure 7-4
Closure

Principles such as proximity, similarity, and closure help to provide us with a stable view of the world around us. Such principles help to explain why, in many situations, we tend to see the same things in similar ways.

OBJECT CONSTANCY

We all know from experience that a house seen at a distance does not resemble a play house but retains its actual size. A friend standing a block away does not appear to be a midget. Actually, the further away an object is from us, the

Figure 7-5
Size Constancy. All the students appear to have approximately the same height. However, when we look at the lines next to them, we realize that their actual sizes are very different. This ability to judge sizes of known persons or objects correctly regardless of their distance from us is known as size constancy. The photograph, as well as our eyes, reports what is actually present. It is we who interpret what is there.

Courtesy of Fullerton Junior College

smaller is the image of the object in the retina of our eyes. The fact that objects do not seem to change in size as the distance increases is known as *size constancy*.

How do we explain size constancy? Size constancy depends on several factors. Learning plays a very important role. Have you ever seen children on a bridge trying to reach down to pick up the "toy" boats or automobiles? Or a child stretching and reaching for the stars? The explanation that size constancy is based solely on memory of familiar objects does not explain why unfamiliar objects also maintain, although to a lesser degree, size constancy. The size of an unfamiliar object is judged by its relative size to familiar objects around it. If a spaceship from Mars were to land in your city, you could judge its size by comparing the spaceship to the buildings and trees next to it. In other words, size constancy depends on the surroundings as well as on learning. Size constancy would tend to disappear if a strange object landed in a strange desert with no familiar objects around it.

There are other factors that contribute to size constancy. For example, if you were to make left turns in front of a yellow car and a black car, the chances of an accident would be greater while turning in front of a black car. The reason is that a dark object always seems further away than a bright object when both are really equidistant from us. (Lawrence, 1949)

Object constancy refers not only to size but also to shape and color. When we have become familiar with an object we tend to recognize its characteristics no matter where it is placed. *Shape constancy* is seen when we look at a circular object such as a doughnut. The doughnut always looks round even when placed on a table and seen at an angle. The image produced by such a doughnut on the retina of the eye is an ellipse, but we report a circle. Figure 7–6 illustrates

213

Figure 7-6

Shape Constancy. The piece of cake and the plate retain their respective shapes when observed from many different sides. Actually, the shape changes as we change our angles of observation. Again, it is we who interpret what is out there.

shape constancy with a piece of cake on a plate. *Color constancy* is seen when a black cloth looks black regardless of the light in the room. (Wallach and Galloway, 1946)

It is well to keep in mind that object constancy is not perfect, but it helps to explain why the world about us seems to be relatively stable.

DISTORTED PERCEPTION

Most of the time we can depend on what we see. However, there are situations in which we all tend to misinterpret reality. In such cases, seeing is *not* believing. Figures 7–7 and 7–8 are photographs of a model of the distorted room created by Ames. (Ittleson, 1952) In both photographs, the same room, the same girl model, and the same doll were used. Impossible? Turn the page to the other photographs. The room is not the normal rectangular room that we expected. It is distorted into the shape of a trapezoid. A person or an object placed at the extreme left of the room appears to be smaller because of the greater distance from the viewing point. An object placed at the extreme right appears to be bigger than it really is because it is closer to the viewer than it appears to be if one is assuming the room to be rectangular. The oddly shaped windows lend themselves to further distortion. The left window was made larger than the right to create the optical illusion that both are at the same distance from the viewer. We are so used to conventional rectangular rooms that we assume this room is the same. Even when we know that the room is distorted, we are still victimized by the distortion and keep seeing and reporting what is not true. When objects that are familiar are placed in the room, we distort the objects rather than accept the fact that the room is distorted.

This distorted perception tells us something important about the effect of experience on perception. Husbands and wives do not see their partners as being distorted by the room. They see each other as normal and the room as distorted! In other words, very familiar objects are not distorted by a distorted environment. (Gregory, 1966) It would seem that the degree of loyalty to ideas, people, and ideals may depend also on the amount of actual experience we have had with them on a personal level.

Another way to overcome distortion from the outside is to become more familiar with the situation. If you were permitted to experience the distorted room even with a probing stick, the room would gradually begin to look like what it really is—just a distorted room! Experience is truly an eye opener!

We can learn a very important lesson from the distorted room experiment. In certain situations, verbal information or warnings are not enough to change our behavior; rather, we must personally learn more about the situation before our perception and behavior change. Can you think of any situation in which the only way to learn is by actively participating? Do you think that you can become a good dancer just by reading about dance routines?

Intermediate Summary

Perception is the process of observing and interpreting the world around us. Although the outside social and physical world presents the same stimulation, the perception of it also depends on the individual's past experiences, emotions, and motivations on the conscious and unconscious levels. Therefore, no two people view events in exactly the same ways.

The objective factors in the external world that help to determine perception are motion, organization, grouping, similarity, constancy, and distortions.

Subjective Factors in Perception

THE SELF-CONCEPT AND PERCEPTION

Of all the subjective factors affecting the way we see the world, the self-concept is perhaps the most influential. That is, how a person typically tends to view himself will have much to do with how he views the world, and particularly other people in the world. This relationship between the self-concept and perception has been considered by some psychologists to be so important that an entire theory has been developed around this principle (see cameo).

This point of view, called *perceptual* or *phenomenological psychology* (Combs and Syngg, 1959), has as its central concern the following ideas:

In the personal, or perceptual, frame of reference we attempt to observe behavior from the point of view of the individual himself. People do not behave according to the facts as others see them. They behave according to the facts as they see them. What governs behavior from the point of view of the individual himself are his unique perceptions of himself and the world in which he lives, the meanings they have for him. (pp. 16–17)

Figure 7-7

At times seeing is not believing. In some instances our eyes do deceive us. The sizes of the doll and the dog have not changed. The false perceptions are produced by placing the objects in a special room that distorts the sizes of the objects within it. We know that something is wrong with our judgment of size, but we cannot help ourselves because the fault lies in the room and not in ourselves.

Figure 7-8

Courtesy of Research Media, Inc. Photos by Don Sakall

Figure 7-9

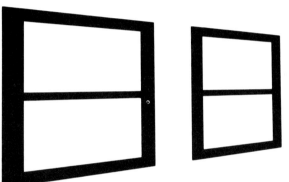

Figure 7-10

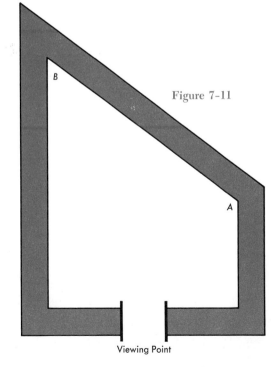

Figure 7-11

Now we see the true sizes of the doll and the dog, and we can understand that it was the distorted room and windows that produced the incorrect perception of sizes. An object at the right of the room is much closer to the viewing point than an object placed at the extreme left, and therefore appears to be larger than it really is. The incorrect sizes and shapes of the windows add to the distortion. The left window should appear smaller because it is farther away; but it was constructed to be larger to make it appear closer to the viewer. Window shapes, normally rectangular, were made trapezoidal for the same reason.

The self provides the frame of reference from which all else is observed.—The meaning of an object or event is thus his definition of the relationship between the object and himself. We have already seen in an earlier chapter that perceptions have a bearing upon the individual's behavior in the degree to which they seem to him to be related to the self. (p. 145)

Effects on Perception of Positive and Negative Self-Concepts

Whether the person likes himself or dislikes himself has a great deal to do with how he perceives the world, especially other people. A person who tends to feel inadequate will often misinterpret the intentions of others and will often perceive other people in a threatening manner.

On the other hand, people who tend to have a positive self-concept will view their world and people in a much more realistic way. This is why mentally healthy persons seem to be more effective in their lives; they like themselves and therefore are able to see reality as it is without trying to distort it.

Proximity of Events to the Self

Situations that directly affect our self-concept tend to be attended to much more readily than events that have little relevance to us. (Combs and Snygg, 1959) For example, if you were watching a television news report and saw the results of a flood in another state, you would feel sorry for the families involved. However, if the report were to give the name of the town where your grandparents live and showed film of the devastation in their neighborhood you would certainly be more affected. And if your younger sister were visiting your grandparents at that particular time you would probably become even more involved. Or, maybe, if your mother and father and other relatives were there for a family reunion, you might even get aroused and nervous enough to place an immediate long-distance telephone call.

Circular Effect of Self on Perception

Another very important aspect of the effect of self on perception has to do with the fact that people perceive in ways that are consistent with concepts of self. For example, people who feel inadequate about their ability to do well in a certain school subject or a certain skill, such as fixing a car, often behave in ways that will ensure that they do not succeed in these areas.

They may feel that they have a reputation to live up to (or down to?). The poor speller explains his low grade in English with "You know I'm a poor speller." This student may avoid the very situations in the future that could help him to become a good speller. In this case there is a negative circular effect of perception on learning. On the other hand, a good speller may seek situations in which he can demonstrate his talent and, thereby, become a better speller. In this case, there is a positive circular effect of perception on learning.

PAST EXPERIENCES AND PERCEPTION

Our past experiences play a major role not only in what we perceive, but in the manner in which we perceive it. For example, studies with children who undergo eye surgery and can see for the first time in their lives (Hebb, 1949) demonstrate the difficulty they have in identifying objects by color, size, and shape. Because they have had no previous visual experience with colors, sizes, or shapes, they must learn it. Chimpanzees, for example, who have been reared in total darkness and then placed in a lighted environment take several months to learn simple discriminations. (Reisen, 1949)

Opportunities for Common Perceptions

Probably one of the most important limitations on our own perceptions of the world has to do with our limited individual experiences in our own particular environment. Because perceptions are built upon previous experiences, there must be opportunities for the perceptions to occur. To understand others we need to study the experiences on which their perceptions were based. According to Cameron (1965):

There are many such worlds. Some are completely different from ours—radically, complexly different, interlocking in their differences so completely as to form consistent wholes, built as each believes, on the most obvious self-evident truths that no one in his senses would think of questioning. There stands the vanishing world of the Navahjo, of the Yoruba, the Eastern Islander—in a word, of every culture in the world. (p. 313)

For example, if parents wish to understand the seemingly unusual behaviors of their teen-agers, the first step would be to carefully observe and study their particular youth culture. For better understanding, the parents should participate actively in the culture of their offspring. Perhaps this participation is too much to ask of parents. Nevertheless, it is the similarities of individual experiences that provide the common ground for the formation of mutually agreed-on perceptions. Many of our problems arise because we forget that individual experiences, which form the basis for our perceptions, are never identical.

INTELLIGENCE AND PERCEPTION

In a sense, one might say that intelligence tests really measure the individual's ability to adequately perceive the environment (particularly factors surrounding the school environment). Combs and Snygg (1959) feel that intelligence is really a measure of the effectiveness of an individual's behavior. Because one's perceptions of the world around him affect how he behaves, intelligence then becomes a question of how adequate and how varied are one's perception of the world around him.

Looking at intelligence as related to perception means that our intelligence is not an inborn or fixed ability as many psychologists have previously believed (Burt *et al.* 1934). Instead, it means that intelligence can be improved through changing the perceptions of people. Studies show that intelligence scores can be changed by changing the environments of children deprived of love. Certain types of stimulating environments can also produce changes in intelligence test scores, whereas restricted environments can actually lower performance on intelligence tests. (Wellman, 1940; Flint, 1966)

Another important factor relating to the limits in intelligence testing has to do with the fact that most intelligence tests measure a certain type of perception.

> By whose standards, then, shall we take our sample—yours, mine, society's, the subject's own? For the most part our intelligence tests are based on the assumption that academic, upper-middle-class, intellectual perceptions are important. But are they? Can we assume that the expert machinist, who can perceive things "out of this world" for most of the rest of us about a piece of stock on his lathe, is less intelligent than a diplomat who perceives many things about foreign affairs? Can we be so sure of our values as to call one bright and the other dull? Can we blame the machinist for his lack of perception about foreign affairs without asking the diplomat to be equally skilled in the machinist's field of perceptions? (Combs and Snygg, 1959, p. 220)

We now know that it is possible to raise the level of thinking by providing the necessary experiences. Mead (1966) describes such a change among the Manus of the Admiralty Islands.

> In 1928 the Manus were a Stone Age people who had no knowledge of geography or history, whose political organization could hold together a group of no more than about two hundred people, who had no script and whose mnemonic devices consisted of such things as sticking small twigs into a larger twig in order, for example, to add up the number of pigs killed for a ceremony. But only twenty-five years later, in 1953, when I returned to the Admiralties to make a restudy of the Manus, I could say to a man who had been a little houseboy during my earlier stay, "Start the generator and take this informant out and make a bilingual tape on the Magnicorder."

MOTIVATION AND PERCEPTION

Think about the last time you were on a trip. You became hungry and couldn't find a restaurant. What happened to the way you perceived the environment? You probably became very aware of road signs advertising food objects; you probably became more sensitive to the smell of a canned food factory as you drove by; and you probably looked at every store building that you thought might be a restaurant.

This simple illustration shows how our motives affect the way we perceive the world. Our needs and motives interact strongly with our perceptions of the world. One dramatic example of this relationship occurred during a study on the effects of a starvation diet on a group of conscientious objectors during World War II. The authors vividly tell about the results on the subjects' behavior as follows (Guetzkow and Bowman, 1946):

There can be no doubt that by the end of the semi-starvation period the hunger drive had become the dominating dynamic factor affecting the behavior of the subjects. Food, either directly or indirectly, dominated the conversation, reading, leisure activities, and day-dreams. More than half of the men devoted their spare moments to reading cookbooks and collecting recipes. Others became intensely interested in such subjects as dietetic agriculture, and frozen food lockers. Some subjects even gave serious consideration to the idea of changing their occupations and becoming cooks.

Other examples of this relationship between our motives and how we perceive the world would include the fact that people with a high need for achievement typically " . . . tend to perceive their parents as relatively distant rather than close. Similarly, students with a high achievement need perceived themselves as more independent of authority in general than did those with a low need for achievement." (McClelland, *et al.*, 1953) Children from wealthy homes tend to perceive a half-dollar to be much smaller than do children from poorer homes. The learning of pro-Communist and anti-Communist material is affected by the political motives of a person. (Combs and Snygg, 1959)

EMOTIONS AND PERCEPTION

Think of the last time you were angry; or the last time you had a "bad day." How did your emotion of anger or depression affect how you perceived the world around you, especially other people. You may have felt that people were being hostile to you or that people were against you. That is, your emotions seemed to color your view of the world.

Think of your first "true love," when you met someone that you felt very good just being around. You probably felt that life was beautiful and that all people were good and loving. Maybe you even began to treat your parents or your little brothers or sisters differently!

Figure 7–12   Figure 7–13   Figure 7–14

Intermediate Summary

Perceptions are also influenced by subjective factors within the person. How a person views himself has much to do with how he views the world and other persons. Important subjective factors are the nature of self-concept, proximity of events to the self, opportunities for common perceptions, intelligence, motivation, and emotion.

Integrating Principles of Perception

HUMANS MUST HAVE A MINIMUM DEGREE OF SENSORY STIMULATION. In a series of studies in which sensory stimulation is reduced to practically nothing, it was consistently found that people tend to get very disoriented. In fact, *hallucinations* (perceptions that have no basis in the external world) can occur. (Heron, 1961) This phenomena was also noticed during high-altitude flying (Jones, in Hebb, 1960):

> A pilot on routine high altitude test flying was forced to descend by a "feeling of dissociation from earth and machine." He had the impression of being detached from the aircraft, of looking at himself and the machine from outside and of the aircraft itself being greatly diminished in size like a "toy suspended in space."

It seems that for adequate development of the human personality, sensory stimulation, especially during infancy, is most important.

THE MANNER IN WHICH WE PERCEIVE THE ENVIRONMENT IS LEARNED. As we mentioned earlier, no two persons perceive the world in exactly the same manner. Through learning, we tend to be selective in what we see and do not see in the world around us.

Illustrative of this point is the following experience of one of the authors and a friend, "We were driving through mountains with strange rock formations. The writer noted how beautiful they were and commented on some of the colors. His friend, on the other hand, noted the causes of the rock formations as a result of earthquakes, the reasons for the colors (heat and pressure), and how difficult it was to climb such mountains."

The writer's experiences with mountains had been purely aesthetic; he had seen them on vacations with friends and family. His friend's previous experience had involved the study and collection of rocks; he had worked with the Boy Scouts in hiking, camping, and mountain climbing.

OUR LEARNED PERCEPTIONS OF THE WORLD CAN BE CHANGED. Even though our learned perceptions tend to make the world quite stable, we do alter our view of it. There are many ways to change our perceptions. Let's discuss some, namely social pressure, cognitive dissonance, crisis situation, therapy, persuasion, and education.

SOCIAL PRESSURE

There are many studies indicating that social pressure can change perceptions—particularly attitudes, opinions, and beliefs. (Lipset, 1959) The results of these studies suggest that when persons are under pressure from many social groups they will tend to change their attitudes on a particular subject. For example, people who belong to different groups with conflicting political views tend to change their voting intention more readily than people who belong to one party only.

COGNITIVE DISSONANCE

Another way our perception of the world may change is brought about when there is an imbalance or disequilibrium in a situation. Festinger has developed a number of ways to see what happens when you can get a person to say one thing and really feel another way about it. For example:

> Confirmed cigarette smokers are more likely to deny that any relationship has been established between cigarette smoking and lung cancer. Recent car buyers read advertisements that confirm them in the wisdom of their decisions. (Festinger, 1957)

In other words, it seems that perceptions of the world can and do change *after* behavior changes; if you can get someone to commit himself either verbally or by doing something, his attitudes and perception of the situation may also change.

CRISIS SITUATION

Sometimes one's perceptions of the world change drastically after a crisis occurs in his life. Death in a family may bring the stray and alcoholic father back home and turn him into a model father. Religious conversions of drug addicts and alcoholics seem to alter their perceptions of themselves and others drastically.

THERAPY

Many people who undergo psychotherapy tend to come away viewing themselves and the world differently. Rogers (1961), for example, has found that patients who go through therapy change their perceptions of themselves considerably. He states that in general they tend to be less critical and more accepting of themselves at the end of therapy than they were at the beginning.

PERSUASION

People can be persuaded to change their views of other people, whom to vote for in an election, or whether to buy a specific item the next time they are in a store. The source of the persuasion tends to be an important variable in changing opinions. For example, when people hear an idea from a source that they have faith in, they will tend to change their opinion. (Hovland *et al.*, 1953, p. 139)

Incentives given in the appeal to change also tend to help alter the way a person views a particular argument. Several studies (Hovland *et al.*, 1953, pp. 139–147) on the effects of opinion change conclude the following:

1. Strong emotional appeals (especially fear) are not too effective in changing opinions.
2. People who identify strongly with a group will resist accepting ideas which are contrary to the standards of the group.
3. When people are asked to participate actively in the exposure to a new idea (either by role playing or spoken agreement) they tend to accept the ideas more readily.

EDUCATION

There is no doubt that education plays a major role in changing our perceptions of the world. For example, in a large-scale study at three American colleges of different types, it was found that education tends to bring about changes in values over the four-year period. However, at the end of the four years, seniors tend to have more of the same values. It was also found that the over-all college atmosphere itself tends to be responsible for value changes, rather than the college courses themselves. (Jacob, 1957)

Perceptual Generalizations About the World and Other People in It. We cannot attend to everything in our environment at the same time. That is, we tend to be highly selective about what we perceive around us. One common way that we handle all the stimuli being fed into us through the various sense organs is by making perceptual generalizations of what we see. Essentially, this means that we tend to oversimplify or generalize the world around us. Examples of this would be these: We don't tend to look at every detail of a car before we learn to classify it as a car; we do not have to examine every detail of a tree to know that it is a tree; we don't look at every detail of a woman's figure and dress to know that she is a woman.

Admittedly this is a convenient and necessary way for us to save a lot of time and energy. Yet, it also gets us in trouble when, for example, we do this with other people, such as people in certain occupations (teachers, doctors, ministers); or with certain races (Negroes, Orientals); or with people who live in a certain city or portion of a city (people in the slum areas of a large city, farmers from the South).

Cultural Patterns and Group Pressure Can Affect Our Perception. Membership in social, religious, or political groups tends to affect perception because of the values and attitudes developed while participating in their activities. For example, in one study a group of students was given a test to measure their interest in religious, social, economic, aesthetic, political, and theoretical matters. Thus, it could be determined for each student his strongest value, his next strongest value, and so on. Then words related to each area of interest were exposed to each student for varying durations of time. It was found that words related to the strongest value were seen in the shortest period of time. If a student had a very strong interest in economics, he would recognize very quickly such words as price or cost. In other words, perception tends to be better and faster when it is related to topics held in high esteem by one's own group or groups. (Postman *et al.*, 1948)

MUCH OF WHAT WE PERCEIVE IS SELECTIVE. The world of perception resembles a kaleidoscope of sights, sounds, and physical sensation. No one can see all, or hear all, or feel all. Although people tend to perceive the same things when the signs are big and bold, or the voices loud, or the physical wounds deep, much of what they perceive is selective. Only certain parts of the total perceptual field available are chosen by the individual. Figure 7–15 indicates that men and women respond differently to pictures they consider to be important (Hess and Polt, 1960). Notice the increase in pupil size (eyes) of the females when viewing pictures of a baby or a mother with her baby as compared to males. In short, each person tends to perceive what is important for him.

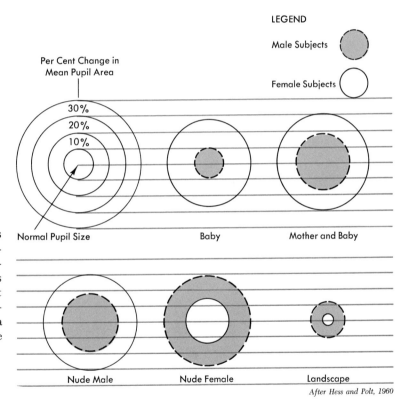

LEGEND

Male Subjects

Female Subjects

Per Cent Change in Mean Pupil Area

30%
20%
10%

Normal Pupil Size   Baby   Mother and Baby

Nude Male   Nude Female   Landscape

After Hess and Polt, 1960

Figure 7–15
The size of the pupil varies in relation to different pictures. Men and women respond differently to pictures that they find interesting. It is not surprising that men respond more to a picture of a nude woman than to a picture of a nude man.

OUR PERSONALITY AFFECTS OUR STYLE OF PERCEIVING THE WORLD. People behave, the circumstances permitting, according to the facts as they see them. How they see the facts is partly determined by their personality characteristics. In a study, people were asked to locate a simple figure hidden in a larger, more complex figure. Some persons found this to be a time-consuming task. They found the task of separating the simple figure from the background in which it was embedded difficult. It seems that for some people, perceptions are dependent largely on everything they see in their environment. Individuals whose judgments were based more on the visual surroundings took a longer time to find the hidden figures. (Witkin, 1950)

In a second study, the subject was seated in a chair that could be tilted. The room, which was darkened, could also be tilted. The subject had to decide when he was in the upright position. This decision could be based on what he saw in the room or on the feelings of the pull of gravity on his body. Subjects who depended on what they saw instead of on their bodily feelings were the same ones who took a long time to discover the hidden figures. These subjects were called *field-dependent* because they depended more on the perceptual field than others. (Witkin *et al.*, 1954)

It was found that the field-dependent persons differed from the *field-independent* with respect to certain personality characteristics. The former were more passive, more submissive, more dependent on others. They also had lower self-esteem. These results support the idea that our personalities have an effect on how we see the world.

Intermediate Summary

Some integrating principles that help us to better understand perception are (1) We must have a minimum of sensory stimulation. (2) The manner in which we perceive the environment is learned and can be changed. (3) Social pressures can change perceptions. (4) Cognitive dissonance, crisis, psychotherapy, and persuasion can change perceptions. (5) Education plays a major role in changing perceptions as well as membership in social, religious, and political groups. (6) Much of what we perceive is selective and reflects our personality characteristics.

APPLICATION

Living with Yourself

The realization that all persons do not perceive the world in the same way should further encourage us to be unique, alive, and growing individuals.

IT'S NORMAL TO SEE THINGS DIFFERENTLY

Have you ever read a book that put you to sleep every time you picked it up? Have you ever seen a painting in a museum that resembled something done by children while wiping brushes clean? If so, you probably suffered from deep feelings of guilt or anxiety. You may have asked, "What is wrong with me? Why can't I see the wonders of these masterpieces?"

These feelings are understandable, for we continually compare our standards and opinions with those of others. Such comparisons are often valuable; for one thing they can lead to a more realistic appreciation of normal individual differences. However, if we always accept the standards of others as being the only correct ones, then we will suffer, needlessly, from feelings of inadequacy.

Today more than ever before, because of the strong influence of the mass media of communications and advertising, we need to maintain the dignity and integrity of individual difference and to avoid the idea that there is only one correct answer or interpretation.

AT TIMES IT IS ALL RIGHT TO CHANGE OUR PERCEPTIONS

There are situations in which our perceptions are inaccurate and therefore lead to continual failure or to rejection. Capable students can fail college work because of an inaccurate estimation of the amount and caliber of the scholarship required for satisfactory grades. Usually, warnings and lectures do not help because their perceptions, although wrong, are based on successful experiences in high school situations. Therefore, many college students do poorly until their perceptions change.

Changing our perceptions is common when we meet new situations. We are most vulnerable to failure when we enter situations that are significantly different but seem to resemble old circumstances. For example, newly married couples have to undergo many changes in their perceptions of themselves and what is expected of them. Their new home may physically resemble that of their parents, but their social roles have changed profoundly. Now it is necessary at times to accept another's view willingly for the good of one's partner and children. As the couple share in more common experiences in the new situation, their perceptions of life and problems become more and more similar.

Living with Others

INTRAFAMILY PERCEPTIONS

Can you apply some of the ideas of this chapter to yourself and your family? Have you ever tried to look at the world or an event from your parents' viewpoint? Two of the most frequent problems students have are those of living at home while they are in college and having difficulties in communication with their parents. Part of this problem lies in the fact that our perceptions of the world, being based on the learning process, are difficult to change.

Imagine yourself as a parent, relating to your infant in a relationship of almost pure dependency. As your child grows, he still retains this dependency on you as his parent. Then one day, he tells you that he doesn't need you much anymore and he'll probably be moving out into an apartment with friends. It might be very difficult for you to suddenly change your perceptions of him, to see him all at once as a grown adult!

Think about other areas in your family's experiences where shared perceptions are important. What about your ways of perceiving such things as money and finances; pleasure and entertainment; conflict and display of aggression; love and expression of other emotions; learning and education; religion; use of leisure time; and assuming responsibilities and the world of work. If you consider each member of your family, and look at each of these areas as he does, you may better understand why in certain areas there are general agreements, whereas in others there may be a serious lack of understanding.

FRIENDSHIP PERCEPTIONS

Do you tend to select friends who have similar perceptions of the world and others? Or, do you tend to have some friends with perceptions quite different from your own? You might look at some of your relationships with others and try to better understand why some of your friends are quite close and others quite distant.

Now that you have a better understanding of individual differences in perception, perhaps you can become more tolerant of others and be able to relate with them on a more open and accepting basis.

MALE-FEMALE PERCEPTIONS

The fact that our cultural patterns and groups influence the way we view the world accounts for the wide and often contradictory perceptions we find among males and females. In a class that was discussing male-female relations, one student remarked, "Girls go out with a guy just for his looks and his car!" A young girl jumped up, retorting "Yeah! *All* you guys have on *your* minds is *one* thing!"

This incident illustrates how we tend to make perceptual generalizations about other people or other groups on the basis of some prior personal experiences. Often our perceptions of the opposite sex change considerably after some positive experiences in dating over a period of time.

Living with Society

Most of us are secure in the knowledge that most people around us tend to see the world as we see it. This is because persons from similar socioeconomic groups have similar backgrounds and values. Often we are unaware of how our group affiliations influence the way we view situations and problems. As long as we remain in a stable and homogeneous neighborhood, we tend to find relatively few sharp disagreements. However, now that our society is extremely mobile, we are continuously dealing with persons with different backgrounds and values, people who often see things differently from the way to which we have become accustomed.

It is important to realize that all social behavior is learned; that all social behavior makes sense if one studies the social nature from which the behavior stemmed; and that, although behavior and perception differ, these differences merely represent different ways of satisfying the same basic human needs common to all of us.

If you were asked to write an opinion of President Jackson, the chances are that you would praise him as an outstanding American hero and statesman. However, would your opinions be the same if you had studied history in Mexico and had read passages such as:

> They (Americans living in Texas) resolutely determined to acquire Texas, counting upon the aid of President Jackson, an unscrupulous man who, as a proprietor of slaves, was personally interested in the matter and resorted to every sort of means, even the most immoral, to accomplish his ends . . . . (Rogers, 1967)

Certainly, if we realize that the "stupid and crazy" opinions of others, can be accounted for just as logically as ours, there will be a firmer base for mutual understanding and for eventual reconciliation. Because perception is determined by a number of factors, the more of these factors that we share with others, such as common experiences and goals, the greater the chances that we will learn to see "the other side" as others learn to understand ours.

Final Summary

Perception is the process of observing and interpreting the social and physical world around us. Perception is determined by objective as well as subjective factors. Therefore, no two people view the world in exactly the same ways.

Objective factors include motion, organization, grouping, similarity, closure, constancy, and distortions in the environment. It is when the external events are vague, unfamiliar, and distorted that the subjective factors within the observer have their greatest influence on perception. Important subjective factors include the nature of self-concept, proximity of events to the self, opportunities for common perceptions, intelligence, motivation, and emotion.

There are important integrating principles that help us to better understand our perceptions of the world. Human beings must have a minimum of sensory stimulation for the adequate development of personality and to maintain a realistic orientation. The manner in which we view events is learned and can be changed by social pressures, cognitive dissonance, crisis, psychotherapy, and persuasion. Education plays a major role in developing and changing perceptions. Much of what we perceive is selective and reflects our personality characteristics as well as our social, religious, and political memberships.

Specific Chapter References

Burt, C., Jones. E., Miller, E., and Moodie, W. *How the mind works.* New York: Apple-ton-Century-Crofts, 1934.

Cameron, D. E. Adventures with repetition: the search for its possibilities. In R. H. Hoch and J. Zubin (eds.), *Psychopathology of perception.* New York: Grune and Stratton, 1965.

Combs, A. W., and Syngg, D. *Individual behavior.* New York: Harper & Row, 1959.

Festinger, L. *A theory of cognitive dissonance.* New York: Harper & Row, 1957.

Flint, Betty M. *The child and the institution.* Toronto: University of Toronto Press, 1966.

Gregory, R. L. *Eye and brain.* New York: McGraw-Hill, 1966.

Guetzkow, H. S., and Bowman, P. H. *Men and hunger.* Elgin, Ill.: Brethren Publishing House, 1946.

Hebb, D. O. *The organization of behavior.* New York: Wiley, 1949.

Heron, W. Cognitive and physiological effects of perceptual isolation. In P. Soloman *et al.* (eds.), *Sensory deprivation, a symposium at the Harvard Medical School.* Harvard University Press, 1961. Pp. 6–33.

Hess, E. H., and Polt, J. Pupil Size as Related to Interest Value of Visual Stimuli, *Science,* 132 (1960), 349–350.

Hovland, C. I., *et al. Communication and Persuasion.* New Haven, Conn.: Yale University Press, 1953.

Ittleson, W. H. *The Ames demonstrations in perception.* Princeton, N.J.: Princeton University Press, 1952.

Jacob, P. E. *Changing values in college: an exploratory study of the impact of college teaching.* Harper & Row, 1957.

Jones, G. M. Personal communication to D. O. Hebb. In D. O. Hebb, The American Revolution, *American Psychologist,* 1960, 15, 735–745.

Lawrence, M. *Studies in human behavior.* Princeton, N.J.: Princeton University Press, 1949.

Lipset, S. M. Political sociology. In R. K. Merton *et al.* (eds.), *Sociology today: problems and prospects.* New York: Basic Books, 1959. Pp. 81–114.

McClelland, D., Atkinson, J. W., Clark, R. A., and Lowell, E. L. *The achievement motive.* New York: Appleton-Century-Crofts, 1953.

Mead, M. Culture and personality development: human capacities. In H. A. Otto (ed.), *Explorations in human potentialities.* Springfield, Ill.: Charles C Thomas, 1966. Pp. 137–153.

Postman, L., Bruner, J., and McGinnies, E. Personal values as selective factors in perception. *Journal of Abnormal and Social Psychology,* 1948, 43, 142–154.

Reisen, A. H. The development of visual perception in man and chimpanzee. *Science,* 1949, 106, 107–108.

Rogers, C. R. *On becoming a person.* Houghton Mifflin, 1961.

Rogers, C. R. Ethnocentrism and the social studies. *Phi Delta Kappan,* 1967, XLIV(4), 208–211.

Vernon, M. D. *Backwardness in reading.* New York: Cambridge University Press, 1957.

Wallach, H., and Galloway, A. The constancy of colored objects in colored illumination. *Journal of Experimental Psychology,* 1946, 36, 119–126.

Wellman, B. L. Iowa studies on the effects of schooling. *Yearbook of the National Society for the Study of Education,* 1940, 39, 377–399.

Wertheimer, M., *Experimentelle* Studien über das Sehen von Bewegungen. *Zeitschrift für Psychologie,* 1912, 61, 161–165.

Witkin, H. A. Individual differences in the ease of perception of embedded figures. *Journal of Personality*, 1950, 19, 1–19.

Witkin, H. A., Lewis, H. B., Hertzman, M., Machover, K., Meissner, P. B., and Wapner, S. *Personality through perception*. New York: Harper & Row, 1954.

Recommended Further Readings

Paperback Books

Alpern, M., Lawrence, M., and Wolsh, D. *Sensory processes*. Belmont, Calif.: Brooks-Cole, 1967.

Blum, G. S. *Psychodynamics: the science of unconscious mental forces*. Belmont, Calif.: Wadsworth, 1966.

Candland, D. K., and Campbell, J. F. *Exploring behavior*. New York: Premier Book, 1961.

Fitts, P. M., and Posner, M. I. *Human performance*. Belmont, Calif.: Brooks-Cole, 1967.

Foss, B. M. (ed.) *New horizons in psychology*. Baltimore: Penguin Books, 1966.

Hildum, D. C. *Language and thought*. Princeton, N.J.: Van Nostrand, 1967.

Hochberg, J. E. *Perception*. Englewood Cliffs, N.J.: Prentice-Hall, 1964.

Leibowitz, H. W. *Visual perception*. New York: Macmillan, 1965.

Milner, P. M., and Glickman, S. E. (eds.). *Cognitive processes and the brain*. Princeton, N.J.: Van Nostrand, 1965.

Mueller, C. G. *Sensory psychology*. Englewood Cliffs, N.J.: Prentice-Hall, 1965.

Segall, M. H., Campbell, D. T., and Herskovits, M. J. *The influence of culture on visual perception*. Indianapolis: Bobbs-Merrill, 1966.

Skurnik, L. S., and George, F. *Psychology for everyman*. Baltimore: Penguin Books, 1964.

Vernon, M. D. (ed.). *Experiments in visual perception*. Baltimore: Penguin Books, 1966.

Weintraub, D. J., and Walker, E. L. *Perception*. Belmont, Calif.: Brooks-Cole, 1966.

Hardcover Books

Association for Supervision and Curriculum Development. *Perceiving behaving becoming*. Washington, D. C.: Association for Supervision and Curriculum Development (A department of the National Education Association) 1962.

Bartley, S. H. *Principles of perception*. New York: Harper & Row, 1958.

Bruner, J. S., Olver, Rose R., Greenfield, Patricia M., *et al. Studies in cognitive growth*. New York: Wiley, 1966.

Dember, W. N. *The psychology of perception*. New York: Holt, Rinehart and Winston, 1960.

Epstein, W. *Varieties of perceptual learning*. New York: McGraw-Hill, 1966.

Forgus, R. H. *Perception*. New York: McGraw-Hill, 1966.

Geldard, F. A. *The human senses*. New York: Wiley, 1953.

Gibson, J. J. *The senses considered as perceptual systems*. Boston: Houghton Mifflin, 1966.

Graham, C. H. (ed.) *Vision and visual perception*. New York: Wiley, 1965.

Solley, C. M., and Murphy, G. *Development of the perceptual world*. New York: Basic Books, 1960.

Soltis, J. F. *Seeing, knowing and believing*. Reading, Mass.: Addison-Wesley, 1966.

Von Fieandt, K. *The world of perception*. Homewood, Ill.: Dorsey Press, 1966.

Part III The Dynamics of Human Behavior

Thus far we have taken a look at you, as a unique and potentially self-actualizing individual. We have discussed the role of learning and problem solving in your growth as well as in your day-to-day existence.

Next, in Part II, we explored the development of human behavior from childhood into the present. We also discussed why people behave the way they do, how emotions affect our behavior, and the importance of perception on our behavior.

In this section, Part III, we plan to bring together the various segments (learning, thinking, problem solving, motives, emotions, and perception) and to discuss the human person as a whole. We hope to show you how the total person behaves as an integrated unit; we call this *personality*.

After a look at the personality of the individual, we plan to discuss certain minor problems that affect personality—problems that are encountered by all people in the day-to-day world: stress, frustration, anxiety, defensive reactions, and mild neurotic symptoms. Then we shall explain how major personality problems develop, as a result of various stresses, into what are called *neuroses* and *psychoses*. We shall talk about the ways used to help people overcome both minor and major personality problems, and in conclusion we shall discuss what is perhaps the most important question of all: How can we prevent the human suffering caused by these personality problems?

Chapter 8 Understanding Personality

Chapter Outline

Study Guide

The study of personality is a very profound topic. All we can do is to observe behavior and guess at what lies beneath the surface. The depths of personality remain unseen. Through the study of personality we cannot even hope to understand completely, but we can learn to appreciate more the complexities of human behaviors.

REVIEW
Read the Table of Contents for the entire book. *This procedure will permit you to see the relationship between personality and the other topics. There is better*

understanding when we know how separate parts fit together to make a meaningful and complete picture.

PREVIEW

Study the structure of the chapter by reading the prelude, chapter outline, headings, cameos, and summaries. Now read to fill in the contents of the structure.

READING

Read the chapter straight through following study guide suggestions. Practice outlining as you read.

REVIEW

Review by practicing recall. Use your chapter outline. Use the book's chapter outline. Reread all summaries. Reread the entire chapter.

REVIEW TIP

How to skim read. Skimming is useful for locating specific information and answers to questions quickly. Skimming is NOT reading. We read after locating what we want. Skim by looking at three lines of print at one time while going from left to right; return to the left margin by looking at the next three lines going from right to left. Each time center your vision on the middle line only. You will be able to see enough of the other two lines to recognize the word or the topic for which you are searching.

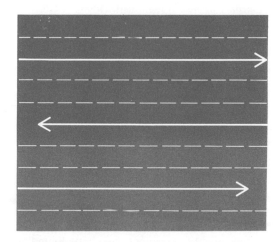

Figure 8-1
Eye Movement in Skim Reading.

Prelude

Personality is one of those words that we all use but that no one really understands. Even psychologists in their attempts to define personality resemble the blind men in the story about describing the appearance of an elephant. One blind man, you will recall, was certain that an elephant was like a large snake. Another blind man insisted that an elephant was like a tree trunk. A third blind man was confident that the other two were really blind because an elephant was like a wall. Of course, all of us try to see the whole elephant. We all want to know all we can about our own personalities and those of other persons around us.

A question that we all ponder is this: What am I really like? Behind the roles we act, the games we play, the façades we build, what are we really? In our attempts to understand personality, whether our own or those of others, we will be like the blind men describing the elephant. Please note, however, that when the observations of each blind man are put together, the composite picture provides a far better description of the elephant. In this chapter, we plan to put together for you various descriptions of how personality develops and suggest ways of studying the various dimensions of human activities. In this book, *personality* refers to all the factors within the person that influence his characteristic ways of behaving, thinking, and feeling.

Students' Viewpoints

To most people, personality is defined in the remark, "He has a lot of personality," or "She's nice looking, but she has no personality." A coed may exclaim after a date, "Gee, I thought I knew him well!" We judge personality by physical appearance, manner of talking, and behavior patterns. In turn, others view our personalities in the same general ways.

Once others have decided on the nature of our personalities, they tend to treat us accordingly. Often the judgment is based on a first impression and it doesn't change even though the interpretation was erroneous and our behavior has changed dramatically. This unchanging opinion of others based only on a first general impression is known as the "halo effect." For example, during the first day of class, a student may inadvertently make an inappropriate remark to the instructor. The instructor, in turn, labels the student a wise guy for the rest of the semester, even though the student behaves himself appropriately after the first day.

In life we tend to accept or reject others according to what we think about their personalities. Employers often tend to hire and promote a person more on personality than on what he knows about the job. The popular student is usually the one judged to have a "good" personality. People often fall in love and marry because they believe their personalities match well. They enjoy the same activities and their opinions are similar. We see that the opinions formed by others about our personalities have far-reaching effects on our lives.

WHY IS IT IMPORTANT?

What does the study of the human personality have to do with you and your daily life?

The study and better understanding of the human personality could very well be one of the most significant studies for you not only now, but in the future as well. For it is through the understanding of the personalities of your fellow-man that the world is going to be a better place.

If you were to ask people of various ages and walks of life what their most pressing personal problem is many of them would say: Understanding my fellow-man; or understanding my wife or husband; or understanding my parents; or understanding my boyfriend or girlfriend; or understanding a particular minority group; or understanding the people of another nation or cultural group.

Most of us see only a small part of the true personalities of those around us; we only see the roles people play: the parent, the son or daughter, the teacher, or the salesman. In other words, what we see in surface behavior may not really represent the major part of the personality of the individual.

Mistakes in personality assessment are often one of the major causes for the interpersonal problems involved in marriage, dating, business partnerships, or relations between friends.

It is the authors' hope that by studying some of the research and theories developed by psychologists about the human personality, you will be better able to understand not only your personality, but also the personalities of other people.

BASIC THEORY AND RESEARCH

Levels of Personality Description

The adequacy of a personality description depends on its purpose. In a casual conversation between two acquaintances, the following description of a third party might be adequate: "She's very friendly and helpful. Everybody likes her."

On the other hand, a description of a potential employee to an employer must be more detailed: "Miss Jones is a dependable and efficient office manager. Her previous employers have given her excellent recommendations. Her ability to plan and to control the work flow of a large business firm has been proven. The morale of the clerical and typist pools under her supervision has been consistently rated as excellent." A mental hospital's requirements for an adequate personality description are so demanding that the services of clinical psychologists are needed. The following personality evaluation is that of a 15-year-old recently committed to a mental hospital.

John is a large, pleasant-looking boy of 15 years. During the examinations he gave the impression of being tense, anxious, and confused. He was very verbal and critical against society in general, the hospital, his mother, and particularly against his father. He displayed extreme apprehension and defensiveness concerning the examination because he felt that their findings could keep him in the hospital. His reasoning was

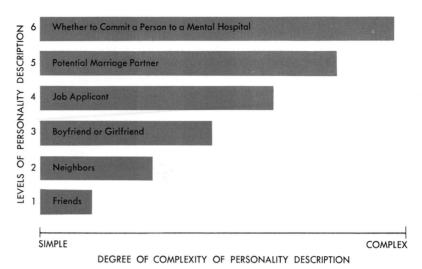

Figure 8-2
Levels of Personality Description

mostly illogical and unrealistic. His role was that of a "big man" who knew everything and who needed help from no one. Interesting to note were his frequent modifications and denials of his own hostile and contradictory statements.

The tests reveal that John is functioning within the normal range of intelligence with little or no impairment. There were no definite indications of organic brain damage, although the possibility cannot be ruled out. It is believed that organic brain damage, even if present, is not a major contributing factor to the patient's present illness.

Although he denies having problems, the tests suggest a great deal of inner tension, concern, and an awareness that something is wrong with him. His apparent lack of superego, the immaturity of his impulses, and his lack of adequate control over his emotions suggest recurrent difficulties in adjusting to his environment and the possibility of impulsive, uncontrolled reactions to emotionally loaded situations.

He is ruled more by immediate needs to gratify his strong instinctual needs than by any long-range goals or inner system of values. His preoccupation with inner conflicts prevents him from adequate handling of outside stimuli. Instead of reacting freely to his environment he tends to restructure reality in terms of his own needs. In so doing, his contact with reality becomes very tenuous.

John is a severely disturbed boy. He often lets past experiences influence his present perception. His preoccupation with his own aggression and hostile feelings prevents him from using his creativity for useful purposes. His unwillingness to accept common standards has led him to approach things in unique ways. In so doing, he reveals many unusual and even strange ideas. He would prefer to do things differently even if it meant doing poorly. In a few words, John is a social rebel.

In apparent overcompensation for deep-seated feelings of inadequacy, he has developed unrealistic levels of aspiration. What seem to him to be constant rejections have made him exceedingly distrustful of people, particularly authority figures. Undoubtedly he can make himself especially obnoxious in an effort to be sure that the persons involved are sincerely interested in him. Because of this, the establishment of

239

an adequate working relationship will be difficult, time-consuming, and will require infinite patience and understanding.

Nevertheless, John has a strong longing for closeness and dependency upon others. Despite his aggressive, hostile feelings and all his efforts at being a "big man," he would like to be a little boy and to be the recipient of tender affection. He is not as rigid as he seems. In the tests and during the interview he corrected mistakes and modified his statements. He feels, however, that the passive role is not adequate and that aggression is the only basis for interpersonal relations.

Presently he seems too disturbed to settle down to sociopathy. He is more concerned with his inner conflicts than with outer reality. He has strongly developed paranoid ideation and could be moving in the direction of a borderline paranoid schizophrenic with a sociopathic orientation.

It is believed that he could profit from long-term supportive psychotheraphy. Initially, however, he could benefit by associating with a warm, accepting, understanding, non-professional person. Situational assistance could be provided through giving him some worthwhile tasks to perform. He mentioned that he has ability and interest in numbers, repairing automoblies, and gardening.

Everyone has engaged in personality description, whether or not he is aware of having done so. How much time and effort should be spent evaluating another person's personality depends on how important that evaluation is. Certainly, prior to a formal marriage engagement, the young couple should get to know each other as well as possible. For example, marriage counselors recommend a courtship period of at least six months.

Studying Factors That Determine Personality

It is possible to classify all the determinants of personality into two broad categories: (1) heredity and (2) social-environmental. At birth, we arrive endowed with a complex set of genes that provide for potential physical and psychological development. Although heredity may set the limits, a person's potential is achieved or not achieved within his social environment.

BIOLOGICAL DETERMINANTS OF PERSONALITY

At the moment of conception, when the *sperm* (male sex cell) unites with the *ovum* (female sex cell), the thousands of genes from each parent unite to form a unique organism. Each parent normally passes on twenty-three *chromosomes* (the gene-carrying bodies found in the nucleus of cells) to his or her offspring, which accounts for children's looking like their parents. The chromosomes contain the *genes*, which are thought to be the trait-carrying elements of heredity. However, only identical twins, who develop from a single fertilized ovum, have an identical genetic inheritance. Individual differences are great even at birth because the twenty-three chromosomes from each parent can unite in 8,388,608 different ways. Therefore, the chances of any brothers or sisters having the same combination of genes is practically nil.

There have been many attempts to estimate the relative importance of heredity and environment to personality development. We have evidence that children reared in impoverished environments generally suffer deficient language and intellectual development and general personality defects, such as lack of emotional responsiveness and inadequacy in relating to other persons. (Dennis, 1961; Deutsch, 1963) Nevertheless, not all the children reared in impoverished environments are equally defective. Twins who are reared in separate environments show a greater equality of scores on intelligence tests than unrelated children reared in separate environments. The greater similarity of intelligence between twins is explained on the basis of greater similarity in genetic endowments. Yet, there is ample evidence that intelligence scores of children are influenced by environmental circumstances (Bloom, 1964, Chapter 3).

The safest conclusion, at the present time, is that the effects of heredity and environment cannot be separated one from the other.

SOCIAL-ENVIRONMENTAL DETERMINANTS OF PERSONALITY

As we discussed in Chapter 4 ("Childhood and Adolescence"), the most important aspect of the social-environmental determinants of personality development includes the family interactions that occur very early in life. Because we have already discussed the effects and some of the consequences of such factors as developing the capacity to love, developing the capacity to learn, socialization, and so on, they will not be repeated here. In this section, then, we will focus more on the effects of social groups and social pressure on personality development.

The preceding section on the effects of heredity on personality development was brief because relatively little is known about how genetic factors influence personality. However, more is known of the social-environmental influences on personality development. *Social psychologists* focus their study of personality development on those aspects of human behavior influenced by the presence of other persons. Notice that behavior changes depend on the social situation. Usually it would not be appropriate to tell to a minister a joke that was told at a party. A person behaves quite differently among strangers than he does among friends.

Table 8–1 shows some of the influences of urban, suburban, and rural environments on behavior.

Of the hundreds of acts that most persons carry out each day, the vast majority are carried out in accordance with the requirements of one's social group. There are a number of things that one would not do because of the presence of another person, such as being very boisterous or scratching certain parts of the body. Yet, there are behaviors produced by the presence and actions of others that one would never do if alone. Consider the behavior of individuals in riots, revolutions, and lynching mobs. The day after, they find it very difficult to explain their behavior; indeed, some persons cannot even remember what happened, and a few are known to have committed suicide.

Table 8-1
Some Significant Characteristics of Folk, Urban, and Suburban Cultures

Folk Culture	Urban Culture	Suburban Culture
I. Tradition-oriented: resistant to new ideas, prefer old ways	I. Future-oriented: accept rapid change, conflict of values results	I. Comfort-oriented: group adjusts to change, similarity of values
II. Informal education: stress practical knowledge, not formal schooling	II. Mass education: "diploma" for all, illiteracy disappearing	II. College education: stress on higher education
III. Tradition-directed personalities: guided by custom, habits, rigid social-classes	III. Rugged individual: emphasis on individual achievement, experimentation, progress	III. Other-directed personalities: emphasis on cooperation and team work, harmony
IV. Male-dominated families: stable marriages, sex roles rigidly prescribed	IV. Families in conflict: male not dominant; similarity of sex roles, family loses its central role	IV. Democratic families: cooperation, companionship, more stable marriages, sex roles more and more alike
V. Long-lasting social relations: warm, intimate, limited to small homogeneous groups.	V. Temporary social relations: impersonal, superficial, meet a great variety of different people	V. Selected social relations: based on common values and interests, more personal and less temporary

Adapted from Hodges in Kallenback and Hodges, 1963, p. 57.

The crucial importance of social context has been demonstrated in laboratory situations. (Asch, 1955) A group of eight individuals were instructed to match the length of a given line with one of three unequal lines. All but one student was informed to give the same wrong answer before the "innocent" subject. This situation placed the "innocent" student in the predicament of denying the evidence of his own senses or going against the judgment of the group. Under such group pressures over one third of those used as innocent subjects made incorrect judgments over 99 per cent of the time. It is well to remember that about 25 per cent of the students stuck with their original judgments despite group pressure and suggestion. Other studies on self-actualizing persons have shown that more mentally healthy people tend to be more independent of group pressures (Maslow, 1962; Rogers, 1961).

Intermediate Summary

Personality refers to all the factors within the individual that influence his characteristic ways of behaving, thinking, and feeling. The different theorists attempt to select and measure what they believe to be the most important personality factors. The length and depth of a personality description are dependent on the purpose for which it was done. The purposes may range from curiosity about friends, to personnel procedures for hiring employees, to the detailed descriptions required by a mental hospital for diagnosis and treatment of a patient. Determinants of personality may be classified into the broad categories of heredity and social-environmental.

Personality Theories

Now that we have examined the two major determinants of personality (the biological and social-environmental), how do psychologists explain the development of such a variety of personality patterns that we see in the people we interact with everyday? Because psychology is a relatively young science (in comparison with the physical and natural sciences), we are still in the process of testing out various theories of personality.

In one of the major texts on personality theory (Hall and Lindzey, 1957), seventeen different theories are discussed that have been postulated and studied by psychologists for more than seventy-five years. This is mentioned to show you that psychologists are far from deciding on a single theory as being the most accurate. For our purposes we will discuss four theories (Self, Psychoanalytic, Trait, and Learning) that we feel are representative of the majority of approaches. In addition, we will briefly summarize some of the other theories for those of you who may wish to do further study in these areas.

SELF-CONCEPT PERSONALITY THEORY

Definition of Self

How one characteristically feels about himself (the self-concept) is believed by many psychologists to be the focus around which our personality is formed, maintained, and through which it changes. This theory has already been mentioned in several of the earlier chapters (see pp. 14, 41, and 71).

The self theory of personality as presented by Rogers and others has the following basic postulates: (Hall and Lindzey, 1957)

(a) The self develops out of the organism's interaction with the environment.
(b) It may introject the values of other people and perceive them in a distorted fashion.
(c) The self strives for consistency.
(d) The organism behaves in ways that are consistent with the self.
(e) Experiences that are not consistent with the self structure are perceived as threats.
(f) The self may change as a result of maturation and learning. (p. 478)

Parts of Self

Jersild suggests that our self actually consists of three basic components: the perceptual, the conceptual, and the attitudinal. (Hamacheck, 1965. Pp. 196–197)

Perceptual Component

This includes the way a person views himself; such considerations as how the person feels about his body and how others perceive him.

Conceptual Component

This includes what a person thinks about his abilities, assets, and limitations. It also includes feelings about his past (including his origin and family background) and about his future.

Attitudinal Component

This component includes the attitudes that a person has developed about himself such as self-esteem or self-reproach, or whether he views himself with pride or shame. As the person gets older this component encompasses values, ideals, and convictions. (The resulting expression of these is often called a person's philosophy of life.)

Summary of Self Theory of Personality

This is but one theory about the human personality. It essentially says that one can understand the behavior of another person and can even make predictions if one can study all aspects of the self-concept of that person: the perceptual, conceptual, and attitudinal. For example, if we find a person with a very negative self-concept, we may be able to predict that he probably has difficulty letting people get very close to him; that he probably very rarely lets his real self show; that he often plays a role or different roles; that he may often exhibit hostilities to other individuals or groups of individuals.

FREUD'S PSYCHOANALYTIC PERSONALITY THEORY

Perhaps one of the best-known, most influential, and most controversial theories of personality is the psychoanalytic theory developed by Sigmund Freud. (Hall, 1954)

Freud was a brilliant medical doctor who developed not only a theory of human personality, but a method (psychoanalysis, see Chapter 11) for helping mentally ill persons to get well.

Freud's View of Man

Freud viewed man as essentially an *unconscious being* (see p. 150) whose behavior was often based on unconscious factors. It has been expressed this way: "He likened the mind to an iceberg in which the smaller part showing above the surface of the water represents the region of consciousness while the much larger mass below the water level represents the region of the unconsciousness." (Hall and Lindzey, 1957, p. 30)

To Freud, the human personality consists of dynamic organization made up of three basic elements: the id, ego, and superego. In order to better visualize Freud's theory, we will use a house to illustrate the dynamics.

CAMEO

Figure 8-3
Sigmund Freud (1856–1939), M.D.,
Psychiatrist, Psychoanalyst

Academic Career
  Graduated from the Gymnasium
  Medical student, University of Vienna
  Studied hypnosis under Charcot in Paris

Professional Experience: Physiologist,
Neurologist, Psychoanalyst

Areas of Interest
  Early in his career, Dr. Freud became interested in hypnosis in treating hysteria. He discovered that the success of hypnosis in psychotherapy depended too much on an emotional relationship with the patient. The practice of hypnosis was abandoned. He encouraged his patients to remember forgotten material, but to his embarrassment he discovered that he was encouraging the patients to invent unreal sexual episodes from their past. Freud's own verbal interactions of commentary and question proved detrimental in that the patient was interrupted in his train of thought. Freud eventually established his method of *free association,* which allowed the patient to say whatever entered his mind.

Courtesy of The Bettmann Archive

  Freud developed the first comprehensive theory of personality, the structure of which is composed of three major systems: (1) the id, (2) the ego, and (3) the superego. The id is composed of an individual's basic, primitive drives, which strive only for pleasure. The ego comes about as the internal needs of the organism (the id) must deal with the world that is external (outside) to the person—it acts as a mediator. The superego is constituted of the social values that are taught us.

Selected Readings

Freud, S. The major works of Sigmund Freud. In R. M. Hutchins (ed.), *Great books of the western world.* Chicago: Encyclopedia Britannica, 1947.

Freud, S. *The standard edition of the complete works of Sigmund Freud.* Vol. 14. London: Hogarth, 1957.

Hall, C. S. *A primer of Freudian psychology.* Cleveland: World Publishing, 1954.

Lauzun, G. *Sigmund Freud: The man and his theories.* Greenwich, Conn.: Fawcett, 1962.

Jones, E. *The life and work of Sigmund Freud.* New York: Basic Books, Vol. 1, 1953; Vol. 2, 1955.

245

THE ID. In the house (Figure 8–4), the id is symbolized by the basement. What do you find in a basement? Often you will find such things as rats, mice, spiders, snakes, old storage trunks, coal, and dirty clothing. On the other hand, you sometimes find a game room, where people play games, drink alcoholic beverages, listen to TV, or, in general, let themselves go and have fun. Figure 8–4 illustrates this.

Figure 8–4
The Basement of the Freudian "House"

To Freud, the id (basement) represents the parts of the personality that we are born with: instincts, inherited potentials, and our physiological body processes. Essentially it operates on *life instincts* (essentially sexual in nature) and *death instincts* (destructive and hostile impulses). These tendencies create tensions and energy within the id that must have release. The release comes (in the diagram) through the opening of the trap door into the main part of the house.

THE EGO. The main portion of the house represents the reality-oriented part of the human personality. Freud called this the ego. This is the part of us that is guided by our intellect; the part of us that thinks, makes decisions, plans ahead, and so on. In the diagram (Figure 8–5), we see this as the part of the house that has a front door, an opening to the outside world. It is also the portion of the house that has control over the opening and closing of the trap door.

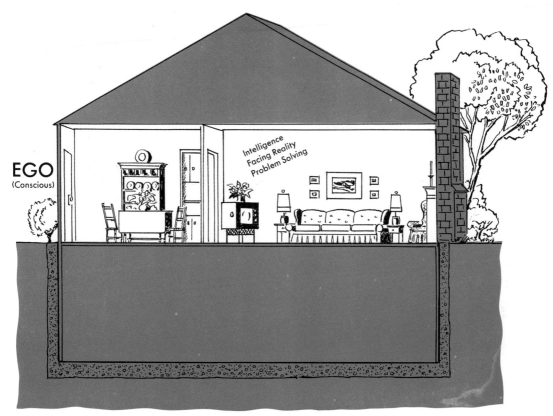

Figure 8–5
The Ground Floor of the Freudian "House"

THE SUPEREGO. The roof of the house represents the restraining forces of society, the family, and the church. That is, the roof (or superego) represents the conscience or moral values that each of us develops through the learning process as children. To Freud, then, the superego was the restraining force put on the instincts of the id; without it, man would not be able to control his hostility and his sexual impulses.

Freud's View of the Total Person
Freud viewed man's personality as consisting of these three major segments. He also felt that there was a constant battle going on among these three segments. On the one hand, we have the id impulses (snakes, spiders, sexual impulses) trying

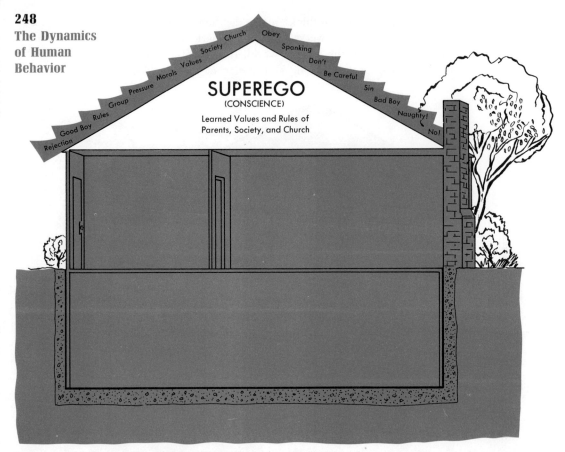

Figure 8-6
The Roof of the Freudian "House"

to push open the trap door and to seek expression to the real world. On the other hand we have the roof exerting pressure down on the ego and indirectly extending to the trap door. At the same time, the ego is trying to get the person through daily life and the real world situations confronting him. Thus, the ego is viewed as the go-between for the id and the superego.

Extremes of the Freudian House

Although the Freudian House analogy has limitations, it does help us understand (from a psychoanalytic basis) some extreme forms of personality functioning. For example, what type of personality pattern might a person have according to the Freudian House shown in Figure 8-7? You might hypothesize that this person's superego is so strong that he is weighted down by feelings of guilt and shame. Furthermore, his ego is very small, thus he has little control in his relations with the real world. You might also notice that his trap

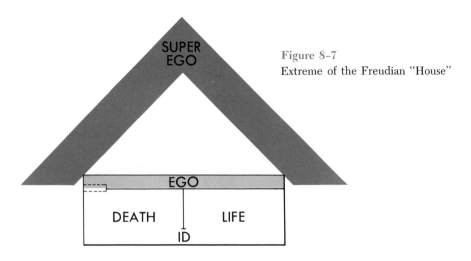

Figure 8-7
Extreme of the Freudian "House"

door is virtually sealed shut, because the pressure from the superego combined with a weak ego does not allow it to open very often.

Sometimes a pattern like this leads to a *personality explosion* whereby the trap door blows off (as a result of the energy that builds up in the id). As a result, the person may go on a killing spree or seek a variety of sexual activities.

Another extreme personality pattern is shown in Figure 8–8.

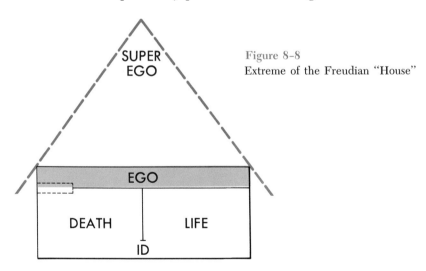

Figure 8-8
Extreme of the Freudian "House"

What kind of a person might this represent? Our jails are often filled with men like this. This would be a psychoanalytic representation of the individual with very few morals or values (a very light roof with few shingles). Notice also that such a person has a very weak trap door, so that any and all impulses (sexual or hostile) are acted on without much concern for the moral values of society.

Other Features of the Freudian House

IMPORTANCE OF EARLY CHILDHOOD IN PERSONALITY DEVELOPMENT. Freud believed that it is during the first few years of life that our basic personality develops. It is also during this period when many of our problems begin to develop in the form of various conflicts between our basic physiological needs and the satisfaction of these needs. It is the time when mother and father are considered to be the providers of all our wants and desires, and yet they often frustrate our wants by denying them or punishing us when we say or do certain things that they or society believe are "bad."

REPRESSSION AND THE ID. As a result of these conflicts, which often produce strong emotional feelings of love and hate, the child hides these feelings from awareness. (The process was earlier called *repression*, see p. 187). Using the Freudian House model again, you might say that the basement (id) gets cluttered with many of these early childhood repressed feelings. Those stay with us and continue to affect our behavior at an unconscious level later in life.

DEVELOPMENT OF THE SUPEREGO. It is also during early childhood that Freud believed we form the basis of our value system (superego). Thus, some people who have lived in homes where rules (both religious and social) were rigidly enforced may carry with them a strong superego that may produce strong feelings of guilt for any violation of these rules.

DREAMS. Freud felt that dreams were a valuable source of material to help the psychoanalyst understand some of the conflicts in the id. In a sense, Freud believed that the ego was not as strong during sleep, thus allowing conflicts and repressed material to come into awareness. For a further discussion of dreams and some of the current research see the appendices.

Psychoanalysis and the Healthy Personality

One criticism of Freud's theory is that it was built around the "sick" personality. What to Freud would be a healthy personality? Using the Freudian House you might say that the healthy person is one who is able to lift the trap door and take a walk into his basement (id) so that he can throw out some of the repressed conflicts from early childhood. Furthermore, this person is also more aware of his life and death impulses lurking in the unconscious.

The healthy personality also is able to crawl up on the roof and examine the shingles (the superego) and maybe even throw a few of them off the roof if they do not appear to be important to him now.

The healthy person also has enough ego strength to face reality and the world around him. He has control over his id impulses and can open and close the trap door without being afraid of what may sneak out. This person also knows the composition of his superego, so that he understands how far he will go before he violates his ethical code.

How does a person become a healthy personality? Freud believed that in order to have the courage to do all of the preceding, a person must undergo psychoanalysis (a lengthy and costly process; see Chapter 11 for further discussion of this form of therapy). That is, he felt that for the average person to delve into the basement or go up on the roof of his "house" alone was too much; that one needs a guide (a trained psychoanalyst).

THE TRAIT APPROACH TO PERSONALITY

Human behavior is so infinitely variable that it is very difficult to find order in it or to make sense of it. A person may behave with good judgment in one situation and behave with poor judgment in another. All of us have this tendency to think clearly at times and poorly on other occasions. The *trait approach* to understanding personality is based on the idea that all persons are different, and that the key to a person's personality consists of knowing his unique pattern of traits, which are revealed with relative consistency by his everyday behavior. (Guilford, 1959)

Figure 8-9
Self-actualization. The desire to help others when translated into action is an important characteristic of the self-actualizing person. Here Herb Alvarez, a VISTA volunteer, helps to launch a campaign to rehabilitate slums in New York's lower West Side.

Photo by VISTA

Psychologists who use the trait approach to understanding personality have the task of defining and selecting the traits most useful in describing personality. Psychologists do not simply make up labels and call them traits. They observe behavior carefully in laboratories and real life situations and describe traits that they believe explain the observed behaviors. For example, if a person has few friends, avoids social contacts, and rarely speaks to others unless spoken to first, trait psychologists may characterize him as introverted or withdrawn. A person who is interested in people and who expresses his feelings and thoughts openly may be characterized as extroverted or very expressive. In other words, a *trait* is simply a report of an observed consistency in the acts or behaviors of persons.

Finally, there is the organization of traits into broad, general areas that can be used to describe personality categories such as the following:

1. Intelligence: skills, information storing, and competencies
2. Temperament: typical emotional behaviors
3. Interests: likes and dislikes, particularly in important areas of life
4. Character: values and morals
5. Aptitude: potential for doing well in particular areas of school, work, or life activities
6. Physical characteristics: body structure, complexion, height, and weight

Once traits and related areas for important life activities have been defined, the psychologists try to determine the amount, the durability, and the frequency of each trait present in a person. The psychograph on page 253 shows how a personality profile may appear when comparing two different persons.

LEARNING THEORY APPROACH TO PERSONALITY

Learning principles, discussed in Chapter 2, have proved extremely useful in describing human behavior. All theories of personality use learning principles, explicity or implicitly, to some extent. Although psychoanalytic theory deemphasizes learning principles in favor of inborn biological tendencies to explain behavior, Freud and his disciples do not deny that the consequences of inborn forces are sharply modified by social learning. In fact, in his later life, Freud stated that if an individual's personality is to be understood, it must be studied biologically, psychologically, and sociologically.

An illustration of the learning-theory viewpoint is the following passage from Dollard and Miller (1950):

The field of human learning covers phenomena which range all the way from the simple, almost reflex, learning of a child to avoid a hot radiator, to the complex processes of insight by which a scientist constructs a theory. Throughout the whole range, however, the same fundamental factors seem to be exceedingly important. These factors are: drive, response, cue, and reinforcement. They are frequently referred to with other roughly equivalent words—drive as motivation, we as stimulus, response as act or thought, and reinforcement as reward (pp. 25–26).

Although the Dollard and Miller approach appears deceptively simple, the four factors can be used to explain much behavior that, in turn, can be used to describe aspects of a person's personality.

Figure 8-9

J. P. Guilford (1897–   ), Ph.D., Clinical Psychologist, Personality Theorist, Statistician

Academic Career
   B.A., M.A., University of Nebraska
   Ph.D., Cornell University

Professional Experience
   Instructor, University of Illinois
   Assistant professor, University of Kansas
   Associate and, later, professor, University of Nebraska
   Aviation psychologist, USAF
   Professor, University Southern California

Areas of Interest
   Assessment of intelligence has been a major area of interest for Dr. Guilford. Based on several studies using the factor analytic method of reducing the quantity of items to those most important, Guilford constructed a model of the basic processes that are demonstrated in what we call intelligence. His model is called the *structure of intellect.* The model provides us with a pictorial idea of intellectual activities as they appear in tests of abilities.

   Personality is the facet of psychology with which Guilford involves himself. He has promoted the use of factor analysis as a research tool. Work in psychometric methods that involves mathematical or measurement phases of psychological experimentation is another facet Guilford has dealt with, particularly concerning mental testing.

Selected Readings
Guilford, J. P. Three faces of intellect. *American Psychologist,* 1957, 14, 469–479.
———. *Personality.* New York: McGraw-Hill, 1959.
———. Factorial angles to psychology. *Psychological Review,* 1961, 68, 1–20.
———. *Psychometric methods* (2nd ed.). New York: McGraw-Hill, 1964.
———. *Fundamental statistics in psychology and education* (4th ed.). New York: McGraw-Hill, 1965.

C A M E O

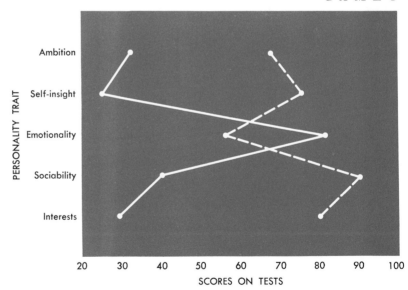

A Personality Psychograph. The dotted line represents scores of one student on a personality trait test; he scored high on the Sociability Trait and low on the Emotionality Trait. The solid line represents another student who scored low on the trait of Self-insight and high on the trait of Emotionality.

Timidity or shyness in a college student could be explained in terms of learning. As a child he liked to play with other children (motivation). Whenever he saw other children playing (cues), he would dash over to play. Because he never learned to share and to take turns, the other children usually rejected him (negative reinforcement). As we learned in Chapter 2, behaviors that are repeatedly negatively rewarded tend not to be repeated. The early rejection by his peers, in turn, prevented him from learning other social skills required for effective interpersonal relationship. His later attempts to engage socially with others (renewed motivation) led to even greater failure experiences (generalization of feeling of inadequacy to increasingly larger groups). Eventually, ignoring social activities (cue) becomes a positively reinforcing procedure (reward).

The preceding illustration is intended to give the reader a bird's-eye view of the manner in which learning theorists approach the study of personality.

OTHER PERSONALITY THEORIES

These four theories (Self, Psychoanalytic, Trait, and Learning) are representative of the major theoretical approaches that psychologists have used to study personality. Table 8-2 summarizes some additional theories that you may find interesting to pursue on your own.

Intermediate Summary

The self theory suggests that how one characteristically feels about himself is the focus around which personality develops. The basic components of self are perceptual, conceptual, and attitudinal. Psychoanalysis emphasizes the unconscious factors of personality and the dynamic organization of id, ego, and superego. The trait approach consists of knowing the unique pattern of traits that reveals itself with relative consistency in everyday behavior. Learning theories emphasize the central importance of learning principles in the development of personality.

Other Ways of Describing and Studying Personality

Some psychologists believe that certain individuals tend to display a dominant personality pattern that is so overpowering that it pervades the behavior of the total person. Among these, the following patterns have been studied by different social scientists: the authoritarian personality; the inner-, other-, and traditional-directed person; and moral character types.

Table 8-2
Other Theories of Personality

Name	Approach	Emphasis	Major Ideas
William Sheldon (1942)	Temperamental traits	Hereditary (especially body physique)	The structure (physique) of a person's body and his behavior are highly interrelated. With each body type there is a related personality pattern (temperamental traits).
Carl Jung (1939; Hall and Lindzey, 1957, pp. 76–113)	Psychoanalytic	Hereditary (man's racial background throughout history) and environment	Man's personality is primarily a function of: (1) his biological and racial history, which were genetically passed on from one generation to the next; (2) his aims and aspirations for the future.
Harry S. Sullivan (1953; Hall and Lindzey, pp. 134–156)	Social psychological	Environmental (especially interpersonal relations)	The individual cannot exist apart from his interpersonal relationships because they are so interrelated. The personality is largely a function of the kinds of interpersonal relationships the person has had and is having in his life.
Kurt Lewin (1935; Hall and Lindzey, pp. 206–256)	Social-psychological (emphasis on models found in chemistry and physics)	Environmental (especially the psychological field or life space of the person—how the person views his environment and persons in it)	Personality and the behavior of a person are highly related to the situation (field or context) within which it operates at the given moment. You can represent the person in his environment for purposes of analysis by using mathematical and physical symbols.
Gordon Allport (1937; 1955; Hall and Lindzey, pp. 257–295)	Self and trait	Environmental (conscious control man has over his behavior)	Personality is in a constant state of growth and change; personality can be understood in terms of a series of individual and common traits.

THE AUTHORITARIAN PERSONALITY

In 1950, Adorno and others were studying personality patterns of people who were highly prejudiced. One of their major findings was that the group that was highly prejudiced tended to be characterized by a particular personality syndrome. This study and others have led one researcher to conclude that the prejudiced person does not merely have a particular negative attitude toward others, but actually represents a *prejudice-prone* personality structure.

The general findings indicate that prejudiced individuals tend to manifest: (a) "conventionalized" social conformity with deep ambivalence toward social norms and the authorities enforcing them; (b) a puritanical conscience; (c) repressed hostility toward parents; (d) admiration of power and strength; (e) advocacy of severe punishment; (f) status-anxiety; (g) repressed sexuality; (h) a rigid dichotomous style of thinking; (i) a tendency to distrust other people; (j) a tendency to view the world as evil and dangerous (Suchman *et al.*, 1958, p. 59).

TRADITION-, INNER-, AND OTHER-DIRECTED PERSONALITIES

Reisman (1953, 1954) believes that the basic personality of Americans is changing because of changes in social and economic conditions. Man's personality changes as he adapts himself to social change. Although he speaks of three basic directions of personality development, it is well to remember that all three are found in varying degrees in all people.

Tradition-Directed

The tradition-directed person's personality is largely determined by the demands, customs, and beliefs of his particular social group, especially those of his family. Such a person finds that his uniqueness is submerged and that he is governed moreso by the rules and pressures of the group. How a young man earns his living is decided by his father's present occupation. His social group membership dictates who he will court and marry. His education is informal and depends more on his family and neighbors than attendance at schools.

Today, few Americans are predominantly tradition-directed, whereas countries relatively untouched by industrialization and mass education tend to produce many persons whose behavior is externally directed. At what level would you place the tradition-directed person on Maslow's hierarchy of needs? Do you believe that such a person will have much opportunity to become self-actualizing?

Inner-Directed

The inner-directed person's personality is largely determined by the *internalized* demands, customs, and beliefs of his particular social group in the form of a strong conscience or superego. In other words, the guiding principles of socially acceptable behavior are within the person. Such a person is no longer completely at the mercy of external forces, pressures, and sanctions.

The basic idea behind the development of inner-directed persons is that living in a highly complex and mobile society requires the establishment of a strong internalized set of values to serve as a constant reminder of what is socially accepted behavior. Failure to behave according to the dictates of one's conscience results in the feelings of guilt. Therefore, there is less need for external controls. Furthermore, with his strong code of ethics, the inner-directed person knows what to do in the face of ever-changing requirements.

According to Reisman, (1953, p. 41) ". . . the inner-directed person has early incorporated a psychic gyroscope which is set going by his parents and can receive signals later from other authorities who resemble his parents. He goes through life less independent than he seems, obeying his internal piloting. Getting off course, whether in response to inner impulses or to the fluctuating voices of contemporaries, may lead to the feeling of guilt." Such persons when faced with decisions often decide what they ought to do is more important than what they really want to do.

Implicitly, such a person believes his real self is an unreliable guide to conduct, and so he represses, suppresses, or ignores his real self. Instead of following his real self, he habitually follows some inflexible moral code or some stringent ideals which he believes he must conform with. The net consequences of ignoring the real self in favor of the conscience and self-ideal is that the person may behave in a moral and exemplary fashion, but his real needs are ignored, and he will be perpetually thwarted. (Jourard, 1963, p. 159)

Other-Directed

The other-directed person's personality is largely determined by his parents and social group membership, but the number and kind of influencing groups is much larger. He is sensitive to changing social pressures and requirements and adapts readily to them. The typical young American of today seems to be other-directed. An example of this may be seen in the young people of the Peace Corps who elect to live within the foreign culture instead of seeking the companionship of other Americans. He seems to be at home everywhere and with everybody.

It may be said that the other-directed person finds stability in mobility by learning to adapt rapidly to change; the tradition-directed by staying home; the inner-directed by remaining in familiar surroundings or by following the dictates of his conscience when in new situations. A person with an other-directed personality may behave traditionally when living or working with one group, but if required to move or to change jobs, he will quickly adapt to new demands, customs, and beliefs. Thus, he gains the social approval of the new group. If he fails to adjust to the new situation rapidly, he tends to experience anxiety, which, in turn, spurs him on to increased efforts. He can adjust quickly because his parents did not emphasize a rigid code of behavior but rather stressed the skills necessary for getting along successfully with others.

The other-directed person appears to be very well adjusted. He may be popular and the recipient of much social approval. He is a good mixer. Nevertheless, it is possible that success was purchased at the price of ignoring and denying what he feels as an individual. Gradually, he may become incapable of establishing warm, long-term human relationships; his approach to life may become somewhat superficial because it is based mostly on a chameleon-like adjustment to his changing environment.

Regarding the interpretation of the three directions that personality development may take, it is necessary to remember that:

. . . there can be no such thing as a society or a person wholly dependent on tradition-direction, inner-direction, or other-direction: each of these modes of conformity is universal, and the question is always one of the degree to which an individual or a social group places reliance on one or another of the three available mechanisms. Thus, all human beings are inner-directed in the sense that, brought up as they are by people older than themselves, they have acquired and internalized some permanent orientations from them. And, conversely, all human beings are other-directed in the sense that they are oriented to the expectations of their peers. (Reisman, 1953)

According to Reisman, all of us have, in varying degrees, components of the three directions that help guide our behavior. However, the authors believe there is a fourth direction, *self-direction,* that characterizes the behavior of the self-actualizing person. The self-directed person achieves stability in motion by basing his decisions on what he believes and feels. Rogers (1961) explains it clearly:

In choosing what course of action to take in any situation, many people rely upon guiding principles, upon a code of action laid down by some group or institution, upon the judgment of others (from wife and friends to Emily Post), or upon the way they have behaved in some past situation. Yet as I observe the clients whose experiences in living have taught me so much, I find that increasingly such individuals are able to trust their total organismic reaction to a new situation because they discover to an ever-increasing degree that if they are open to their experience, doing what "feels right" proves to be a competent and trustworthy guide to behavior which is truly satisfying. (p. 91)

If society hopes to develop more young people who have trust in themselves, then parents and teachers must begin to encourage this attitude from early childhood on. The fortunate individual who feels that it is "OK" to trust himself as the best guide for behavior possesses a powerful tool for increasing his inner strength, self-confidence, and poise.

MORAL CHARACTER AND PERSONALITY

Moral character is an important determinant of behavior and, therefore, of personality. It generally refers to the system of values, ideas, and attitudes that helps a person decide what is right and wrong and what his duties and responsibilities ought to be. Certainly, a person with the attitude "all's fair in love and war" is likely to be consistently inconsiderate of others. In contrast, a person with the attitude "do unto others what you would have them do unto you" is likely to treat others with kindness and charity.

Table 8-3
Personality Directions

DOMINANT SOCIAL PERSONALITY	SOCIAL CONDITIONS	METHODS OF DEVELOPING PERSONALITY	PRINCIPLE EMOTIONAL SANCTIONS	REACTIONS TO CHANGE	CHILD-REARING PRACTICES
Tradition-directed	Little social mobility; industry and education; people born into a fixed caste	By established custom, caste, or ritual	Shame: Individual had a very well-defined role and he was not expected to deviate from that role	Tends to band together to preserve traditional patterns; tends to live in ghettos	Children trained to follow parental roles in society
Inner-directed	Dynamically growing society; new opportunities; industrial empires; America from 1900 to 1950	By psychological gyroscopes (set of values) which were intended to keep the individual straight on to his goals regardless of environmental stresses and changes.	Guilt: Failure to live up to his internalized code of behavior led to feelings of guilt (a built-in policeman)	Tends to ignore change because he is not dependent on his environment to guide his behavior.	Formal character training to develop strong conscience to serve as model for all future behavior
Other-directed	Great wealth, natural resources; production exceeds consumption; automation; more leisure time; America today	By developing great awareness of others; learn to get along with all groups; conform to changing pressures	Anxiety: Failure to obtain social approval from all his groups produces anxiety	Tends to adapt to changes, although perhaps superficially	Parents are not sure what to teach because they cannot predict rapid changes; schools and peer-group influence is greater than ever; teach social sensitivity and adjustment techniques.

Adapted from Reisman, 1953.

Peck and Havighurst (1967), in their attempt to define moral character, have hypothesized five different types based on the developmental stages of human beings from infancy to adulthood, as outlined in Table 8–4. Their study of moral character revealed the presence of all five types among high school students. While studying the five types of moral characters, the caution expressed by Reisman regarding personality classifications should be remembered: the question is always one of degree regarding personality characteristics or types.

Table 8–4
Developmental Levels of Character

CHARACTER TYPE	DEVELOPMENTAL PERIOD
1. Amoral	1. Infancy
2. Expedient	2. Early childhood
3. Conforming (or Irrational-Conscientious)	3. Later childhood
4. Rational-altruistic	4. Adolescence and adulthood

Adapted from Peck and Havighurst, 1967.

Amoral

The amoral person follows his whims and impulses, without regard for how this affects other people. He considers himself the center of the universe, and sees other people or objects as means to direct self-gratification. (Peck and Havighurst, 1967, p. 5) The amoral character gives the impression of a spoiled child who tries to get what he wants immediately without any regard for the welfare of others.

The following account by a prison psychiatrist illustrates the possible behaviors of an amoral character if he turns to a life of crime (McCord and McCord, 1964):

At eight, he began stealing from his grandmother, who had taken care of the abandoned child. He stole throughout adolescence, but still he graduated from high school. During service with the navy, B. T. rolled drunks, picked up homosexuals, and smoked "reefers." Following his discharge, B. T. passed from job to job, forging checks and staying with relatives until he stole from them. Once, after robbing his grandmother, he borrowed $300 from her and skipped town. At his mother's request, he was brought to jail.

After setting fire to his cell, he was transferred to a state hospital for observation. There, psychologist Weber began his counseling, but not soon enough to prevent B. T.'s escape. B. T. stole a horse, soon abandoning it for a stolen airplane. Although he had not studied flying, B. T. somehow got the plane off the ground and later landed it.

Returned to the State Hospital, B. T. boasted of his exploits, while Weber tried to reach him through counseling interviews. B. T. turned every friendly overture to his own advantage. When the psychologists—upon the patient's request—gave him a model airplane kit, B. T. secretly poured the kit's glue into "cokes" to make his own bootlegged liquor. Gradually, however, Weber made progress with the case. Under Sodium Amytal B. T. spoke about hatred of his parents and shock over his father's suicide.

After release from the prison hospital as legally "sane," B. T. went to the counselor's home three times each week. At the counselor's urging, the patient went to work and began to repay the airplane damage. Although he lost his first job, B. T. did well as a clerk in a grocery store. . . . The interviews tapered off as B. T. assumed more control over his life. (pp. 105–106)

Expedient

A person of this type is primarily self-centered, and considers other people's welfare and reactions only in order to gain his personal ends. He tends to get what he wants with a minimum of giving in return. He behaves in ways his society defines as moral, only as long as they suit his purpose. (Peck and Havighurst, 1967, p. 5) Hence, the expedient-oriented person may interest himself in the problems of others, but only if this brings him maximum gratification of his own wishes in the long run. He resembles the young child who needs external controls. When the teacher, policeman, or employer is not present, his behavior tends to become socially irresponsible. He lacks the internal controls or conscience to govern his own behavior properly.

Conforming

"This kind of person has one general, internalized principle: to do what others do, and what they say one 'should' do. He wants to and does conform to all the rules of his group." (Peck and Havighurst, 1967, p. 6) The conformist has internalized a few moral principles into a childlike conscience that is still dependent on external controls. He tends to follow rules in a black-or-white fashion with no middle ground for disagreement and with no exceptions to the rules. He lives by the letter of the law not by the spirit. "Righteousness" is following the rules. Unlike the expedient-oriented person, the conformist accepts all the rules as good even when contrary to his welfare or to that of other people. He differs from the amoralist in that he feels shame and guilt when his behavior departs from the expected.

Irrational-Conscientious

"In the adolescent or adult of this type, conformity to the group code is not the issue. Rather, it is conformity to a code he has internalized and believes in. . . . An act is 'good' or 'bad' to him because he defines it as such, not necessarily because it has positive or negative effects on others." (Peck and Havighurst, 1967, p. 7) The irrational-conscientious person is no longer dependent on external controls. In fact, in case of conflict between what the group believes to be right and what his own code (taken originally from those around him) tells him is right, he will tend to follow the dictates of "his" code. If he fails to follow the dictates of his code, he suffers from feelings of guilt. He believes that violations of the code mean that he has been untrue to himself. Hence, he is like a child who has accepted the rules of his parents as being "inalienable truths" without realizing that his parents are only human and that the rules were made for him to follow in certain situations, not in all situations and for all time.

Rational-Altruistic

The rational-altruistic type describes the highest level of moral maturity. Such a person not only has a stable set of moral principles by which he judges and directs his own behavior, he objectively assesses the results of an act in a given situation and approves it on the grounds of whether or not it serves others as well as himself. (Peck and Havighurst, 1967, p. 8) He does not blindly follow his principles or impose them on others. He lets circumstances alter cases. When confronted with decisions, he studies the situations carefully and mentally experiments with alternate solutions and their implications before deciding on the most appropriate course of action. His final actions depend on what he believes to be morally right in light of careful study, not because it is "the thing to do."

The rational-altruistic represents the self-actualizing person. He is the ideal toward which all of us aspire. In the words of Peck and Havighurst (1967) "Who would say that he prefers to live with people who cannot be reasoned with? Who would really want to live with people who are undependably erratic and unpredictably unstable? Who would choose to live with unscrupulous, untrustworthy people on whom one dare not turn his back? No one in his right mind, anywhere, seriously wants this kind of life." Based on observations of family life that produced rational-altruistic behavior in young people, Peck and Havighurst (1967) offer three recommendations:

1. If we wish others to be dependably stable, sincerely motivated, and ethically oriented, treat them in exactly these ways.

2. If we wish others to be genuinely friendly for any length of time, treat them in the most genuine, warmest, and kindest ways consistently.

3. If we wish others to be reasonable, rational, and effective in their thinking, provide them with a model of these behaviors and give them the opportunity and trust for them to develop these desirable characteristics. (p. 200)

Intermediate Summary

Some individuals display personality patterns that dominate most of their behavior. The authoritarian personality represents a prejudice-prone personality with unique characteristics. Reisman believes that there are three basic directions that personality direction may take: inner-, tradition-, and other-directed. Peck and Havighurst stress the crucial importance of moral character in determining personality.

Integrating Principles of Personality Development

Now that we have looked at some of the theories that psychologists use in attempting to study personality, the authors conclude this chapter with a few important integrating principles of personality development that seem to have support from most psychologists regardless of the particular theory they follow.

PERSONALITY IS RELATED TO EXPERIENCES WITH PARENTS AND SIBLINGS. As we mentioned earlier, it is out of our interactions with those who are close to us (usually our parents) that we learn: (a) who we are (our self-concept); (b) what is important to us (our values); (c) how to satisfy certain needs (our motives); (d) ways to solve problems (thinking); and (e) ways to handle our feelings (emotions). The sum total of all these would be our total personality.

THE CENTRAL CORE OF OUR PERSONALITY DEVELOPS VERY EARLY IN LIFE. Most psychologists would agree that our basic personality structure is formed very early in life (probably within the first five years). This does not mean, however, that our personality always stays the same. As we will see in Chapter 10, for some individuals who have developed inadequate personality patterns that get them in trouble, personalities may undergo drastic changes during treatment in a mental hospital or clinic.

PERSONALITY PATTERNS CAN CHANGE. Even though much of our personality is set early in life, experiences in later life do have an influence on our behavior. Sometimes a serious event, such as a death in the family or failure or success in life, may bring about drastic changes in personality patterns.

Our discussion on the development of healthy personalities in Chapter 1 offers further ideas on how personality patterns can and do change in the self-actualizing person. As we shall later see in Chapter 11, even mentally ill persons often undergo very dramatic personality changes as the result of various treatment programs.

SOCIETY AND CULTURE HAVE A DIRECT INFLUENCE ON OUR PERSONALITY. As mentioned earlier in this chapter, our culture (particularly groups with whom we identify) has a great influence on our behavior. Such institutions as the church, the political and economic system, and the educational systems also play a major role in the development of human personality.

APPLICATION

Living with Yourself

There can hardly be a more important subject than the study of yourself. The questions that haunt us are, "What am I really like? Beneath the surface, what are my abilities, talents, and strengths?" Yet it seems that educators throw everything into the curriculum except self-understanding.

Psychologists use tests, questionnaires, and interviews to evaluate personalities. However, most of us cannot afford the expense of such a personality evaluation. Instead we must depend on other ways of evaluating ourselves.

SELF-APPRAISAL

All of us are constantly evaluating and modifying our behavior in the light of successes and failures. All of us could write extensively about our perceptual, conceptual, and attitudinal selves. We all have some ideas concerning our ego strength, the power of our superego, and the vitality of our id. What may bother us is the accuracy of our self-appraisal. Are we realistic? Have we overestimated our abilities? The answers lie in our future interpersonal relations and in the tasks required of us as we seek to accomplish our goals.

The key point is that self-appraisal will help us to do a better job in the future. As Rogers (1947) states:

It would appear that when all the ways in which the individual perceives himself are accepted into the organized conscious concept of the self, then this achievement is accompanied by feelings of comfort and freedom from tension which are experienced as psychological adjustment. (p. 358)

In other words, the process of self-analysis allows one to bring together all that one knows about himself. So informed, one is less likely to commit many errors, or to take on impossible tasks.

IMPROVING YOURSELF

What you think you are—whether true or false—is a product of your past. What you can become, then, depends on your future experiences. An active person—taking on new responsibilities, learning new competencies, undergoing new emotional feelings—is one who is in the process of constructing a more dynamic, exciting, and profound personality.

Remember you are the architect of your own personality. The building blocks for the personality structure contain diversities of experiences. The more you get involved in the world and the more you accept its challenges, the greater will be the opportunities to test out what you believe to be true about yourself and to build your personality.

Living with Others

Perhaps the discussion of personality has given you at least a slightly different perspective about other people, and you now have a better understanding of why two personalities (even those of identical twins) are never the same.

**TECHNIQUES FOR BETTER UNDERSTANDING
THE PERSONALITIES OF OTHERS**

How can you better understand the personalities of others? Part of this task has already been accomplished when you begin to realize how we all develop our unique personality styles. However, there are certain techniques (some of them still exploratory) that seem to help people become more sensitive and empathetic toward their fellowmen. Let's look at some of these now.

Sensitivity Training

A rather new approach to helping people become more understanding of their fellowman is called sensitivity training. Essentially, this involves a group of people who interact together on many different levels over a period of time. On one level, they may interact with each other on a purely physical basis by touching one another without any verbal communication. On another level, they may speak very openly to each other, telling each other just how they feel. Although these techniques are still highly exploratory, they seem to help people work better together, particularly in business and educational organizations. (Gunther, 1968; Bradford, Gibb, and Benne, 1964)

Self-Disclosure

Another approach that seems to help develop a better integrated personality, which in turn helps one become more effective in understanding others, is the process of self-disclosure. This involves letting yourself go and letting your feelings show. You stop hiding your feelings and attitudes. People who are more open, more self-disclosing, tend to be more self-actualizing. (Jourard, 1964)

Role Playing

Another technique often used in helping people understand the personalities of others is through role playing. Here, you take the part of another person (a teacher, husband, wife, mother, father, or child) and try to see how the world is viewed from his or her point of view.

Travel

Even though this is not commonly recognized as a method for understanding the personality of others, there is no doubt that persons who travel to other parts of the United States and the world will tend to be more understanding and accepting of their fellowmen. By seeing how different cultural and racial groups differ, as a result of many factors (weather, religion, cultural mores and customs, political systems), one becomes more tolerant and aware that all people really have the same basic motives, but their ways of satisfying these motives may differ.

UNDERSTANDING THE PERSONALITIES OF YOUR FAMILY MEMBERS

How can you better understand the personality patterns within your own family? You probably have a fairly good idea of the more consistent patterns and will want to expand this understanding so that more effective communication can occur.

One of the authors' parents, when he was a child, had a monthly "gripe session," during which each member of the family had a chance to express his feelings about the actions of the others. These sessions often seemed to clear the air. Each had a better understanding of the likes and dislikes of the others.

When traveling together a family has opportunities to see each other in new environments and sometimes in a new light. Discussions in the car can give all of the family members new insight about each other's feelings and personalities.

When do you get a chance to observe your family members in different roles? Have you ever seen your father as he plays the worker role on his job? Have you ever observed your mother in any role besides that of mother? One way to help better understand each other's personality is to observe each play the different roles required: student, employee, boyfriend or girlfriend, member of a peer group, and so on.

Families who sometimes work and play together have an additional opportunity to interact. Working on a family project as a team often allows a chance to freely express one's feelings.

Family arguments, although not to be encouraged to the point of a daily occurrence, often allow for an expression of feelings that have been held back for a period of time; as a result, they often bring better understanding of the needs that we each have.

Living with Society

Living with society refers to our ever-increasing need to live with people in other cultural groups and institutions such as schools, churches, places of employment, and government agencies. In a sense, each of these segments of society tends to have a distinct personality; that is, it has its ways of getting things done, its ways of rewarding desirable behavior, and its ways of punishing those who violate established rules. Group membership means that one is willing to accept certain ways of behaving and thinking. Should one wish to change some of the characteristics of the social group, one will follow the established procedures for change.

LIVING IN A SMALLER WORLD

We expect people from other parts of the world to behave differently than we do, but these differences are not really important. If we expect to understand others, we must get away from superficial characteristics such as eating habits and ways of talking. For example, a gaucho from Argentina may look strange to us, but change his dress to that of a Texas cowpoke and substitute a lasso for his lariat, and, ipso facto, we have an American. Or, take an Indian Guru to a barber, buy him a suit from a local department store, and he becomes indistinguishable in a crowd of Americans.

In other words, superficial behaviors are merely different ways of achieving the basic human needs common to all of us. We should expect people from different cultural backgrounds to react differently to identical situations. If we wish to avoid shock or feelings of discomfort when living with persons from a different background we should study the experiences on which their behavior is based, namely, their history and their present culture.

The inner experiences of other people cannot be observed directly unless we have lived with them and shared in their experiences.

Because behaviors also depend on the particular social context, we expect people to display patterns peculiar to the situation. The behaviors of teachers and students are determined by social expectancies. Although we are able to characterize those we know personally in terms of their distinctive traits, most of our school contacts are with strangers. Strangers are usually conceived in terms of stereotypes. A *stereotype* is a rough way of grouping other people together on the basis of some preconceived and prejudiced idea of what they are like. If we allow stereotyped thinking to guide our behavior toward others we are bound to make many incorrect assumptions and to find ourselves in disagreeable circumstances.

It is informative to note that in one study, schoolchildren's perceptions of their teachers' feelings toward them was significantly related to their self-perception. The child with a favorable self-image tended to perceive his teacher's feelings toward him more favorably. Furthermore, the more positive the child's perception of his teacher's feelings, the better was his academic achievement, and the more desirable was his behavior as rated by the teacher. (Davidson and Lang, 1965)

Final Summary

Personality is the study of the factors within the individual that influence his characteristic ways of behaving, thinking, and feeling. The different theories select and measure what they believe to be the major personality factors. Self, psychoanalytic, trait, and learning are representative of the major theoretical approaches to the study of personality.

Some individuals display personality patterns that dominate most of their behavior. Such personality patterns include: the authoritarian; the inner-, tradition- or other-directed; and moral character.

There are some important integrating principles of personality that seem to have support from most psychologists regardless of their personality theory: (1) Personality is a result, largely, of our experiences in the home with parents and siblings. (2) The central core of our personality develops very early in life. (3) Personality patterns can change. (4) Our society or culture has a direct and important influence on our personality.

Chapter References

Allport, G. W. *Personality: a psychological interpretation.* New York: Holt, 1937.
Allport, G. W. *Becoming: basic considerations for a psychology of personality.* New Haven: Yale University Press, 1955.

Asch, S. Opinions and social pressure. *Scientific American*, 1955, 193, 31–35.

Bloom, B. S. *Stability and change in human characteristics.* New York: Wiley, 1964.

Bradford, L. P., Gibb, J. R., and Benne, K. D. (eds.). *T-group theory and laboratory method.* New York: Wiley, 1964.

Davidson, Helen H. and Lang, G. Children's perceptions of their teacher's feelings toward them related to self-perception, school achievement, and behavior. In D. E. Hamacheck (ed.), *The self in growth, teaching and learning.* Englewood Cliffs, N.J.: Prentice-Hall, 1965. Pp. 424–439.

Dennis, W. Causes of retardation among institutional children: Iran. *Journal of Genetic Psychology*, 1960, 96, 47–59.

Deutsch, M. The disadvantaged child and the learning process. In A. H. Passow (ed.), *Education in depressed areas.* New York: Columbia University, 1963.

Dollard, J. and Miller, N. E. *Personality and psychotherapy.* New York: McGraw-Hill, 1950.

Guilford, J. P. *Personality,* New York: McGraw-Hill, 1959.

Gunther, B. *Sense relaxation below your mind.* New York: Collier Books, 1968.

Hall, C. *A primer of Freudian psychology.* Cleveland: World, 1954.

Hall, S., and Lindzey, G. *Theories of personality.* New York: Wiley, 1957.

Hamacheck, D. E. (ed.). *The self in growth, teaching and learning.* Englewood Cliffs, N.J.: Prentice-Hall, 1965.

Hodges, H. M., Jr. The folk-urban-suburban continuum: a conceptual overview of America yesterday, today, and tomorrow. In W. W. Kallenbach and H. M. Hodges (eds.), *Education and society.* Columbus, Ohio: Charles E. Merrill, 1963.

Jourard, S. M. *The transparent self.* New York: Van Nostrand, 1964.

Jung, C. G. *The integration of personality.* New York: Farrar and Rinehart, 1939.

Lewin, K. *A dynamic theory of personality.* New York: McGraw-Hill, 1935.

Maslow, A. H. *Toward a psychology of being.* New York: Van Nostrand, 1962.

McCord, W. and McCord, Joan. *The psychopath.* Princeton, N.J.: Van Nostrand, 1964.

Peck, R. F., and Havighurst, R. J. *The psychology of character development.* New York: Wiley Science Editions, 1967.

Reisman, D., Glazer, N., and Denney, R. *The lonely crowd.* New York: Doubleday, 1953.

Reisman, D. *Selected essays from individualism reconsidered.* New York: Doubleday, 1954.

Rogers, C. R. Some observations on the organization of personality. *American Psychologist*, 1947, 2, 358–368.

———. *On becoming a person.* Boston: Houghton Mifflin, 1961.

Sheldon, W. H., and Stevens, S. S. *The varieties of temperament.* New York: Harper, 1942.

Suchman, E. A., *et al.* Desegregation: some propositions and research suggestions. New York: Anti-Defamation League of B'nai B'rith, 1958.

Sullivan, H. S. *The interpersonal theory of psychiatry.* New York: Norton, 1953.

Recommended Further Readings

Paperback Books

Allport, G. W. *Becoming.* New Haven: Yale University Press, 1955.

Argyle, M. *The psychology of interpersonal behavior.* Baltimore: Penguin Books, 1967.

Aronoff, J. *Psychological needs and cultural systems.* Princeton, N.J.: Van Nostrand, 1967.

Freud, S. *Psychopathology of everyday life.* New York: Mentor Books, 1914.

Honigmann, J. J. *Culture and personality.* New York: Harper, 1954.

Jahoda, Marie, and Warren, N. (eds.). *Attitudes.* Baltimore: Penguin Books, 1966.

Jersild, A. T. *In search of self.* New York: Teachers College, Columbia University, 1952.

Kaplan, B. (ed.). *Studying personality cross-culturally.* Evanston, Ill.: Row, Peterson, 1961.

Lazarus, R. S. *Personality and adjustment.* Englewood Cliffs, N.J.: Prentice-Hall, 1963.

Linton, R. *The cultural background of personality.* New York: Appleton-Century-Croft, 1945.

Loehlin, J. C. *Computer models of personality.* New York: Random House, 1968.

McCurdy, H. G. *Personality and science.* Princeton, N.J.: Van Nostrand, 1965.

Nixon, R. E. *The art of growing.* New York: Random House, 1962.

Nuttin, J. *Psychoanalysis and personality.* New York: Mentor-Omega, 1953.

Queen, S. A., Habenstein, R. W., and Adams, J. B. *The family in various cultures.* Chicago: Lippincott, 1961.

Royce, J. R. *The encapsulated man.* Princeton, N.J.: Van Nostrand, 1964.

Semeonoff, B. (ed.) *Personality assessment.* Baltimore: Penguin Books, 1966.

Southwell, E. A., and Merbaum, M. (eds.). *Personality.* Belmont, Calif.: Brooks-Cole, 1964.

Tallent, N. *Psychological perspectives on the person.* Princeton, N.J.: Van Nostrand, 1967.

Van Kaam, A., C. S. Sp. *Religion and personality.* Garden City, N.Y.: Doubleday, 1968.

White, R. W. *Lives in progress.* New York: Holt, Rinehart and Winston, 1966.

Whiting, J. W., and Child, I. L. *Child training and personality.* New Haven: Yale University Press, 1953.

Hardcover Books

Allport, G. W. *Pattern and growth in personality.* New York: Holt, Rinehart, and Winston, 1961.

Bischof, L. J. *Interpreting personality theories.* New York: Harper, 1964.

Blum, G. S. *Psychoanalytic theories of personality.* New York: McGraw-Hill, 1953.

Burton, A., and Harris, R. E. (eds.). *Clinical studies of personality.* Vol. 2. New York: Harper & Row, 1955.

Byrne, D. *An introduction to personality: a research approach.* Englewood Cliffs, N.J.: Prentice-Hall, 1966.

Cameron, N. *Personality development and psychopathology: a dynamic approach.* Boston: Houghton Mifflin, 1963.

Coleman, J. C. *Personality dynamics and effective behavior.* Glenview, Ill.: Scott Foresman, 1960.

De Levita, D. J. *The concept of identity.* Paris: Mouton, 1965.

Dreger, R. *Fundamentals of personality.* Philadelphia: Lippincott, 1962.

Endleman, R. *Personality and social life.* New York: Random House, 1967.

Gordon, J. E. *Personality and behavior.* New York: Macmillan, 1963.

Guilford, J. P. *Personality.* New York: McGraw-Hill, 1959.

Harris, I. D. *The promised seed.* London: Free Press of Glencoe, 1964.

Jourard, S. M. *Personal adjustment* (2nd ed.). New York: Macmillan, 1963.

Kluckhohn, C., and Murray, H. A., and Schneider, D. M. (eds.). *Personality in nature, society and culture* (2nd ed.). New York: Knopf, 1953.

Lundin, R. W. *Personality.* New York: Macmillan, 1961.

Maddi, S. R. *Personality theories: a comparative analysis.* Homewood, Ill.: Dorsey Press, 1968.

Maher, B. A. (ed.). *Progress in experimental personality research.* Vol. 4. New York: Academic Press, 1967.

McCurdy, H. G. *The personal world.* New York: Harcourt, Brace and World, 1961.

Millon, T. *Theories of psychopathology.* Philadelphia: Saunders, 1967.

Rethlingshafer, Dorothy. *Motivation as related to personality.* New York: McGraw-Hill, 1963.

Sahakian, W. S. (ed.). *Psychology of personality: readings in theory.* Chicago: Rand McNally, 1965.

Sanford, N. *Self and society.* New York: Atherton, 1966.

Sarason, I. G. *Personality: an objective approach.* New York: Wiley, 1966.

Shibutani, T. *Society and personality.* Englewood Cliffs, N.J.: Prentice-Hall, 1961.

Smith, H. C. *Personality development.* New York: McGraw-Hill, 1968.

Stagner, R. *Psychology of personality* (3rd ed.). New York: McGraw-Hill, 1961.

Toman, W. *Family constellation.* New York: Springer, 1961.

Chapter 9 Coping with Normal Personality Problems

Chapter Outline

Study Guide

This chapter will be easier to read. The topics are based on familiar life experiences and are relatively few in number. This permits the authors to use a more narrative style of writing and to provide more illustrative examples. Understanding this chapter thoroughly is important because it is very closely related to the following chapter.

REVIEW

Glance at the major chapter headings in the Table of Contents.

PREVIEW

Learn the main ideas and structure of the chapter before you read (read prelude, chapter outline and headings, and all summaries).

READING

Read the chapter through, following the study guide suggestions (adjust your speed of reading to difficulty levels; check mark topics not understood; reread after reading the entire chapter; after major topics, stop reading and repeat everything you can remember). Practice outlining as you read the chapter.

REVIEW

Review by practicing recall. Use your outline of the chapter. Use the book's chapter outline. Reread all summaries. Reread the chapter.

STUDY TIP

Making up test questions. The practice of constructing and answering your own examination questions is an excellent study and review technique. It also prepares you psychologically for taking tests in class. By now you know enough about the organization, contents, and style of the book to make up good test questions. With practice you will begin to predict the questions asked in classroom examinations.

Prelude

A part of everyday living involves coping with problems that we face. Sometimes we are successful in dealing with problems that produce tension, strain, and anxiety within each of us. At other times we deal more ineffectively with these situations. This chapter should help you learn to understand that:

1. Everyone sometimes gets involved in situations that produce personality problems.
2. There are both effective and ineffective ways of solving these problems.
3. There are built-in defense mechanisms we tend to employ in these problem situations.
4. Sometimes defense mechanisms are rational, but often they are irrational, so that they lead to feelings of inadequacy.

5. If carried too far, defense mechanisms can lead to more serious personality problems.

6. The best thing we can do to cope successfully with personality problems is to move on toward becoming self-actualizing persons.

Students' Viewpoints

The psychiatrist of a large western university recently stated, "One out of nine [college students] is sufficiently emotionally disturbed to need hospitalization, or extensive and intensive psychiatric treatment." (Paulsen, 1964, p. 96)

Students in the authors' classes were asked to describe problem areas that they faced. Some students described their major problems as follows:

My chief problem is my parents. They have very old-fashioned ideas, especially my mother. I cannot sit down with her and talk about sex because she changes the subject. She is very jealous about any boys liking me; she also hates the idea of me wanting to leave home.

I am not sure of what I am or what I'm going to be. Everything is confused. I want something out of life, not just enough to get by. I would like to get myself straightened out on many matters: religion, overcoming shyness with others whom I first meet, why my parents won't realize that I'm old enough to know what's right and what's wrong and to decide for myself instead of them restricting me to things I want to do and therefore missing the chances to solve some of my problems. I have to learn who I am and what I want.

Figure 9-1
Learning to cope successfully with problems is a major step toward self-actualization. Here is a gentleman, young at heart, exchanging ideas with another college freshman. Mr. Smith says, "I feel it is necessary to contribute to my society." In the face of such spirit, our "impossible" problems, become, somehow, a little less unsolvable.

Photo by Charles Gibbs

I love someone that doesn't love me. I am getting so that I don't care about anything anymore. I am becoming more withdrawn from life and other people.

It seems clear that college students have a special set of problem areas, partly because of their age and partly because of their circumstances. How you cope with these problems will govern how you will solve your problems later in life, in most cases.

WHY IS IT IMPORTANT?

Throughout life you will be faced with problem situations. One cannot avoid stress and frustrations. Facing problems and learning to cope with them successfully is a necessary condition if we are to continue to move toward self-actualization.

Efforts toward self-actualization, to become whatever we are capable of becoming, require that our creative energies be directed toward activities that will provide us with the competencies needed to achieve our goals. However, continuous and prolonged stress tends to wear us down and to tie up our creative energies. Constant frustrations block our progress by narrowing our perceptual field to what could be relatively insignificant matters. In other words, persons in the midst of constant frustration can drown themselves, literally, in a cup of water!

BASIC THEORY AND RESEARCH

Problems in Satisfying the Hierarchy of Needs

Basically, all personality problems occur as a result of our attempts to satisfy those basic needs expressed by Maslow on his stepladder, or hierarchy, of needs. To review these briefly, see Figure 9-2.

Thus, the individual is constantly trying to meet his needs. In our society, in general, the lower needs are satisfied to a relatively adequate degree. That is, most people in our society have enough food, water, and the like to meet the basic physiological needs. As you move up the ladder, you, as a college student, may find problems in satisfying the higher needs.

Barriers to Goal Attainment

What kinds of barriers prevent us from satisfying certain needs? The barriers to the attainment of a certain goal that will satisfy a particular need or set of needs would include: ourselves, other people, or factors in the environment.

Figure 9-2
Hierarchy of Needs (Stepladder
Theory)

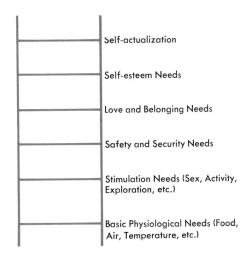

Self-actualization

Self-esteem Needs

Love and Belonging Needs

Safety and Security Needs

Stimulation Needs (Sex, Activity,
Exploration, etc.)

Basic Physiological Needs (Food,
Air, Temperature, etc.)

OURSELVES AS BARRIERS TO GOAL ATTAINMENT

It has been said about some people that they are their own worst enemies.
Many often behave in ways that suggest that they are working against themselves.
A male student with long hair came to the authors very depressed because he
couldn't stand living at home any more. "I have to move out or I'm going to
have a nervous breakdown," he said. "Why can't you move?" they asked. "Because I can't get a job due to my long hair." "Well, why not cut your hair?"
they suggested. "Are you kidding!" was his angry reply.

Frequently the successful satisfaction of a particular need requires that we
do something about ourselves, that we change our behavior in some way.

OTHER PERSONS AS BARRIERS TO GOAL ATTAINMENT

Often, other people interfere, sometimes on purpose, other times inadvertently,
with the satisfaction of your needs. This occurs in the business world, when for
example, there may be only one promotion and several persons to fill the vacancy.
It may happen to you when you like a girl very much, but she is engaged to
another.

ENVIRONMENTAL BARRIERS TO NEED SATISFACTION

Certain rules, regulations, or laws of society often prevent us from the immediate satisfaction of our needs. Many criminals spend years in jail because
they overlooked this truth. They may have needed money for a new car right
away, and robbed a bank in order to get some satisfaction of their self-esteem
needs. Less dramatic is the willingness of college students to spend years in
college to achieve goals that they also would like to enjoy much sooner.

THE EFFECTS OF BARRIERS ON THE INDIVIDUAL

The results of being blocked in attaining satisfaction of a need will vary according to the importance of the need; the *length of deprivation* (how long the
person has been blocked); the nature of the barrier (within himself, another

person, or within the environment); and the consequences if he does not have the need satisfied.

Generally, however, people will display one or more of the following responses if they are blocked in their attainment of a particular goal: frustration, anxiety, hostility, or guilt. As was mentioned earlier, these emotional reactions tend to make us feel uncomfortable so we attempt to reduce the strength of these feelings.

Conflicts

Conflicts result when there are two desirable goals, or two undesirable goals, one of which we must choose, or when one goal contains both negative and positive aspects. In a conflict, we are threatened with frustration regardless of which course we choose. However, although conflicts are inevitable, there are techniques and information that will help us to resolve conflicts more successfully.

CONFLICTS ARE LEARNED

In the chapter on learning principles, we found that our basic attitudes toward activities, people, and material objects were developed gradually through the process of rewards and punishments. For example, we *learn* to prefer steak over fish, sports over music, or education over immediate rewards of getting a job. A conflict occurs when we have to choose between a steak dinner and going to a baseball game, because we do not have the money or the time for both activities. When a college student is torn between love of country, which requires serving in the armed forces, and love of God, which requires love for all humanity, he too has a dilemma.

GOAL GRADIENTS

To understand our behavior in conflict situations we first must understand how goal gradients operate. A *goal* refers to an object, place, or activity that we may either like or dislike or toward which we have mixed feelings. A *gradient* refers to the amount of feeling felt or expressed as we approach or retreat from a goal. If we have a date with an exciting member of the opposite sex, our emotions gradually build up to a high peak. The positive goal gradient shows that the tendency to approach the desired object increases more sharply the closer we get to the desired object. (See Figure 9-3.)

The effects of the negative goal gradient can be illustrated by the behavior of a student who hates school. The closer he gets to the school, the strength of the negative feelings increases more and more rapidly. It is important to note that the negative goal gradient increases more rapidly than the positive. Figure 9-4 further illustrates this point.

APPROACH-APPROACH CONFLICT

An approach-approach conflict occurs when there are two desirable, but mutually exclusive, goals. There are two excellent marriage partners, but bigamy

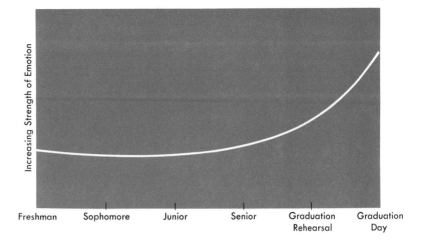

Figure 9-3
Positive Goal Gradient

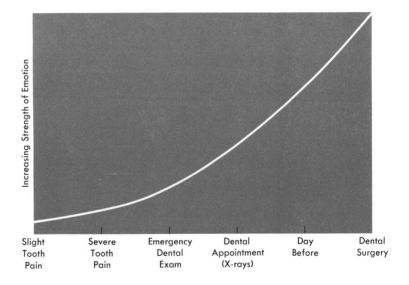

Figure 9-4

Negative Goal Gradient

is unlawful. A student is offered two jobs with good potential, but he cannot be in two places at the same time. An approach-approach conflict is illustrated in Figure 9-5. A young man's desires to go to a movie and a ball game are equally strong; therefore, the attraction of each goal is equally strong and he is caught in a conflict situation.

The young man at position (A) is midway between going to the movies (goal 1) and the ball game (goal 2). Any behavior that would bring him closer to either goal will resolve the conflict. The behavior may consist of moving closer physically to one of the goals or thinking more about the benefits of one over the other. Typical major approach-approach conflicts are choice of career and selection of marriage partners.

277

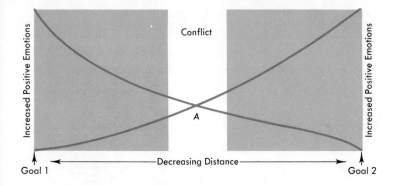

Figure 9-5
Approach-Approach Conflict

AVOIDANCE-AVOIDANCE CONFLICT

In the avoidance-avoidance conflict the person is faced with two unpleasant situations so arranged that moving away from one brings the other closer (Figure 9-6). A husband dislikes his job, and his wife is continually nagging him. The happiest moment in his miserable existence arrives when he is midway between his place of work and his home. Some students find living at home intolerable and college work meaningless. Their happiest times seem to be those when they have just cut classes.

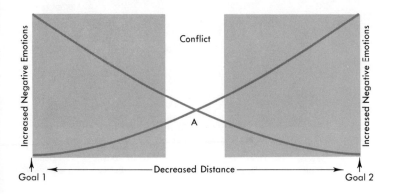

Figure 9-6
Avoidance-Avoidance Conflict

A common resolution to avoidance-avoidance conflict occurs when the person escapes the entire situation. A husband may simply disappear, a student may join the armed forces, or a coed may agree quickly to a marriage proposal. However, there are other solutions. A person may tolerate a temporarily bad situation in expectations of rich future rewards. Or he may find that one situation changes and becomes more agreeable and pleasant.

APPROACH-AVOIDANCE CONFLICT

Many goals are at once desirable and undesirable. A girl likes candy, but doesn't want to get fat. A student wants a college education, but he doesn't like to study. The attitude of liking and disliking something at the same time is called *ambiva-*

278

lence. Ambivalent attitudes are common; surgery, bad-tasting medicines, employment, and feelings of love and hate toward parents and friends suggest examples.

Have you ever heard of a person being stood up on the day of her wedding? Figure 9-7 illustrates what can happen. A couple begin to date because they

Figure 9-7
Approach-Avoidance Conflict

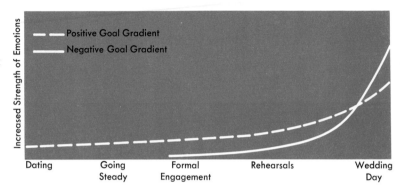

like each other (positive feelings). After going steady, they announce their formal engagement (the positive goal gradient increases). Finally, the preparations for the wedding begin. At this moment, close to the point of no return, the negative goal gradient may begin. The husband-to-be begins to realize the responsibilities of marriage and raising a family. The future bride realizes that she will no longer be able to say "No" to his advances, that child-birth is now a definite possibility and that she may not have picked the best man. Because the negative goal gradient increases more rapidly than the positive, there is a possibility that the negative may become stronger prior to the wedding. To avoid this possibility, the couple may need strong support and encouragement from their families and friends.

Consequences of Unresolved Frustrations and Conflicts

If every need could be satisfied, then there would be no frustration, no conflicts. But we do not live in an ideal world. There are always obstacles to overcome, deficiencies among our competencies, and difficult choices to be made. All of our problems cannot be resolved successfully all of the time. Even the healthiest people psychologically are confronted with feelings of guilt, aggression, depression, and anxiety resulting from failure to resolve all their frustrations.

The fact that all people suffer the consequences of unresolved frustrations and conflicts doesn't mean that they all suffer to the same degree or as frequently. We must bear in mind that:

1. People react differently to the same stressful situation.

2. Some have developed a high toleration; they can withstand higher levels of anguish, pain, or failure than others.

3. Some have developed greater intellectual and emotional competencies so that they can solve problems more successfully than others.

4. Some are fortunate in that their life situation produces fewer frustrations and conflicts because of richer resources and helpful friends and associates.

5. As a result of their greater understanding of human behavior, some do not suffer needlessly over shortcomings that are common to us all.

Intermediate Summary

Facing problems and learning to cope with them successfully is a necessary condition for moving toward self-actualization. Personality problems result from attempts to satisfy physiological and psychological needs. Barriers that can block the satisfaction of needs are ourselves, other people, or environmental factors. In some situations, conflicts result when we are threatened with frustration no matter on which course of action we decide. Conflicts are inevitable, either approach-approach, avoidance-avoidance, or approach-avoidance.

Defenses Against the Consequences of Frustration and Conflicts

Feelings of guilt, hostility, depression, and anxiety are destructive to positive self-concepts, much like germs are destructive to our bodies. Just as our bodies have physiological defenses to combat bacterial invasion, so do we have psychological defenses to ward off self-destructive tendencies. These psychological forces are called *reality-oriented defense mechanisms.*

REALITY-ORIENTED DEFENSE MECHANISMS

Reality oriented defense mechanisms have three principle characteristics:

1. They are ways of maintaining self-esteem in situations in which we feel inadequate or have already failed.

2. They are ways of reducing feelings of anxiety, guilt, hostility, and depression.

3. They are ways of convincing people that we are really adequate and worthwhile.

It is well to keep in mind that reality-oriented defense behavior is geared to protecting the self against emotional hurt and not to problem solving. At this point the original problem, such as getting a job or a date, is no longer the important matter. We feel hurt. We are under the stress of attack, and it is the hurt that we are trying to overcome.

In discussing reality-oriented defense mechanisms, it is convenient to look at them in terms of three modes of coping with the consequences of failure: verbal-oriented defenses, action-oriented defenses, and emotion-oriented defenses.

VERBAL-ORIENTED DEFENSES

Rationalization

By rationalization is meant the process of attaching what we believe to be logical reasons to our behavior. Very early in life we all learned that reasons for behavior can be just as important as behavior itself. Because people interpret behavior in so many different ways, it is important to be able to correct mistaken perceptions by providing appropriate rationalizations. For example, suppose a father had threatened his child with a spanking the next time he broke a window with his baseball, and the next day the baseball crashed through the window. As the father began to spank him, the boy remarked, "If I hadn't blocked the ball that broke the window, the ball would have hit little Mary on the head." The father immediately embraced his son and praised him. That child learned that, at times, actions are not as important as the reasons for them. What couple hasn't experienced the anxiety of suddenly realizing that their petting has lasted way past the time to be back home. By the time they arrive home, a great number of rationalizations have been processed and a "good" one selected.

One of the authors recalls that after his first year in college he was to be dropped because of poor grades unless he could explain adequately the *reasons* for his failure. The college accepted his reasons for failure and allowed him to continue his studies. In other words, the college agreed that the reasons were good enough to excuse the poor scholarship. Thus, the author saved face, removed emotional hurts, and remained a worthy person in the eyes of his peers and relatives.

Undoing

In this defense we reduce our emotional hurts, such as guilt and anxiety, by admitting the disapproved desire, idea, or behavior; apologizing for our misdeeds; or offering compensation for the damage we have done. The first step in undoing is to admit to one's self and to others our transgressions. One study found that children who readily admitted their faults were judged by their teacher to be more mentally healthy than children who admitted few or no faults. (Taylor and Combs, 1952) In other words, self-actualizing persons tend to be those who are able to look at everything about themselves, even what they don't like, without distortion. Religion has long recognized the value of undoing for mental health by encouraging its members to confess their sins and to do penance.

Fantasy

An immediate approach to many conflicts and frustrations is the use of fantasy. At first, we can tentatively seek solutions in fantasy. During fantasy, we can transcend all physical and personal barriers. We can, through the use of imagination, seek the unusual and the innovative. Such anticipation of future success can boost our sagging motivations during periods of prolonged stress such as serving in the armed forces, attending college, or waiting for a promotion. Of course, we must be careful not to use fantasy as a crutch too frequently, or at the expense of not understanding or improving our behavior.

ACTION-ORIENTED DEFENSES

Acting Out

One way to reduce mounting tension, especially that resulting from frustration, is to give it direct physical or verbal expression. However, acting out should be expressed within socially acceptable limits. Among the acceptable outlets are physical training or any activity requiring a large expenditure of energy. The actual expression of justifiable anger is reality-oriented. A person should show anger when he has been deliberately and maliciously lied to. A student should become resentful when his test scores have been unfairly downgraded. As you may remember from the chapter on learning, a high level of tension or anxiety usually interferes with effective problem solving.

Identification

Identification is the process of imitating the behaviors and values of persons or groups we admire and respect. A child's behavior resembles that of his parents because he identifies himself with them. In other words, parents serve as ideal models of how to behave in many life situations. As we develop socially we take on other roles of many persons such as older *siblings* (brothers or sisters), teachers, or coaches. The moral and ethical codes of organizations such as clubs, churches, schools, and our country help us too. Through identification we may learn new ways of coping with problems and emotional hurts by imitating the behavior of others in similar situations.

Compensation

All of us, at one time or another during our lives, have attempted to excel in some area essentially because we felt inadequate in another area; psychologists call this action-oriented defense mechanism *compensation*. That is, the person compensates for being inadequate in one area by becoming proficient in another.

When he was a high school student, one of the authors remembers some of the students in the Honor Society who were achieving very well in scholastic work essentially because they were rather poor in athletics. Often students who are doing very poorly in school may at the same time be outstanding officers in student government. It seems sometimes that our educational system forces

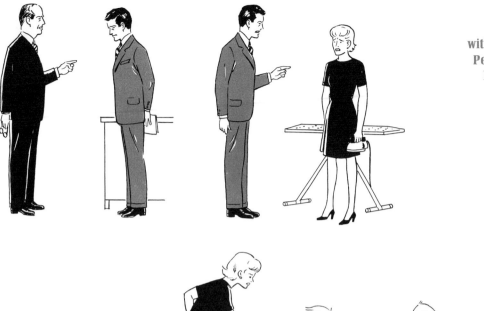

Figure 9-8
Displacement

students who are not successful in our academic programs to compensate by turning to sports, hot rods, or other pursuits.

Frequently one of the compensatory reactions people engage in when they are having difficulty in reaching a goal is to increase their effort and to work harder. We often see this in students who have reading problems; they are willing to work five or ten times harder in order to succeed in school, rather than fail.

Displacement

You have probably already been the recipient of a defense mechanism called *displacement*. Have you ever come home only to have a member of your family verbally attack you for some very minor thing that you said? There is a good chance that this was an example of displaced aggression. (See Figure 9-8.)

One convenient way—although it is not too fair—for us to release some of our feelings of anxiety or hostility caused by frustration is to displace it onto someone else. Most wives, after a few years of marriage, can tell when their husbands have had a bad day at work and need to displace some of their feelings. "Don't take it out on me," is a common expression of feelings in many families at the end of a hard day. Perhaps if more husbands and wives would realize the important release function that displacement serves, there would be fewer tendencies to file for a divorce.

EMOTION-ORIENTED DEFENSES

Projection

One of the most common emotionally based defense mechanisms is called *projection*. Essentially this takes place when the individual projects certain of his own emotions or behaviors onto another person or other people.

Often we do something or have a desire to do something that goes against our morals or those of society, such as a free expression of sexual behavior. Many a person who has been trained to look on sexual feelings as bad, finds such feelings so frightening that he begins to accuse his boyfriend or girlfriend, husband, or wife of looking at others in a lustful manner or, even, of being unfaithful.

This defense mechanism, like all others, keeps us from feeling inadequate; in a sense, to defend our self-concept. This is a very natural and quite understandable defense mechanism, because no one likes to feel inadequate. In our society, this mechanism is encouraged particularly around the area of failure. We are not trained to accept failure; in fact, we are rewarded for achievement and success. So, when a person fails at something (a course in college, a job, learning a new skill, or the like) he finds it painful to admit it. Often the immediate response is to project the blame for his failure onto something or someone else. We all tend to use this mechanism in our everyday life. Frequently, after the negative experience is over, we may realize what we have done and begin to admit to ourselves that we did fail or make a mistake.

Regression

Another defense that we all tend to use to protect ourselves against the realities of the world, especially when they become harsh, is called *regression*. (See Figure 9-9.) Essentially regression involves the use of behavior from an earlier age. We regress to an earlier form of behavior when, for example, we become frustrated and throw a temper tantrum. Or, if we cannot get what we want, we pout for several hours.

Even though this type of behavior often worked in childhood to manipulate our parents into giving us what we wanted, it may not be quite as successful in adult life. However, it is a convenient mechanism to use and probably one of the most natural for us to engage in because of the strength of this type of emotionally based learning. In many cases, it allows us to retreat from present reality and to vent some emotions freely in a safe, comfortable manner. Like projection, after a period of time we frequently can more realistically face the situation that produced the regressive behavior (Kris, 1952).

Suppression

Frequently life gets very complicated and we may do or say something that we are sorry for later. If we had to carry all of these things around with us in our conscious awareness, life would be very painful; to be constantly reminded of our embarrassing or bad experiences would be harmful. What most of us do, then, is to purposely forget these situations; we call this process *suppression*. It is called a defense mechanism, because by forgetting our mistakes, we feel better about ourselves.

Figure 9-9
Regression

An advantage of this mechanism is that it allows us to focus our thoughts and energies on facing realities of the moment, rather than to worry about some of our past mistakes.

Emotional Insulation

Do you remember your first "love affair"—the first time you related to another person in a free and emotionally open way? Because you had been taught that you could trust those you love, you brought real trust to this new relationship. Suddenly, you were jilted; that wonderful, almost superhuman person let you down. The relationship was over. You became bitter, "I'll never love anyone again" is a frequently heard comment by parents after their sons or daughters fail in their first real emotional encounter with a boyfriend or girlfriend.

Usually, however, this bitterness does not last too long. However, there begins to develop a holding back, a tendency not to get so emotionally involved next time. We call this type of reaction *emotional insulation.*

A degree of emotional insulation takes place in all of us as we grow up and learn not to get too emotionally involved in a pending situation or actual situation with other persons. Frequently what we hope for may not occur and we have invested a large amount of emotional energy that tends to take a lot out of us.

On the other hand, a person who has experienced much hurt early in life uses this mechanism to remain aloof and detached from others so that he won't be hurt again. Such a person is often very lonely; he fails because he is unwilling to take the chance of getting emotionally involved with others.

Catharsis

When we are blocked in our progress toward a particular goal, we often develop a variety of emotional reactions that make us feel very uncomfortable. Too, they often prevent us from effectively solving a problem or thinking about another way to reach our goal. A mechanism that is very helpful in releasing some of these stored up feelings is called *catharsis*. Essentially this involves "talking it out" with another person, usually someone to whom we feel very close. By releasing some of our true feelings, we are able to face a particular problem more effectively. A good bull session with friends is another example of catharsis.

Intermediate Summary

Just as there are physiological defenses to combat bacterial attacks on the body, there are defenses at the psychological level against self-destructive tendencies. These psychological defenses, called reality-oriented defense mechanisms, are geared to protect the self against emotional hurts such as guilt, fear, and anxiety but not to solve the problem producing the stress. The defenses can be verbally oriented, action-oriented, or emotion–oriented.

APPLICATION

Living with Yourself

A DEGREE OF FRUSTRATION AND CONFLICT IS A PART OF LIFE

It should be clear by now that one aspect of being an alive, growing, and stepladder-climbing person is to be aware that we are not always going to be able to reach goals we desire or meet all of our needs immediately. A part of life involves the frustration of need satisfaction. We all have to learn to accept and deal with such feelings as anxiety, hostility, and guilt. Furthermore, we must be aware that we will find conflict situations arising out of our need for certain, sometimes conflicting, goals. Also, it is clear that we all must resort to the use of one or more of the reality-oriented defense mechanisms in order to continue to be able to function in the real world.

WHAT ARE SOME GENERAL AREAS OF NEED DEPRIVATION AND CONFLICT THAT RELATE TO YOU?

Before we begin to look at some of your own specific areas of need deprivation and conflict, let's discuss some overall problem areas that the authors have found to be important for their own students.

Blocks to Self-Actualization

We all want to climb the stepladder to reach self-actualization; we all want self-esteem, prestige, and feelings of love and belonging. Yet, in a sense we are all bound to be frustrated in our attempts to meet these needs fully and completely. Many students feel a general discouragement when all these higher needs in the hierarchy cannot be met immediately. They need to be reminded that it takes time to climb this ladder, that they can't do it all at once.

Conflicts Produced by Changes in Values

Many inner conflicts within our students occur (1) because of the nature of our fast-moving and changing society; (2) because in college they are hearing new points of view from teachers and fellow students; and (3) because they share a rather natural desire to break away from their parents and to discard some of the values they have had "imposed" on them.

Inner conflicts tend to make a person insecure and anxious. You want something to fill the void; you want to adopt a new value to take the place of a value in question. But frequently it takes time to build in a new value—you need data, information, experiences, and sometimes discussions and support, before you feel that the new value is right for you. Too often the pace of classes in college does not allow you time to do all these things.

Independence Versus Dependence

Another area that produces frustration and some of the emotional results is that of independence. There seems to be in all of us a need to become independent, to become at least somewhat free, so that we can grow and live a life that is meaningful to us. However, parents find it hard to give us this freedom and independence because it makes them feel anxious and uneasy.

Many students are waging a constant battle between being independent and doing and saying what they feel is right, and being dependent on parents—or others—and allowing them to make the decisions for them. This ambivalence arouses a high degree of anxiety, hostility, and even guilt, for their parents often make them feel as if they are ungrateful and do not love them anymore.

Satisfaction of Immediate Needs Versus Satisfaction of Long-Range Needs and Goals

Probably one of the most frequent conflicts for students arises out of the desire to satisfy some of their pressing needs immediately, and, at the same time, think about and plan for the satisfaction of needs through long-range goals and planning. The life of a student is difficult. On the one hand there is the desire to satisfy some of the lower needs on the stepladder, such as needs for exploration, sexual stimulation and satisfaction, and affection and belonging. Yet, parents, teachers, and society say that he must delay those immediate gratifications to attain success, prestige, and self-actualization through college learning and career.

So you constantly fight the battle between "doing what comes naturally"— now—and putting these desires aside for a few years. Most students end up with a compromise. For example, a student came to see the authors looking as though he was ready for a hospital (both mentally and physically). They asked him what was wrong and he said that he hadn't slept in two days because he was studying for finals. Then he went on to explain that he had been "partying it up" most of the semester and suddenly he decided to "hit the books." Perhaps this is not the best type of compromise!

General Reaction Among Students to Emotions Aroused by General Conflicts

As a result of some of these more common conflicts found among students, there seem to be more common defensive reactions to them. Among these are emotional insulation, rationalization, and suppression.

Emotional Insulation

This defensive reaction seems to take the form of passivity and lack of emotional involvement with others. "I've been hurt once, so why get involved," is a common attitude that emerges. This emotional insulation also seems to pervade relations with school and the learning process. Perhaps at one time a student was involved and enthusiastic about school work and the learning process; however, he was hurt, perhaps by an insensitive teacher, somewhere along the way.

Rationalization

Another common reaction of students is to rationalize their inadequate performances in the learning process. This reaction seems logical enough when we consider that college students are learning to become more confident and self-reliant. It is much easier to blame the school, teacher, or exam for inadequacies.

Suppression

Many of the general conflicts of students cannot be resolved on the spot; they take time. Therefore, by forgetting some of these conflicts, students are able to function much better and face the demands of reality more skillfully. Thus, suppression, at this age and stage of life is very common.

ANALYZING YOUR OWN SPECIFIC NEED DEPRIVATIONS AND CONFLICTS

What are your major need deprivations at this moment? What are some of the types of conflicts that you face? Perhaps you, like many other students, face some of the general need deprivations and conflicts mentioned earlier. You could perhaps begin to find out by listing now what to you are your major unfulfilled needs. Look at p. 275 to see that you include all the needs on the hierarchy of needs.

Then, you might identify the types of blocks that are preventing you from satisfying these needs. You could make a list of the major conflict situations present in your life. What kind of defensive reactions do you typically make to some of these need deprivations and conflicts? A way to begin is to keep a defense-mechanism diary in which you list the conflict situation and the type of response you made to it. Soon you will probably find a pattern emerging that may help you evaluate whether your defensive behavior is reality-oriented or not.

Perhaps, too, you will come to better understand why you react in certain ways to conflict and frustration. Most of all, it is possible that you will be able to have more understanding of other people's defensive reactions.

Living with Others

Usually we live happier lives with people with whom we have shared common experiences. Shared experiences permit us to know the "why" of behavior. For example, when a close friend leaves for a certain date, we can predict that she will have a miserable time if we know she accepted the date in order to make another young man jealous of her popularity. However, if the young man does not react with jealousy, the young woman's positive feelings for him may weaken as her neutral or negative feelings for other men become increasingly more positive. Knowing the "why" of behavior and how goal gradients operate in conflict situations enables us to understand others and to live better with them.

DIFFERENCES IN REACTIONS TO STRESS

People react differently to stress. The same failure situation produces different reactions depending on the person's previous experience with similar problems, the intensity of his emotional feelings, and group membership. People from lower socioeconomic groups tend to respond with action-oriented defense mechanisms, such as acting out. (Sherif and Sherif, 1965) Others, usually from the middle and upper socioeconomic groups, tend to react with verbally oriented defenses, such as rationalization. In general, boys tend to make more openly expressed aggressive responses than girls. (Henry and Sharpe, 1947)

Intensity of Reaction to Stress

All people react to stress. However, an important difference in such reactions is the intensity of the reaction and the longevity of the hurt or shock. Figure 9-10 shows possible relationships between stress and intensity of reaction among individuals.

Figure 9-10
Individual Responses to the Same Stress.

In general, the more intense the response to stress, the greater the use of defense mechanisms to reduce the emotional hurt and to justify the ways in which we responded.

The duration of emotional hurts usually depends on how often one has failed in a similar situation and the consequences of these failures on our life situation. Figure 9-11 shows individual differences in the longevity and intensity of emotional hurts to the same stress. Prolonged intense reactions to stress can cripple a person psychologically and physically. (Levine, 1960) The more resources a person has psychologically, biologically, and socially, the better he is able to cope with stress.

School Stress

A student who has received failing grades several times in a row may develop prolonged and intense feelings of anger or depression. In such a situation, he may try harder to improve, may drop out of school, or may develop emotional insulation so that future failure will not produce even a normal response. Emotional insulation in students can be seen in general apathy and in remarks such

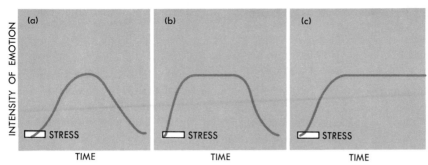

Figure 9-11
Individual Differences in Duration of Reactions to the Same Stress Situation.

as "I don't care." Of course, underneath the cover-up of the defense mechanism, most of them really do care. But, at the present moment they feel unable to do anything but to protect themselves from further emotional hurts.

Parental Stress

Some college students complain that they do poorly because of conflicts at home. Prolonged reactions to stress drain away energies essential for problem solving at school, on the job, and in other social relations.

Parental conflicts can be better understood if one realizes that parents often identify with their children. In so doing, parents tend to project onto those they love their thoughts, tastes, ideas, and aspirations. Parental identification can become stronger as parents become older and as their world becomes smaller and their chances for success diminish. Such parents may see in their children their last chance to achieve worthy goals and satisfaction. Indirectly, through their children, they hope for the success they were unable to achieve directly. Their efforts, if too great, can hamper the young person's efforts toward self-actualization. However, for most parents the process of identification is a form of love for their children. The conflicts arise because their values and aspirations differ from those held by their children. Solutions to such problems often come out of frank "man-to-man" discussions. Parents may find increased satisfactions apart from those achieved through identification with their children. If not, the young person may leave the home in order to develop his own competencies, freely.

Courtship and Marriage

The basis for conflicts and frustrations during courtship and marriage can be reduced if both persons take the time and effort to evaluate themselves and each other in terms of their present and future needs and how they plan to meet them.

They should consider objective information that is predictive of success in marriage, such as the evidence that the more successful marriages are not the very youthful marriages (Landis, 1963, p. 153) and that the shorter the acquaintance period before marriage the greater the chance of poor marital adjustment. (Burgess and Cottrell, 1939) Too, the engaged couple might well consider some factors predictive of marital happiness, such as the happiness of the parents' marriage, childhood happiness, and a positive relationship with parents.

Nevertheless, conflicts will be inevitable because needs change. A young wife may need the security of a strong and dominant husband. As she matures and grows, her husband's dominancy may become the obstacle to her self-actualization. The husband, in turn, may at first be extremely pleased to find his wife so dependent on him. It makes him feel important and wanted. However, after gaining his self-confidence, he may find that he no longer enjoys a clinging wife. Other conflicts can center around a wife's strong identification with her husband's success. She thrives on his accomplishment, yet she fails to grow herself. Eventually the gulf between the two can become so great that they have little in common with each other. Her needs have stabilized while his needs have changed almost completely.

It is important to become sensitive to signs of stress such as chronic anxiety, depression, and hostility. These indicate that all is not well, that the couple must find the roots of their hidden conflicts and frustration, and then do something constructive to change. In the same way that one should not ignore a high fever, one should not ignore signs of psychological stress.

But more important than later treatment is early prevention. Putney and Putney (1964) describe what may happen to an engaged couple who seek marriage prior to confronting each other as they really are.

Because each wants to be loved, each agrees to love the other (not that the bargain is explicit, of course, but it is understood all the same). Like most lovers, these two form a mutual admiration society, dedicated to indirect self-acceptance. No romance is ever open and candid, for both parties are intent on making and maintaining a good impression. Mary seems a faultless angel to John because he is seeing what he has projected onto her—a view she encourages by seeking to conceal less flattering characteristics and by trying to fit his picture of her. Anything he praises, she seeks to emphasize, and because he compliments her on what he expects to see (independently of reality) she finds herself cultivating new and exciting self-potential.

All of this could lead to self-discovery on Mary's part. As realists have long noted, the appearance and disposition of an unattractive, shrewish girl can be remarkably improved by daily assertions that she is beautiful and sweet tempered. Mary would like to believe the image of herself that she sees reflected in John's eyes. But she knows that she is concealing other facets of herself (perhaps ill-tempered or slovenly proclivities) and, moreover, she finds it hard to believe that the charms John attributes to her are real. Any changes which she does perceive in herself she believes are elicited by John and she fears that if she lost him she might turn into a pumpkin. So she clings to him as a prop for a masquerade she hopes will never end. Her self-discovery remains unrecognized. (Pp. 115–116)

Possibly the saying that "love is blind" is true as well as is "beauty is in the eye of the beholder." In any case, young couples should delay marriage until they can know each other as they really are without the façades and masquerades. Young people must learn that the highly exciting romantic period is only temporary and that they must seek the enduring qualities in each other that could last a lifetime. A study by Burgess and Wallin (1953, p. 7), based on 1,000 engaged couples, revealed this trend. Young people are emphasizing companionship and compatibility instead of just romantic love as the bases of mate selection.

Living with Society

REALITY-ORIENTED DEFENSIVE BEHAVIOR AND THE WORLD OF WORK

Certain types of jobs have built into them certain need deprivations and conflicts; as a result there will tend to be an increased probability that people in those jobs will use certain types of defensive reactions. Think for a moment of the differences in conflicts common in the jobs of a policeman, minister, auto mechanic, and medical assistant.

You might think for a moment about the job or occupation you have selected or are considering selecting. Do you think you can handle the types of conflicts and emotional reactions that are almost built into the job? Most counseling

Table 9-1

Some Relationships Between Occupation and Stress

OCCUPATION	CONFLICTS	DEFENSES
Medical work	Treatment A vs. B Temporary cures for terminal cases Death and suffering when no cures	Defenses turned inward: suppression emotional insulation rationalization
Policework, military	Self-sacrifice vs. duty Duty vs. personal beliefs	Defenses turned inward and outward: suppression emotional insulation rationalization acting out
Business world	Routines vs. self-expression Profits vs. ethics	Defenses turned inward: suppression emotional insulation rationalization
Manual labor	Routines vs. self-expression	Defenses turned outward: acting out compensation (horseplay) rationalization

Occupations are characterized by different stresses. The chart illustrates some of the possible stresses and corresponding defensive reactions.

centers have much data about the salary, requirements, and needs for certain occupations, but few have any information on the type and degree of conflicts built into a job. Discussions and observations of persons already in the occupation of your choice can provide valuable insights into the kinds of problems they face. Books and publications on occupations also illustrate some of the common conflicts and frustrations. The following are brief comments from young people in the world of work:

When I came down here to work, I tried my damndest to work, to get along with everyone. I'll do all that's expected of me, but I gotta have some help. Well, I came down here and I was trying. I was new and I didn't know the job, even though I have worked down here off and on as a roll shafter. I was trying to work out on the job, so Charlie and I got along pretty well at first, but then he clammed up, so I went up to him, "What's the matter, Charlie? Have I done something wrong?" Charlie laughed and said, "Naw, naw, I'm just teed off with these damn machines here. I'm OK." And what happened? Everything went swell from then on. But up to that time, boy, I didn't feel so good. (Zaleznik and Moment, 1964, p. 195)

I like the work here. I like the variety, the moving around. There are some personal clashes that I get into, and I see inconsistencies in management once in a while. I just don't think they're using their talent efficiently. (*Ibid.*, p. 428)

I don't have anything to complain about. The money is good; the work isn't too hard. You know, I like seeing people, but you can get too much of it. It's when these people come through at the end of the day, and they start adding up their bills, and I have to stand there and wait for them—the women especially. They really get me. As far as being a full-time job, there's just too much worry to it. All these customers at you all the time. I couldn't take it. (*Ibid.*, p. 429)

I enjoy teaching, but I have so many students with so many difficult problems. I have a student who cannot speak one word of English and another who cannot read or spell although he is in high school. Another student is literally "climbing the walls" with anxiety. What can I do when I have thirty other students who need my help? At times I feel so frustrated and depressed. (Authors' interview with a teacher)

REALITY-ORIENTED DEFENSIVE BEHAVIOR AND SOCIETY

Our society, like all others, tends to produce within the individual certain types of need deprivations and conflicts. As we go up the stepladder of needs, we are most fortunate to have most of our basic needs satisfied, to a relative degree at least. However, our competitive society, particularly in the world of business, sometimes presents blocks to the attainment of prestige and success. This is partly because money and prestige are the only ways for measuring success for a large segment of our society. Thus, many people in our society, particularly minority group members, find their lives continually filled with frustration and conflict. It is no wonder that many of our poor and "unsuccessful" people engage in the extensive use of defense mechanisms—particularly identification, emotional insulation (almost an apathy to ever doing better financially), and rationalization (blaming others for their ills). (Kaufman, 1966)

DEFENSIVE BEHAVIOR IN A DEMOCRATIC SOCIETY

From a psychological standpoint, a democracy such as ours offers a man, perhaps more than any other political system, an opportunity to become self-actualizing. On the other hand, it tends to produce certain types of frustrations. The fact that we must adhere to majority rule in the making of certain laws and in electing officials, means that we often cannot have our way.

In such a large society, there is also a tendency for group affiliations to exert pressures on us to conform to certain expectations and values. Frequently, we tend to introject what the group thinks is good or bad, and so lose some of our individuality.

REALITY-ORIENTED DEFENSIVE BEHAVIOR AND THE SCHOOL

As was mentioned earlier, the student in school is "neither fish nor fowl." He is treated by his parents ambivalently, one day as a child and the next as an adult; unfortunately, at times, he is treated by the school and by many teachers as being a lower form of humanity; he finds it difficult to be accepted as a participant in the community. Thus, many of his needs, particularly for self-esteem, success, and prestige, are frustrated. He is bound to react to the feelings of anxiety and hostility by using some of the reality-oriented defense mechanisms. This is normal.

Final Summary

Everyday living means coping with problems that produce tension, grief, and anxiety. Facing problems and learning how to resolve them successfully are necessary conditions for continual growth toward self-actualization.

There are psychological defenses against emotional hurts just as there are physiological defenses against infections and diseases. We are just as concerned with maintaining self-esteem as we are with protecting our bodies against physical damage and pain. The psychological defense systems for coping with normal personality problems are composed of reality-oriented defense mechanisms and have three principle characteristics: (1) They are ways of maintaining self-esteem in situations in which we feel inadequate or have already failed. (2) They are ways of reducing feelings of anxiety, guilt, hostility, or depression. (3) They are ways of convincing people that we are really adequate and worthwhile. Reality-oriented defense mechanisms can be verbally oriented, action-oriented, or emotionally oriented.

Specific Chapter References

Brown, J. S. Gradients of approach and avoidance responses and their relation to level of motivation. *Journal of Comparative and Physiological Psychology*, 1948, 41, 450–465.

Burgess, E. W., and Cottrell, L. S. *Predicting success or failure in marriage.* Englewood Cliffs, N.J.: Prentice-Hall, 1939.

Burgess, E. W., and Wallin, P. *Engagement and marriage.* Philadelphia: Lippincott, 1953.

Henry, M. M., and Sharpe, D. F. Some influential factors in the determination of aggressive behavior in pre-school children. In J. M. Seidman (ed.), *The child.* New York: Holt, Rinehart, and Winston, 1966. Pp. 187–205.

Hoch, P. H. State care. *Atlantic Monthly*, 1964, 214(1), 82–85.

Kaufman, S. S. Economic status as a factor in the etiology of the neuroses. In J. H. Merin and S. H. Nagler (eds.). *The etiology of the neuroses.* New York: Science and Behavior Books, 1966. Pp. 110–121.

Kris, E. *Psychoanalytic explorations of art.* New York: International University Press, 1952.

Landis, J. T., and Landis, M. G. *Building a successful marriage.* Englewood Cliffs, N.J.: Prentice-Hall, 1963.

Levine, S. Stimulation in infancy. *Scientific American*, 1960, 202(5), 80–86.

Paulsen, James A. *Atlantic Monthly*, July, 1964, 94–101.

Putney, S., and Putney, Gail J. *The adjusted American: normal neuroses in the individual and society.* New York: Harper Colophon Books, 1964.

Sherif, M., and Sherif, Carolyn W. *Problems of youth.* Chicago: Aldine, 1965.

Taylor, C., and Combs, A. W. Self-acceptance and adjustment. *Journal of Consulting Psychology*, 1952, 16, 89–91.

Zaleznik, A., and Moment, D. *Casebook on interpersonal behavior in organizations.* New York: Wiley, 1964.

Recommended Further Readings

Paperback Books

Freud, S. *The psychopathology of everyday life* (trans. by A. A. Brill). New York: Macmillan, 1914.

Krutch, J. W. *The measure of man.* New York: Charter Books, 1954.

Maslow, A. H. *Toward a psychology of being.* Princeton, N.J.: Van Nostrand, 1962.

Miller, D. R., and Swanson, G. E. *Inner conflict and defense.* New York: Schocken Books, 1960.

Redlich, F., and Bingham, June *The inside story.* New York: Vintage Books, 1953.

Rodman, H. (ed.). *Marriage, family, and society.* New York: Random House, 1965.

Ruitenbeek, H. M. (ed.). *The dilemma of organizational society.* New York: Dutton Paperback, 1963.

Smith, H. (ed.). *The search for America.* Englewood Cliffs, N.J.: Spectrum Book, 1959.

Tallent, N. *Psychological perspectives on the person.* Princeton, N.J.: Insight Book, 1967.

Hardcover Books

Allport, G. W. *Personality and social encounter: selected essays.* Boston: Beacon, 1960.

Arkoff, A. *Adjustment and mental health.* New York: McGraw-Hill, 1968.

Bennis, W. G., Schein, E. H., Steel, F. I., and Berlew, D. E. (eds.). *Interpersonal dynamics: essays and readings on human interaction.* Homewood, Ill.: Dorsey Press, 1968.

Bernard, H. W. *Toward better personal adjustment* (2nd ed.). New York: McGraw-Hill, 1957.

Christensen, H. T. *Marriage analysis.* New York: Ronald Press, 1950.

Horney, Karen. *Our inner conflicts.* New York: Norton, 1950.

Jourard, S. M. *Personal adjustment.* New York: Macmillan, 1958.

Lazarus, R. S. *Psychological stress and the coping process.* New York: McGraw-Hill, 1966.

Lazarus, R. S. *Patterns of adjustment and human effectiveness.* New York: McGraw-Hill, 1968.

Lehner, G. F. J., and Kube, Ella. *The dynamics of personal adjustment* (2nd ed.). Englewood Cliffs. N.J.: Prentice-Hall, 1964.

McKinney, F. *Counseling for personal adjustment: in schools and colleges.* Boston: Houghton Mifflin, 1958.

McKinney, F. *Understanding personality: cases in counseling.* Boston: Houghton Mifflin, 1965.

Miller, D. R., and Swanson, E. G. *Inner defense and conflict.* New York: Holt, Rinehart and Winston, 1960.

Offer, D., and Sabshin, M. *Normality.* New York: Basic Books, 1966.

Reik, T. *Curiosities of the self.* New York: Farrar, Straus and Giroux, 1965.

Schneiders, A. A. *Personality dynamics and mental health* (rev. ed.). New York: Holt, Rinehart and Winston, 1965.

Selye, H. *The stress of life.* New York: McGraw-Hill, 1956.

Shaffer, L. F., and Shoben, E. J., Jr. *The psychology of adjustment: a dynamic and experimental approach to personality and mental hygiene* (2nd ed.). Boston: Houghton Mifflin, 1956.

Smith, H. C. *Personality adjustment.* New York: McGraw-Hill, 1961.

Symonds, P. M. *The dynamics of human adjustment.* New York: Appleton-Century-Crofts, 1946.

Yamamoto, K. (ed.). *The college student and his culture: an analysis.* Boston: Houghton Mifflin, 1968.

Chapter 10 Understanding the Unhealthy Personality

Chapter Outline

Study Guide

The study of abnormal behavior requires special and concentrated efforts. The topic itself is complex with many new ideas and terminology; students often have erroneous preconceptions; while reading about mental illnesses, the reader is often reminded of his own problems and griefs that can interfere with effective learning.

REVIEW

Review the last chapter by reading the summaries. Restudy now what is not clear.

PREVIEW

Study the main ideas and structure of the chapter before reading by following study guide procedures.

READING

Read the chapter in detail by following the study guide procedures. Construct and answer your own examination questions.

REVIEW

Practice recall by following the study guide procedures.

STUDY TIP

Group study techniques. Learning and reviewing in a give-and-take social situation with other students can be very rewarding. (1) Find three or four students interested in group study. (2) Reserve a library room for several hours on certain dates. (3) Assign each student a chapter for intensive study. Each student presents his chapter orally, or orally and written, to the group. A question and answer session follows. (4) Each student prepares examination questions for the other members. Exchange questions and practice taking tests. A question and answer session follows. (5) Offer tutoring services to those having difficulty, or to any international students or handicapped students.

Prelude

In the previous chapter, we discussed normal reality-oriented reactions to the stress produced by unresolved conflicts and frustrations. We saw that under such conditions, we become more concerned with the removal or reduction of emotional hurts than with the immediate solutions of the problems at hand. Such reactions are common because we cannot resolve all of our problems adequately at the same time. In real life, problems do not occur one at a time, as in textbooks; rather, problems bunch up and can overwhelm our adjustive capacities unless we utilize reality-oriented defenses to keep some of our problems in abeyance while we learn to develop more effective problem-solving methods.

In this chapter, we are going to discuss the psychologically unhealthy personality and abnormal reactions to prolonged or intense stress as a result of unresolved conflicts and frustration. We should keep in mind that this chapter is really a continuation of the last. It is particularly significant for persons who are unable at present to resolve their problems despite extensive usage of reality-oriented defense mechanisms.

Students' Viewpoints

Think for a moment about the people you now know or have known during your lifetime; think about the way they behaved and how you and others felt about them. Who do you believe is or was the most mentally unhealthy person you have known? Write a detailed description of this person.

This is an assignment the authors have given classes for the past several years. Here are some of the descriptions of student nominations:

(1) I have known a young man for seven years. For those years I have never seen him express sorrow, pleasure, misery, or happiness.

A loss of a friendship will not turn the corners of his mouth. A car accident will not shake his composure.

Someone will call him the lowest names on earth and he will not show any anger.

(2) This person that I consider mentally unhealthy always seems depressed and nervous. She often gets into states of mental depression, where she feels no one loves her or cares. Often her actions are done irrationally without really thinking through the situation. It is hard for her to really do something on her own for she was a spoiled child and always had someone to do things for her. She demands her own way on many issues, and when things do not go her way she becomes moody and will not speak for a long period of time. Her opinion once expressed to me was that "Life is a challenge to live and death is the easy way out."

(3) In the club that I belong to there is a boy who I feel is mentally unhealthy. He has caused a lot of trouble in the club and has obtained a bad image because of his loud mouth.

He always wants to be the center of everything and wants everyone to look on him as their best friend when they're in trouble. He is especially good at twisting the truth to suit himself and has caused discord between those who are going steady in the club.

(4) This man has a terrible complex. He is afraid to take responsibility at all so he lets the other person assume it is their duty. He has a way of not answering or when and if he answers he leads you to think one thing when actually the answer is just the opposite.

He has a way of playing one person against another that is often harmful.

He also lies even on the most important issues.

He tries his hardest to impress outsiders while his immediate "friends" are treated with no consideration whatsoever.

Obviously, it would be dangerous to say that these persons are mentally ill based solely on such brief descriptions. However, some of these patterns of behavior are found in people who have emotional problems requiring professional treatment.

Experiences with first-year psychology students have consistently revealed that most of them can readily detect when a person is experiencing emotional problems. Descriptions such as the preceding are examples of this sensitivity to people who are hurt emotionally. Certainly, students cannot always know the reasons for disturbances, or how to help, but they are aware that problems exist.

All of us, the authors believe, possess a sensitivity to the emotional needs of others. Yet, this awareness often produces conflict within us, because we don't understand why a person has these feelings and we don't know how to help him. The authors of this chapter will give you a better understanding of the emotionally troubled person, so that you will be better able to understand people you meet who are in need of professional help; hopefully you will be able to help them get some professional help before their problems become even more serious.

WHY IS IT IMPORTANT?

Mental illness is the Number One health problem in the United States. More than one-half of all our hospital beds are occupied by mental patients, and the majority of all people who go to see medical doctors are suffering from illnesses related to emotional problems. Furthermore, millions of Americans seek relief from nervous tensions through the use of drugs and alcohol. (National Association for Mental Health, 1967)

Although it is common to believe that "It can't happen to me," it has been estimated that one college student out of ten will need help because of emotional problems that interfere with their college work. (Roche Laboratories, 1965) The incidence of maladjustive behavior runs into the tens of millions in the United States. (Coleman, 1964)

Truly, mental illness is a major catastrophe. It is the single greatest impediment to self-actualization and happiness. It can take the joy and enthusiasm out of living and turn human beings into cringing animals and dull robots.

The authors believe that if we all learn more about how people become mentally ill, how to recognize the early signs, and where to seek help, the awesome number of persons who develop unhealthy personalities can be reduced.

BASIC THEORY AND RESEARCH

Who Is Mentally Healthy or Unhealthy?

All of you who are, at this moment, reading this sentence with glasses on are mentally ill! What did we say? Yes, you read it correctly. Go back again and reread it.

How do you feel about that statement? Does it make you mad? Are you asking, "Who the hell do you think you are?" Well, you should.

However, it won't do you any good. You see, we are psychologists, experts on mental illness. We believe that people who wear glasses are disturbed! And that's that!

But is it? What kind of authority gives us the privilege of locking up all those who wear glasses? You're right this time, no authority! And yet right at this moment there are many people in court about to be committed to a mental hospital. On what basis? By whose authority?

By now, you have probably guessed we were really pulling your leg (or glasses) in the first paragraph. There are important ethical and value judgments implicit in any discussion defining mental illness. That's the point we were making indirectly. Therefore, we must ask, "By whose standards do we judge a person to be mentally ill? By a psychologist's, a psychiatrist's, society's, a dictator's, yours?" There have been a number of different answers. Among these, two of the more common hinge on statistical norms and the criteria of personality adjustment.

Criteria Used in Defining Mental Illness

STATISTICAL NORMS

This approach essentially says that any behavior that most people in a given society engage in is considered "normal"; conversely, behavior that is exhibited by only a small minority is considered "abnormal," or bad. (Offer and Sabshin, 1966) Thus, Nazis who went along with Hitler's policies or who didn't disapprove of the atrocities would have been considered "healthy" in Nazi society. Those who objected or rebelled were obviously "sick." The tribesmen in a primitive, head-hunting village who refuse to hunt heads are also "sick." As you can see, this criterion leaves much to be desired.

PERSONAL ADJUSTMENT

This view says that those who "adjust well" to the demands of a society have healthy personalities. (Jahoda, 1958) Thus, people who show anxiety, depression, or hostility are considered "maladjusted." This position too is less than adequate, because many people who are merely "existing" and are happy all of the time often cannot be considered especially "healthy." This theory also leaves out the question of man's responsibility to the group. Certainly one who protests social injustices such as lynchings and religious and racial bigotry is demonstrating the behavior of the mentally healthy.

WHICH CRITERION IS BEST?

Coleman (1964) summarizes his discussion of problems involved in defining "abnormal" and "normal" as follows: "Until needed research data become available, however, definitions and criteria of mental health will of necessity depend heavily upon pragmatic considerations." (p. 15)

In a sense, the authors agree. However, for the time being they feel that the research on self-actualizing persons is a very promising area and may lead us into a better understanding of both the mentally healthy and unhealthy.

Thus, the authors' criteria of mental health are related to the following characteristics of self-actualizing persons that were discussed in Chapter 1.

1. They accept others as they are.
2. They can express intense and warm feelings.
3. They see others as *they* are.
4. They have the capacity to respond to life.
5. They maintain a serenity and calmness.
6. They apply a creative approach to living.
7. They show a democratic orientation to life.

Mental illness, then, constitutes the opposite. Persons who do not accept others, who express little or no feelings, who tend to distort their perceptions of others, who fail to respond to life, who are constantly tense and nervous, who tend to be rigid and uncreative in their behavior, and who have an *authoritarian orientation* (demanding complete obedience without question) to life—these are the mentally unhealthy.

From this point of view, then, it is possible to develop a humanistic approach to mental health. This suggests that a society that allows man to develop into his full potential by climbing the ladder to self-actualization is the healthy society, and the society that holds man back from attaining such goals is the unhealthy society. (Fromm, 1955)

Now that we have briefly discussed mental illness, first in general and then in more philosophical terms, let's discuss which factors are involved in the development of mental illness. As we have done previously, we shall look at both the objective (external) factors contributing to mental illness and the subjective (internal) factors.

Subjective Factors Leading to Mental Illness

FAILURES IN DEVELOPMENTAL TASKS

As was mentioned in the discussion of children (see Chapter 4) the evidence is now quite clear that early childhood is a period when many crucial stages of personality development occur. Of particular importance are the development of the self-concept and the ability to relate to others. One of the most frequent characteristics of persons who experience emotional problems is a negative self-concept. This often manifests itself in an inability to relate well to others or to express affection and love toward others. (Quay, 1968)

FAILURES IN PROBLEM-SOLVING TECHNIQUES

Frequently people with mental illness have had very little experience in effectively solving their problems. As children, they may have been extremely over-protected and may never have been allowed to work through problems that arose. As was mentioned in Chapter 3, these people are continually frustrated in their attempts to overcome barriers that are blocking certain goals. They may attack obstacles that are too great for them; they may set unrealistic goals for themselves; or they may simply fail to define their problems accurately.

FAILURES IN EXPRESSING EMOTIONS

The behavior of mentally ill persons is often characterized by the display of inappropriate emotional responses. That is, as a result of the inconsistent expectations of their parents or of a lack of warm emotional responses in the home, children may fail to relate to others on an emotional level. (MacFarlane, Allen, and Honzik, 1954).

Another frequent behavior pattern of people with emotional problems is an inability to control emotions. Thus, the person may literally "explode" into a fit of rage if he is blocked in the attainment of a particular goal. (Plutchik, 1962)

We also find that the mood swing, the emotional variations, in these persons may vary considerably from day to day. One day they may feel very elated about life; the next they may feel extremely depressed, ready to attempt suicide. Usually their emotional variations occur with little relevance to the events in the real world. Figure 10–1 gives a visual picture of the mood swings of the "normal" and the mentally ill person.

FAILURES IN PERCEIVING REALITY

Persons with personality problems tend to display an inability to perceive reality accurately. That is, they cannot tolerate the real world, particularly other people. To defend themselves, they do not allow the "real world" to enter into their perceptions. So they frequently distort reality and thus are often at odds with it.

You might say these people view the world and others by means of a thick mask through which they "filter reality." If the mask gets too thick, the person may not perceive reality at all and react instead to what the mask is built of (hallucinations or delusions).

FAILURE TO ACHIEVE CERTAIN BASIC NEEDS IN THE HIERARCHY OF NEEDS

Persons constantly living in a state of basic need deprivation (lack of adequate food, water, and protection from the elements; lack of a sense of security and safety; lack of a sense of belonging and affection) tend to be much more prone to the development of mental illness than those who have an adequate degree of basic need satisfactions.

One of the most extensive studies to illustrate this relationship was the Midtown Manhattan Study (Langer and Michael, 1963), which found a definite relationship between low socioeconomic status and proneness to mental illness. However, persons at all levels of society do become mentally ill.

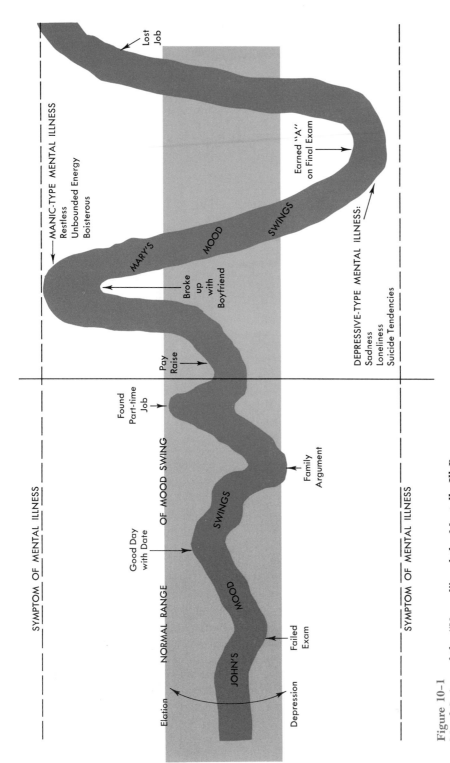

Figure 10-1
Mood Swings of the "Normal" and the Mentally Ill Person

305

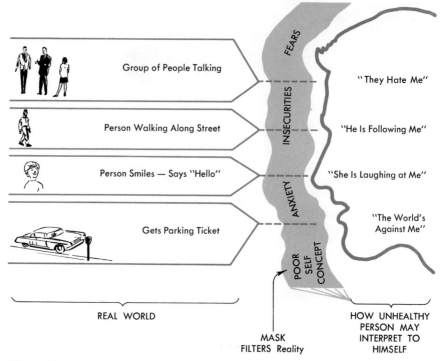

Figure 10-2

The Mentally Unhealthy Person May Filter Reality Through a Thick Mask

In a sense, this again verifies the importance Maslow places on the idea that we must *first* satisfy the more basic needs before we can become concerned with the satisfaction of higher needs. It also helps to explain why we have difficulties in our ghetto areas, where many of the residents are still on the bottom rung of the ladder.

SUMMARY OF EFFECTS OF SUBJECTIVE FACTORS ON THE PERSON

As a result of the previously mentioned subjective factors, the individual experiences a general lack of confidence in himself as a dignified being and begins to perceive himself as inadequate. He, thus, becomes highly prone to the effects that stress, anxiety, and frustration can have on his mental health. He becomes the first to break down. In a sense, he becomes unable to tolerate the following situations, which often occur in real life: delay in the gratification of needs, frustration in achieving goals, competition, failure, and meeting the demands of society, parents, and friends.

Intermediate Summary

Mental illness is the Number One health problem in the United States. It has been estimated that one college student out of ten will need help because of serious personality difficulties. Mental illness is the single greatest impediment to self-actualization. Up to now all mental health workers have not agreed on a common definition of mental illness. In this book mental illness is defined as behavior that is directly opposite to that of self-actualizing persons. Subjective factors leading to mental illness are failures to master developmental tasks, failures in problem solving, failures in expressing emotions, failures in perceiving reality, and failures in satisfying needs in the hierarchy of motives.

Objective Factors Leading to Mental Illness

DELAYS IN NEED GRATIFICATION

A person who has experienced some of the subjective failures listed previously is unable to tolerate a waiting period before he can satisfy a particular need. Frequently he must have immediate satisfaction or he becomes very upset. Such persons tend to stress the importance of immediate attainment of needs over waiting for a period of time before they receive satisfaction. Thus, they are oriented toward need satisfactions of the moment and are almost compulsively driven by their basic needs to behave in certain ways. They may have little control over their own behavior and are driven by their various needs.

FRUSTRATIONS IN GOAL ACHIEVEMENT

Some people are so insecure and have experienced so much frustration already in life that they become very upset if things do not go their way. Thus, they seem to "go to pieces" over small blocks to the achievement of minor goals. The emotional response given in these situations seems all out of proportion to the real life situation; therefore, their behavior many times is inappropriate. People who are close to them may shy away, thus increasing their feelings of isolation and insecurity.

COMPETITION FROM OTHERS

For those persons prone to mental illness, all situations that involve competition with other persons pose major threats. If one feels insecure and inadequate as a person already, the thought of comparing performance or behavior with that of others produces a lot of anxiety and fear. It is no wonder, then, that many of our poor people and people from minority groups find school a threatening place to be.

FAILURE

The personality-problem prone person has already experienced failure in so many forms that he tries to be very careful not to place himself in situations that will increase his chances of failure. In so doing, he limits even more, his opportunities for success.

Another factor operating here is that such a person may be unconsciously trying to fail. As Coombs (1962) puts it: "People who think that they are no good are continually trying to prove it to themselves through their behavior."

DEMANDS OF SOCIETY

Another objective factor that may lead to mental illness for some individuals relates to the demands of society. A result of living in a complex society such as ours (or any for that matter) is that we are pressured into behaving in certain ways that we feel are not reasonable. That is, we cannot always do what we want to when we want to because of the necessity to conform to certain expectations.

For the persons who feel insecure and inadequate and have little control over his behavior, this presents another dilemma. Also, these people may tend to feel that many of the demands of society are unreasonable and rebel by refusing to conform. This may lead to criticism and rejection by others, which only makes them feel more alone and insecure. You can see how easy it becomes to set a vicious cycle in motion.

DEMANDS OF PARENTS AND OTHERS

Society, of course, includes our family, friends, and groups to which we belong or identify. The same problems tend to emerge in these areas as with society as a whole. In order to get along in living with others, we must expect to conform to certain expectations; or, putting it another way, we all play different roles as son, daughter, friend, or group member.

People who are prone to mental disorders find it difficult to relate to others and therefore may reject the standards set by others. Thus, they are considered rebels and are discriminated against for their behavioral deviations.

Physiological Factors Leading to Mental Illness

Certain forms of mental illness are caused principally by physiological malfunctions of the body. Often they are caused during birth, by disease, or by physical injury to the central nervous system or other part of the body. Brain injury can produce such disturbances in thinking, perceptual, and emotional behaviors as to require hospitalization. Injuries to the brain can occur before, during, and after births. According to Coleman (1964) the majority of these people are not so seriously disturbed as to require hospitalization. However,

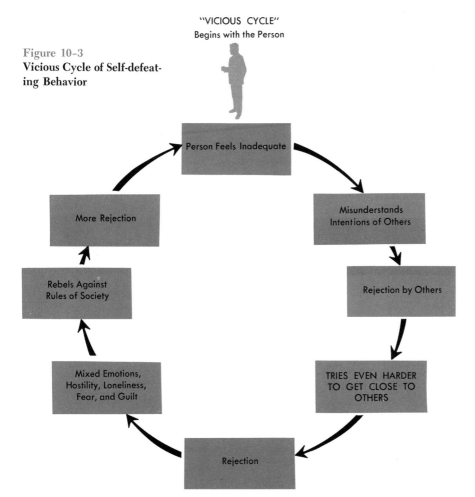

"VICIOUS CYCLE"
Begins with the Person

Figure 10-3
Vicious Cycle of Self-defeating Behavior

persons with disorders of the nervous system account for over one third of all first admissions to mental hospitals.

Other physiological factors that can cause or contribute to disturbances in behavior are endocrine disorders, severe malnutrition, and infectious diseases. Endocrine disorders result in the over- or undersecretions of hormones. Hormones have a widespread effect on many bodily functions such as level of activity, sexual activity, metabolism rate, physical growth, and general reactions to stress. In Chapter 7, we noted the widespread effect of hunger on behavior. Food, either directly or indirectly, dominated the subjects' thinking, perceptual, and emotional behaviors. Infectious diseases such as syphilis and epidemic encephalitis, if untreated, produce sufficient damage to the nervous system to cause personality disturbances.

The Three Stages of Personality Decompensation

What happens to the person when he experiences some of the subjective and objective failures mentioned on the previous pages? Does he "lose his mind" all of a sudden? Does he go down the street screaming and have to be put in a straitjacket? This is the impression that many television programs and motion pictures often give.

But the process is actually quite subtle and time consuming. Essentially, as the pressure because of failures, frustration, and anxiety builds up within the person, the individual tries to defend himself from his feelings. A person may go through as many as three stages of *personality decompensation* (ego defense mechanisms, neurotic defenses, and psychotic defenses) before treatment is received. Another may have to endure only the first stage (the use of ego defense mechanisms). That may be enough to help him realize that he is losing control of his behavior and send him in search of help from a friend, teacher, counselor, psychologist, or psychiatrist. Other persons may actually develop some neurotic defenses before they or those close to them realize that help is needed.

EGO DEFENSE MECHANISMS

When the extensive use of reality-oriented defenses fails to diminish the anguish of emotional hurts, a more powerful psychological defense system gradually comes into action. It is the ego defense mechanism. In this defense system, the motives for behavior are at the unconscious level. That is, although the person knows *what* he is doing, the *reasons* for his behavior remain unknown to him. Ego defensive behavior is self-deceptive, whereas reality defensive behavior is intended to deceive other persons. Indulging in self-deceptive behavior is a major step toward distorting reality and mental illness; nevertheless, it serves the purpose of reducing emotional hurts by blocking from consciousness the unresolved problems and transgressions.

Thus, although ego defenses against anxiety and tension may contribute to the person's emotional equilibrium, they are, when used extensively and unsuccessfully, responsible for the symptoms that can cripple and lead eventually to mental illness. Still, the occasional use of ego defenses during periods of unusual stress is normal. They can provide us with a breather until we can gather the resources and energies to face the problems.

REPRESSION

Repression is the ego defense whereby the unresolved problem is pushed into the unconscious level. At first, one tries not to think about the problem. This process is suppression. However, suppression may not be sufficient, and the problem keeps coming into awareness along with its crippling anxiety and tension. The next step is repression; it occurs automatically and without conscious effort.

Repression provides only temporary relief. Whatever is repressed into the unconscious level is always pushing up toward the conscious level, acting much like a cork in water. If the person is not ready to cope with the anxiety and the unresolved problem when they threaten to come up again to consciousness, he must bring up reinforcement, in the form of additional ego defense mechanisms.

For example, a young girl developed feelings of hatred toward her mother for divorcing her father, whom she deeply loved. Because this emotion was incompatible with the love she still felt for her mother, the hatred was eventually repressed. Subsequently, she experienced hate for her mother at unexpected moments. These experiences produced excessive anxiety. At this point the girl began to develop negative feelings toward teachers, who are more acceptable substitutes. Of course, when others asked why she disliked teachers, she had to develop rationalizations to make her otherwise unreasonable behavior appear acceptable to herself and to others.

IDENTIFICATION

Identification as an ego defense mechanism is similar to identification as a reality-oriented defense except in that it is an unconscious process. A student who feels extremely inadequate and unable to improve himself may join many organizations on and off campus. He carries with him many membership cards, his car windows are plastered with signs, and his conversation revolves around the accomplishments of his organizations. He then begins to feel that he was responsible for the great deeds, whereas in reality he accomplished nothing.

RATIONALIZATION

Rationalization, as an ego defense, consists of finding what seem to be logical or plausible reasons for behaviors whose underlying motives have been repressed. Lying, however, is reality-oriented because it is conscious and deliberate. Persons who use rationalization really believe what they are saying even though their reasons are false, distorted, or not really the whole story. Consider the following example of rationalization.

A wealthy childless Caucasian couple adopted an Indian youngster. They quickly became heartbroken, for their friends and neighbors rejected their adopted son. Other boys and girls would either not play with him or would call him names.

They asked in righteous indignation, "How can people who go to church every Sunday be so inhuman? Even our neighbors, whom we've known and respected for years, reject our little boy. How is this possible? What makes people who are decent, educated, and religious, hateful toward an innocent child?" Finally, a psychologist suggested that they stop telling everybody that their son was of Indian heritage and to simply refer to him the way they would if he were really their own son. The father replied rather indignantly. "We can't do that! We must tell everybody that he is an Indian; otherwise, they may mistake him for one of those dirty Mexicans!"

Now we can understand their behavior better. This couple apparently was as prejudiced toward minority groups as their neighbors. However, they loved their adopted son as an individual human being. An approach-avoidance conflict developed. Love and hate were directed at the same time. By repressing their prejudiced feelings and through rationalization, they had solved their conflict temporarily. Their insistence on the same theme and their indignant protests were efforts to strengthen their defense system against their own repressed feelings, which were unacceptable because the negative feelings were directed against a person they loved.

Rationalizations, whether true, reality-oriented, or ego defensive, are very common because they enable individuals and organizations to "justify" everything they have done, are doing, or propose to do.

COMPENSATION

Compensation is the effort to make up for deficiencies that have been repressed. Because the deficiencies are beyond awareness, the efforts are not directed toward improvement but rather to cover the feeling of inadequacy. Consequently, the efforts are usually absurd, like the behavior of the class clown. The student with third-grade reading ability talks and dreams of becoming a lawyer or a neurosurgeon. The unpopular girl may turn to sexual behavior as a means of attracting attention. Such behaviors are doomed to fail because they do not improve competencies, nor do they remove the roots of the problem.

REACTION FORMATION

In reaction formation, a person represses his unacceptable attitudes or behaviors and develops at the conscious level attitudes and behaviors that are just the opposite. A person who is extremely frightened by his strong impulses to steal may eventually become a policeman or a criminal lawyer. Typically, they are so harsh in dealing with the suspect or the accused that one would think that the crime had been committed against them. At times such staunch defenders of the law startle the community by committing crimes. People who crusade against the evils of alcohol are often protecting themselves from such evil behavior. However, this does not mean that all or most crusaders are engaging in reaction formations. Typically, defensive behavior may be distinguished when the person ignores other obligations, such as the needs of his family, becomes openly hostile when his motives are challenged, and has emotions and rationalizations that are not entirely appropriate.

EMOTIONAL ISOLATION

Emotional isolation is a more complex ego defense mechanism. Illustrations are a policeman who is a burglar, a model housewife who is sexually immoral while working part time outside of the home, or a pillar of the church who may also be a dishonest and ruthless businessman. Emotional isolation involves repression, rationalization, and emotional insulation. An example is a woman reared with the idea that sex is evil who marries a man with similar ideas; consequently, sexual intercourse is rare between them. However, sex urges that had been repressed may come to the surface when she finds night employment with members of the opposite sex who openly express their sexual urges toward her. Her sexual promiscuity results in deep-seated anxiety and guilt. To thwart the tensions she develops rationalizations (everybody is doing it) around her sexual behavior and insulates herself from such feelings while at home.

There are other ego defense mechanisms not included in this discussion. A list of such mechanisms is theoretically limitless, because ego defenses are elaborations of normal human behavior. In other words, we can take any normal human behavior and carry it to such an extreme that the behavior becomes pathological. For example, washing one's hands is commendable behavior, but when a person washes his hands fifty to sixty times a day he shows abnormal behavior.

MAKING DISTINCTIONS BETWEEN EGO AND REALITY-ORIENTED DEFENSES

In real life situations, it is very difficult, or nearly impossible, to decide if a behavior is reality-oriented or truly ego defensive. A student who does feel adequate may join many organizations because he wishes to learn new ideas and meet new people. In fact, he may make many valuable contributions to these organizations. Here are a few guidelines that may help you make a distinction between the true ego defenses and normal reactions.

Inconsistencies in Behavior

A teacher claims to love her job, but avoids her students whenever possible. The authors recall one teacher who "loved" to teach. A student accidentally spilled ink on her desk. She looked at her desk and tears rolled down her face. A year later she quit teaching.

Overreactions to Questions

When one questions the reasons for ego defensive behavior, the person is likely to overreact emotionally. For example, a student who is rejected frequently by members of the opposite sex may buy an expensive sports car because he "needs transportation." An inquiry suggesting the real reason for his behavior may elicit a violent reaction of denial.

Constant Protests and Excuses

The student with latent homosexual tendencies, which frighten him, often viciously attacks and condemns homosexuals' behavior. The unfaithful husband may overwhelm his wife with tokens of love, constant telephone calls, and gifts.

Behavior That Doesn't Make Sense

Behavior that just doesn't make sense may be indicative of an ego defense mechanism. A young woman may turn down a marriage proposal from a man she loves because "mother needs me." A man who condemns sex may be seen reading pornography. If questioned about his inconsistent behavior, he may answer, "Well, someone must read it to see if it is dirty."

The following incident of a father's behavior toward his son may be understood in terms of identification. Try to decide if the father's behavior is reality oriented or ego defensive.

A father brought his 13-year-old son to a well-known reading clinic for diagnosis of his reading problem. To the amazement of the clinic staff, the boy's reading test scores were equivalent to a college freshman's. They informed the father, but he wanted reading lessons for his son anyway. "Everybody can improve his reading skills!" was his basic argument. Finally, the reading clinic agreed to provide lessons three times a week and the father filled out the application forms. However, the application forms revealed that the family lived over 150 miles from the reading clinic. Because of the great distance, the father was informed that his son would not be accepted under any circumstances.

The father's unreasonable behavior would seem indicative of an ego defense mechanism. The sacrifice of driving six hours a day three times a week for reading lessons for an eighth-grader who was already reading at the college freshman level does not make good sense.

DECOMPENSATION

As a person uses more and more ego defense mechanisms, he blocks out more and more reality. In so doing, he decreases more and more his chances of constructive solutions to his problems. Eventually, if the use of ego defenses has not reduced the mounting tension and anxiety, other defense systems called neuroses and psychoses develop. At this point, the person enters the range of abnormal behavior, as shown in Table 10-1.

Table 10-1

Sequence from Normal to Abnormal Behavior

Problem-Solving Behavior	$\longrightarrow$	Reality-Oriented Behavior	$\longrightarrow$	Ego-Defensive Behavior	$\longrightarrow$	Decompensation (1) Neurotic (2) Psychotic

Intermediate Summary

Continuous severe failure and stress can gradually overwhelm a person's total adjustive capacities. At this point, personality decompensation begins. The first stage is the extensive use of ego defense mechanisms; the second, the development of either neuroses or psychoses. Ego defense mechanisms have three essential characteristics: (1) The true motives for the behaviors are always at the unconscious level. (2) The person engages in self-deceptive behavior. (3) The level of anxiety is reduced.

Neurotic Defense Systems

Neurotic defense systems are stable and strong defenses against unbearable emotional hurts. Such a defense system is welcomed by the person because the intolerable anxiety, fear, and tension are removed. After becoming neurotic, a person feels much better, although the neurotic defense does nothing to solve his real problems.

A neurotic defense, seemingly a blessing at first, eventually complicates the real problems. The neurotic person has become less able to help himself, because his attention and energies are now directed toward strengthening and protecting the neurotic system. He has to be continually on the defensive. He is like the man on a tightrope who has little freedom of movement, or the poker player who can't take any more chances because he has only two chips left with which to play.

Although there are many ways to develop neurotic defenses, a typical sequence goes something like this: (Coleman, 1964)

1. Circumstances with which the individual cannot cope.
2. Failure in the solutions of the problems after some unsuccessful attempts.
3. Replacement of problem-solving efforts by defense-oriented behavior.
4. Development of neurotic defenses.

GENERAL SIGNS OF NEUROTIC BEHAVIOR

To decide whether a person is a neurotic requires the services of a professional person. However, the troubled person must know what some of the general signs are before he is sufficiently motivated to seek help. A major difficulty is that many of the general signs of neurotic behavior are present in all of us during times of unusual stress. Therefore, the diagnosis of a possible neurosis depends not on just the presence of the general signs, but on the frequency and intensity of the symptoms as well. The following are some of the general signs of a neurotic defense system.

Lowered Intelligence

The neurotic often suffers from a loss of intellectual ability. The more severe the illness, the greater the loss. The reason is that the development and maintenance of a complex defense system requires a constant expenditure of energy and effort. (Hall, 1954)

Disturbing Tensions

Neurotics often complain of sleeping badly, nightmares, restlessness, and tensions that do not seem related to any existing problem. The reason is that the real problems have been repressed and, from time to time, they break through the neurotic defense system.

Very Self-Centered

All of us are concerned about ourselves, but the neurotic is chronically and overly concerned with himself, his problems, his feelings, his belongings, and so on. He shows little interest or concern for the problems and feelings of other people.

Great Need for Love

Neurotics tend to have an almost insatiable need to be loved. They cling to others in a desperate search for affection. Of course, it is difficult for others to love a person who shows little concern for their welfare.

Oversensitive

Reactions to ordinary frustration are exaggerated. An outburst of uncontrollable crying may result from an unannounced change in a favorite television program, purchase of wrong-sized shoes, or some other trivial matter.

Inability to Make Decisions

Conflict situations, even simple ones, are much more difficult for neurotics. A coed may change her dress so many times that it becomes too late to go to the party. An outburst of tears follows because her desire to go to the party has been thwarted.

Rigid and Conservative

A neurotic gears his life activities so that he knows ahead of time what to expect. He avoids new ideas and situations because he must gear life to protect his defense system and not to meet new challenges or to explore new frontiers.

Difficult to Help

Neurotics have some insight into their inappropriate behavior. They are generally unhappy about their life situation and wish to get rid of their symptoms. However, to get rid of their symptoms they must face again the same problems from which they are running away.

It is difficult to help neurotics. They tend to find reasons for rejecting helpful suggestions and advice. Most neurotics seek help only when their neurotic system deteriorates and the anxiety becomes too much for them to cope with.

THE THREE CLASSIFICATIONS OF NEUROTIC BEHAVIOR

There are three major classifications of neurotic behavior: (1) psychoneurosis, (2) character disorders, and (3) situational transient neurosis. Within each classification there are various kinds of specific neurotic patterns.

Psychoneurosis

In order to develop a psychoneurosis, a person must undergo the long-term process from unsuccessful problem solving to reality-oriented defenses and ego defenses. The specific neurosis developed depends on the individual's past experiences, the nature of his problems, and the kinds of defenses previously used.

ANXIETY REACTION. This neurotic reaction is temporary. All neurotics first go through it before developing a stable neurosis. In the same way that a very high fever can be the final warning of a serious medical problem, an anxiety reaction is our last warning of serious psychological illness. This is the last opportunity to seek help if we are to avoid the sufferings of a neurosis.

Anxiety reactions are the simplest neurosis because repression is the only ego defense mechanism involved. It is characterized by anxiety for which one cannot account. In some cases, there is a mild anxiety that is present constantly, no matter where the person goes or what he does. In other cases, the mild chronic anxiety is interrupted by a wild anxiety attack. With no warning, heart palpitation increases rapidly, breathing becomes difficult, the hands and lips tremble. The terrified person may feel that he is going to die. He may call a doctor and a minister. However, the attack usually lasts but a few minutes. He may undergo a few more anxiety attacks before he moves on to a stable neurosis, seeks psychological help, or, by some miracle, resolves his own problems through good fortune or intensely increased efforts.

Obsessive and Compulsive Neuroses

OBSESSIVE NEUROSIS. Obsessive neurosis is the process wherein a person is forced to think about things that he does not want to think about. Has this ever happened to you? Of course it has! While in church or school you may get an urge to shout an obscenity. Or, without provocation, the thought flashes in your mind, "I wish mother would die." Such irrational thoughts occur in all of us. What distinguishes neurotic obsessive thoughts from normal, is that normal persons feel guilty about them. These same thoughts do not put guilt feelings and tension in the neurotic because the constant flow of irrational thoughts keeps the repressed problems from consciousness.

Obsessive thoughts interfere and interrupt learning and daily activities. With time, the thoughts become more intense and frequent until the person is so miserable that he seeks professional help.

COMPULSIVE NEUROSIS. Compulsive behavior consists of doing things one does not want to do. Yet, not to go through the activity would mean being overcome with anxiety. Have you ever stepped on every crack on the sidewalk, or counted every car similar to yours while driving? You did it for fun. The neurotic, however, must do such things or suffer overwhelming anxiety.

Compulsive behavior becomes more serious when a person washes his hands fifty to sixty times a day. A compulsive housewife maintains an extremely rigid routine, keeps everything in very exact order, and her home is meticulously clean. A small spot of dirt requires immediate removal. A book slightly out of line will be straightened with care. The purpose of such meticulous behavior is to protect herself from any change or disorder that could threaten her neurotic defense system.

In some cases obsessive thoughts precede compulsive acts. Some types of obsessive-compulsive behavior can be serious from the viewpoint of society. A pyromaniac is one who starts fires because of the sexual gratification it produces. In fact, the bigger the fire the more intense the sexual reaction. It is interesting to note the frequent association between passion and love in such common statements as, "We had a hot time last night" or, "You set me on fire."

Kleptomaniacs are also obsessive-compulsive neurotics. They steal objects for which usually they have no material need, but that are symbolic for them of sex. The stealing of these sex symbols—the excitement and suspense—produces sexual excitement and gratification.

In general, the personalities with obsessive-compulsive neurosis are rigid, introverted, and highly conventional and moral. (Shapiro, 1965) Typically, they tend to repress sexual and aggressive feelings. Therefore, we would expect that their neurotic defenses would serve the purpose of keeping these feelings from being expressed at all, or expressed only in ritualistic or symbolic forms.

PHOBIC NEUROSIS. Phobias are irrational fears of objects or situations that present no actual danger. All of us have unwanted and unwarranted fears that are the result of previous learning and hurts. We may fear to look down from a tall building or take an ocean cruise because of previous frightening experiences or because of our reading about persons who have committed suicide by jumping from high places and the terrifying episodes of survivors of shipwrecks. Such fears are learned and have become exaggerated from fantasies, misunderstandings, or the incubation process (discussed in Chapter 2). In a true phobic neurosis, the person does not really fear the specific object or situation itself, but rather what is symbolized. For example, fear of snakes because of their symbolic nature is a phobic neurosis; fear of snakes because one was bitten is a learned fear. Two students may fear bees to the same extent. However, in one case there is an exaggerated fear of the dangers of a sting and, in the other, bees represent a repressed problem. That the fear is symbolic means that it has been displaced to another object, person, or situation having nothing to do with the original fear or fright. In either case—exaggerated response to early stress or response to symbolic fears—professional assistance should be sought. If the fear turns out to be a learned response, the treatment is relatively simple; if the fear is symbolic, more intensive psychotherapy will be required.

ASTHENIC NEUROSIS. An asthenic neurosis consists primarily of being very tired, physically and mentally. Significantly, such persons show an abundance of energy for selected activities not related to their repressed problems. All of us are, to a degree, asthenic. A student who can barely keep his eyes opened during a late afternoon class can be observed shortly afterward energetically polishing his car for an evening of frenzied dancing.

The asthenic is not fatigued because of actual work done or physical exhaustion. His "tiredness" is produced by the prolonged emotional stress related to unresolved problems. According to Coleman (1964, p. 202), a well-known authority in the field of abnormal behavior:

> Asthenic reactions are especially common among so-called nervous housewives who feel neglected by their husbands and frustrated and cheated by life. Frequently, such women reveal a history of delicate health and parental overprotection in childhood. Their life situation seems hopeless to them, and they react with discouragement, bitterness, and preoccupation with various somatic (bodily) complaints.

> Relatives and friends frequently reinforce their illness by feeling sorry for them and helping them to escape from responsibilities and chores. Asthenics need to

develop their competencies, to use them to cope with problems, and to get back into the battle of life.

HYPOCHONDRIACAL DEFENSE. A hypochondriac is one who is utterly convinced that he is physically ill when there is nothing wrong organically. He is not pretending illness. He sincerely believes that he is in need of medical care. Most of us are interested in our health, but the hypochondriac's interest is abnormal.

Typically, hypochondriacs are middle-aged people who believe that they are failing in life. Their "illness" gets them attention and provides an acceptable excuse for failure. In their backgrounds we find parental overconcern and acceptance of illness as excuses for not doing what is expected of them.

Hypochondriacs are difficult to cure because they do not accept their need for psychological treatment, but insist on undergoing medical treatment, which only reinforces their neurotic defense.

CONVERSION DEFENSE. A conversion defense, also known as a *psychosomatic disorder,* consists of organic symptoms with or without underlying organic disease produced primarily by emotional stress and tension. As in the other neurotic defenses, the symptoms protect from failure and at the same time they provide attention and sympathy. Few persons would condemn a sick man for shirking his duties and responsibilities.

Conversion defenses include a wide variety of physical disorders such as headaches, stomach ulcers, diabetes, arthritis, high blood pressure, blindness, paralysis, loss of sense of touch or pain, skin disorders, and hyperthyroidism. In cases with no organic damage, the symptoms are still real; the person is not faking. The paralysis of the legs may last for years. The skin disorders may resist all medical treatments by dermatologists. In other cases, the symptoms are equally real but there is true organic damage. Stomach ulcers result in actual bleeding in the stomach lining. The blood chemistry and other organic changes of the hypersomatic hyperthyroid patient are as real as hyperthyroidism produced by a diseased thyroid gland.

As yet, no one has been able to explain satisfactorily how chronic emotional stress is converted to physical ailments and symptoms. Yet, there are more conversion disorders than all other neuroses put together. It is our most common ailment.

The following are ways to distinguish a conversion defense from an organic disease:

1. The person's emotional state does not correspond to that of a patient with an organic disease. If you were informed that you would never walk again, you would suffer intense and prolonged emotional feelings. The person using a conversion defense typically would not.

2. A case history reveals that the conversion served as a way out of an intolerable life situation. For example, a machine-gunner may develop a paralysis of the hand used to fire his weapon or a ditch digger may become incapacitated by back trouble.

Understanding the Unhealthy Personality

3. The family doctor may find no underlying organic reason for the disease; the symptoms are impossible to explain medically.

4. Careful observation may reveal "impossible" activities. A blind person may duck to avoid a rock. The man with a paralyzed arm may use it while sleeping. A hospitalized veteran may recover "miraculously" as soon as peace is declared.

DEPRESSIVE DEFENSE. A depressive defense consists of admitting defeat and developing feelings of unworthiness and apathy. Severe depressive defenses can lead eventually to suicide. Such defenses serve as an excuse for not trying anymore. By admitting that he's stupid, incompetent, lazy, and no good, the person puts an effective brake on his efforts and those of others to motivate him toward efforts to improve and to solve his problems.

Typically, depressive defenses are used by persons who have thought that it is wrong to feel anger toward loved ones and to express hostility outwardly toward others. Therefore, he turns feelings of hostility inward, toward himself. If things go wrong, it is always his fault. This inner hostility toward one's self becomes destructive of one's self-confidence and adequacy. To avoid depressive defenses, we must accept the fact that even those we love are not perfect and do wrong things. Therefore, it is all right to feel anger and to express it to those we love. One cannot love everything a loved one does or love him all of the time. To do so, would be to distort reality.

Prolonged failure in many life situations can also produce depressive defenses. Sometimes we feel that we "have had it" and that the world is against us. Such conditions can and should cause a temporary depressive state. Actually such temporary states are not considered to be neurotic.

DISSOCIATIVE DEFENSES. Dissociative defenses consist of repressing those acutely unpleasant situations from which there seems to be no escape. The repression may cover large segments of a person's life, or it may include all past experiences. In psychological amnesia, one suddenly represses almost everything about himself. Usually he is taken to a hospital where he is kept until memory returns. More dramatic are fugue defenses, in which a person has amnesia but moves to a new place, changes his name, and begins an entirely new life that may last for days, weeks, or years. When he finally recovers his memory, he returns home, with an amnesia for the fugue period.

A dramatic form of dissociative defenses that has attracted much attention is the multiple personality. In this defense, a person demonstrates two or more contrasting personalities, each unaware of the other. The Robert Louis Stevenson story, "Dr. Jekyll and Mr. Hyde" was based on this defense reaction. Actually all of us have multiple personalities, but we call them social roles. The behavior of a college student out to have a good time in a neighboring city does not usually resemble the student's behavior while on campus.

Cases of multiple personality are extremely rare. The best publicized was the case of Eve White, who had two major distinct personalities, one carefree and witty and the other serious and conventional. After psychotherapy, a third personality developed. (Thigpen and Cleckley, 1957)

Somnambulism refers to sleepwalking, a symbolic escape from unresolved conflicts. One study of 1,808 college students revealed that 5 per cent suffered from somnambulism. (Jenness and Jorgensen, 1941)

Character Disorders

Character disorders are similar to the psychoneurosis in that they represent what people do after their previous defenses against emotional hurts break down. Character disorders may take as long as psychoneurosis to develop. They differ in that the symptoms are either antisocial or far more disturbing to others.

CRIMINAL DEFENSE. Criminal defense, or criminal insanity, consists of breaking the law as part of a neurotic attempt to solve problems. To prove insanity legally is difficult, for it must be proven that at the time of the crime the person was unaware of what he was doing or of the consequences of his behavior. However, there are some general indications of criminal defensive behavior:

1. The accused has no previous record of criminal behavior.
2. His crime doesn't make sense (for example, a wealthy man stealing a few dollars or a car dealer stealing a used automobile).
3. The accused offers no alibis or reasons.
4. He wants to be found guilty and to go to prison.

An example of criminal insanity is the case of an insurance agent who collected death claim checks for clients who were still living. He had no previous criminal record and, as an insurance agent, he knew that he would be caught. During the court proceedings, he made no attempts to justify his behavior. A court-appointed psychologist found that the accused was suffering from intense guilt feelings because his wife had undergone three consecutive stillbirths. Somehow he felt responsible, so he was seeking a way to punish himself. Committing a "crime" and going to prison is one way of atoning for sins, real or imagined.

PSYCHOPATHIC DEFENSE. Psychopathic behavior consists of taking undue advantage of other people and engaging in antisocial and illegal activities without any feelings of guilt or concern. On the contrary, psychopaths seem to go out of their way to make a burlesque of society, its values, and morals.

Apart from their lack of conscience and feelings, they appear to be normal, particularly in everyday behavior. They are unlike the normal person in their psychopathic activities, which seem purposeless or that satisfy only immediate needs without regard for long-range satisfaction. Essentially the psychopath is an asocial, aggressive, highly impulsive person, who feels little or no guilt and is unable to form lasting bonds of affection with other human beings. (McCord and McCord, 1956)

SEXUAL DEFENSES. Another type of behavior that the individual who feels extremely inadequate may engage in has to do with expressions of sexuality.

Because sexual release is one of our basic physiological needs, and because sexual attractiveness ("sex appeal") is one of the values consistently rewarded in much of our advertising, it is understandable why a person who feels badly about himself might turn to sexual outlets as a defense system. Some of the more common expressions of this defensive pattern include: homosexuality, pedophilia, and exhibitionism.

HOMOSEXUALITY. Homosexuality (sexual interest in and/or achieving sexual orgasm with a member of the same sex) is in our society one of the most misunderstood and controversial forms of sexual defense. Kinsey (1948) made discussion of the topic even more heated. In his study, *Sexual Behavior in the Human Male*, he showed that 4 per cent of American men are exclusively homosexual, but that about 50 per cent of the male population had at one time had some homosexual experiences.

In our discussion here it should be made clear that we are not talking about the person who may have had one or two exploratory homosexual experiences in adolescence or young adulthood. According to many psychiatrists and psychologists, this is within the range of normality. For example, Blain and McArthur (1966) state:

Because adolescence is the time when the first strong outwardly directed sexual impulses are experienced there is a good deal of confusion in the minds of college boys as to what sort of outlet is most healthy and appropriate. Sexual feeling is at its strongest at this period also, so whatever degree of homosexuality one may have inherently or as a result of environmental influences is felt more powerfully and urgently during these years. Many students feel and do things at this time which they never repeat again during their adult life. (p. 121)

There appears to be evidence that many homosexuals do use their behavior as a defense system against feelings of inadequacy. As to the causes of this form of sexual behavior, the evidence seems to support the theory that homosexuality is a result of learned patterns of behavior. Two of the more common patterns seem to be: (1) a dominant mother figure and a passive father (here, the male fails to identify with masculine patterns of behavior and adopts a feminine role) or (2) a beautiful, rather seductive mother, who may be very close to the son; thus, the son, in his relations with other females, unconsciously relates to them as his own mother and finds it too threatening to develop a close relationship. (Bieber, 1962)

Homosexuality is still considered a form of illness according to the norms in our society; in addition, it is illegal in many states of the union. Therefore, in general, individuals who seek out members of the same sex are bound to be affected by the hostility and prejudice against them.

A recent study suggests that within the context of a homosexual society, certain homosexuals may lead productive lives. (Hooker, 1962)

PEDOPHILIA. Pedophilia (child molesting, using a child as a sex object) is another, more serious form of sexual defense because it involves children. Coleman (1960) lists three possible patterns:

1. Individuals who feel inadequate and inferior and focus their attention on children to avoid possible failure and self-devaluation in normal adult relationships.

2. Older men with fears about their potency, who have a basically psychopathic make-up.

3. Mentally ill individuals whose ethical restraints have been lowered by their mental disorders. (p. 241)

EXHIBITIONISM. A person who has low self-esteem or who feels inadequate in normal sexual relationships may turn to exhibitionism (exposing genitals to members of the opposite sex in public) as a defense. Another common pattern among male exhibitionists is the person who feels questionable about his masculinity; by exposing himself and getting a response from the opposite sex, he feels more like a man. Treatment for exhibitionism is generally quite effective.

ALCOHOLIC DEFENSE. Alcoholism consists of the consumption of alcohol to the extent that it interferes seriously with daily living. It is another example of an unsatisfactory way of trying to cope with failure. Yet there are some 5,000,000 Americans who may be classified as alcoholics and each year 200,000 more join them. (Coleman, 1964) At present, alcoholism ranks as the fourth most prevalent disease in the United States.

Most persons engage in social drinking, but only a certain percentage continues beyond this normal stage. The person who does is thought to have built up greater tension from unresolved problems. Therefore, social drinking may be more tension reducing for this person and, therefore, more rewarding. However, there are experts who feel that the reason some like alcohol better than others is because of individual physiological reactions to the alcohol. Whatever the reason, some people enjoy alcohol more than other persons.

From a study of 2,000 alcoholics, the following stages of alcoholism have been derived: (Jellinek, 1952) (1) The alcoholic-to-be shifts from social drinking to constant drinking to reduce tension. (2) He suffers blackouts, that is, loss of memory, of a drinking episode. At this point, too, he rationalizes his drinking, denies it, or projects the blame onto others. He may now become more concerned with drinking and hiding his activity from others than with his responsibilities at home or on the job. The ideal time for seeking help is at the second stage, because by stage three, control over drinking is lost. (3) The individual begins to drink and cannot stop until he is completely intoxicated. During this period, he may lose his job, friends, and family. All this adds to his original struggle for self-esteem. (4) The alcoholic admits defeat, may seek help, or may allow himself to be committed to a hospital for alcoholic psychosis.

DRUG ADDICTION DEFENSE. The drug addict is a person who has selected drugs as a way of coping with his problems. Of course, to select drugs as a way of avoiding the realities of life there must be access to drugs. Almost all accounts of people who are dependent on drugs stress that they have, continuously, a very bad opinion of themselves and their abilities. (Ausubel, 1954)

As with alcoholism, drug addiction does not solve the problems, but rather temporarily covers them up. In the long run, the person still has his original problems, in addition to the new one of drug addiction.

Neuroses can be seen essentially as efforts to ward off the anxiety and stress resulting from problems that persons could not cope with, despite all their efforts. Each is an example of interrupted learning, because the person is more concerned with his feelings and self-esteem than he is with solving the problems.

SITUATIONAL TRANSIENT NEUROSES

Situational transient neuroses are caused by unusually severe crisis or by prolonged external stresses. In either case, the person responds neurotically to circumstances that are beyond his ability to handle. The neurotic behaviors produced by severe or prolonged life situations should not be confused with the chronic neuroses that are the results of long-term failures to difficulties that may no longer even be present. The situational transient neurosis depends on present major catastrophes, such as deaths in the family, the severity of unexpected illnesses, or a series of incredably bad breaks in life.

Although the symptoms of situational transient neurosis often resemble those of the chronic neurosis, the symptoms will typically disappear when the crisis ends or shortly afterward. Therapy, when given, is usually brief and mild. In many cases it is not difficult for an outsider to realize that someone else is suffering from a situational transient neurosis. However, in some cases, the crisis is the last straw in a long series of previous failures producing a chronic neurosis. Therefore, it is best to seek professional advice regarding all kinds of neurotic behaviors.

Combat Neurosis

Stress under military conditions can produce situational transient neurosis. After World War II, it was found that 34 per cent of medical cases were neurotics. (Menninger, 1948) Some would have become neurotics under the normal stresses of civilian life, but others became neurotics as a result of the severity of combat. The following is a description of combat-produced neurosis. (Saul and Lyons, 1953, pp. 152–153)

The typical picture seen in the last war is a fighting man recently returned from combat or the front areas. His features are distorted with fear and wan with fatigue. His normal co-ordination is troubled with gross tremors, and excessive perspiration dampens his body. Even in the quiet of the rear area, his biologic mobilization for fight or flight remains. He overreacts to ordinary noises; a low-flying commercial plane sends him into a frenzied dive for shelter. The sudden ringing of a telephone may send him leaping out of his seat, followed by hysterical crying and extreme rage at himself for such an emotional display. He is alternately passive and clinging and equally aggressive and combative on slight irritation. War movies and usual civilian noises send him into a panic, so that he becomes seclusive and prefers to remain in the ward rather than take part in the rehabilitation program. Night becomes a time of terror, when every shadow threatens danger. Even the escape into sleep is hampered by insomnia, or, when sleep does come, it ends with nightmares of his horrible experiences. His waking hours are further plagued by tension, indecisions, difficulty in concentrating, headaches, gastro-intestinal disturbances, dizzy spells, and other psychosomatic disturbances.

Who will develop neurosis, whether transient or chronic, depends on many individual factors such as the man's personality, previous experiences, the kind of life to which he must return, the morale of his buddies, and his degree of loyalty to fighting the war.

College Problems

Although college life can have moments of great joy and excitement, it can also produce many conflicts and frustrations. Some students find it very difficult when they try to be serious, work part-time, placate parental ambitions, and maintain their images as "great lovers." Some students feel that they are being manipulated by colleges into studies they believe to be meaningless. Some react with apathy or emotional insulation. Others act out their frustrations in anger and rebellion.

Here again, we find large individual differences. Whereas some students can adjust to or tolerate problems of college living, others respond with transient situational neuroses of varying degrees of severity. Considering all the pressures that students must face, the presence of neurotic symptoms is understandable. However, students with severe problems should seek professional help because the emotional turmoil interferes with effective thinking and learning. Failure to do so may result in a vicious circle of failure-tension, more failure, more tension, and so forth. Some of these problems are illustrated in the following case (Walters, 1948 p. 181):

A freshman was asked to go to the psychiatric clinic by a dean because of poor grades, cutting classes, and failure to meet physical education requirements. The patient stated he began to lose interest in his studies in his senior year in prep school. He had been sent away to a boarding school for preparation for a "name" college by his father, a self-educated executive in a large company, who wished his son to have the "best" education, the success of which the father could measure only by achievement. The patient hated to leave home where he felt secure among friends and family but after much argument acceded to the wishes of his father and the pleas of his mother. Soon after his arrival at school he learned that his mother had her first attack of a gradually debilitating, ultimately fatal, disease. The patient consciously felt that arguments associated with persuading him to go away to school plus the strain of moving to another city the year before (because of the father's promotion to an executive position) were responsible for her illness. . . . The patient made it clear that he shared with the father the responsibility for this injury, but that due to his complete lack of action and argumentativeness he could no longer be held responsible for further injury. He also used the apathetic defense as a means of punishing himself by failing his courses, and punishing his father by failing to satisfy his father's own vicarious pleasure in his son's education.

The student was using apathy as a defense against previous problems as well as present school difficulties. For some students, school adjustment is made far more difficult because they bring to college unresolved personal problems. Other students find their studies are being sabotaged by the cold indifference found in many colleges. These students need to feel that someone does care about them. The following case points this out clearly (Blaine and McArthur, 1966, p. 92):

> A sophomore, who had been doing little or no work during his second year at college, came to see the dean in order to resign from college. Previously he had been a good student, but during the summer following his freshman year his father had died. The boy had tried to continue to do his studying conscientiously, but he had begun procrastinating and gradually the mountain of work became too great and he had decided to withdraw from college and planned to tour throughout the West, doing odd jobs on the way. The dean told him that it was perfectly all right to withdraw and added that he would like very much to hear from the student as he traveled about the country and hoped that he would send postcards back regularly. He offered to write the boy from time to time if he would give him addresses to which mail could be sent. The student showed great surprise at this interest on the dean's part, tears came to his eyes, and he said, "I did not know that you cared that much about me."

The fact that this student did not drop out of college should surprise no one who has worked with college people. All of us need to know that we are wanted. It is difficult to think of a greater punishment than to be systematically ignored by others, to walk down the halls and have no one notice, to speak and have no one listen.

College Marriages

Although college marriages are more acceptable today, they do present additional problems not found in other marriages. That a successful marriage does not come easily is apparent from the fact that one of every four marriages in the United States ends in divorce. For college students, already in the midst of academic struggles and strivings for complete independence from the home, the decision to marry is a serious one. For some it is the straw that breaks the camel's back; for others it is the oasis that satisfies. Landis and Landis (1963) describe some of the alternatives in college marriages:

> When both members of a married couple are attending classes and perhaps working part-time, or when one is in school and the other working, their lives become very full; they find it necessary to organize their activities with great efficiency. If, in addition, there are children to care for, couples need to be supermen and superwomen in order to meet all of their responsibilities adequately. The success of college marriages means that many young couples are adequate for all these requirements. But a man or boy who expects to be waited on, who considers it beneath his masculine dignity to do dishes, scrub floors, or diaper babies, is likely to be a problem husband in a college marriage. And a girl who wants to be free from hard work and struggle, and who cannot be happy if she has to miss any of the whirl of college social life should not marry while she is still in college. For even if there is plenty of money and there are no babies, working at marriage while both are students requires unselfish cooperation and some sacrifice of personal preferences. (p. 152)

It is important to realize that situational transient neurosis may develop at any time as a result of a series of bad breaks or the great suffering produced by such factors as severe illnesses, economic depressions, divorce, unemployment, or the onset of old age. Such unusual pressures can temporarily overwhelm our adjustive capacities.

Intermediate Summary

Neuroses are stable defenses against the unbearable emotional hurts produced by prolonged severe failures. General signs of neuroses are lowered intelligence, disturbing tensions, extreme self-centeredness, great need for love, oversensitivity, difficulty in making decisions, rigidity, and difficulty in accepting help. The three major classifications of neuroses are (1) the psychoneuroses, of long-term development, consisting of symptoms usually kept within the person, (2) the character neuroses, of long-term development, consisting of symptoms usually acted out in society, and (3) the situational transient neuroses, produced by short-term severe crisis and resulting in symptoms that resemble those in psychoneuroses or character neuroses.

Psychotic Defense Systems

Psychotic patients are much further removed from social contact than neurotic patients. They appear immune to all ordinary efforts to influence them psychologically. They seem, somehow, removed from this world. They say, do, see, and think strange things. In so doing we say that they have broken with reality. The term *insanity* is a legal term and not a psychological one. Insanity means that the patient is dangerous to himself or dangerous to society.

Typically a patient is called insane after a legal court procedure. At times when he does, or says, or thinks strange things, we find that his emotional feelings are inappropriate or absent. He may speak of incest or reveal strange, completely unrealistic ideas ("I am God"); these ideas could be embarrassing for the normal person to tell, but not for the psychotic. Some psychotics seem to have dropped the social façades maintained so seriously and meticulously by ordinary persons. In other words, there may be a complete or partial deterioration of personal or moral control; the patient just doesn't seem to care.

The strange things that psychotics speak or think are called *delusions* and *hallucinations*. *Delusions* are false beliefs, which the patient defends despite all contrary evidence. He may believe that he is some great leader appointed by God to save the world and that is why he has so many enemies. *Hallucinations* are sights, smells, or sounds without any appropriate external stimulations. A patient may feel bugs under his skin, hear voices, or taste poison in his food. It helps to understand these behaviors when we realize that all of us have beliefs and ideas that are not supported by clear-cut evidence, such as religious views, prejudiced feelings, and ideas of superiority.

It cannot be overemphasized that the psychotic is not psychotic all of the time and in all areas of his life or in all aspects of his personality. The psychotic is disturbed only part of the time, only in certain situations, and only in certain aspects of his total personality. We add this: Within a hospital setting the normal individual might react in a similar manner to that of the psychotic. But in the outside world, this is not the case. The psychotic cannot function well or at all when confronted with the demands and stresses of ordinary daily life. Yet, within the safe and highly structured hospital situation, his behavior can fall within the normal range.

CLASSIFICATIONS OF PSYCHOTIC DEFENSES

There are two major classifications of psychotic defenses: (1) functional psychoses, which are the strongest defenses that humans have against the unbearable emotional hurts of unresolved conflicts and frustration and (2) organic psychoses, which are caused by injury to the nervous system. The most common psychoses by far are the functional ones. It is important to realize that the psychiatric labels used for differentiating types of psychoses have little meaning. Even experts in mental hygiene disagree as to which labels to use with hospitalized patients. Far more important than labels is understanding the patient and his unique problems. No one wants to be treated as if he were an item in a Sears catalogue!

Functional Psychoses

The most common psychotic defenses are those called the *schizophrenic disorders*. Like all psychotics, the schizophrenics tend to have the same general symptoms of unrealistic contact with the world, inappropriate emotions, delusions and hallucinations, and a deterioration of personal habits.

In addition to these four general characteristics, there are additional distinguishing characteristics, which so far have produced nine subtypes. Because psychotic symptoms are not always clear and because the textbook descriptions rarely fit what the average person actually sees of abnormal behavior, we will provide descriptions of only a few of the subtypes.

SIMPLE SCHIZOPHRENIA. The principle defense is indifference or lack of interest. The victims seem to have little or no enthusiasm about any activity or topic. They are withdrawn, secluded, and asocial. They seem content to live simple, irresponsible existences. Such people are not really psychotic but rather borderline. Under additional pressure, they may decompensate further and require hospitalization.

PARANOID SCHIZOPHRENIA. This is the most common schizophrenic defense. It consists of trying to maintain feelings of self-esteem by projecting the blame for all failures on others. Such faulty thinking can lead to illogical delusions of persecution, which in turn can lead to delusions of grandeur. How else can he explain all the attention that he receives? But such delusional defenses do not hold up well. Thus, the paranoid develops more bizaare delusions and hallucinations.

CHILDHOOD SCHIZOPHRENIA. Childhood schizophrenia is relatively rare, but it has attracted much attention because it is one of the very few mental illnesses that can be helped, but for which there is no known cure. From infancy, these children are strange; they seem incapable of establishing interest in people or objects. In general, they are passive and withdrawn, but they suffer from inexplicable and unrestrained outbursts of uncontrollable behavior. One of these authors recalls a fifteen-year-old childhood schizophrenic who had received intensive treatment. His outbursts consisted primarily of tapping on the table with one finger, then two, then one hand, and then finally smashing on the table with both arms. Subsequently, he would calm down. However, one night he frightened his parents by practicing this procedure on their bedroom door.

Although there is some disagreement, most experts stress that the backgrounds of schizophrenics reveal overprotective parents who do not allow their children to develop the skills necessary to solve their own problems. Therefore, they take on the role of the "good child," who accepts without question the roles parents, teachers, and others had chosen for them. Upon reaching adolescence, they find that they are psychological cripples who cannot solve problems on their own. Mounting feelings of failure produces fairly rapid decompensation because they have so few competencies with which to protect themselves.

PARANOID DEFENSE. The paranoid's defense consists primarily of a logical and intricate delusional system. However, his personality remains so sufficiently intact that he avoids hospitalization. Because of superior intelligence, he is able to present cogent rationalizations for this behavior that make him sound most convincing. For example, the wife of a paranoid who is accused by him of being unfaithful lives a terrible existence. She is innocent, but his accusations are so detailed and logical that others may believe what he is saying.

Typically, the paranoid is arrogant, rigid, and suspicious. He quickly projects the reasons for his failure experiences onto others. In so doing, he does not permit the learning of new skills. His only defense is to blame others. The paranoid defense can break down under continuous failure in many areas of life. His defense system becomes overextended and his behavior begins to become absurd and even dangerous.

MANIC-DEPRESSIVE DEFENSE. Manic-depressive defenses consist of either extreme elation and a high level of activity or a depressive reaction, or an alternation between the two. All of us have mood swings from passivity to overenthusiasm, depending on how we feel and what we are doing. Manic-depressive defenses are gradual exaggerations of these moods until they become dangerous to the person or to society. The terminal stage of depression may be a vegetable existence, suicide, or—as in the manic type—a swing back to mild and then extreme manic excitement.

It is informative to note that the more violent and depressed the defenses, the better the chances of recovery. It seems that the release of pent-up emotions is helpful. Some manic-depressives may never undergo the extreme moods of activity and do not require hospitalization.

INVOLUTIONAL DEFENSE. An involutional defense consists of depressed feelings accompanied by increased activity. The person feels miserable, unworthy, and may want to commit suicide. At the same time, there is restlessness, insomnia, crying, and excessive worry about minor matters. Typically, an involutional defense occurs in later life, and is much more common among women, especially after menopause. To understand the involutional defense we must be aware of the psychological and physical meaning of becoming old. The middle-aged and the aged can see the beginning of the end. Women can no longer bear children and physical beauty is already declining. A man begins to tire easily, his sex drives lessen, and he can no longer dream of starting all over again. Some can accept aging gracefully. Others find this a most trying period. Even the well-adjusted individual may suffer a mild involutional defense at this point, especially if he has failed to achieve some of his dreams and goals.

APPLICATION

Living with Yourself

By now you should have a better understanding of the unhealthy personality and how it develops through the ego, neurotic, and psychotic defense systems. Your knowing about how mental illness develops may help you to detect the development of certain defensive patterns within yourself, and, hopefully, to be able to prevent the development of serious mental illness within yourself.

Another point to be emphasized is that we all suffer from temporary decompensation at times during our lives when a series of events may exert tremendous pressure on us (that is, death in the family, divorce, serious illness, or a series of failures). In addition, it is important to recognize that there is a good chance that you will experience a period of transient neurosis, in which your behavior will resemble that of some of the neurotic defense systems. Such periods of time as adolescence, early marriage, middle age, and old age often produce these temporary neuroses. As long as you can explain some of your neurotic responses on the basis of real life stress and strain, there is a good chance that it is of a temporary nature; however, if you begin to repress or cannot explain why you feel a certain way, be aware that you may have a more serious illness.

One thing you can do to help yourself become less susceptible to mental illness is to get to know yourself very well. You might, as a psychiatrist put it, begin "listening to yourself with the third ear." That is, you might take an inventory of yourself to determine areas of oversensitivity. These would include areas of your life that tend to produce a high degree of anxiety or tension.

From talking with their students, the authors say the following are some more common sensitive areas: competition, premarital sexual experiences, failure, arguments with parents, and trusting others. What they are not saying is that you should avoid these areas of life completely; however, if you are under pressure already, it might be wise to temporarily pull back from experiences such as these that may produce additional pressures. Try to "know" your limits: to notice when you are trying to do too much, too fast.

Certainly by now you have learned to observe certain danger signals that tell you when you are getting overburdened. Keep an eye open for these and know when to stop or say, "No!" What are some of your ego defensive patterns? Knowing these should help you reduce considerably the chances of moving from the use of reality-oriented defenses to the use of ego defenses.

Another way to help you become less prone to mental illness is through the development of frustration tolerance. By being able to tolerate some degree of frustration and anxiety in life, you will be much more able to cope with the problems that we all face in trying to climb the stepladder toward self-actualization.

Living with Others

If nothing else, it is hoped that this chapter will give you a compassion for, as well as an understanding of, the mentally ill person who has to resort to neurotic or psychotic defenses. Perhaps now you won't react to mental illness as some strange and bizarre disease, but will recognize it as merely an extension of some of the reality-oriented defense mechanisms that we all use in our everyday lives.

You should now be in a better position to recognize signs in others who may be starting to use ego and/or neurotic defensive patterns of behavior. When you do recognize these behavior patterns in others, you can aid them by being a *therapeutic helper* (one who listens with compassion and advises another person who may be undergoing a period of severe stress). By actively and empathetically listening to another person who is beginning to use ego or neurotic defenses, you help him to maintain a sense of relatedness to at least one other person. In addition to listening, another responsibility you have is to help the person maintain contact with reality. You can do this by pointing out things the person is doing or saying that are not in response to the real-life situation in which the person finds himself.

There is sometimes a fine point between the use of reality-oriented defensive behavior and the development of that behavior into ego or neurotic defensive behavior. At what point the person needs professional help will always be difficult to determine, because it depends on so many problems. However, it would be safe to say that if a person begins to feel extremely anxious and fearful with no apparent reason, he may be in the early stages of an ego defense pattern that could become more serious.

Living with Society

It is good to see that our schools are beginning to recognize among students the existence of unhealthy defensive behavior resulting from pressures; this is particularly true of colleges. Most colleges today have a large, well-staffed counseling center where students can go for help.

Perhaps you will be more prone to recommend these services to friends of yours who may be exhibiting symptoms of unhealthy personality defensive patterns. Much of the counseling in schools is done in the light of the realization that the student's behavior is based on a situational or transient neurosis. Thus, it is easy for students to get an appointment with a counselor in crisis situations. Fees, by the way, are either nonexistent or very reasonable.

THE UNHEALTHY PERSONALITY AT WORK

The business world, like education, is slowly becoming more aware of the emotional problems of its workers. Many corporations now provide psychiatric help right on the job, with trained counselors available on a 24-hour basis. Many insurance programs now pay for part of, or all, psychiatric services.

Certain jobs (as was mentioned in the last chapter) have certain built-in strains that may increase the chances of the development of unhealthy defensive patterns. This is something you should assess carefully as you begin to survey your own sensitive areas.

THE UNHEALTHY PERSONALITY AND SOCIETY

Fortunately, our society is developing a realistic and humane attitude toward the mentally ill. We now have mental hospitals and clinics where patients can and do get well after certain treatment. There is a trend toward more short-term mental health facilities in the community so that the patient does not have to leave his friends and family by going to a state hospital miles away.

You can aid in society's concern for the mentally ill by supporting legislation to improve local and state mental health facilities and by supporting such groups as the National Association for Mental Health, Family Service Agencies, Catholic Welfare, Big Brothers, Help, Inc., and the like.

Final Summary

Mental illness is our Number One health problem. It produces untold misery and is the single greatest block toward self-actualization. Mental illness is the consequence of the unbearable hurts produced by prolonged failure to achieve satisfaction of our basic human needs. When this happens our psychological defense systems go into action to protect our self-esteem from further destruction. The first line of defense is the ego defense mechanisms, which are self-deceptive, reduce anxiety, and operate on the unconscious level. The second line of defense is the neuroses or the psychoses. When the first or second line of defense is operating, the person is said to have undergone personality decompensation.

Neuroses are stable defenses against the unbearable emotional hurts produced by continuous failure experiences. The general signs are reduced intellectual ability, disturbing tensions, self-centeredness, exaggerated need for love, over-sensitivity to minor frustrations, difficulty in making decisions, rigidity, and resistance toward help from others that may help them face their problems realistically. The three major classifications of neuroses are the psychoneuroses, which are of a long-term development with symptoms typically internalized; the character neuroses, which are of a long-term development with symptoms typically externalized; and situational transient neuroses, which are short term and are produced by a severe ongoing personal crisis. The symptoms are similar to those of either the psychoneuroses or the character neuroses.

Psychoses are also stable defenses against unbearable emotional hurts. The symptoms are usually so severe that hospitalization is required. Psychotics are much further removed from social contact than neurotics. At times they do, see, feel, and think strange things. Nearly all psychoses result from psychological causes and are called *functional*. Organic psychoses are the result of injuries to the nervous system.

Specific Chapter References

Ausubel, D. P. *Drug addiction: physiological, psychological, and sociological aspects.* New York: Random House, 1954.

Bieber, I., *et al. Homosexuality: a psychoanalytic study.* New York: Basic Books, 1962.

Blain, G. B., Jr., and McArthur, C. C. *Emotional problems of the student.* New York: Doubleday, 1966.

Coleman, J. C. *Abnormal psychology and modern life.* Chicago: Scott, Foresman, 1964.

Coleman, J. C. *Personality dynamics and effective behavior.* Chicago: Scott, Foresman, 1960.

Coombs, A. W. *What can man become?* Address to the Association for Supervision and Curriculum Development, National Education Association, 1962.

Emotional problems of college students. Roche Laboratories, Nutley, N. J., 1965.

Facts about mental health. National Association for Mental Health, 1967.

Fromm, E. *The sane society.* New York: Rinehart, 1955.

Hall, C. S. *Freudian psychology.* New York: World, 1954.

Hooker, E. *The homosexual community.* In Proceedings of the XIV International Congress of Applied Psychology. Vol. II. Personality research. Copenhagen: Munksgaard, 1962.

Jahoda, M. *Current Concepts of Positive Mental Health.* Joint Commission on Mental Illness & Health. Monograph Series No. 1. New York: Basic Books, 1958.

Jellinek, E. M. Phases of alcohol addiction. *Quarterly Journal for the Study of Alcohol,* 1952, 13, 673–678.

Jenness, A., and Jorgensen, A. P. Ratings of vividness of imagery in the walking state compared with reports of somnambulism. *American Journal of Psychology*, 1941, 54, 253–259.

Kinsey, A. C., Pomeroy, W. B., and Martin, C. E. *Sexual behavior in the human male.* Philadelphia: Saunders, 1948.

Landis, J. T., and Landis, M. G. *Building a successful marriage.* Englewood Cliffs, N. J.: Prentice-Hall, 1963.

Langer T. S., and Michael, S. T. *Life stress and mental health.* New York: Free Press, 1963.

MacFarlane, J. W., Allen, L., and Honzik, M. P. *A developmental study of the behavior problems of normal children between twenty-one months and fourteen years.* University of California Publications in Child Development, Berkeley: University of California Press, 1954.

McCord, W., and McCord, J. *The psychopath.* Princeton, N. J.: Van Nostrand, 1956.

Menninger, W. C. Facts and statistics of significance for psychiatry. *Bulletin of the Menninger Clinic*, 1948, 12,1.

Plutchik, R. *The emotions: facts, theories, and a new model.* New York: Random House, 1962.

Quay, H. C. *Children's behavior disorders: selected readings.* Princeton, N. J.: Van Nostrand, 1968.

Saul, L. J., and Lyons, J. W. Acute neurotic reactions. In F. Alexander and H. Ross (eds.), *Dynamic psychiatry.* Chicago: University of Chicago Press, 1953.

Shapiro, D. *Neurotic styles.* New York: Basic Books, 1965.

Thigpen, C. H., and Cleckley, H. M. *Three faces of eve.* New York: McGraw-Hill, 1957.

Walters, P. A. Student apathy. In G. B. Blaine and C. C. McArthur *et al.* (eds.), *Emotional problems of students.* New York: Doubleday, 1948.

Recommended Further Readings

Paperback Books

Eaton, J. W., and Weil, R. J. *Culture and mental disorders.* New York: Free Press, 1955.

Hoffer, E. *The true believer.* New York: Mentor Books, 1951.

Hunt, R. (ed.). *Personalities and cultures: readings in psychological anthropology.* Garden City, N. Y.: Doubleday, 1967.

Klausner, S. Z. (ed.). *Why man takes chances.* Garden City, N. Y.: Anchor Books, 1968.

McGee, R. *Social disorganization in America.* San Francisco: Chandler, 1962.

Nunokawa, W. D. *Human values and abnormal behavior.* Glenview, Ill.: Scott, Foresman, 1965.

Southwell, E. A., and Feldman, H. (eds.). *Abnormal psychology.* Belmont, Calif.: Brooks-Cole, 1968.

Stengel, E. *Suicide and attempted suicide.* Baltimore: Penguin Books, 1964.

Stoor, A. *Sexual deviation.* Baltimore: Penguin Books, 1964.

Sullivan, H. S. *Concepts of modern psychiatry.* New York: Norton, 1953.

Zax, M., and Stricker, G. *Patterns of psychopathology.* New York: Macmillan, 1963.

Zax, M., and Stricker, G. (eds.). *The study of abnormal behavior.* New York: Macmillan, 1964.

Hardcover Books

Cameron, N. *The psychology of behavior disorders.* New York: Houghton Mifflin, 1947.

Carroll, H. A. *Mental hygiene: the dynamics of adjustment* (4th ed.). Englewood Cliffs, N. J.: Prentice-Hall, 1964.

Cattel, R. B., and Scheier, I. H. *The meaning and measurement of neuroticism and anxiety.* New York: Ronald Press, 1961.

Dellard, J., and Miller, N. E. *Personality and psychotherapy: an analysis in terms of learning, thinking, and culture.* New York: McGraw-Hill, 1950.

Eysenck, H. J. (ed.). *Handbook of abnormal psychology.* New York: Basic Books, 1961.

Foulds, G. A., and Caine, T. M. *Personality and personal illness.* Philadelphia: Lippincott, 1965.

Frazier, S. H. and Carr, A. C. *Introduction to psychopathology.* New York: Macmillan, 1964.

Pronke, N. *Textbook of abnormal psychology.* Baltimore: Williams and Wilkins, 1963.

Quay, H. C. (ed.). *Research in psychopathology.* Princeton, N. J.: Van Nostrand, 1963.

Stone, A. A., and Stone, Sue S. *The abnormal personality through literature.* Englewood Cliffs, N. J.: Prentice-Hall, 1966.

Szasz, T. S. *The myth of mental illness.* New York: Hoeber-Harper, 1961.

White, R. W. *The abnormal personality* (3rd ed.). New York: Ronald Press, 1964.

Chapter 11 Diagnosis, Treatment, and Prevention of Unhealthy Personalities

Chapter Outline

Study Guide

It is not the purpose of this chapter to develop a complete understanding of the diagnosis and treatment of the mentally ill. Therefore, much of this information is summarized in table form. The major purpose is to develop an appreciation of the importance of diagnosis, treatment, and prevention.

337

Diagnosis,
Treatment,
and Prevention
of Unhealthy
Personalities

REVIEW

Read the summaries for Chapters 9 and 10. Restudy what is not clear.

PREVIEW

Study the main ideas and structure of the chapter. *Read the tables carefully.*

READING

Read the chapter following study guide procedures.

REVIEW

Practice recall. *Practice group study techniques.*

STUDY TIP

Outside readings. Read over the extensive bibliographies of references including paperbacks and prepare a book or research report. Continuous outside reading by students is the single best indicator of the success of a book, a course, or a college education. Your instructor will greatly appreciate evidence of this kind of behavior.

Prelude

You should now have a better understanding of how people get into emotional difficulties through the use of various defensive patterns. Beginning with our common, everyday reality-oriented defenses, you should be able to appreciate your behavior and that of others more effectively. Perhaps, now you will be seriously aware of how and why people, at times during their lives, use more ego defensive patterns of behavior. And, finally, maybe it is clearer now how persons may begin to show signs of more acute psychotic defensive patterns that often lead to mental illness.

You may be asking yourself such questions as: "How can we help people who are mentally ill to get well again?" Or, "How can we prevent the development of serious mental illness, so that people can move toward greater self-actualization?" This chapter will answer questions like these.

Students' Viewpoints

At times when I feel terribly alone, I feel as if I would rather die or be somewhere where there are no familiar surroundings. At times I want to stand on a table and say: "Hey! Someone come and talk with me."

I have strange feelings of being able to fly. I wish I could so badly that I really feel as if I am. There is such a strong urge of jumping off tall buildings and just flapping my arms, that at times it really scares the hell out of me.

Sometimes I've gotten so worked up that I've wanted to kill or physically harm the object of my anger. (Anonymous statements from college students.)

I just had to do something! I've been scared to death; I don't know what's happening to me! I think I'm completely coming apart—sometimes I'm afraid I already have. I can't go on this way. . . . (Statement from a person who has decided to get professional treatment to help her solve her problems. Fitts, 1965, p. 16.)

These comments are representative of statements people have made when they are experiencing emotional problems. These feelings raise a number of questions: At what point in our lives do we seek help? When have we had enough? What happens when we go to a psychiatrist or psychologist? Is mental illness curable? How can we prevent mental illness?

Perhaps you have felt the way some of these students have felt. Perhaps you have felt a need to talk with a counselor or teacher about some of your problems. This chapter will give you some insight into how persons with emotional problems receive help and become more self-actualizing, thus being able to solve more competently the problems that being alive pose.

WHY IS IT IMPORTANT?

There is a good chance that at least one out of ten of you reading these words may, during your lifetime, require some form of help for mental or emotional illness! (National Association for Mental Health, 1967) There is also a good chance that you have already known personally someone who has experienced emotional difficulties requiring professional help.

It is important for you to realize that persons with emotional problems can and do receive help in a variety of forms and that mental illness is not necessarily a life-long illness. But, even more important, the authors feel that it is especially significant for you to become more aware of how you can help prevent the chances of mental illness from developing within yourself or your family.

BASIC THEORY AND RESEARCH

What Can Be Done to Help the Mentally Ill?

Now that we have discussed (1) some of the causes of mental illness; (2) what actually occurs to a person as he moves toward mental illness; and (3) some of the major forms of mental illness found in neurotic and psychotic defensive behavior patterns, we will look at some of the ways that mental health workers try to help people who are experiencing these kinds of difficulties.

Let us say that a friend of yours is beginning to show signs of using psychoneurotic or psychotic defenses frequently, that he gets scared and decides to get

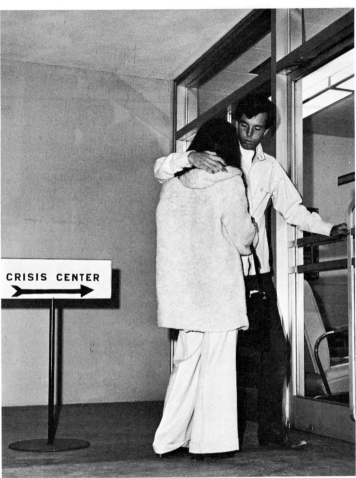

Figure 11-1
During periods of unusual stress, we may need emergency care. Crisis centers provide immediate help during these critical moments.

Photo by Ron Sakall

help. To whom and where should he go—to a mental hospital, a private sanitarium; his family doctor; to his minister, his priest, or his rabbi? This question is difficult to answer because it would depend on many factors: how serious the illness is; how much money he has to pay for treatment; and the availability of mental health facilities.

Table 11-1 tells you a little about some of the people who work with the mentally ill.

Where Does a Mentally Ill Person Go for Help?

This question depends a lot on where you live, because in many parts of the United States there are very few facilities. In Table 11-2 some of the more common places that people with emotional problems can go for help are described.

339

Table 11-1
Mental Health Workers

Name	Degrees Required	Total Years of College (Approximately)	Major Functions	Employed by
Psychiatrist	M.D. (Medical Degree)	9–11	• Psychotherapy • Diagnosis of physiological malfunctions • Prescribes medications and program of rehabilitation	Private practice Public and private hospitals Public and private clinics Industry°
Clinical or Counseling Psychologist	Ph.D. (Doctor of Philosophy)	8–10	• Diagnosis of emotional problems with psychological tests • Psychotherapy • Research in mental illness	Private practice Public and private hospitals Public and private clinics Industry°
Psychoanalyst	M.D.	10–15	• Psychoanalysis (special type of therapy based on Freud's theory of personality).	Private practice
Psychiatric Social Workers	M.A. or M.S. (Master's Degree)	6	• Family therapy • Develops case study on person • Group and individual therapy	(Same as above)
Psychiatric Nurse	R.N. (Registered Nurse)	2–4	• Follows orders of psychiatrist regarding diet, medication, and activities of patient • Informal therapy through patient interaction	(Same as above, except private practice)
Psychiatric Attendent	A.A. preferred; none in many states	0–2	• Works directly with patient in various forms of therapy	Same as above, except industry and private practice.

° Sometimes

How Do Mental Health Workers Help the Mentally Ill?

Once a patient (1) realizes he is mentally ill; (2) goes to a clinic or hospital; and (3) finds a mental health worker or workers to help him, the next logical questions might be: How do these people help him to get well? What goes on in a clinic or hospital?

Table 11–2
Facilities for Helping the Mentally Ill

Facility	Types of Service Provided	Advantages of Facility	Disadvantages of Facility
Family physician	Prescribe medication Referral to another facility (clinic or hospital)	Many patients confide in their family doctor when they are troubled	Some doctors have little training in helping the mentally ill
Private mental health clinic	Diagnosis, Therapy (all types)	Fast service and more intensive treatment Usually has team of mental health workers Can live at home and get treatment	High costs ($25–35 per hour)
Public mental health clinic	Same as above	Low cost (pay what you can afford) Team of mental health workers Can live at home	Long waiting list
Private hospital, psychiatric ward, or sanitarium	Same as above	Fast service Good for mental illness Associated with physiological problems	High cost
Public hospitals (psychiatric ward)	Same as above	Low cost	Often overcrowded with a waiting period
State mental hospital	Same as above	Therapeutic community Can get away from poor environment	Often overcrowded and understaffed Not as much therapy as private
College counseling and health center	Same as above	Specialists who only work with student problems In groups can see that others have similar problem Keeps you in school	Often understaffed and overcrowded Student may not want to divulge himself
Public agencies • (Family service agency) • Juvenile Hall • Welfare department • Probation department	Varies with agency	Low cost Available in your own community	Often a long waiting period More group than individual therapy Often understaffed and overcrowded
Private agencies • Mental Health Association • Churches • Big Brothers of America • Salvation Army • Goodwill Industries • Alcoholics Anonymous • Recovery, Inc.	Varies with agency	• Low cost • Available locally	• Waiting period • Sometimes staff not trained professionally (use volunteer workers) • Understaffed • Overcrowded

It wasn't too long ago that the mentally ill were treated as if they were possessed by demons or were being punished for their sins (Deutsch, 1949). Here is what Dorothea Lynde Dix, a retired New England schoolteacher who crusaded for humane treatment of the mentally ill, reported to the Legislature of Massachusetts in 1843:

> I come to present the strong claims of suffering humanity. I come to place before the Legislature of Massachusetts the condition of the miserable, the desolate, the outcast. I come as the advocate of helpless, forgotten, insane and idiotic men and women . . . of beings wretched in our prisons, and more wretched in our Alms-Houses.
>
> I proceed, Gentlemen, briefly to call your attention to the state of Insane Persons confined within this Commonwealth, in cages, closets, cellars, stalls, pens: Chained, naked, beaten with rods, and lashed into obedience! (Deutsch, 1949, p. 165)

Her report continued with some of the following observations that she made at various jails and poorhouses:

> Lincoln. A woman caged.
> Medford. One idiotic subject chained, and one in a close stall for 17 years.
> Concord. A woman from the hospital in a cage in the almshouse. In the jail, several, decently cared for in general, but not properly placed in a prison.
> Savoy. One man caged.
> Lenox. Two in jail; against whose unfit condition there, the jailor protests.
> Dedham. The insane disadvantageously placed in the jail. In the almshouse, two females in stalls, situated in the main building; lie in wooden bunks filled with straw; always shut up. One of these subjects is supposed curable. The overseers of the poor have declined to give her a trial at the hospital, as I was informed.
> Franklin. One man chained; decent.
> Taunton. One woman caged. (Deutsch, 1949, p. 166)

A long time has passed since those days, and today we find quite a different situation for those who have emotional problems. There are essentially two phases or steps that all persons with emotional problems go through: diagnosis and treatment.

How Do Mental Health Workers Find Out What Is Wrong with the Mentally Ill?

One of the first things a medical doctor does when you go to him with an illness is to take your temperature, for your body temperature often reflects the seriousness of your illness. Mental health workers also attempt to measure the degree of illness in a mental patient when he comes for help. Rather than with thermometers and other medical instruments, psychologists, psychiatrists, and social workers measure the illness through a variety of different diagnostic instruments. In Table 11–3 some of the most frequently used diagnostic techniques are summarized.

Table 11-3
Kinds of Diagnostic Instruments Used with the Mentally Ill

Area of Person	Who Does It?	Type of Instrument(s)	Purpose of Instrument(s)	How Good Is It?
PHYSIOLOGICAL	Psychiatrist	Complete physical exam; especially neurological and glandular factors	To determine if there are any organic causes to the mental illness	Good: if there is a definite cause e.g., brain tumor, nerve tissue damage, glandular imbalance. Otherwise, difficult to tell if mental illness is causing physiological disturbance or vice versa
PSYCHOLOGICAL Personality	Psychologist	Personality tests	To determine degree of illness and areas of feelings or personality that is disturbed	Fair: often they are easy to fake
Perception of reality	Psychologist	Projective tests	To determine degree of illness and areas of disturbance	Good: difficult to fake. Depends on training and experience of person administering them
Level of intellectual functioning	Psychologist	Intelligence tests	To see if illness has impaired patient's level of intellectual functioning	Good: if given to individual by trained person
Emotional control	Psychologist	Projective tests (TAT, Rorschach, Sentence Completion, Thematic Apperception test, etc.)	To determine amount of control person has over his emotions. To determine areas of emotional sensititivity (anxiety, hostility, etc.)	Good: if given by experienced and trained person
Unconscious feelings	Psychologist	Projective tests (TAT and Rorschach, Sentence Completion)	To determine and tap kinds of unresolved conflict areas person has repressed	Good: if given by experienced and trained person
Family background	Psychiatric social worker	Case study	To get background of person in his relationships with others in and out of his immediate family	Good: often gives clues as to causes of problem areas
Present behavior	Psychiatric nurse and psychiatric attendent	Observation and anecdotal accounts in a daily log kept on ward	To determine present level of patient's functioning	Good: gives reliable indication of patient's present level of functioning

As can be seen from Table 11–3, adequate diagnosis of mental illness requires the services of a team. Each member of the team contributes valuable information. When all the information is compiled, a complete picture of the patient and his problems is available for the final diagnosis.

THE HOLISTIC APPROACH TO DIAGNOSIS.

The use of experts from different fields such as psychology, biology, and sociology to determine what is wrong with a person is called the *holistic approach*. The basic idea underlying this approach is that whatever happens or has happened in one part of a person's life affects the whole person. (Goldstein, 1939) In other words, if we really want to understand a person, we must study everything we can about him. For example, a person may be extremely jittery for several reasons: (1) a hyperactive thyroid gland; (2) severe stress on the job and at home; or (3) unconscious conflicts. Therefore, before starting treatment, it is essential that the underlying causes be known.

Biological Factors

Medical doctors or psychiatrists with the assistance of specialists such as neurologists and ophthamologists study the patient biologically to find organic defects that may be contributing to the mental illness. Among the biological factors are infections, glandular imbalances, inadequate diets, brain tumors and dysfunctions, and nerve tissue damage.

Sometimes students have visual problems that interfere with effective study and that, in turn, produce additional stress. (Berner and Berner, 1938) A study of the visual problems of college students in a remedial reading class revealed that 40 per cent had untreated visual difficulties related to the reading process. (Lugo and Hershey, 1966) The remedial reading techniques would have been more effective if the visual handicaps had been treated first.

Sociological Factors

Case studies by psychiatric social workers to get background information on the patient in his relationships with others in and out of his immediate family often provide clues as to possible causes of his behavior. Such factors as childhood deprivations and physical beatings, divorce, broken homes, unemployment, constant sickness in the family, and extreme poverty may compose the roots of the mental illness.

Psychological Factors

Psychologists, whether clinical, counseling, or school psychologists, study the many characteristics of the person's personality including forms of intelligence, typical ways of learning and coping with stress, self-concepts, psychological defenses, and unconscious conflicts and motives. In order to describe these characteristics, they use interviews and standard objective and projective tests. An illustration of their use in practice may provide the reader with a greater understanding of their usefulness. The following psychological report concerns a woman who was committed to a state mental hospital because of behavior at home that was considered to be indicative of insanity:

345

Diagnosis,
Treatment,
and Prevention
of Unhealthy
Personalities

F. B., a deaf-mute, is a small, physically unattractive woman who was very cooperative during the interview and testing. Communication was possible through the combined use of pantomime and illustrations. Once she understood directions, she worked with diligence and persistency. Even when confronted with very difficult problems she would seek out cues that would lead to some reasonable answers.

The tests did not reveal any definite signs of organicity. On the contrary, there were signs which strongly counter-indicated organicity. The possibility of some degree of brain damage cannot be definitely ruled out (need for the services of a neurologist) although her performance was not that of a typical organic patient.

The tests did not reveal any responses typical of a psychotic. Although her written work contained what seemed to be strange wordings, they should not be taken as indications of psychosis because the patient can hardly read or write. Her reading level is equivalent to that of a child in the fifth month of the first grade. She cannot read even a simple sentence. It is of utmost significance that this woman, who cannot read a primer or tell time, has what appears to be a superior intellectual capacity. Her present intellectual functioning is average or better.

F. B. has a remarkable ability to integrate visual perceptions with motor manipulations in a very fast and accurate manner. In addition, she possesses such remarkable artistic ability that one wonders why this talent has not been put to use. The patient, who at first presented a picture of a dull, sad, and lifeless person, turns out to be a bright and talented person when shown sincere interest and attention.

If the patient and her problems are to be understood, her home situation must be investigated (psychiatric social worker). She conveyed the impression that her home was an unhappy and confusing place to live in. It would be essential to know the stresses and frustrations which this woman has faced. Possibly her mental illness is appropriate to the conditions under which she has been living all her life.

Due to difficulties in communication it is difficult to make a definite diagnostic statement, but perhaps she is an emotionally unstable person due to the strong frustrations she encounters without having the means for solving her problems. Perhaps if provided with special schooling and kindness, she could lead a normal and productive life.

From this report we see the value of stressing what is positive about others as well as what is negative. Too often we tend to stress faults and mistakes.

PSYCHOLOGICAL TESTING

Psychological tests are essentially shorthand ways for understanding why people behave as they have in the past, as they do in the present, and how they will in the future. Tests are constructed to measure enduring and important ways of thinking, feeling, perceiving, and learning. For example, if we know how well a child reads in the fourth grade, we can predict with a relatively high level of accuracy how well he will read in the eighth grade. (Alexander, 1961) Of course, predictions such as this one are based on the assumption that there will be no radical changes in the person's environment during the time period between the testing and the moment of the predicted behavior. Furthermore, the results of testing are made far more meaningful when the scores of the individual are compared to the scores obtained from other persons on the same test who have had similar experiences and education. To state that a person has a high degree of intelligence on a particular test is not too meaningful. However, if we can say that his scores on a test are higher than other college freshmen who take the same test, then we know that he performed more intelligently in comparison to others. Nearly all psychological tests have scores from others with which to compare the score of an individual. Such tests are referred to as *standardized tests* because they permit comparison of the individual's performance with that of a large number of persons who are somewhat like him. In other words, the performance of a five-year-old is compared to that of other five-year-olds with similar backgrounds.

For diagnostic purposes psychologists use three major types of tests: (1) *intelligence tests;* (2) *objective standardized tests;* and (3) *projective tests.* Figure 11–2 shows examples of the three kinds of tests used to measure the degrees of consciousness of the individual's personality.

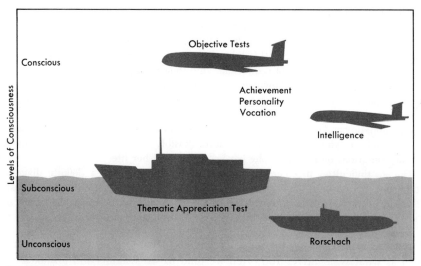

Figure 11–2
Measuring Personality with Tests

Intelligence Tests

Intelligence tests provide us with a fairly accurate measure of the individual's learning and thinking abilities. The tests consist of a series of different tasks such as word definitions, general information about the world and society, and motor and visual skills. Each intelligence test constructor assumes that its particular tasks are measuring the important and enduring characteristics that determine effective thinking, learning, and memory. However, as yet there is no general agreement as to which tasks are most predictive of present or future intelligent behaviors. In 1961, Buros listed 238 different tests of intelligence. (Buros, 1961)

The best and most widely used intelligence tests are the Stanford-Binet and the Wechsler Intelligence Scales for children and adults. These tests are individually administered and require considerable clinical experience for accurate analysis. Although intelligent behaviors are only one aspect of personality, they are crucial for understanding the development and treatment of mental illnesses. In general, the greater the capacities for thinking and learning, the easier it will be for the person to master new adjustive techniques for coping with frustrations, threats, and conflicts. On the other hand, a person with limited intellectual abilities may have developed a mental illness because of his inability to cope with the problems of everyday living. In some cases, problems develop because the environment is not sufficiently challenging and the bright individual responds with justifiable anger and hostility toward a monotonous existence.

Objective Personality Tests

Objective personality tests are designed to measure the complex ways of behaving, thinking, and feeling that determine the total personality. The various measures are obtained by having the person answer questions about his behavior, thinking, and feeling in a wide variety of different personal and social situations. The California Test of Personality attempts to measure personal adjustment by asking questions about self-reliance, personal worth, personal freedom, feelings of belonging, withdrawing tendencies, and nervous symptoms. Social adjustment is measured through questions on social standards; skills; family, school, and community relations; occupation relations; and antisocial tendencies. The person's responses are compared with the responses of others who have been judged

347
Diagnosis,
Treatment,
and Prevention
of Unhealthy
Personalities

Figure 11-3
A Projective Test. Look at the ink blot. What do you see? People see different things. These differences tend to reveal the internal experiences, emotions, and ways of thinking that make up personalities. Turn the page to find what others see.

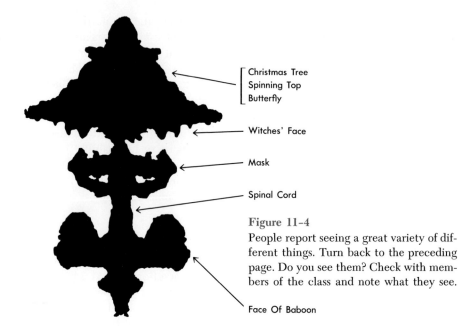

Christmas Tree
Spinning Top
Butterfly

Witches' Face

Mask

Spinal Cord

Figure 11–4
People report seeing a great variety of different things. Turn back to the preceding page. Do you see them? Check with members of the class and note what they see.

Face Of Baboon

to be well-adjusted or poorly adjusted in the different areas of personality being measured. A person may be judged poorly adjusted in certain areas of life, marginal in others, and well-adjusted in some personal and social situations.

The most widely used objective personality test for evaluating personality and mental illness is the Minnesota Multiphasic Personality Inventory (Starke and Meehl, 1951). It is designed to measure some of the common symptoms of selected neuroses and psychoses. However, there are hundreds of other personality tests. (Buros, 1961)

Projective Tests

Projective tests are designed to measure the more unconscious levels of personality, the person's private world. In these tests there are no "right" or "wrong" answers. The interpretation of answers depends on the clinical experience of the psychologists, which is one of the major weaknesses of projective tests. (Sanders and Cleveland, 1965) A person is presented with vague and unstructured stimuli such as inkblots, incomplete sentences, and drawings. He is asked to respond with whatever comes to mind because there are no right or wrong answers. The interpretation of the responses is based on the assumption that they were determined more by what is inside of the person than the actual outside stimuli. Taking a projective test is similar to deciding what cloud formations remind one of. In other words, the person projects his inner feelings and ideas onto the ambiguous stimuli presented to him.

The most widely used projective tests are the Rorschach Inkblot Test

349

**Diagnosis,
Treatment,
and Prevention
of Unhealthy
Personalities**

(Rorschach, 1942) and the Thematic Apperception Test (Murray, 1938). In the Rorschach Test the person is presented with a series of standard inkblots and is told, "Here are some inkblots. Different people see different things. We want to know what you see. There are no right or wrong answers." People produce a great variety of different answers and the psychologist has to judge which responses are psychologically healthy and which are not. Examples may provide the reader with greater understanding. A young man applied for admission to a reading clinic that accepted candidates who had no symptoms of mental illness. A common response to one of the inkblots is that it resembles a U-shaped island when seen from high above. The young man replied that it resembled a highway, which is a reasonable response. However, when asked to explain and to point out his response, he explained that because highways are straight he had to force the U-shaped inkblot into a straight line. The psychologist, correctly or incorrectly, interpreted the response as psychologically unhealthy because the young man had twisted the inkblot (reality) to conform to the way that he wanted it to be. Another case involved a 14-year-old boy who was referred to a psychologist because of disciplinary problems at school. On a particular inkblot he saw a penis. His response was reasonable because a segment of that inkblot does resemble a penis. However, he described in detail that the penis was surrounded by fire and that flames were shooting out of it. This response, together with data from the interview and other tests, suggested the presence of pyromania, a neurosis in which the person receives sexual satisfaction from watching and starting fires.

In the Thematic Apperception Test a set of pictures that are not clearly drawn is used. Each picture can be described in a variety of different ways. If a person repeatedly makes up stories of failure, he is revealing how he feels about his own relations to the world, whether he realizes it or not.

Although projective tests are not as scientific as objective standardized tests, when used with caution by highly trained clinical psychologists, they can provide valuable insights into behavior that are not available as readily through any other means.

Intermediate Summary

Today there are many ways to cure and to help the mentally ill. Diagnosis is the key to treatment because it reveals what kinds of treatments are best for the individual patient and his unique problems. The best way to understand a patient completely is to study him holistically—that is psychologically, biologically, and sociologically. Psychologists use tests as shorthand ways of analyzing personality characteristics. Intelligence, standardized, and projective tests provide valuable insights into a patient's typical ways of behaving, learning, feeling, and solving problems.

Treatment of Mental Illness

After the diagnosis is made, some form of treatment program is recommended to help the patient function more fully. The general name for treatment given to those with emotional problems is *therapy*.

In general, the purpose of all types of therapy is to strengthen the individual's feelings of adequacy and competence (self-concept) so that he feels strong enough to cope with reality without using the various systems of defense (ego, neurotic, or psychotic) that he has built into his (often unconscious) behavior. In viewing therapy, there are essentially two ways to look at it: The therapist may work on the stress that has helped produce the defensive system. He can do this by changing the person's environment and/or his goals. Or, he can look at therapy as an organized effort to build up the person's feelings of competence.

Basically, all forms of therapy help the person to develop competencies in the various aspects of his behavior. These would actually include most of the areas we have discussed up to this point. Thus, the therapist helps the person to learn to solve problems more effectively; to perceive the world and himself more realistically; to learn how to control and release his emotions more effectively; to get to know what he, as a unique person, wants in life (goals and motives); to unlearn ineffective behavior patterns that are getting him into trouble; to alter his self-concept so that he accepts himself more; and to look at his childhood and family experiences so that he understands how he got the way he is.

In Tables 11–4 and 11–5 some of the more common forms of psychological, sociological, and biological therapy are described. It should be pointed out that mental health workers differ in their therapeutic approach. That is, some exclusively use one form of therapy (for example, a psychoanalyst may use essentially the techniques developed by Freud), whereas others may use parts of all forms of therapy. The important thing to remember, however, is that although their techniques vary, their goal is the same.

OTHER FORMS OF THERAPY

During the past twenty-five years, a number of new and promising developments have taken place in the treatment of the mentally ill. In Table 11–5 a summary of some of these developments is made, aimed at the social and biological aspects of the individual. Most clinics and hospitals use one or a combination of these types.

Other specialized techniques of therapy being used but not included in the table are *play therapy* (Mann, 1957), used with disturbed children to help them release emotions and to help the therapist get clues as to the areas of conflict; *psychodrama* (Moreno, 1959), in which patients act out short scenes playing different roles (their own mothers, fathers, brothers, sisters, employers, or other patients) in order to gain insight into their particular problems as related to other people; and *remotivation* (American Psychiatric Association, 1964), used by psychiatric attendants as a technique for remotivating patients to take renewed interest in their surroundings.

Table 11-4
Psychological Forms of Therapy Used in Helping the Mentally Ill

TYPE OF THERAPY	DESCRIPTION	WHERE USED	WHO USES IT	ADVANTAGES	DISADVANTAGES
Directive (McKinney, in Pennington and Berg, 1954, p. 502)	Therapist actively probes and makes specific suggestions	Clinics and Hospitals	Psychiatrists and clinical psychologists	Faster at getting at specific problem areas Patient has specific suggestions for action	May threaten patient Does not allow patient to make decisions
Nondirective (Rogers, 1951)	Therapist acts as mirror; reflects back to patient what he is feeling or saying	Clinics and Hospitals	Psychiatrists and clinical psychologists Social workers	Patient does work and gets insight on his own; tends to build his self-confidence	Takes longer than directive
Psychoanalysis (Hadfield, 1967)	Emphasis on patient's past Focus on patient's relationship to his parents Dreams and free flow of thoughts used	Clinics and Hospitals	Psychoanalysts	Patient gains insight as to possible causes of problems	Long process (2–5 years) Expensive Understanding cause of problem may not change behavior
Behavior (Eysenck, 1960)	Uses learning principles and techniques (reward and punishment) Works with immediate behavior only; not concerned with past history	Clinics and Hospitals	Clinical psychologists; some psychiatrists	Usually produces fast changes in behavior	Patient may feel manipulated
Group (Luchins, 1964)	Patient works out problems with help and insight of others Work in groups of 5–10 Complete freedom to express feelings (toward self and others) Often used with patients and their families	Clinics and Hospitals	Clinical psychologists; some psychiatrists Social workers	Can work with several patients at same time Patient gets honest reactions of other persons	May be difficult for withdrawn patients

351

Table 11-5

Sociological and Biological Forms of Therapy Used in Helping the Mentally Ill

Type of Therapy	Description	Where Used	Who Uses It	Advantages	Disadvantages
SOCIOLOGICAL					
Therapeutic community (Calif. Dept. Mental Hygiene, 1965, p. 28)	Patient is a member of the "team" (psychiatrist, social worker, psychologist, nurses, and attendants) Patient "government" on wards helps make decisions	Hospitals	Patient and staff	Patient feels he plays a role in his treatment Patient develops responsibility for himself and others	Transition into "real world" is sometimes difficult
Occupational (Coleman, 1964, p. 583)	Patient may do work around hospital (related to his occupation before he entered hospital); patient may be trained for job when he leaves hospital	Hospitals	Occupational therapists	Patient builds job competencies Patient gains self-confidence	Hard to get some patients involved Patient may be inefficient
Recreational (Coleman, 1964, p. 583)	Patient engages in various activities: sports, crafts, dancing, drama, etc. to help build self-confidence, release tensions, and learn to work with others	Hospitals	Recreational therapists	Patient builds self-confidence; releases tensions; learns hobbies and skills to help him in later life	Hard to get some patients involved
BIOLOGICAL					
Drug (Coleman, 1964, p. 559)	Various drugs administered to help patients relax (tranquilizers) or to help them to be less depressed (energizers)	Hospitals and clinics	Psychiatrists	Helps patient control emotions so that he can receive and participate in therapy Helps maintain order in hospital	Only treats symptom of illness Possible dependence on drugs
Electro-shock (Cameron and Cameron, 1951, p. 596; and Coleman, 1964, p. 556)	A brief (0.1–0.5 sec.) electric shock is given to the patient through electrodes. This is followed by unconsciousness (10–30 min.)	Hospitals	Psychiatrists	Used as a quick treatment to help extremely depressed patients Especially useful in patients who do not respond to drug therapy	Fear of treatment by patient Short-term memory loss

353

Diagnosis,
Treatment,
and Prevention
of Unhealthy
Personalities

Therapy seeks to strengthen the patient's self-concept and his problem-solving techniques so that he will be able to cope with his past and future problems more effectively and without the need for the crutches of psychological defense systems. Basically, therapy seeks through personalized education programs to develop the patient's competencies required to achieve satisfaction of his basic needs and to continue his interrupted growth toward self-actualization.

DOES TREATMENT HELP THE MENTALLY ILL?

Now that we have briefly looked at some of the ways that the mentally ill are helped, the next questions might be: Does it work? Do people who are mentally ill get better? Are those in mental hospitals able to return home to their families and friends?

Even though there is much research that still needs to be done to fully evaluate different forms of therapy, the fact is that, in general, people are getting help faster than ever before and are being released from mental hospitals much sooner than they ever were before. However, we still have a long way to go. In Table 11–6 a summary of recent facts about mental illness is given.

A dramatic example of the improved picture of the treatment and release of

Table 11–6
Facts About Mental Illness

QUESTION	ANSWER
1. What is the extent of mental illness?	° At least 1 person in every 10 (19 million in all) has some form of mental illness (from mild to severe) ° More people in hospitals with mental illness, at any one time than with all other diseases combined. ° At least 50% of all the medical and surgical cases treated by private doctors and hospitals have a mental illness complication.
2. How many enter and leave mental hospitals?	° Over 1,500,000 persons are hospitalized for mental illness during the year. ° On any one day of the year about 760,000 persons are under psychiatric care of hospitals.
3. What are chances of leaving a mental hospital?	° 75% of those admitted for the first time leave the hospital within the first year. ° With good care and treatment, at least 7 out of 10 patients can leave partially or totally recovered. ° The chances of release within a year of patients suffering from schizophrenia has jumped from about 20% to about 80% within the last 40 years.

° Adapted from: Facts About Mental Illness (National Association for Mental Health, 1967).

mental patients is found in California where there are actually fewer patients in state mental hospitals today than there were in 1959! The California State Department of Mental Hygiene explains it this way:

How did it happen? Most directly, through a modernized plan of attack on mental illness made possible through support of the California State Legislature, and waged on many different fronts. It has been said that if there is a "miracle drug" for mental illness, it is probably "money": funds to enable scientific application of known principles for treatment and planned research, yet which in the long view represent savings in both financial and humanitarian terms.

Four major developments backed by the Legislature which have made today's results possible are: (1) the enriched staffing and intensified treatment programs that afford a higher level of hospital treatment than previously possible; (2) discovery of the popularly-designated tranquilizing drugs and their availability to an increasing percentage of patients; (3) application of the open-door, therapeutic community approach to treatment with its strong involvement of the patient in his own recovery process; and (4) the steady strengthening of those community-based extramural programs which hold an important key to the future.

These multiple fronts are strongly interrelated. In accordance with modern psychiatric principles, they have closed the gap between institutions and home. They also share an important mutual objective: That the patient functions as a whole person in the community he calls home. (1965, pp. 21–22)

Mental Illness from a Personal Point of View

You should now have a better understanding of some of the things that happen to persons who suffer from mental illness as they go through the different types of diagnosis and treatment. However, you still might ask: How does it feel? What is it like to the patient who is experiencing it?

The following account was written by a former mental patient (the mother of one of the authors' former students). It gives a very humanly sensitive, yet realistic, idea of some of the feelings a patient in a mental hospital may experience.

"My Little Saint," by Virginia Harvey

The sun was warm on the patio. The patio was small and enclosed by a high eight-foot, chain-link fence. It was planted with shrubbery but no flowers. We had been thinking of putting flowers in and had decided it would be a good project for all of us.

Ann was sitting on the patio with us, but she was miles away. She was very withdrawn. Ann was a pretty girl. She had long dark hair which I had plaited that morning for her. Her eyes were very dark, almost black and she had a gentleness in her face that gave her an expression of saintliness.

Nancy came out of the day room and joined us on the patio. She had been working on the medical ward helping to feed and bathe patients. Nancy had been a nurse. Ann had worked in a factory making belts, and I had been a bookkeeper for a wholesale nursery; now, we were all patients in a large state hospital. We no longer belonged to the outside world.

We were on Ward 1, for the very disturbed patients. Some of us were in the very worst part of a severe mental illness.

All of the other patients loved Ann, there was something about her that drew you to her. Perhaps it was her gentle expression and her extreme youth. Nancy and I were in our thirties, but Ann was just 21. So young and yet so very ill.

Nancy and I were assigned to help her. Ann could no longer care for herself. She must be taken to the toilet, dressed, and fed. We never minded our assignment; it wasn't just another task. Ann needed us.

Our ward was a very small one and could only accommodate twelve. We had single rooms down a long hallway. Each room contained a bed and nothing else. The thick steel doors on the rooms had a small window of only about four inches in diameter, this was just enough for the attendants to keep an eye on each of us. There was one window in each room, it must have been at least eight feet above the floor and was covered by heavy-duty screening. If we were not too disturbed, the doors were left open at night so that we could get a breeze. This was July, and it was very warm. When the doors were closed it was stifling.

Ann had been in the hospital nearly two months and had made no progress. She saw visions and was constantly making the sign of the cross. She was of Mexican decent and from a large family. All the other brothers and sisters had left home and it was Ann's duty to care for her elderly mother and father. She had been doing most of the housework plus earning a living for all three of them. She had been doing this for three years with never a complaint, but, underneath, her mind demanded freedom and when finally it could find no way out that her conscience would allow, it gave way to a serious mental illness. She had finally found her freedom.

Actually, the doctor told us, mental illness is a way to escape. If we were wealthy we could take a long extended trip and perhaps keep the illness from taking hold, but our conscience wouldn't let us run away so we did the next best thing. Our minds had taken as much as possible and we had finally reached a breaking point. We had to escape, so we did—to a terrifying world of our own making. This world is a hell all of its own. There are hallucinations of both sound and sight—terrifying delusions. It's inhabited by the damned. We have punished ourselves far worse than anyone else could possibly have conjured up as torture.

Ann's world made her sacrifices worthwhile. Some will go to this other world and never return. I've seen and lived with these patients that have given up the outside world forever. The outside world only means hurt and frustration. We all hoped that Ann would not be one of those who would give up completely.

Thursday was to be the day that she would start shock treatments. All other types of therapy had failed and this was a last resort. Our hospital, fortunately, wasn't too fond of the use of shock treatments.

I had managed to pull myself out of the worst and missed the shock treatments by only a small margin. Nancy had had her last one the week before. (Shock treatments are given in a series). We all hoped this would turn the tide for Ann.

I was now well enough to be assigned to work outside of our ward and so therefore was gone until four o'clock Thursday afternoon. I rang the bell at the door of our ward and waited in the hallway for the sound of heavy keys, which would be the sound of the nurse coming. You know you actually get used to these keys and don't mind them. As a matter of fact sometimes I think it's less locking the patient in and more locking the world out.

The nurse greeted me and I asked immediately how Ann was. She said the same. I went into our little day room and there sat Ann, silent. She had never spoken a word in all these months. Well, maybe the next one would work. I put my hand on her shoulder and spoke encouragingly to her. I knew that she could hear me but was unable to answer.

Nancy and I took her to supper and fed her. Later we undressed her and put her to bed.

Tuesday came and another shock treatment for Ann. This time she spoke my name, I could have wept with joy. She had spoken. She was going to get well.

You who read this may wonder what either Nancy or myself were doing taking care of Ann, but this is a lesson well learned on the very disturbing wards. There is always someone much worse off than yourself and the sick need someone to care for. They always seek out those worse off than themselves. There are always too many patients and not enough help. This is true throughout the whole hospital, and I imagine any state hospital. After caring for a patient like Ann you begin to feel that you're needed and wanted. This is an important feeling. One you lost at home.

After many shock treatments and much patience, Ann started to come out of her world of dreams, and those whom she trusted most were Nancy and myself. You see even though she was living in a world of her own she remembered those who had cared for her.

Within a few weeks she was able to join in our conversations in the evening and able to tell us what she saw and felt. This was a great stride forward for her. She was still very ill and acted much as a small child—insecure if alone, frightened with strangers, and clinging to those she trusted.

Somewhere along the way of our friendship, I came to love Ann as one loves a child. Her simple acceptance that she was destined to be a saint was part of her. Well maybe this may sound like an off-balance thought to you, but you would have had to know Ann. Sometimes I began to wonder if maybe she wasn't right. She had all the innocence, gentleness, and sweetness of a saint; who were we to say she wasn't right.

Reason of course told me that this couldn't be true. Reason also told me that this delusion was caused by an inability to cry out against the sacrifices she was forced to make in caring for her parents. Ann needed to become angry and speak her piece instead of withdrawing from the whole world and being afraid that she had no right to complain.

As time went on, Ann did become angry and she did begin to realize that the world had given her a pretty large cross to bear all alone. It was high time some of her brothers and sisters accepted some of the responsibility of their parents and that Ann be allowed to have some sort of life of her own.

Ann never had time for parties, or boyfriends or any of the things a girl of 21 should have. All she ever knew was work and responsibility.

Suddenly one day Ann took her stand against the world; she was getting well and we were glad to see the anger. She was living again. She made new plans for a different sort of life, one that would allow her a chance for happiness.

Weeks had gone by and I was being allowed to go home for good, on the condition that I be placed under the care of a psychiatrist. My family agreed and I made preparations to return to life outside.

When the day came for me to leave I found that it was hard to leave my friends that I had become so close to. The nurses had been good to me; they had supported my delusions when they knew I needed a friend and had given me time to break them myself. They didn't laugh at the disturbed thoughts or confusing conversation. Sometimes looking back, I certainly wouldn't have blamed them, because they were some pretty weird ideas. When I was terrified and screaming at my hallucinations, they sat and held my hand knowing that I was so terribly frightened and alone. The patients had

357

**Diagnosis,
Treatment,
and Prevention
of Unhealthy
Personalities**

accepted me as I was. If I had a bad day they overlooked it and were glad when I was feeling better.

Nancy would be leaving too, the following week.

All of my things were together and the nurse took me to the door. Ann ran and put her arms around me and wept quietly. She gave me a piece of embroidery that she had been making. We each wished the other well knowing that this would be the last time we would see one another.

I've thought of Ann many times and prayed that she be happy. She was my little saint.

APPLICATION

Living with Yourself

What insights can we learn from those who have experienced some form of mental illness, received some type of therapy, and returned to their families and jobs to lead productive lives? It seems that if mentally ill persons can gain better insights of self and others through various treatment programs, then the implications for healthy persons are far reaching.

One therapist describes some of the changes that occur in his patients as they successfully reach the end of therapy:

Feeling Free—"For the first time I have discovered that delightful sensation of expressing my own real feelings and reactions."

Feeling New Strength and Capacity—"I still have problems, but somehow they don't have the weight that they once had. . . ."

Accepting and Valuing Self—"And *you* becomes very important. It *becomes important* to know who you are, and why you are, and *WHAT YOU WANT TO BE! . . .*"

Feeling More Alive—"I was more or less a lifeless, existing mechanism operated from the outside. Now I am able to face life, to feel, to make decisions and to operate this mechanism myself. . . ."

Feeling Responsible for Self—"I don't want to crawl into a hole and hide. I want to stand out in the open and accept the best life has to offer and to stand up under the weight of the worst." (Fitts, 1965, pp. 148–151)

Actually, the work of Rogers on self-actualizing persons is a description of the characteristics that many of his patients have displayed as they have moved along in therapy. As you remember, these characteristics include a willingness to accept what they experience, a trust in themselves, self-reliance, and the willingness to continue to grow as a person.

How can we now translate some of these subjective results of therapy into our own lives to help us live more productively? It seems to us that the various forms of therapy are actually ways of relating to ourselves and others and tend to help keep us somewhat sane in this fast-moving world. What can we deduce from these?

**THE PREVENTION OF MENTAL ILLNESS: SOME
THERAPEUTICALLY BASED INSIGHTS FOR EFFECTIVELY
LIVING WITH OURSELVES**

1. People need to live in an atmosphere of acceptance and trust (from non-directive therapy).
2. People need to feel some sense of responsibility and choice within their own lives (from the therapeutic community concept).
3. People need to be allowed to express their true feelings (from nondirective therapy).
4. People need to have various outlets for recreation and play (from recreation therapy).
5. People need to have a meaningful job through which they can express their individuality (from occupational therapy).
6. People need a close and deep relationship with at least one other person (from nondirective and directive therapy).
7. People need to learn to accept their past lives as they happened and not to live in self-pity or blaming of others—their parents (from psychoanalysis and behavior therapy).
8. People need to explore their unconscious feelings and should get to know and accept all aspects of themselves (psychoanalysis).
9. Sometimes people have to get away from problems in a safe and non-threatening environment for a period of time in order to gain strength to cope with the world (from the therapeutic community).

Living with Others

What can we learn from the various approaches to therapy about living effectively with others? A few patients express it as follows:

Other People Seem Different—"This time when I went home they didn't seem the same. Maybe it's because I wasn't afraid of them, but anyway I realized that I was really enjoying being with them."

My Relationships Are Better—"And I just tell them now. I say, 'Nope, I don't want to do that.' Now the nice part is that I can do this and feel all right about it—and I do. Also it doesn't matter to them. They still like me. In fact, they probably like me better."

The Future—"I can now feel some hope for the future, some reason for living, some purpose. . ." (Fitts, 1965, pp. 151–153)

EFFECTS OF THERAPY ON FAMILY INTERACTIONS

359

Diagnosis,
Treatment,
and Prevention
of Unhealthy
Personalities

Carl Rogers (1961) has noted a number of changes that occur in his patients as they undergo therapy; particularly changes in their family interactions:

It appears that an individual finds it satisfying in the long run to express any strong or persistent emotional attitudes in the situation in which they arise, to the person with whom they are concerned, and to the depth to which they exist. . . . It seems that the individual discovers that it is more satisfying in the long run to live a given family relationship on the basis of the real interpersonal feelings which exist, rather than living the relationship on the basis of a pretense. . . .

It is in these ways, I believe, that a therapy which results in the individual becoming more fully and more deeply himself, results also in his finding greater satisfaction in realistic family relationships which likewise promote the same end—that of facilitating each member of the family in the process of discovering, and becoming, himself. (pp. 327–328)

THE PREVENTION OF MENTAL ILLNESS: SOME THERAPEUTICALLY BASED INSIGHTS FOR EFFECTIVELY LIVING WITH OTHERS

Again, let us try to summarize what some of the implications of therapy are for living with others:

1. Man needs to realize that he is not alone; that in time of stress other persons are willing and able to help him (from directive therapy, group therapy, therapeutic community, and the story, "My Little Saint").

2. Man needs to be aware that many of us at times suffer from similar feelings of inadequacy and are overwhelmed by problems in the environment (from group therapy).

3. We all need to identify to some degree with our fellowman in some form of group effort (occupational and recreational therapy).

4. It is helpful for us to try and put ourselves in another person's position at times to better communicate and develop empathy for our fellowman (psychodrama).

5. It is healthy for us to realize why our parents did what they did to us when we were younger, and not to go on blaming them for our present inadequacies (psychoanalysis).

6. As responding organisms we must expect to receive certain types of reactions from others when we react in certain ways. We must sometimes force ourselves to act in responsible ways so that we don't get into trouble with others in the world (behavior therapy).

7. When groups (for example, family, job, or friendship) interact in a climate of mutual trust and freedom of expression, people seem to become more alive, productive, and creative (from nondirective therapy and group therapy).

Living with Society

In discussing the plight of the mentally ill in society, Lucy Freeman (1953) observes:

These are among the troubled. Part of a silent army, they walk alone even in the largest crowd. They may escape for the moment into tavern, dance hall or theater, but when they come out into darkness, once again they face inescapable loneliness.

There is no one they can tell what they feel, no one who listens and understands. Their tears fall unseen, their words go unheard, their wishes unfulfilled.

It does not matter whether a man lives in a Park Avenue penthouse or an East Side slum. Trouble does not respect the dollar sign.

Nor whether he wears a Phi Beta Kappa key or has never opened a book. Trouble spares neither the educated nor uneducated.

And it does not matter whether he is ready for the tomb or just out of the womb. Trouble holds no reverence for years.

The troubled hold little faith in the future. They lack the vision that enables man to walk his way in wisdom and comfort.

"Where there is no vision, the people perish," warns the Bible.

The troubled feel themselves slowly perishing. (pp. 5–6)

Miss Freeman portrays a rather gloomy picture of those suffering from various degrees of mental illness in the year 1953 at least. What about the situation today? Has there been much change, or do the troubled still feel themselves "perishing"? What about you and your future family? Will this hopeless situation change in the future?

ACTION FOR MENTAL HEALTH

One of the most significant developments in the area of mental illness in the United States occurred on July 28, 1955, when the Senate and the House of Representatives approved the Mental Health Study Act. (Joint Commission on Mental Health and Illness, 1961)

This act established a joint commission on mental illness and health to conduct the first large-scale study in history regarding the mentally ill in our society. Thirty-six organizations participated in the five-year study, which resulted in a number of recommendations to meet the needs of the mentally ill. This report created quite a controversy because of some of its drastic suggestions for immediate action:

1. That the amount of money spent on mental illness by local, state, and federal agencies be doubled in the following five years and tripled in the next ten!

2. That the system of the large state mental hospital is obsolete and should be replaced by local community clinics and hospitals.

3. That we are drastically short of trained mental health workers at all levels and that a national campaign be launched to interest more persons to pursue a career in the mental health field.

Even though the tone of the report suggests that we are in need of immediate solutions to these problems, the committee does see some hope:

> The evidence from which we derive hope and conviction is of several sorts: Mental health information, whatever its vehicle, has had positive effects on the educated public's ability to recognize and seek help for psychological problems. The public demand for the services of mental health experts is clear-cut, and has not been met. Congress and some of the State Governors and legislatures have assumed leadership in providing increased support. Many communities have evinced eagerness to establish and pursue mental health problems. All signs over the past fifteen years indicate that a trend has been established, which, if wisely and boldly fostered, could continue. Innovations and experiments are sufficiently numerous to make us believe that old retrogressive directions, prejudices, and resistances can be reversed if frontally assaulted. In the name of patient care and despite personal rivalry and honest differences in opinion, psychiatrists, psychologists, social workers, nurses, occupational therapists, volunteers, and others are learning to work together, and may become more disposed to do so as time passes. (Joint Commission on Mental Illness and Health, 1961, p. 247)

361

Diagnosis,
Treatment,
and Prevention
of Unhealthy
Personalities

Since the publication of this report, many positive changes have occurred in the prevention and treatment of many mental illnesses. Many of the changes may have a profound effect on you and your family in the future as you face the everyday problems of working, raising a family, and living in the community and world.

POSITIVE TRENDS IN LOOKING FOR A MENTAL HEALTH RESOURCE

The Family as a Mental Health Resource

Perhaps no other institution in our society is more important for the prevention of mental illness than the family. For it is in the daily family interactions (particularly those of the first five years) that the seeds of mental illness are often implanted.

The early case histories of thousands of persons suffering from emotional illness later in life are practically identical in that they contain either one or more of the following factors: broken home, social instability (drinking, separations, family arguments, loss of job), and/or actual mental illness within the family itself.

Chapter 4 discussed some of the important factors for the development of healthy personalities. Sometimes students say that one thing they learned from psychology class is never to get married! What they really mean is that they never fully realized the responsibilities involved in married life—particularly in rearing children.

The authors hope that they do not give you a similar negative view of marriage. They do also hope that you now more fully appreciate the role that you as a future parent must play in order to give your children the basic foundation to develop into mentally healthy individuals. The Children's Bill of Rights (see Chapter 4) is one of the best statements of some of the responsibilities that parents should be ready to undertake.

The Job as a Mental Health Resource

Freud defined mental health, among other things, as the ability to love and work. It is at our jobs where we spend most of our waking hours. Naturally, if we find our work exciting and challenging it will be an asset to help us develop into self-actualizing persons. However, all too often people find themselves in a rut, tied, because of their age, education, and/or the training requirements, to a job that they do not enjoy. These are frequently the ones who develop patterns of behavior that could lead to various forms of mental illness.

There are many hopeful signs that industry and labor are assuming part of their responsibility for the mental health of their workers. Most personnel departments use psychological tests to help employees find jobs that they are capable of handling.

Many companies and unions now have counselors available for workers to go to in times of emotional stress. Many fringe benefits for workers in the larger unions include fully paid insurance for treatment (in or out of the hospital) of mental illness. Many companies offer employees and their families various forms of free recreation both on and off the job to help them keep in better physical and mental condition. Workers are being brought into company discussions before major changes in working conditions actually occur. Various forms of incentive awards are now given to employees for outstanding service.

The School as a Mental Health Resource

No where else outside the home is the opportunity for the development of healthy personalities in children available than in the school system. For it is here that the child can actualize his potential and channel his creative energies in many directions. This is also the place where far too many children meet failure, frustration, and defeat. So the school does have a significant role in acting as a resource for mental health.

Teachers are smarter these days, as far as assuming some responsibility for the mental health of their students. Most teacher-training programs include courses in psychology so that the teacher will be able to detect early symptoms of possible emotional problems of students in their classes.

In addition to teachers, most high schools and colleges have full-time counseling centers where students can go for help with a variety of problems. School psychologists offer specialized services to teachers and parents with children having emotional problems.

The Community as a Mental Health Resource

One of the most significant trends in the treatment and prevention of mental illness is taking place within many communities throughout the United States today. The shifting of responsibility from the large "warehouse" type of state mental hospital to the local clinics and hospitals has revolutionized treatment programs. For example, in the State of California's long-range plan for treatment of the mentally ill it is stated:

363
**Diagnosis,
Treatment,
and Prevention
of Unhealthy
Personalities**

Figure 11-5
**College students visit a psychiatric unit to entertain patients. It is important for the
patients to maintain social contacts with members of the community.**

No longer will it be necessary for the mentally ill and retarded to be farmed out
to a distant state for want of community-based programs. Instead, they will be guided
toward recovery through services available in or near their hometowns.

As is now the case with physical ailments, a psychiatric patient, or his family, will
in the future have a choice of various local treatment resources. And in most cases he
will be able to pay at least part of the treatment cost himself.

In some cases the patient may be admitted to a psychiatric unit in a local general
hospital. In others it may be a locally operated clinic or day treatment center financed
with federal, state and local funds. Often the patient will be treated by a local psychiatrist or physician in private practice, much as the person with a broken leg receives
treatment from the family doctor.

Many developing emotional problems will be identified through services provided
by the schools, welfare departments, correctional institutions, general medical services,
and other non-psychiatric agencies. Professional personnel of such agencies will be
trained to recognize needs for psychiatric treatment among those they serve.

Preventive services through nonpsychiatric agencies will be directed toward prevention of prenatal maldevelopment, premature births, and birth damage: toward promotion
of healthy growth and development in the general population, and toward alleviating
pressure on individuals in trouble or with serious personal problems. (California State
Department of Mental Hygiene, 1965, p. 47)

It will be up to you as a citizen of your community to work with your local hospital, clinics, and mental health associations to encourage them to develop facilities and programs.

The Nation and World as a Resource for Mental Health

Our government is providing matching state and local funds to help establish some of these local facilities. In addition, the National Institute of Mental Health is supporting research and training programs in all areas of mental health.

Through the United Nations, for the first time in history, cross-cultural studies of mental illness are being conducted. Information and research findings on the prevention and treatment of mental illness from countries all over the world are being gathered and shared. Through such fine programs as VISTA and the Peace Corps young people are trying to do something to help people *before* they develop more serious emotional illnesses.

Again, it is up to you as a future citizen of your country to ask yourself what you can do (whether it be writing letters to your congressman, supporting mental health programs, or joining the Peace Corps for one year) to help in the treatment and prevention of mental illness.

Final Summary

Nearly all neurotics and psychotics can be treated successfully. Today there are many different kinds of therapy for the mentally ill. The principle goals of therapy are to strengthen the patient's self-concept and to develop his competencies so that he can satisfy his needs and meet the demands placed on him by society successfully without using the crutches of psychological defense systems.

Major developments in the field of treatment such as therapeautic communities, drugs, better-qualified staffs, and local mental hygiene clinics have significantly reduced the number of patients in the state mental hospitals. There will be even greater public interest in the prevention and treatment of the mentally ill when there is better understanding of what it is really like to be mentally ill. The authors hope that after reading "My Little Saint," you will agree also that a mental patient is far more normal than abnormal and that he is a human being who has reacted to unbearable hurts in the same way that you would have if placed in similar dire circumstances that seemingly offered no hope or salvation.

Specific Chapter References

Alexander, M. The relation of environment to intelligence and achievement: a longitudinal study. Unpublished master's thesis, University of Chicago, 1961.

American Psychiatric Association. *Remotivation: basic facts about a useful mental hospital program* (pamphlet). Philadelphia: Smith, Kline and French Laboratories, 1964.

365
Diagnosis,
Treatment,
and Prevention
of Unhealthy
Personalities

Berner, G., and Berner, D. Reading difficulties in children. *Archives of Ophthalmology,* 1938, 20, 830.

Buros, O. K. (ed.). *Tests in print.* Highland Park, N. J.: Gryphon Press, 1961.

California State Department of Mental Hygiene. *Pattern of Progress.* Sacramento, Calif. 1965.

Cameron, N., and Cameron. Margaret A. *Behavior pathology.* Boston: Houghton Mifflin, 1951.

Coleman, J. C. *Abnormal psychology and modern life.* Chicago; Scott Foresman, 1964.

Deutsch, A. *The mentally ill in America.* New York: Columbia University Press, 1949.

Eysenck, H. J. (ed.). *Behavior therapy and the neuroses.* London: Pergamon Press, 1960.

Fitts, W. H. *The experience of psychotherapy.* Princeton, N. J.: Van Nostrand, 1965.

Freeman, L. *Hope for the troubled.* New York: Cardinal, 1953.

Goldstein, K. *The organism.* New York: American Book, 1939.

Hadfield, J. A. *Introduction to psychotherapy.* London: Allen and Unw , 1967.

Joint Commission on Mental Illness and Health. *Action for mental health.* New York: Basic Books, 1961.

Luchins, A. S. *Group therapy.* New York: Random House, 1964.

Lugo, J., and Hershey, G. L. College reading difficulties. Unpublished study, Fullerton Junior College, Calif., 1966.

Mann, L. Persuasive doll play: a technique of directive psychotherapy for use with children. *Journal of Clinical Psychology,* 1957, 13, 14–19.

Moreno, J. L. Psychodrama. In S. Arieti (ed.), *American handbook of psychiatry.* Vol. II. New York: Basic Books, 1959. Pp. 1375–1396.

Murray, H. A. *Explorations in personality.* New York: Oxford University Press, 1938.

National Association for Mental Health. *Facts about mental illness. 1967 Fact Sheet* (pamphlet). New York, 1967.

Rogers, C. R. *On becoming a person.* Boston: Houghton Mifflin, 1961.

Rorschach, H. *Psychodiagnostics,* P. Lemkau and B. Kronenberg (trans.). Berne: Hans Huber, 1942.

Sanders, R., and Cleveland, S. E. The relationship between certain examiner personality variables and subject's Rorschach scores. In B. I. Murstein (ed.), *Handbook of projective techniques.* New York: Basic Books, 1965.

Starke, R. H., and Meehl, P. E. *An atlas for the clinical use of the MMPI.* Minneapolis: University of Minnesota Press, 1951.

Recommended Further Readings

Paperback Books

Allport, G. W. (ed. and interpreter). *Letters from Jenny.* New York: Harbinger Book, 1965.

Bettelheim, B. *Paul and Mary: two case histories from "truants from life".* Garden City, N. Y.: Anchor Books, 1961.

Beukenkamp, C., Jr. *Fortunate strangers.* New York: Grove Press, 1958.

Boisen, A. T. *The exploration of the inner world.* New York: Harper Torchbooks, 1936.

Braceland, F. J., and Stack, M. *Modern psychiatry: a handbook for believers.* Garden City, N. Y.: Doubleday, 1963.

De Kruif, P. *A man against insanity.* New York: Black Cat Book, 1957.

Evans, Jean. *Three men.* New York: Black Cat Book, 1954.

Fitts, W. H. *The experience of psychotherapy.* Princeton, N. J.: Van Nostrand, 1965.

Freeman, Lucy. *Hope for the troubled*. New York: Avon Book Division, Hearst Corporation, 1957.

Freud, S. *Three case histories*. New York: Collier Books, 1963.

Goffman, E. *Asylums: essays on the social situation of mental patients and other inmates*. Garden City, N. Y.: Anchor, 1961.

Goldstein, M. J., and Palmer, J. O. *The experience of anxiety*. New York: Oxford University Press, 1963.

Green, Hannah. *I never promised you a rose garden*. New York: Signet Book, 1964.

Greenwald, H. (ed.). *Great cases in psychoanalysis*. New York: Ballantine Books, 1959.

Gross, M. L. *The brain watchers*. New York: Signet Book, 1962.

Guthrie, R. V. (ed.). *Psychology in the world today*. Reading, Mass.: Addison–Wesley, 1968.

Hoffman, B. *The tyranny of testing*. New York: Collier Books, 1962.

Lepp, I. *Health of mind and soul*. Garden City, N. Y.: Anchor, 1966.

Lindner, R. M. *Rebel without a cause*. New York: Grove Press, 1944.

Luchins, A. S. *Group therapy, a guide*. New York: Random House, 1964.

May, R. *Man's search for himself*. New York: Signet Book, 1963.

McCord, W., and McCord, Jean. *The psychopath*. Princeton, N. J.: Van Nostrand, 1964.

McNeil, E. B. *The quiet furies*. Englewood Cliffs, N. J.: Prentice-Hall, 1967.

Menninger, K. *Man against himself*. New York: Harvest Book, 1938.

Mowrer, O. H. *The new group therapy*. Princeton, N. J.: Van Nostrand, 1964.

Nixon, R. E. *The art of growing*. New York: Random House, 1962.

Nunokawa, W. D. (ed.). *Human values and abnormal behavior*. Chicago: Scott Foresman, 1965.

Redl, F., and Wineman, D. *Children who hate*. New York: Collier Books, 1951.

Rogers, C. R. and Stevens, B. *Person to person: the problem of being human*. Lafayette, Calif.: Real People Press, 1967.

Shostrom, E. L. *Man, the manipulator*. New York: Bantam Books, 1967.

Sohl, G. *The lemon eaters*. New York: Dell Books, 1967.

Hardcover Books

Ball, J. *By reason of insanity*. London: Hutchinson, 1966.

Crow, L. D. *Psychology of human adjustment*. New York: Knopf, 1967.

Davis, J. A. *Education for positive mental health*. Chicago: Aldine, 1965.

Deutsch, A. *The mentally ill in America*. New York: Columbia University Press, 1949.

Ford, D. H., and Urban, H. B. *Systems of psychotherapy; a comparative study*. New York: Wiley, 1963.

Glasser, W. *Reality therapy*. New York: Harper & Row, 1965.

Harper, R. A. *Psychoanalysis and psychotherapy: 36 systems*. Englewood Cliffs, N. J.: Prentice-Hall, 1959.

Menninger, K., Mayman, M., and Pruyser, P. *The vital balance*. New York: Viking Press, 1963.

Mowrer, O. H. (ed.). *Morality and mental health*. Chicago: Rand McNally, 1967.

Nannaly, J. C., Jr. *Popular conceptions of mental health*. New York: Holt, Rinehart and Winston, 1961.

Riessman, F., Cohen, J., and Pearl, A. *Mental health of the poor*. New York: Free Press, 1964.

Ringness, T. A. *Mental health in the schools*. New York: Random House, 1967.

Robinson, R., DeMarche, D. E., and Wagle, M. K. *Community resources in mental health*. New York: Basic Books, 1960.

Rokeach, M. *The three christs of Ypsilanti: a narrative study of three lost men.* New York: Knopf, 1964.

Rotter, J. R. *Clinical psychology.* Englewood Cliffs, N. J.: Prentice-Hall, 1964.

Sundberg, N. D., and Tyler, Leona E. *Clinical psychology: an introduction to research and practice.* New York: Appleton-Century-Crofts, 1962.

Thorpe, L. P. *The psychology of mental health,* New York: Ronald Press, 1960.

367
Diagnosis,
Treatment,
and Prevention
of Unhealthy
Personalities

Part IV Understanding the Future Development of Human Behavior

Chapter 12
Challenges of Tomorrow

This section of the book was written especially for the subculture of youth. The future is highly relevant to young people because, like them, its existence is just beginning and opened to change and new ideas. On the other hand, the past has been set hard "in cement" and the present is already solidifying. Young people realize that many of their ways of living were determined by decisions made a long time ago by others. Many of them feel that our present institutions have not made this a better world in which to live. They feel that these institutions have not and will not be able to keep pace with the revolutions occurring in science, technology, education, communication, politics, and social living. The rush of change was too great.

Dissatisfied with the past and doubtful about the present, youth wants a voice in deciding and shaping the future. Perhaps their vitality and creativity combined with the wisdom of the ages represented by present institutions can produce the kind of society that will allow for continual renewals and innovations necessary for man's continuous efforts to achieve self-actualization.

John W. Gardner, former Secretary of Health, Education, and Welfare, in his book *Self-renewal* discusses some of these issues:

An individual cannot achieve renewal if he does not believe in the possibility of it. Nor can a society. At all times in history there have been individuals and societies whose attitudes toward the future have been such as to thwart, or at least greatly impede, the process of renewal.

There is a readily discernible difference between the society (or individual) that is oriented to the future and the one that is oriented to the past. Some individuals and societies look forward and have the future ever in mind, others are preoccupied with the past and are antiquarian in their interests. The former have a vivid sense of what they are becoming, the latter a vivid sense of what they have been. The former are fascinated by the novelty of each day's experience, the latter have a sense of having seen everything.

No society is likely to renew itself unless its dominant orientation is to the future. This is not to say that a society can ignore its past. A people without historians would be as crippled as an individual with amnesia. They would not know who they are. In helping a society to achieve self-knowledge, the historian serves the cause of renewal. But in the renewing society the historian consults the past in the service of the present and the future. (1963, pp. 105–106)

Chapter 12 Challenges of Tomorrow

Chapter Outline

Study Guide

At first, good readers form tentative conclusions, generalizations, and inferences. They maintain these tentative notions until they have gathered further supporting evidence. However, in reading about future trends and developments, tentative ideas and opinions must remain more open to change and modification, because confirming evidence, if any, will come only in the distant future.

The interdisciplinary nature of this chapter adds another dimension of difficulty. Information from many other sciences and fields of study have been included because man's future depends on the changes in all areas of life.

1. Study this chapter following study guide procedures. By this time you should be able to do so independently.
2. If you have not done so already, practice applying the study guide procedures in other courses.

372
**Understanding
the Future
Development
of Human
Behavior**

Further Suggestions

If you feel that your academic performance has not been as high as it should be, consider some of these alternatives:

1. Mention this problem to your optometrist or opthamologist and request a thorough visual examination.

2. Mention this problem to your physician and request a thorough physical examination.

3. Discuss this problem with a counselor or psychologist and request a thorough academic and vocational evaluation.

4. Ask your librarian for recommendations on how-to-study books.

Prelude

On the first page of this book one of the authors' students was quoted as saying that "we all play our parts, and hide our feelings." In one sentence that student captured the major dilemma that each of us faces not only today, but also in the world of tomorrow: How to play our part in this highly technologically organized and rapidly changing world and, yet, retain some of our human qualities of love, affection, and compassion for ourselves and our fellowmen.

Many possible answers to this dilemma have been woven throughout the previous eleven chapters in some of the theory, research, and their applications. In this chapter we will study some of the roots of the dilemma facing modern man today and especially in the future. We see many gaps that have been created between the advancement of technology and a "humanized man." Yet, we also see many positive future trends that could allow for the possibility that all men could become free enough to develop their full potential by climbing the ladder toward greater and greater self-actualization.

Students' Viewpoints

Students, like yourself, have one foot in the present century and the other in the twenty-first century. How do you view the world of the year 2000? We asked our students the same question. It became apparent from their responses

Figure 12-1

Challenges of Tomorrow. The world of tomorrow has its roots in the present and the past. As young people look toward the future, they should remember that they are living on the foundations built by their fathers and forefathers. Young people today are literally "standing on the shoulders" of others. In turn, our children will be able to live a better life because they will be standing on our shoulders.

that they are deeply concerned about their future and what can be done to make this a better world in the time that remains. Here are some of their views:

By the time I get to the year 2000, I will be 50-years old, perhaps with grandchildren. Life, then, will be longer and easier than it was for my parents or grandparents. It will be fun to know what they will call "primitive living" is the way I lived when I was growing up. It will also be fun to see if their values are different from mine and what their plans and thoughts for the future will be.

Within the span of the next thirty years many scientific advances will be made which will change life as we now know it. Certainly the world will continue to grow smaller with the ever-increasing speed and availability of jet aircraft. Many diseases which are seemingly incurable will be conquered by medical science. In education, many technological advances will be made enabling instructors to accelerate learning programs. In business the computer will be as common as the mechanical calculator is today.

However, there is one thing that will not change, or at least will not change dramatically, that is man. Although his environment will be rapidly changing, man will only adjust to these changes just as he has done in the past. It may be true, though, that the faster, more complex world of the future may prove to be more difficult to adjust to. This might be evidenced by the many emotional illnesses seen today. But, on the other hand, man might grow in knowledge and emotional strength which may enable mankind to cope with the world of the future.

If mankind is still alive at the turn of this century, he will probably be overwhelmed by the tremendous scientific advancements of his society. But will the same society that spawned the scientific boom of the twentieth century be able to advance as rapidly in curing society's ills? Will the same men who have been trying to destroy one another learn to live in peace as the world grows smaller? The only concern that I have for the year 2000 is whether I will live to see it or not.

These comments reflect some of the basic issues and questions raised by our students. The world of tomorrow is almost upon them and they know it. They seem eager and impatient for an education and a society that will prepare them to live in what will be their world.

WHY IS IT IMPORTANT?

Adequate education and successful living in today's world is no guarantee of success in tomorrow's world. Therefore, a truly adequate education today must include a serious consideration of the frontiers of living that lie just ahead. Once we have developed reasonable ideas about the requirements for successful living in the near future, we can start preparing ourselves and our children with the necessary social, intellectual, and emotional competencies for survival and progress.

Preparation for future living should no longer be left to chance and good fortune. Man should no longer permit himself the luxury of muddling through life. He should plan ahead even though mistakes will be made. The fulfillment of social aims and objectives always allows freedom for the individual in the many acts of day-by-day living. The individual can remain true to the standards and ideals of his society within its broad limits while, at the same time, exercising his own individuality.

BASIC THEORY AND RESEARCH

The basic research and theory in this chapter will be interdisciplinary. That is, information from other fields of study such as anthropology, sociology, medicine, space, weather, and communication will be integrated with psychology. An interdisciplinary approach permits a more complete understanding of man.

The Age of Progress

Possibly historians of the future will refer to the latter part of the twentieth century as the Age of Progress and Material Comfort. Man is no longer a beast of burden. He has harnessed enormous energies to work for him. He continuously develops new machines and processes for making living more comfortable and efficient. Nevertheless, there is a growing sense of urgency everywhere. We all know that we stand at the threshold of dramatic events that will change our ways of living just as events of the early part of the century produced radical changes in our present ways of living.

How does one explain this resurgence of interest in "the future"? Some of this is due, undoubtedly, to the lure of the millennial number of the year 2000, which is but thirty-three years away; two-thirds of all Americans now alive will probably witness the turn of that chiliastic year. Some is due to the romance of space—the awareness that within this generation men will stand upon the moon, and before the end of the century they may even reach out for Venus and Mars. Important as these factors are to the imaginative context of men's efforts—the recurrence of an impulse toward omnipotence—there are more prosaic, yet, paradoxically, more important reasons for this new upsurge. It arises from the simple fact that every society today is consciously committed to economic growth, to raising the standard of living of its people, and therefore to the planning, direction, and control of social change. What makes the present studies, therefore, so completely different from those of the past is that they are oriented to specific social-policy purposes; and along with this new dimension, they are fashioned, self-consciously, by a new methodology that gives the promise of providing a more reliable foundation for realistic alternatives and choices, if not for exact prediction. (Kahn and Weiner, 1967, p. xxv)

376

**Understanding
the Future
Development
of Human
Behavior**

In other words people today are aware that it is possible to change and direct future developments. With the growth of modern mass communications, education, and transportation, new ideas and methods can be exchanged quickly on a worldwide basis. Even more important is the ability to implement rapidly new ideas and methods into everyday living. A new advance in medicine can become a commonly used technique within fifteen years—the time it takes for a college freshman to complete medical studies.

ADVANCES IN THE AGE OF PROGRESS

Man's advancements on practically all frontiers of knowledge have become so great that it is often referred to as the *knowledge explosion*. Table 12-1, compiled from *The Year 2000* (Kahn and Weiner, 1967, pp. 51–57), provides a concise impression of some of the ongoing advancements in science, technology, and the social sciences. An attempt has been made to classify the innovations according to Maslow's hierarchy of human needs.

Table 12-1
Human Needs and Technological Advancements

Physiological needs (food, air, temperature)

1. Generally acceptable and competitive synthetic foods and beverages (e.g., carbohydrates, fats, proteins, enzymes, vitamins, coffee, tea, cocoa, and alcoholic liquor)
2. Intensive and/or extensive expansion of tropical agriculture and forestry
3. More reliable and longer-range weather forecasting
4. New techniques for preserving and improving the environment
5. Relatively effective appetite and weight control
6. New and useful plant and animal species
7. Controlled and/or supereffective relaxation and sleep
8. Practical use of direct electronic communication with and stimulation of the brain
9. Human hibernation for relatively extensive periods (months to years)
10. New techniques for very cheap, convenient, and reliable birth control
11. New, more varied, and more reliable drugs for control of fatigue, relaxation, alertness, mood, personality, perceptions, fantasies, and other psychobiological states
12. Capacity to choose the sex of unborn children
13. Improved capacity to "change" sex of children and/or adults
14. Other genetic control and/or influence over the "basic constitution" of an individual
15. "High quality" medical care for undeveloped areas (e.g., use of medical aides and technicians, referral hospitals, broad spectrum antibiotics, and artificial blood plasma)
16. Simple techniques for extensive and "permanent" cosmetological changes (features, "figures", perhaps complexion and even skin color, and even physique)
17. New techniques for keeping physically fit and/or acquiring physical skills
18. Extensive genetic control for plants and animals
19. New biological and chemical methods to identify, trace, incapacitate, or annoy people for police and military uses
20. New and possibly very simple methods for lethal biological and chemical warfare
21. Artificial growth of new limbs and organs
22. Room temperature superconductors
23. Conversion of mammals (humans?) to fluid breathers

Table 12–1 (Cont.)

377

Challenges of Tomorrow

24. Direct augmentation of human mental capacity by the mechanical or electrical interconnection of the brain with a computer
25. Major rejuvenation and/or significant extension of vigor and life span—say 100 to 150 years

Stimulation of needs (exploration, activity, senses)

1. New airborne vehicles (ground-effect machines, VTOL and STOL, superhelicopters, giant and/or supersonic jets
2. New sources of power for fixed installations (e.g., magnetohydrodynamic, thermionic and thermoelectric, and radioactivity)
3. New sources of power for ground transportation (storage battery, fuel cell, propulsion or support by electromagnetic fields, jet engine, turbine, and the like)
4. Extensive and intensive use of high-altitude cameras for mapping, prospecting, census, land use, and geological investigations
5. New methods of water transportation (such as large submarines, flexible and special purpose "container ships," or more extensive use of large automated single-purpose bulk cargo ships)
6. Three-dimensional photography, illustrations, movies, and television
7. Permanent manned satellite and lunar installations—interplanetary travel
8. Permanent inhabited undersea installations and perhaps even colonies
9. New uses of underground "tunnels" for private and public transportation
10. Individual flying platforms
11. Simple inexpensive home video recording and playing
12. Inexpensive high-capacity, worldwide, regional, and local communication (perhaps using satellites, lasers, and light pipes)
13. Inexpensive worldwide transportation of humans and cargo
14. Inexpensive road-free (and facility-free) transportation
15. Artificial moons and other methods for lighting large areas at night

Safety and security

1. Multiple applications of lasers and masers for sensing, measuring, communication, cutting, heating, welding, power transmission, illumination, destructive (defensive), and other purposes
2. Extreme high-strength superperformance fabrics (papers, fibers, and plastics)
3. New and improved materials for equipment and appliances (plastics, glasses, alloys, ceramics, intermetallics, and cements)
4. More sophisticated architectural engineering (e.g., geodesic domes, "fancy" stressed shells, pressurized skins, and esoteric materials)
5. Automated or more mechanized housekeeping and home maintenance
6. Use of nuclear explosives for excavation and mining, generation of power, creation of high-temperature high-pressure environments, and/or as a source of neutrons or other radiation
7. General use of automation and cybernation in management and production
8. Extensive and intensive centralization of current and past personal and business information in high-speed data processors
9. Automated grocery and department stores
10. Extensive use of robots and machines "slaved" to humans
11. Improved chemical control of some mental illnesses and some aspects of senility
12. Major improvements in earth moving and construction equipment
13. Practical large-scale desalinization
14. Flexible penology without necessarily using prisons (by use of modern methods of surveillance, monitoring, and control)
15. Stimulated and planned and perhaps programmed dreams

378

**Understanding
the Future
Development
of Human
Behavior**

Table 12–1 (Cont.)

Love and belonging (learning, education, group membership)

1. Increased educational opportunities in schools, home, and industry
2. Home education via video and computerized and programmed learning
3. New and more reliable "educational" and propaganda techniques for affecting human behavior —public and private
4. New techniques and institutions for the education of children
5. Chemical methods for improving memory and learning
6. Practical home and business use of "wired" video communication for both telephone and TV (possibly including retrieval of taped material from libraries or other sources) and rapid transmission and reception of facsimiles (possibly including news, library material, commercial announcements, instantaneous mail delivery, other printouts, and so on)
7. Pervasive business use of computers for the storage, processing, and retrieval of information

Self-esteem (adequate self-concept, social success)

1. More extensive use of competitive examinations for occupational advancements
2. Greater opportunities for achieving success regardless of sex, race, or religion
3. More extensive and intensive use of merit systems, rewards, and other symbols of individual and group accomplishments

Self-actualization

1. Greater use of psychotherapy for persons who are not mentally ill (e.g., sensitivity training, T-group methods, brain-storming, and other methods used to increase self-awareness, creativity, cooperation, and group participation)
2. Greater variety of educational courses designed to meet individual needs (e.g., arts, crafts, music, drama, writing, dancing, and small group seminars)
3. Greater leisure time (can be used in self-enhancing ways or can lead to increased boredom)

It is obvious from this impressive but incomplete list of innovations that the impact on our lives in the near future will be great and far-reaching. The knowledge explosion poses many new problems and challenges, but it also promises, for the first time, what may be the great unifying and facilitating force permitting large numbers of people to achieve self-actualization. Literally man can have the "whole world in his hands." The time to act intelligently and compassionately is now. The promise of human fulfillment is so great that we should proceed immediately and willingly to consider seriously the existing blocks toward self-actualization.

Intermediate Summary

As man approaches the year 2000, he finds himself in the midst of a giant informational and technological explosion. He stands at the threshold of dramatic events that promise to radically improve his ways of living. The major problem facing him is to close the gap between technological advancements and his urgent need for self-actualization.

Figure 12-2
Space Travel. Technological advances promise exciting frontiers for man. Space stations will facilitate and popularize space travel. As man probes the reaches of the stars, he should not forget to probe the unexplored potentials that lie within himself.

PROGRESS VERSUS ALIENATION

In spite of all the rapid changes that we have seen in many areas of human life, man still feels lost and alienated—like a puppet being moved about by unknown forces. For example, a recent survey reports the following results:

One-third of the adults in the nation are concerned over not being able to sleep at night. . . . About 25% feel too exhausted to get up in the morning and about the same percentage either lacks an appetite or feels unable to control it. A majority (52%) of the sample poll reports that they are "lonely and depressed" some of the time and 23% said that they have felt "emotionally disturbed." (Nelson, 1968).

In the foreword to one of Erich Fromm's latest books (*The Revolution of Hope: Toward a Humanized Technology*, 1968) he writes:

379

380
**Understanding
the Future
Development
of Human
Behavior**

This book is written as a response to America's situation in the year 1968. It is born out of the conviction that we are at the crossroads: one road leads to a completely mechanized society with man as a helpless cog in the machine—if not to destruction by thermonuclear war; the other to a renaissance of humanism and hope—to a society that puts technique in the service of man's well-being.

Rollo May (1967) expresses his concern over this dilemma as follows:

To begin with, I pose the question, Is not one of the central problems of modern Western man that he experiences himself as without significance as an individual? Let us focus on that aspect of his image of himself which is his doubt whether he can act and his half-aware conviction that even if he did act it would do no good. This is only one side of contemporary man's picture of himself, but it is a psychologically critical aspect—a self-doubt which reflects the tremendous technological power that surges up every moment about him to dwarf overwhelmingly his own puny efforts. (pp. 25–26)

WHAT HAS GONE WRONG?

The question that you might be asking yourself now may go something like this: Why, with all the progress in the past one hundred years that has put man in control of his environment, does he still feel alone, depressed, and alienated from others and the world in general? Of course the answer to such a question is very complex and involves factors of which we are not yet even aware. However, we feel that a large part of the answer has to do with the fact that so many of our changes have been aimed at the satisfaction of our basic needs (the lower rungs of the self-actualization stepladder), while the satisfaction of some of the higher needs has been almost totally neglected.

TECHNOLOGICAL CHANGE AND THE SELF-ACTUALIZATION GAP

We have already documented the enormous changes that have taken place with respect to the basic needs (physiological, stimulation, and safety). Even though the satisfaction of these needs today is far from universal, it is a matter of time before these will be available to all people in the world. In a sense we have solved the problems of meeting man's lower needs: we have enough food, we know how to help countries establish ways of providing safe environments (both physically and socially), and we have developed the means to help people explore their world through such developments as the mass media (television, radio, books, cultural programs, and the like). And, yet, man still fails to adequately feel that he belongs, that he is worthwhile, and that he can actualize his potential.

When the history of man in the twentieth century is written it may be said that our greatest tragedies were not the terrible earthquakes, the series of wars, or even the dropping of the atomic bomb on Hiroshima, but that so many millions of persons lived and died without even realizing the tremendous human potential that lay undeveloped within themselves; that so much of modern man's life centered around being safe, having enough food, and having his senses stimulated

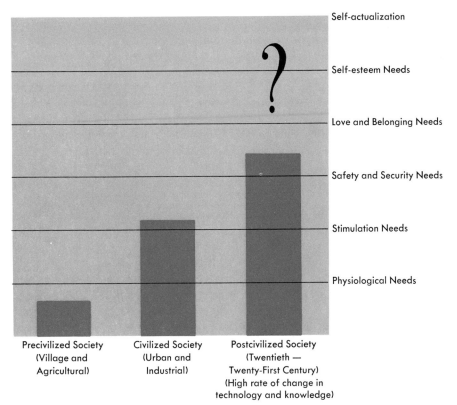

Figure 12–3

The Development of Civilization and the Satisfaction of Human Needs

by television serials and cartoons; that man failed to experience a true sense of belonging, love, and self-esteem; that man never really knew who he was. Figure 12–3 demonstrates the self-actualization gap that technological change has helped produce in modern man.

CLOSING THE SELF-ACTUALIZATION GAP THROUGH THE KNOWLEDGE EXPLOSION

The knowledge explosion, including the demands required for living successfully in a technological society, has produced two major blocks toward self-actualization. No one today can learn all there is to learn. Secondly, man has failed to study himself adequately. The greatest unexplored frontier today is man himself—not the ocean bottom or the ceiling of galaxies. As man probes the reaches of the farthest stars and the depths of the earth, he should not ignore the greatest treasures of all, himself and his children.

Improving the Process of Education

The process of education must be updated to facilitate meaningful communication of the contents of the knowledge explosion to students. Figure 12–4 is a

382
**Understanding
the Future
Development
of Human
Behavior**

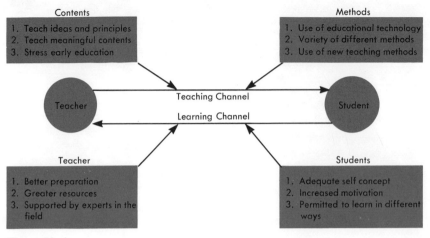

Figure 12–4
Aids to Education.

diagrammatical representation of some ways of improving the channels of teaching and learning.

The basic idea is that school achievement is greatest when the channels of teaching and learning are clear. The successful implementations of educational innovations can remove the "noise" that often blocks the communication channels essential to effective learning.

Contents

Students of the future will not have to memorize endless lists of facts, dates, and numbers. Instead, educators will teach the principles, ideas, and attitudes that underlie the facts and numbers. Once a student has mastered a basic principle, he can use the principle to understand the many facts that earlier he had had to memorize. Furthermore, through the process of generalization, he can apply the principle to similar and more complex problems. For example, in the new mathematics the role of rote learning of number operations is deemphasized in favor of the basic assumptions that underlie the mathematics taught in kindergarten through grade twelve. Researchers have identified the eight basic strands that unite the basic mathematics programs. The following are some of the advantages of the new mathematics: (Strehler, 1964)

1. The students are taught the basic principles in a systematic fashion instead of in a series of unrelated topics.
2. Complex ideas are introduced much earlier in ways that young children can understand.
3. Mathematics has been updated through the introduction of recent and important developments.

Major curriculum improvements in the sciences have proceeded along similar lines. The nation's scientific scholars, who have for so many years ignored the scientific needs of the nation's schoolchildren, have made invaluable contributions toward the science programs to be taught in our schools. Heath (1964) reports that the gap between research knowledge and what is taught in schools is closing. Furthermore, he reports, after studying the publications of the research directors of numerous curriculum projects, that there is now an awareness that the intellectual abilities of children have been seriously underestimated.

The new science programs, as well as the others in mathematics, social sciences, and languages, emphasize teaching the structure of knowledge—the basic ideas, principles, methods, and attitudes that form the meaningful framework of science within which science contents can be taught meaningfully. In other words, students must understand the basic structure of a subject matter before they can learn how it works. Burner (1961) presents four advantages to teaching the structure of knowledge:

The first is that understanding fundamentals makes a subject more comprehensible. This is true not only in physics and mathematics . . . but equally true in the social sciences and literature.

The second point relates to human memory. Perhaps the most basic thing that can be said about human memory, after a century of intensive research, is that unless detail is placed into a structured pattern, it is rapidly forgotten. . . . A scientist does not try to remember the distances traversed by falling bodies in different gravitational fields over different periods of time. What he carries in memory instead is a formula that permits him with varying degrees of accuracy to regenerate the details on which the more easily remembered formula is based.

Third, an understanding of fundamental principles and ideas, as noted earlier, appears to be the main road to adequate "transfer of training." To understand something as a specific instance of a more general case—which is what understanding a more fundamental principle or structure means—is to have learned not only a specific thing but also a model for understanding other things like it that one may encounter.

The fourth claim for emphasis on structure and principles in teaching is that by constantly reexamining material taught in elementary and secondary schools for its fundamental character, one is able to narrow the gap between "advanced" knowledge and "elementary" knowledge. (pp. 23–25)

These newly discovered ways of organizing the contents of the knowledge explosion will facilitate and accelerate the production of the highly educated society needed for living successfully in the world of tomorrow.

New Methods of Teaching

The application of technology to education can provide more efficient ways of presenting the structure of knowledge. Here is a description of an experimental classroom that provides us with notions of what the classroom of the future may be like: (Silberman, 1962, pp. 349–350)

384
Understanding
the Future
Development
of Human
Behavior

Each student in the class has a display unit and a response device. The student typically reads an item on his film viewer and then enters a multiple choice answer on his response device. Answers are recorded and evaluated in the computer, and feedback is supplied by small lights on the response device. The computer then determines what the student should see next. The number of the next item is displayed on the student's response device. The student then turns to the indicated item on his film viewer and repeats the cycle. In this fashion each of twenty students in the class receives simultaneously individualized instruction from the computer.

The teacher has special monitoring equipment to keep track of what is going on in the classroom. When a student is having trouble an alarm light on the teacher's monitor console is activated. The teacher may defer action if he is busy or he may press a button on his console corresponding to that student's position and take a number of actions. For example, one action button will cause his response unit to be connected in parallel with that student's response device. He may then observe that student's responses to each item. Another action button will call up further information, on a cathode ray tube, about this student's performance. This information will assist the teacher in locating the source of the student's difficulty. A brief discussion with the student may help to clear up his problem, and the incident will be recorded for future reference when the program is being revised.

Programming, learning in a step-by-step fashion with constant feedback, has been used by teachers in presenting lessons, in workbooks, and in textbooks. However, the more sophisticated use of complex technology is still in the experimental stages. It is important to remember that instructional aids such as programmed learning, television, language laboratories, and computer-based teaching are designed to help the teacher to communicate more effectively with the individual student and should not be seen as replacements for teacher-student contacts.

A new technology related to education is that of storing or "remembering" information. The ability to store and to transmit information accurately and rapidly constitutes an enormous jump forward. The use of microfilms, magnetic storage, and video films offers a potential for unlimited storage of information. Presently it is possible to show a film with sound tracks in four or five different languages simultaneously using the multitrack system developed by Cinestar Incorporated; computer translation of languages is still in the experimental stage. In other words, it may be possible in the near future to recreate the world of knowledge for the individual regardless of distance, time, or language.

DeCarlo (1968), Director of Automation Research at the International Business Machines Corporation (IBM), summarizes some of the possibilities that may result from recent trends in memory and communication technology in the book, *Toward the Year 2018:*

First, the volume of information that can be electronically sensed, stored, and made available to the mind and senses will be increased beyond our present imagination. . . . In the future it is certain that the individual will have available a great range of sensations and experiences that can be recreated for him.

Second, the development of very small, portable storage units would permit an individual to have, for his individual ownership and use, specific kinds of competencies and experience. Instead of *How to* books, he might have the actual "presence" of experts to teach and direct him. One thing is certain: Learning and education will be completely changed by the existence of such devices. Moreover, the devices could be connected to central banks of experience, permitting the individual to tap an unlimited amount of assistance and experience.

Third, the development of better input/output devices will make recorded experience more directly accessible to the "senses." Communication into the machine through modified spoken languages, by stylized writing and codification, will make the power of electronic technologies available to persons of all educational levels without specialized training. . . . (p. 104)

Increased Demand for Education

Corresponding to the knowledge and technological explosions is the education explosion. More people today than ever before are in the midst of the process of education. It might be that the three explosions together can provide the impetus necessary to propel us into the world of tomorrow. Drucker (1965) discusses the scale of the education explosion:

Thirty years ago only one out of every eight Americans at work had been to high school. Today four out of every five of the young people of high school age in the United States attend high school. Twenty years hence, when today's middle-aged will have retired, practically every working American will be a high school graduate. We have already passed the half-way mark.

Even greater has been the jump in college and university attendance. Thirty years ago it was still an almost negligible 4 per cent or less of the appropriate age group. Today the figure is around 35 per cent for the nation. . . .

On top of all this, adult education is booming. . . . Adult education during the last fifteen years has been growing faster in this country than college enrollment. And now increasingly it means advanced education for the already highly educated. . . . (pp. 117–118)

The process of education, opened to all and supported by modern technology, is perhaps the greatest hope for closing the self-actualization gap. The ever-growing numbers of highly educated persons, freed from the boredom of menial labor, will be able to bring to bear all their energies and know-how to the achievement of the upper rungs of the stepladder of human needs, at the same time, guaranteeing themselves and others the satisfaction of their basic physical and psychological needs.

CLOSING THE SELF-ACTUALIZATION GAP THROUGH EXPLORING MAN'S POTENTIAL

Finally, there are now many signs that we have entered the travail of a major revolution: We are undergoing a change in the image of man. The old images are being discarded, and a new image is in the making—man the shaper of his own boundless potentialities. It is an image of HOPE and of BECOMING. (Otto, 1966, p. xv)

386
**Understanding
the Future
Development
of Human
Behavior**

As the quote suggests, man is still living life with a fraction of his potential. The authors feel a major development in helping to close the self-actualization gap lies in studying man's largely untapped potential. It should be noted that much research in this area is still highly tentative, yet we are exploring areas that man has never touched before and the implications are far-reaching.

Even though there are many areas being explored today, we can focus on only some of the developments within the few that are highly significant. These include the following: (1) explorations regarding the nature of man; (2) explorations in developing man's psychological potential; (3) explorations in developing man's physiological potential; and (4) explorations in developing man's social potential.

Exploring the Nature of Man

We have already discussed some of the theories regarding man's basic nature. We have also discussed Maslow's theory regarding man's inner nature as being "good" rather than "bad". In summarizing a chapter on our conception of human nature, Ashley Montagu (1962), a leading anthropologist, states:

It is becoming increasingly clear that an infant is born not only with the need to be loved, but also with the need to love; he is certainly not born with any need to be aggressive.

This view of human nature makes a picture radically different from the traditional one, the one that conceives of man as born with an aggressiveness which must be suppressed or eradicated by the socialization process; the view that renders rationalizations about the "innate warlikeness" of man, and circulates facile fallacies about man as a "brute." Modern research has shown this view of human nature to be erroneous. Man is not born evil or aggressive—he is rendered so. This being the case, it is incumbent upon us to realize that we can best change human nature for the better not by working on man's biological inheritance but by working on his social inheritance; by changing those conditions which produce disharmony in the person and a corresponding disharmony in his society.

Human nature fortunately holds considerably more promise for man than he has thus far been able to realize on a significant scale. A first step toward a fuller realization of that promise is a fuller understanding of his own nature. (Pp. 33–34)

Thus, there appears to be a reformulation of the basic nature of man, from that of a sinful, rather wild beast that must be tamed, to that of a being with unlimited potential waiting to be developed.

Exploring the Development of Man's Psychological Potential

What new trends are developing to help man uncover and explore his vast psychological potential? In discussing the creation of new human natures, one psychologist puts it this way:

Man's interaction with the things of this world through the methods of the arts and through the methods of science will produce more and more that is new in man as the centuries pass. The very process of interaction with that which was previously unknown produces new content, new stuff, new realities, new things to understand and to love, as well as new instruments of observation, new ways of knowing, new modes of esthetic apprehension. These, too, will change the nature of man, not simply by enriching that which lies under the threshold of his immediate nature but by broadening the doorway through which he passes, so that he may see more of the vista he approaches and may as he does so become always a larger man. It is because of man's capacity for intimate union with the stuff of this world through the methods of science that he may hope to do more than to transcend himself, may hope to become in each new emergent phase of his life a new kind of man. (Murphy, 1965, p. 158)

There are many trends evident that we are on the horizon of helping develop "a new kind of man." What are some of these trends?

AN ENLARGED RESEARCH PROGRAM. An enlarged research program would include not only a better understanding of the unhealthy personality, but more intense studies of the healthy, growing personality.

Evidence of this trend is reflected in the formation of a new professional organization called the American Association for Humanistic Psychology. Back in 1962, a group of psychologists felt that an organization was needed to encourage research and exchange of views regarding man's potentialities. Since that time the organization has grown and now sponsors regional and national meetings as well as a *Journal of Humanistic Psychology*. Their latest pamphlet lists their four major goals as follows:

1. A centering of attention on the experiencing person, and thus a focus on experience as the primary phenomenon in the study of man.
2. An emphasis on such distinctively human qualities as choice, creativity, valuation, and self-realization, as opposed to thinking about human beings in mechanistic and reductionistic terms.
3. An allegiance to meaningfulness in the selection of problems for study and of research procedures, and an opposition to a primary emphasis on objectivity at the expense of significance.
4. An ultimate concern with and valuing of the dignity and worth of man and an interest in the development of the potential inherent in every person. (American Association for Humanistic Psychology, 1969)

Another significant step in this direction is the Human Potentialities Research Center at the University of Utah, where a series of studies is now being conducted and planned. Dr. Herbert Otto (1966), Director of the center, states: "Unquestionably, only a very small fraction of the creative potential of the total population ever finds expression. It is safe to conclude that if a larger fraction of this creative potential were "actualized," this could lead to a renaissance and cultural flowering unequalled in history." (p. 412)

HUMAN GROWTH CENTERS AND CLINICS. The availability of such centers and clinics to help man develop and renew his potentialities cannot be underestimated.

One of the first growth centers for developing man's potentialities was estab-

388
Understanding
the Future
Development
of Human
Behavior

lished at Big Sur, California, in 1961, and is called the Esalen Institute. The purposes of the institute are stated in their yearly bulletin as follows:

> Esalen Institute is a center to explore those trends in the behavioral sciences, religion and philosophy which emphasize the potentialities and values of human existence. Its activities consist of seminars and workshops such as the ones described in this brochure, research and consulting programs, and a resident program exploring new directions in education and the behavioral sciences. (*Esalen Programs*, 1968, p. 31)

Here on a beautiful bluff overlooking the Pacific Ocean one may come for a week or weekend of humanly stimulating interactions involving such topics as: Breathing and Awareness; The Cultivation of Fantasy; Alienation and Loneliness; Words, Feelings, and the Body; Creativity and Awareness; or Body Awareness, Sense of Being, and Encounter.

Since the development of the Esalen Institute, where some 50,000 people have participated in programs, there have been more than thirty other centers founded in all parts of the United States. Although much of the activity here is still highly experimental, a larger number of psychologists, sociologists, psychiatrists, and even priests and ministers are becoming interested in conducting research in this area. It is possible that many more of these programs will be made available to persons living in large urban areas and in the future it will become a part of our daily lives to attend one of these centers for further self-renewal and growth toward self-actualization.

Explorations in Developing Man's Physiological Potential

In this area, we find so many rapid developments, that it would be easy to write an entire book. We will focus on areas that relate more specifically to psychology.

ADVANCES IN THE STUDY OF THE BRAIN AND NERVOUS SYSTEM. Otto (1966) points out that the Russians have become concerned with developing man's potential. For example, an article in a Russian magazine states:

> . . . If we were able to force our brain to work at only half its capacity, we could, without any difficulty whatever, learn forty languages, memorize the Large Soviet Encyclopedia from cover to cover, and complete the required courses of dozens of colleges. (p. xiv)

Brown (1966) lists a number of other possibilities in this area:

> Recent demonstrations that chemical or psychological conditioning would produce drastic changes in behavioral patterns of rats or humans, whether induced by the injection of minute quantities of chemicals including sex hormones or by visual stimulation, leads to the interesting supposition that someday it may be possible to condition the population of a country to a desired situation.
>
> These experiments suggest that pharmacological investigations may result in formulation of drugs which could increase human potential for learning.

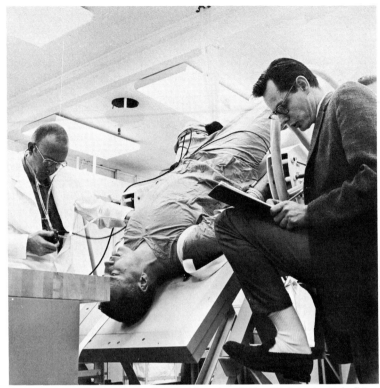

Figure 12-5
The design of complex machines must include research on the limits and potentials of the human machine as well. Because the final product is man and machine together, there is growing need to explore and develop man's psychological potential.

Courtesy of Autonetics, a division of North American Rockwell Corp.

Recent experiments in Cleveland have opened a new vista in the potential of man. The brain has been removed from a Rhesus monkey and kept alive by perfusion for eighteen hours. (pp. 86–87)

ADVANCES IN THE STUDY OF THE AGING PROCESS. One of the most challenging areas of research is that of prolonging man's life and therefore his possibilities for developing his potential over a longer period of time. Brown (1966) lists a number of developments in this area:

The many recent surgical experiments in the transplantation of human organs suggest the eventual possibility of replacement of aged or damaged organs.
Singer's experiments have pointed out the possibility of eventual controls of cells and tissues so that regeneration of a damaged organ or limb may be possible.
The possibility of synthesis of desired proteins within the cell is opened by this discovery and might lead to virus-resistant cells, to cells grown with specific inhibitor or stimulator substances or other alterations of the normal genetic pattern. (pp. 88–89)

Explorations in Developing Man's Social Potential
What possibilities regarding man's social potentials lie ahead in the future world? Will man overcome the conflicts and tensions that separate one race and

389

one nation from another? Will the peoples of the crowded and smaller world be able to live closely together without social unrest? Let's look at some of the projections.

COMPUTERS TO ANALYZE SOCIAL AND INTERNATIONAL RELATIONS. Pool (1968) makes the following predictions:

Computers will permit us to simulate exceedingly complex systems of the many variables of which society and its component organizations are constituted. By 2018, therefore, planners will be able to experiment on computer models, testing out in advance the consequences of various policies.

Widespread use of social indicators thus depends on another breakthrough in behavioral technology, the development of large-scale computerized data systems. By 2018 it will be cheaper to store information in a computer bank than on paper.

Perhaps the most complex cognitive process that will have been analyzed by 2018 is language. We will long since have learned how to program computers to put grammatical sentences together in meaningful response to verbal questions, and to translate these sentences into other languages if so desired. (pp. 90–92)

GREATER COOPERATION AMONG NATIONS AND GREATER HUMAN UNDERSTANDING AMONG MANKIND. With the increase in technology (including travel, communications, and sharing of information stored in computers) man is being forced to interact with his fellowmen all over the world. Margaret Mead (in Otto, 1966) describes this interaction as follows:

Now for the first time, we are having to share political action with peoples of exceedingly varied levels of civilization, whose historic past differs one from another and from our own. We have to include in one forum, one world forum, many peoples who, a generation ago, had cultures without a written language and without any knowledge of the wider world; we have also to include other peoples whose ancient civilizations we have thought to be effete or decadent or mystical, but who are coming into the modern world with quite alarming speed and efficiency. (p. 138)

Perhaps no where else is this spirit of cooperation evident than in the work of the United Nations Educational, Scientific, and Cultural Organization (UNESCO). In her introduction to a manual prepared by the World Federation for Mental Health entitled, *Cultural Patterns and Technical Change*, Margaret Mead (1955) states:

But more urgently, we live in a world which is so haunted by the destructive powers which have been released in the twentieth century that it is of vital importance that we have reason for faith in our world, a reasoned belief in the future of human living. The speed and constructiveness with which the peoples of the world can learn to share in the skills which will free them from their age-long fears is the measure of our right to hope. . . . (p. 7)

In this manual, studies of five different cultures appear in relation to the effects of technical change on various aspects of their lives. As an illustration of the interdependence of nations to help each other, the appendix contains a list of some of the functions of various agencies working with different countries on specific problem areas. Some of these include:

> Appraisal of mineral resources
> Road transport
> Railroad transport
> Budgeting and financial reporting
> Personnel selection and training
> Social-welfare services
> Community, family and child welfare
> Employment, training and migration
> Nutrition
> Technical education
> Environmental sanitation
> Monetary and banking problems
> (Mead, 1955, pp. 318–321)

Intermediate Summary

The self-actualization gap can be closed through the educational process and through the exploration and development of man's potentials. The new process of education includes teaching the structure of knowledge more efficiently to increasing numbers of people by means of educational technology. The explorations of man's potentials include the nature of man psychologically, physiologically, and sociologically.

APPLICATION

Living with Yourself

In spite of all the exciting and humanly challenging changes that are predicted for the world of the future, the final answer to the question of how man will respond to them lies within you as a unique, creative, and growing individual. Peter Drucker (1965), in the concluding paragraphs of his stimulating book entitled *Landmarks of Tomorrow*, puts it this way:

But ours is also a time of new vision and greatness, of opportunity and challenge, to everyone in his daily life, as a person and as a citizen. It is a time in which everyone is an understudy to the leading role in the drama of human destiny. Everyone must be ready to take over alone and without notice, and show himself saint or hero, villain or coward. On this stage the great roles are not written in the iambic pentameter or the Alexandrine of the heroic theater. They are prosaic—played out in one's daily life, in one's work, in one's citizenship, in one's compassion or lack of it, in one's courage to stick to an unpopular principle, and in one's refusal to sanction man's inhumanity to man in an age of cruelty and moral numbness. (pp. 269–270)

The world of tomorrow, automated, computerized, and supersonic, will place much greater value on the individual because only man can provide wisdom and direction. Only man can provide the central guiding principles to which all machines can be programmed—the task of living better in a society geared to the self-actualization of all men.

DEVELOPING A PERSPECTIVE ON YOUR PLACE IN THE WORLD OF TOMORROW

Once, when he was an undergraduate in college, one of the authors was questioning himself and what he was going to do with his life. He stopped by to see a professor whom he liked and respected very much. As they sat and talked about some of the uncertainties that he felt about himself and his future the professor suddenly asked him this question: "When you are an old man ready to die, what will help you to die with a smile?"

"What do you mean?" the author remembers asking in a puzzled voice.

"I mean that so many people die with bitterness, regret, and sorrow written on their faces. 'If I could only relive my life again' I have heard many older people say. What kinds of things do you want to do with your life that will help you to die with a smile; to die saying such things as 'I feel that I have lived a good and personally meaningful life?' "

That question couldn't be answered right then.

But, since that day many years ago, the author has often asked himself that question, especially when he was in doubt about the meaningfulness of what he was doing in his life at that particular time. It helps him to separate the really important and humanly meaningful aspects of his present life from the rote and trivial things that we all get caught up in.

Now, the author mentions this experience because it helped give some direction to a life and helped with the understanding of what was really important and unimportant (his values). The author was at the same point that many of you are now, in your lives; a point where you may be asking such questions as "Who am I?" and "Where am I going in this fast-changing world?"

What the authors hope to do in this section is to discuss with you some of the experiences you will be facing in the future, in light of (1) what you now know about your own behavior and that of others (the first eleven chapters of the book); (2) which types of experiences you will be going through in your world of the future (for example, education, finding a job, marriage, raising children, living in a community, joining groups, playing different roles); and (3) some of the drastic changes mentioned earlier that are occurring and will occur in your lifetime and in your children's.

In addition, we hope that you will be in a better position to answer the profound question that the professor asked one of the authors: How can I live a good and meaningful life?

Self-appraisal

Each person has some realistic ideas as to his strengths and capabilities. In the past he resolved many problems successfully. Other, more difficult problems he has attacked through increased efforts and mastery of new skills. During moments of intense crises, he has learned how to maintain his sense of self-esteem through the limited use of defense mechanisms or by admitting defeat temporarily when confronted with overwhelming odds. Self-appraisal based on these experiences forms the essential core of one's self-concept.

Positive Self-concept

Much of what a person does or refused to do depends on the adequacy of his self-concept. Those who do not regard themselves as talented or worthy usually do not aspire to lofty goals, nor are they overly disturbed when they fail to perform well. Hence, when persons are preparing themselves for the tasks of life it is crucial that they have a positive and realistic view of themselves if they are to increase their chances of success. Often we are better judges of what we are capable of doing because there is much about ourselves that remains hidden from others. However, at times we need feedback from friends and relatives because defense mechanisms may have warped our self-perceptions. In one study, each person in a group was asked to rate himself on certain personality characteristics. At the same time close friends were told to rate each individual in the same way. The results showed clearly that most were unaware of a significant number of their shortcomings. (Frenkel-Brunswick, 1939) Differences between what we think about ourselves and what others believe should be carefully considered. Whenever we accept what others say, we should not experience needless guilt feelings; instead, we should plan to take constructive measures to improve our competencies. In so doing, we tend to raise our level of self-esteem and, consequently, to increase our chances for future success.

Education

The better our education, the more opportunities we will have to develop our potentials. Right or wrong, employers tend to give the promotions to those who have achieved higher levels of education. Without the opportunity, one cannot develop his untapped potentials and talents. Certainly Einstein or Newton could not have developed their creative genius had they been reared on the Fiji Islands or the South Pole. In the United States, education is a major requirement for the exploration and fulfillment of human potential.

Learning to Learn

As a result of the information explosion and the rapidity of technological change, no body of knowledge in any field is immune to radical change. Therefore, education and reeducation will become more and more life-long activities.

Many colleges and universities now have larger enrollments in their evening programs for adults and college graduates than for daytime students. Large businesses have in-service training programs or pay employees to go back to school in order to keep up with new methods and techniques. Therefore, college students today should develop the skills and attitudes toward learning that will enable them to learn new materials more effectively. Among these skills are reading comprehension, listening skills, note taking, library reference skills, effective verbal and written communication, and taking tests. Positive attitudes are developed through successful experiences that have been positively reinforced. In other words, persons successful in college reap rewards for a lifetime; positive attitudes and skills facilitate the future learning so necessary now for living effectively in our changing, complex society.

Occupational Careers

Scientific and technological change have far-reaching consequences for occupations. Years ago, sons followed their father's occupation or began apprenticeships during early adolescence. Daughters merely followed in their mother's footsteps. Today the choices are far greater for both sexes and far more of the choices require mastery of increasingly complex skills. *The Dictionary of Occupational Titles* contains 21,741 separate occupations, with 35,550 different titles. The trend shows an increase in demand for more technical and professional employments.

Selection of an occupation is a highly individualized matter. Selecting and getting an occupation are, in a sense, similar to the processes of courtship and marriage. Both affairs require careful consideration because they are often lifelong engagements. Hughes (1958) in his book, *Men and Their Work* (p. 7) points out: "A man's work is one of the most important parts of his social identity, of his self: indeed, of his fate in the one life he has to live, for there is something almost as irrevocable about choice of occupation as there is about choice of a mate . . . ." The occupational version of dating and courtship consists of education, including electives, part-time jobs, summer work, reading about the newer occupations, and discussions with those already employed in the various fields.

The more we know about ourselves and occupational choices, the more likely are we to make a proper match. Selection will involve many conflicts, such as income versus what we enjoy doing; the demands of the job versus time needed with the family; ethical and moral values; cooperation versus competition; and the emotional tone of occupations such as that felt in hospitals, factories, and places of business. A student nurse may change her ideas of being a nurse after a week's work in an intensive-care unit; or a woman who likes to converse may switch from being a dentist's assistant to social work.

Occupational decision making is an uncertain process for many students. Many change their minds during their college years, which indicates that they have been thinking seriously about their career choices. The student who has learned how to learn effectively, who has a broad base of education and experiences, and who has critically evaluated himself in light of occupational choice, is more likely to select an occupation that will give him the opportunities for self-actualization.

In addition to the careful selection and preparation required for occupational careers, the world of tomorrow will necessitate two important shifts: (1) greater education for leisure; and (2) an increase in careers related to people. Even today, with most of technological advances yet to be felt, in the United States only 38 per cent of the population is "employed", in the Bureau of Labor Statistics' definition of the word, and during their working years, from 16 to 65, they spend less than 23 per cent of their total time engaged in work even if "fully employed" for all those years. . . . Not yet. But perhaps sooner than most of us want to think. What happens when, as some have predicted, two per cent of the American population is employed in producing the necessities of life, and 98 per cent is not?" (Fabun, 1967, p. 17) The answer is to educate man to use his leisure time to explore and to develop his own unique qualities and talents. In short, education for self-actualization must become a major objective of education in the very near future.

If two per cent of the American population can produce the necessities of life, what kind of work will the other 98 per cent do?" Fabun here makes an important distinction between "object-oriented" and "people-oriented" work. Object-oriented work is directed toward the production of some object useful to society. However, because of automation, man has been freed from this tremendously boring work. Man has been freed to engage in people-oriented work such as teaching, social welfare, crime prevention, nursing, and general service to others. What kind of person can work best with others? The answer to the question is the person with the personality characteristics of the self-actualizing man.

Marriage

From early childhood until the time of marriage, most persons are forming their ideas of what an ideal mate should be like. In a study of 373 engaged or recently married persons, it was found that nearly all had some ideas about the ideal mate and that there was a resemblance between the ideal and the actual mates. The resemblance was greater for personality characteristics than for physical features. (Strauss, 1946)

THE SEARCH. The search for a person who resembles the ideal image can produce the false impression that love suddenly appears when the ideal image is finally located. The danger is that of projecting the good qualities that we seek onto the other person. In reality, the qualities may not be there. A person in love may be oblivious to discrepancies because of his high level of emotional involvement and anticipation. We should remember that our perception of the world becomes narrow when we are searching for something to satisfy an immediate need. Sometimes society or relatives, unintentionally, increase the desire toward a person or an object through strong disapproval and threats of severe punishment. There is evidence that forbidden fruit is likely to become more

Technology is rapidly becoming man's "great liberator" as it frees him from the terrible boredom and long hours of menial toil. The near future promises man the time and means to explore and travel extensively. These increases in opportunities will provide avenues for greater self-actualization.

Courtesy of Autonetics, a division of North American Rockwell Corp.

Figure 12-6

attractive. (Festinger, 1962) In such cases, the sheer passage of time may extinguish the feelings of love.

COURTSHIP. Love for another is learned; it requires many warm, happy, shared experiences. A loving person is one who has been loved for a long time. To develop similar feelings for another person also requires an intense period of sharing and caring for one another.

Courtship is provided as an opportunity for arriving at a mutually satisfactory decision through problem solving together. Democratically reared children are accustomed to arriving at decisions together and should have little difficulty in transferring these habits to their own families. However, young people reared in an authoritarian family (rules are made only by the parents or one parent) must learn the give-and-take required for most successful marriages.

PERSONALITY ASSESSMENT. Marriages between two people with contrasting personalities may be just as successful as marriages between couples who are very much alike in their personalities. (Blood, 1957) People with contrasting personalities may find that their different needs are met by the other. A submissive

Figure 12-7

female may find her ideal companion in a strong domineering male, and a couple with similar needs may find togetherness in satisfying similar goals and interests. However, some people do change. The submissive housewife may later gain sufficient self-confidence to seek success on her own. The husband, who has not changed, may then begin to search for another submissive woman to meet his domineering needs. The "perfectly matched" couple may find that there are goals that only one can obtain as a result of limited time and money. The husband may attend graduate school while his wife works overtime to pay the bills.

The important point is that a wise choice of a marriage partner in itself does not guarantee a long and successful marriage. Both must be sensitive to and accepting of each other's changing needs and desires to explore all their poten-tialities.

MARRIAGE IN THE YEAR 2000. Of all areas of living, the greatest resistance of "outside" interference is probably found in marriage. Possibly people feel that the state of marriage is the last frontier of privacy and intimate feelings. It is the only remaining social situation in which they are the absolute rulers. Never-

398
**Understanding
the Future
Development
of Human
Behavior**

theless, the affairs of courtship and marriage are inseparable from society as a whole. Social changes affect all its parts including the state of marriage.

Freed from the boredom of housekeeping, the wife of the future will have far more time to develop and to practice her unique talents and potentials. Having children will not be a major barrier to her self-actualizing efforts because earlier education in the form of nursery schools will be commonplace. Because of greater emancipation from the usual feminine obligations as we know them today, many more women will seek employment in people-oriented occupations. Possibly husbands and wives will seek employment as teams, thereby continuing their companionship in the world of work.

The increase in leisure time will enable married couples to extend their activities into areas of life rarely explored by today's couples. The mutual explorations of their combined talents offer hitherto unimagined possibilities in such fields as art, music, writing, drama, hobbies, world travel, and increased communication with others on a worldwide basis. Increased life span will provide them with the assurance that their long-range plans, ambitions, and dreams can be fulfilled.

Living with Others

A United Nations study predicts that the world's population, which has almost doubled from 1900 to 1960, will more than double again by the year 2000, will soar from its present level of almost three billion to over six billion. (Wrenn, 1962, p. 15)

What does the organization society do to human beings? The modern American has been depicted as being pragmatic, disinclined to think about long-term social goals, satisfied to lump all his personal long-term goals into the single objective of a good job, an adequate income, and a respected position in his firm. (Ruitenbeek, 1963, p. xiv)

It is my impression that no one really likes the new. We are afraid of it. It is not only as Dostoyevsky put it that 'taking a new step, uttering a new word is what people fear most.' Even in slight things the experience of the new is rarely without some stirring of foreboding. (Hoffer, 1952, p. 1)

The preceding statements summarize some of the major problems that you and your children will have to face in meeting the challenges involved in living with others in the world of tomorrow: increase in population, pressures from a highly organized society that tends to force people to conform, and drastic technological, economic, political, and religious changes.

What are the implications of these and the many other changes discussed earlier that will occur in the future for you and your children? Although it is impossible to project ourselves into the future with complete accuracy, we can at least forsee some required personal characteristics that will be necessary for people to develop in order to effectively live through these periods of time.

Openness to Change

One of the first characteristics of people for which this and future days will call is a high degree of openness and flexibility in responding to reality and others in the world. Yet, we know that for many people, this is difficult to do, particularly if they are at all insecure about themselves.

This is why we feel that people must begin to develop, within themselves and their children, some of the characteristics of the self-actualizing person. As was mentioned before, this has to start with a love of self and the development of positive self-concept.

Brotherly Love

The fact that the world is getting smaller and the population is getting larger means that people from all over the world will be interacting even more closely and living together in large urban areas. This will call for a high degree of patience and involvement with other humans of all races and creeds.

From the authors' standpoint, one of the most important characteristics that will be called for in this situation will be the development of brotherly love. A sense of oneness and understanding coupled with respect, care, and responsibility for other people will be necessary. We will rely even more on other persons for our own survival.

As Combs and Snygg (1959) put it:

> Our society is so complex and interrelated that few of us could live more than a very short time apart from his fellows. Whether we like it or not, we are thoroughly dependent upon the good will of others. (p. 4)

Creativity

Creativity will be another important characteristic for the citizen of tomorrow. The type of creativity involved in the effective solving of problems will be of particular importance because fast changes often bring about problems in the satisfaction of many of our basic needs.

Creativity implies new and different ways of doing things; it will also be called for as we interact closely with other persons as individuals and groups.

Responsibility

We are going to have to assume more responsibility as parents as we try to raise our children for the world of tomorrow. We will have to help them gain a sense of competence in meeting their responsibilities as citizens of the world.

We will also have to assume greater responsibility as citizens in a shrinking

400

Understanding
the Future
Development
of Human
Behavior

world, exercise our rights as citizens in a democratic society, and work with groups toward solving mutual problems.

Peter Drucker (1965) summarizes the need for responsibility this way:

> In a time of change and challenge, new vision and new danger, new frontiers and permanent crisis, suffering and achievement, in a time of overlap such as ours, the individual is both all powerless and all powerful. He is powerless, however exalted his station, if he believes that he can impose his will, that he can command the tides of history. He is all-powerful, no matter how lowly, if he knows himself to be responsible. (p. 270)

Living with Society

> Technical change is also as old as civilization and since time immemorial the ways of life of whole peoples have been transformed by the introduction of new tools and new technical procedures, as inventions like the plough, the domestication of animals, writing, the use of steam, the factory assembly line, and the internal-combustion engine, have been diffused from one country to another. (Mead, 1955, p. 12)

> The fact of the great transition is not in dispute. Almost anyone in middle life today has simply to look back to his own childhood, or still more to the days of his grandparents to realize that we are living in a world in which there is an enormous rate of change. If anyone in an advanced society today were to be suddenly thrust back into the world of only a hundred years ago, he would feel utterly alien and strange. A considerable part of his vocabulary would be meaningless to the people around him. He would find it hard to adapt to the inconveniences and to the restricted life which he would have to lead. He would feel indeed in an alien society. (Boulding, 1964, p. 180)

The preceding quotes emphasize the fact that technological change in society has been with us for centuries and will continue to be a part of our lives in the future. The important question is whether we will be psychologically prepared for these changes.

As far as the authors are concerned, there is a great hope for mankind to meet the challenges in the world of tomorrow. They feel psychology has some of the solutions to help people who may become alienated and isolated as a result of these vast changes. Particularly, they feel the relatively new research in the area of self-actualization and mental health may offer mankind an opportunity to tap its vast potential.

In conclusion, the authors feel the best way a person can help himself, his family, and his fellowman; and the best way to live with himself, with others, and with society in the world of tomorrow is by developing himself into a self-actualizing person. The behavior of such a person displays the following characteristics: acceptance of self and others; ability to express feelings; seeing others as they are; responding to the world; creativity; democratic character; trust in himself; self-reliance; and willingness to continue to grow as a unique person.

In the chapter on Childhood and Adolescence, we discussed a Bill of Rights for children. We would like to conclude with suggestions for a new Bill of Rights for the world of tomorrow. However, if we are to enjoy these rights in the future, we must begin to practice and to allow others to practice these rights now.

Each person has the right to be treated and respected as a valuable human being in his own right regardless of race, religion, nationality, wealth, talents, or occupation. A person and his life are valuable and sacred primarily because he is a human being; all the other characteristics are secondary in comparison.

Each person has the right to be given the opportunity to achieve self-actualization. Because no one is truly satisfied unless he feels that he is learning, growing, and improving, the "pursuit of happiness" is not possible unless one is provided with the opportunities to fulfill one's potential.

Each person has the right to be altruistic, that is, to practice the Golden Rule of doing unto others what we would want others to do unto us. Each of us has the right to care for, to help, and to love others. Think for a moment how wonderfully safe and secure you would feel if all the people around you were to be altruistic.

Each person has the right to be different. It is the differences among us that make life so exciting. It is as we learn from others that we can grow. Social pressures to conform have made many of our different citizens into stereotypes of members of the majority culture. Our country, great as it is, has lost much of the richness of the cultures and languages brought to our shores by minority groups: the Germans, the French, the Black man, the Russians, the Greeks, the Brown man, the Italians, the Spanish, the Orientals, and others who have melted undistinguishably into the pot. Now we realize our mistakes and efforts are being made to study other cultures and languages. In so doing, we will learn to cherish, more than ever before, the valuable differences among people. It seems reasonable to conclude that our most important resources lie in the untapped reaches of people—people like you and your neighbors.

Final Summary

Drastic changes require drastic adjustments and accommodations. Man has produced vast and lopsided advancements in the physical world. Now he must shift some of his energies toward filling in the gap psychologically and sociologically before he turns into a cog of the machine he constructed. The self-actualization gap can be closed through the application of new methods in the education process and through the exploration and development of man's potentials.

The new process of education, which emphasizes the structure of knowledge, can be seen in the new mathematics, language, and physical and social science programs. The results of educational technology can be observed in the use of computer-based programs, programmed instruction in textbooks and machines,

402
Understanding
the Future
Development
of Human
Behavior

and novel audiovisual aids. These advances, in addition to increased interest in learning, are producing an education explosion which may match the technological and informational explosion in size and scope.

There is a growing awareness that only a very small fraction of man's potential ever finds expression. It is reasonable to conclude that if a large fraction of this potential were to be actualized that this would lead to an explosive fulfillment of man's untapped talents and creativities.

Trends to help man increase and explore his vast potential include intensive studies of the healthy, growing personality, the formation of the American Association for Humanistic Psychology, increasing numbers of Growth Centers, and research in the chemistry and physiology of the brain and nervous system.

All these accomplishments and efforts to make this a better world to live in will have no meaning unless man learns how to live peacefully with himself and others. Efforts to overcome social conflicts include the use of computers to analyze international problems, the Peace Corps, and the efforts of the United Nations. On the personal level the best way is to develop as many self-actualizing persons as we can.

Specific Chapter References

American Association for Humanistic Psychology. *Membership brochure,* San Francisco, Calif. 1969.

Blood, R. O. *Anticipating your marriage.* Glencoe, Ill.: Free Press, 1957.

Boulding, K. E. *The meaning of the 20th century.* New York: Harper & Row, 1964.

Brown, J. H. U. Physiological parameters of human potential. In H. A. Otto, *Explorations in human potentialities.* Springfield, Ill.: Charles C. Thomas, 1966. Pp. 79–100.

Bruner, J. S. *The process of education.* Cambridge: Harvard University Press, 1961.

Combs, A. W. and Snygg, D. *Individual behavior.* New York: Harper, 1959.

DeCarlo, C. R. In Foreign Policy Association (ed.) Computer technology. In *Toward the year 2018.* New York: Cowles Education Corporation, 1968.

Department of Labor, Bureau of Employment Security. *Dictionary of occupational titles.*

Drucker, P. F. *Landmarks of tomorrow.* New York: Harper & Row, 1965.

Esalen Programs: Fall 1968. Big Sur, California.

Fabun, D. *The dynamics of change.* Englewood Cliffs, N.J.: Prentice-Hall, 1967.

Festinger, L. Cognitive dissonance. *Scientific American,* 1962, 207, 93–107.

Frenkel-Brunswick, Else. Mechanisms of self-deception. *Journal of Social Psychology,* 1939 (X), 409–420.

Fromm, E. *The revolution of hope: toward a humanized technology.* New York: Bantam Books, 1968.

Gardner, J. W. *Self-renewal: the individual and the innovative society.* New York: Harper & Row, 1963.

Heath, R. W. (ed.) *New curricula.* New York: Harper & Row, 1964.

Hoffer, E. *The ordeal of change.* New York: Harper & Row, 1952.

Hughes, E. C. *Men and their work.* Glencoe, Ill.: Free Press, 1958.

Kahn, H., and Weiner, A. J. *The year 2000.* New York: Macmillan, 1967.

May, R. *Psychology and the human dilemma*. Princeton, N. J., Van Nostrand, 1967.

Mead, Margaret (ed.). *Cultural patterns and technical change*. New York: Mentor Books, 1955.

Montagu, A. *The humanization of man*. New York: Grove Press, 1962.

Murphy, G. Human natures of the future. In. W. D. Nunokawa (ed.), *Human values and abnormal behavior*. Chicago: Scott, Foresman, 1965.

Nelson, H. Feelin' groovy? A third of the nation doesn't. Article: *Los Angeles Times*, November 19, 1968.

Otto, H. A. (ed.). *Explorations in human potentialities*. Springfield, Ill.: Charles C Thomas, 1966.

Pool, Ithiel de Sola. Behavioral technology. In Foreign Policy Association (ed.), *Toward the year 2018*. New York: Cowles Education Corporation, 1968, pp. 87–113.

Ruitenbeek, H. M. (ed.). *The dilemma of organizational society*. New York: Dutton, 1963.

Silberman, H. F. The digital computer in education. *Phi Delta Kappan*, 1962, 43, 345–350.

Strauss, A. The ideal and the chosen mate. *American Journal of Sociology*, 1946, 52, 204–208.

Strehler, A. F. What's new about the new math? *Saturday Review*, March 21, 1964, 69–84.

Wrenn, C. G. *The counselor in a changing world*. Washington, D. C.: American Personnel and Guidance Association, 1962.

Additional References

Paperback Books

Arendt, Hannah. *The human condition: a study of the central dilemmas facing modern man*. New York: Doubleday, 1958.
New York: Doubleday, 1958.

Bagrit, Sir L. *Age of automation*. London: Weidenfeld and Nicolson, 1965.

Barnett, H. G. *Innovation: the basis of cultural change*. New York: McGraw-Hill, 1953.

Bohannan, P., and Plog, F. (eds.). *Beyond the frontier: social process and cultural change*. New York: Doubleday, 1967.

Matson, F. *The broken image: man, science and society*. New York: Doubleday, 1964.

Riesman, D. *Abundance for what? and other essays*. New York: Doubleday, 1964.

Von Neumann, J. *The computer and the brain*. New Haven: Yale University Press, 1958.

Weiner, N. *The human use of human beings*. New York: Doubleday, 1954.

Hardcover Books

Chardin, T. de. *The future of man*. New York: Harper & Row, 1964.

Churchman, C. W. *Challenge to reason*. New York: McGraw-Hill, 1968.

Etzioni, A., and Etzioni, E. (eds.). *Social change: sources, patterns and consequences*. New York: Basic Books, 1964.

Mumford, L. *The myth of the machine*. New York: Harcourt, Brace, and World, 1966.

Seligman, B. B. *Most notorious victory—man in an age of automation*. New York: Free Press, 1966.

United Nations. *World population prospects*. New York, 1966.

Woolridge, D. E. *Mechanical man*. New York: McGraw-Hill, 1968.

Appendix A Introduction to Physiological Psychology

The discipline of psychology is interested in understanding or explaining behavior as well as, hopefully, being able to predict it. A psychologist focuses on past and present influences in relation to their effect on living organisms, the highest order of which is man. Physiology is involved with using information gained in the fields of anatomy, biology, chemistry, physics, and fields associated with these, to investigate how cells, organs, and systems function.

Physiological psychology combines aspects of both of the two fields to study relationships between psychological events and the physiological counterparts that accompany them. The physiological psychologist, then, is one who applies the methods of these various disciplines to primarily explain behavior as well as gain knowledge that may allow for prediction.

A physiological psychologist is typically involved in experimentation with animals because certain operations and procedures he uses may damage the organism or include stimulation of locations in the brain. Although his animal experimentation is humanely accomplished, there are ethical restraints against the use of human subjects. An addition to this basic reason is one of allowing the investigator to sacrifice the animal for an autopsy study of the effects of the experimentation. Great caution is involved in making assumptions about animal experimentation as it applies to man; however, the practice does readily provide means for discovering clues.

Structure of the Nervous System

The nerve cell is our body's basic functional unit for communication. Neurons, which are of different shapes and sizes, make up nerves; in turn, these nerves form our nervous system. An impulse or activity of an electrical nature begins in a certain neuron and proceeds or is conducted along the fiber of the cell, called the axon, to other nerve cells. The message of the nerve cell is transferred to another one at the small end fibers of the axon called the *synapse*. Our nervous system has two jobs, one of which is to conduct the message along the nerve fibers, and the second to transfer this message at the synapses. Receptors—which include our senses—and effectors—which are muscles and glands—receive the

407

information being transferred. The effectors create observable action either directly or indirectly.

The nerves in our body consist of bundles (tracts) of axons that connect our brain and spinal cord to our muscles and sense organs. The central nervous system is made up mainly of axons lying within the brain and spinal cord, whereas the peripheral nervous system includes the axons lying in the remaining areas including connectors leading from the receptors to the spinal cord and the brain, and also the connectors leading to muscles and glands from the spinal cord and the brain. The photograph of the physiological model of man shows these two systems.

Our nervous system is divided another way into: the somatic system, effecting skeletal control and involving chiefly the body's voluntary processes; and the

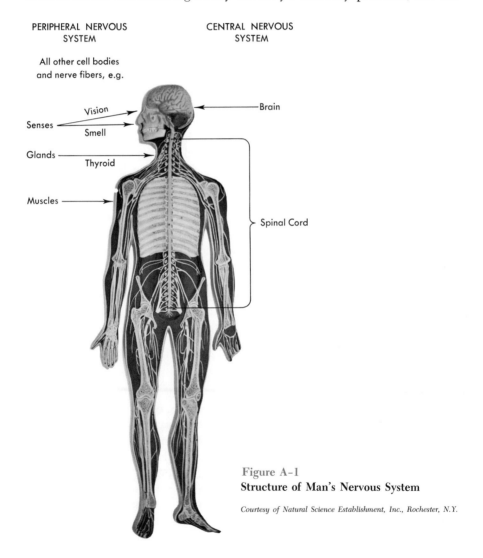

Figure A–1
Structure of Man's Nervous System

Courtesy of Natural Science Establishment, Inc., Rochester, N.Y.

autonomic system, regulating smooth muscle processes that generally do not come under voluntary influence.

The peripheral autonomic system, which is composed of nerves that lead to as well as regulate smooth muscles and glands, is divided into two subsystems. The division can be distinguished by location, function, and method. The sympathetic system is located in the central areas of the spinal cord; whereas the parasympathetic system comes out from the brain stem and also out the tail end of the spinal cord. The two systems are antagonistic in general. The sympathetic system is excitatory and is established for action in incidences of emergency, affecting behaviors such as increased heartbeat rate. Contrarily, the parasympathetic system is a conservation system that would decrease heartbeat rate. In Table A-1 a detailed account of this antagonistic relationship is presented; it also shows you other physiological reactions to rage and fear.

In Table A-2 a detailed account of different theories attempting to explain such a physiological drive as hunger is given.

Table A-1
The Relationship Between Autonomic Function and Emotional Behavior

Rage and Fear
—suppression or stoppage of salivating activity
—restrained stomach movement
—restrained wavelike (peristaltic) contractions of the intestines
—restrained secretion of gastric juices
—slowed or halted digestion as a result of the above restraints
—harder and/or more irregular bladder or colon elimination (except in acute situations when the sympathetic system acts quickly followed by overcontrol of parasympathetic activity causing urinating and/or defecation)
—increased heartbeat rate
—shrinking of blood and gut vessels to send blood from the skin and outer areas toward muscles and the brain
—flushed appearance in *rage*, from dilation of the blood vessels going to the head and face
—sallow or colorless appearance in *fear*, from constriction of the blood vessels going to the head and face (sometimes this situation can become advanced to the point of fainting, which can generally be attributed to a general dilating of the body's blood vessels, thereby causing the head to be deprived of needed oxygen supply by the blood lack produced, and creating a loss of one's consciousness)
—alteration of the blood chemical and endocrine balance, wherein adrenalin is released into the blood in greater amounts, and not only causes faster heart action, but brings about the conversion of a compound in the liver (glycogen, which stores blood sugar, the type of foodstuff energy source more readily used by specialized cells of the body) into sugar, raising that level already present to allow for more energy use of muscles and the brain
—stimulation of the thyroid gland to increased functioning (by the adrenalin) and thereby causing a general increase of oxidation in the body
—sweat glands in the skin (controlled by the sympathetic system) secrete a fluid that provides the means of getting rid of greater amounts of heat that may come about in emotional activity
—hair may become erect from contraction of the muscles at the base, causing "goose pimples"
—breathing takes forms such as panting, gasping, or other forms of hard breathing
—increased size of the air sacs of the lungs to allow for a greater exchange rate of oxygen and carbon dioxide
—increase in the blood of red corpuscles from the spleen to increase the capacity to carry oxygen

Table A-2
Exploring a Physiological Drive

Hunger

—this condition of our body, which indicates that we are in need of food, is not fully understood as yet. Theories form the concepts used to explain the process.

—a feeling of a light pain in the stomach

—a general feeling of weakness may accompany the light stomach pain

—a hunger motive can be inferred to underly the behavior called hunger that is assumed from behavior of the organism as it seeks food—a behavior that can be observed

—stomach contractions may typically accompany the feeling of hunger, but are *not* a necessary counterpart

—the idea of a stomach-regulated phenomena of hunger from stomach contractions or organ distensions is termed a *local theory* of hunger. These theories have generally been replaced

—*central theories* of hunger state that mechanisms controlling food intake are in the *hypothalamus* (an area of the brain deep at its base) and other areas of the brain.

—evidence-based theories promote the idea that the bloodstream is sampled by the hypothalamus, which checks for some element, *possibly* some kind of blood sugar.

—one of the central theories suggests that there is a fast, direct variation between the ratio of glucose in bloodstreams that enter and leave the brain. A low ratio means that the organism's food and glucose storage is low and signals the hunger mechanisms, yet unknown. This theory does not present the complete story of hunger but does recognize the importance of the value of foods, which is learned; and also, that distensions and contractions of the stomach add a signalling function to eating.

—many investigators support the *multifactor theory* of food intake, which combines the local or peripheral theories with the central theories. It suggests that food-intake regulation is performed by both peripheral or local, in addition to central, mechanisms.

—the term is in fact a label applied to a composite of several needs and appetites—it is not *one* concept. There are general hungers and also specific hungers.

—a specialized type of hunger is called specific hunger. Such specific appetites result from dietary deficiencies and are a controlling factor on food intake.

—an intricate result of a web of factors. A need instigates internal organic conditions that create hunger feelings and activates eating behavior. These feelings depend on the perceptions of the stomach contractions and also on neural processes. In either of these cases, the feelings can be added to or subtracted from, by stimulus variables. These stimulus variables affect cortical (brain) processes, which in addition to neural or chemical effects underlie the behavior of eating. Learning plays a basic part of the total system because it organizes and modifies the procedure. Depending on availability of food and cultural practices, we typically eat at regular times regardless of degree of hunger. It is possible a person does not regulate the amount of food intake according to changes in his physical activity or other influences that could be expected to change his objective need.

Recommended Further Readings

Paperback Books

Asimov, I. *The intelligent man's guide to the biological sciences.* New York: Pocket Books, 1960.

——. *The human brain.* New York: Signet, 1963.

——. *The human body.* New York: Signet, 1963.

Landauer, T. K. (ed.). *Readings in physiological psychology: the bodily basis of behavior.* New York: McGraw-Hill, 1967.

Louttit, R. T. (ed.). *Volume IV: research in physiological psychology.* Belmont, Calif.: Brooks/Cole, 1965.

Strange, J. R., and Foster, R. (eds.). *Readings in physiological psychology.* Belmont, Calif.: Brooks/Cole, 1966.

Teitelbaum, P. *Physiological psychology.* Englewood Cliffs, N.J.: Prentice-Hall, 1967.

Hardcover Books

Altman, J. *Organic foundations of animal behavior.* New York: Holt, Rinehart and Winston, 1966.

Deutsch, J. A., and Deutsch, Diana *Physiological psychology.* Homewood, Ill.: Dorsey Press, 1966.

Edwards, D. C. *General psychology.* New York: Macmillan, 1968. (Especially, chap. 2, Physiological Psychology.)

Geldard, F. A. *The human senses.* New York: Wiley, 1953.

Hebb, D. O. *A textbook of psychology.* Philadelphia: Saunders, 1966.

Leukel, F. *Introduction to physiological psychology.* St. Louis: Mosby, 1968.

Morgan, C. T. *Physiological psychology* (3rd ed.). New York: McGraw-Hill, 1964.

Stellar, E., and Sprague, J. M. (eds.). *Progress in physiological psychology.* New York: Academic Press, 1966.

Thompson, R. F. *Foundations of physiological psychology.* New York: Harper & Row, 1967.

Appendix B Introduction to Statistics

Because more and more information is being numerically described today, *statistics* has increasingly become a valuable tool for scientists as well as for educated citizens. In general, statistics permit description, analysis, and evaluation of numerical information. Specifically, statistics serve two major purposes: *descriptive statistics* is used to describe and summarize large sets of numbers, and *sampling statistics* is used for evaluating and predicting from small sets of numbers to larger populations. Sampling statistics, however, is based on the assumption that the data being analyzed is *normally distributed*. This requirement of normality is met when the data used in the statistical analysis were taken from *populations* (well-defined groups that include all the individuals or events we are interested in analyzing) whose scores, if plotted on a graph, would fall into symmetrical bell-shaped curves known as *normal curves.*°

Descriptive Statistics

When presented with a list of numbers describing the frequency or intensity of a behavior, we need a convenient or shorthand way of handling the numbers so that they can be readily analyzed and interpreted. For example, if a large corporation listed the salaries of its 25,000 employees, the information would be practically useless because it is not possible to remember all the numbers. However, the long list of numbers could be made comprehensible through the application of statistical techniques such as central tendency and measures of variation.

CENTRAL TENDENCY

Central tendency or average is a single number that represents a group of numbers with some numbers above and some numbers below. There are three ways of calculating a central tendency.

°When the assumption of normality cannot be met, nonparametric statistics must be used. Nonparametric statistics are discussed in statistics books.

The *mean* or average of a group of numbers is the common arithmetic average. It is obtained by adding all the numbers and dividing by their number. For example, the mean of 4, 5, and 6 is 5, which is obtained by dividing 15 by 3. The mean is the most commonly used measure of central tendency because it is usually required for computation of other statistics and, in general, it is the most accurate of the three ways of calculating an average.

The *median* is the number that divides a group of numbers into two equal parts. The numbers are first arranged in a series from the lowest to the highest. The middle number is the median. It is most useful and accurate when there are extremely low or high numbers in the series.

The *mode* is the most common number in the group. It provides a rough estimate of the central tendency; it tells us the most typical case.

It is important to note that the three averages provide the same answer only when the group of numbers forms a normal curve. In many situations, however, the normal curve is not achieved and the averages are different. For example, in the series 2, 2, 2, 2, 2, 5, 10, 10, 20, 56, 120, the mode is 2, the median is 5, and the mean is 21.

MEASURES OF VARIATION

Measures of variation describe the amount of spread of scores around the average. This statistic is important because it is not enough to know, for example, that the average temperature is 75°. Two cities may have the same mean temperature of 75°, but in one city the temperature remains mild throughout the year, whereas in the other it may be freezing during the winter and terribly hot during the summer.

A rough measure of variation is the *range*. It is obtained by subtracting the highest score from the lowest. For example, using the same preceding group of numbers, the range is 118 (120 − 2).

The most accurate and frequently used measure of variation is the *standard deviation*. The formula for calculating the standard deviation is:

$$\text{Standard deviation} = \sqrt{\frac{\text{Sum of } D^2}{N}}$$

where D = deviation of each score from the mean
and N = number of cases.

The interpretation of a standard deviation depends on the assumption that the data is approximately normally distributed. Thus, the mean or average is at the peak of the curve with most of the cases piling up at each side and gradually tapering off. The number of cases within the range of one standard deviation plus the mean and one standard deviation minus the mean is exactly 68.7 or approximately 68 per cent. Using the preceding example, the mean height is 68 inches and the standard deviation is 5.831 inches; therefore, 68 per cent of the variation in height lies between 68 plus 5.831 and 68 minus 5.831, or between 73.831 and 63.831 inches.

Table B-1
Data Illustrating the Computation of Standard Deviation

Persons	Height (X)	Mean Height (M)	D (X − M)	D²
A	60	68	−8	64
B	64	68	−4	16
C	72	68	+4	16
D	73	68	+5	25
E	75	68	+7	49

$$\text{Sum of } D^2 = 170$$
$$N = 5$$
$$\sqrt{\frac{170}{5}} = 5.83$$

The range between the mean plus-two standard deviations and the mean minus-two standard deviations is approximately 95 per cent. The range between the mean plus-three standard deviations and the mean minus-three standard deviations is approximately 99 per cent. Thus, if the mean temperature in a certain city is 75° and the standard deviation is 5°, then the temperature will be between 65° and 85° 95 per cent of the time, and between 60° and 90° 99 per cent of the time.

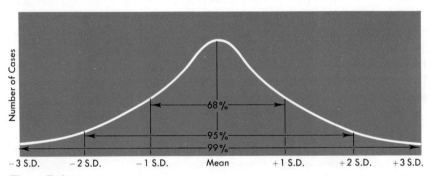

Figure B-1
A Normal Curve

CORRELATION

Much of what goes on in life and science deals with relationships. Typically, we find that as one thing changes, other related things also change. For example, there is a relationship or correlation between the heights of sons and their fathers, education and income, and scores on the college entrance tests and later grade-point averages. A correlation, thus, provides a measure of the closeness of the relationship between two sets of measures. In addition, measures of correlation are used for predictive purposes. If we know the correlation between heights of sons and fathers, we could predict the heights of sons knowing the heights of their fathers with varying degrees of accuracy.

Correlations range from perfect positive (r = +1.00) to perfect negative correlations (r = −1.00). Practically all correlations lie between +1.00 and −1.00, because perfect correlations are extremely rare. Most correlations in psychology range from .30 to .70. The following correlation charts illustrate different correlations between scores on two tests.

An exact interpretation of a correlation requires the use of statistical tables that are not readily available to students. For general purposes, correlations below .20 have little or no significant value, correlations between .20 and .40 indicate a low relationship, correlations between .40 and .60 a moderate relationship, correlations between .60 and .80 a high relationship, and correlations between .80 and 1.00 high to perfect relationships.

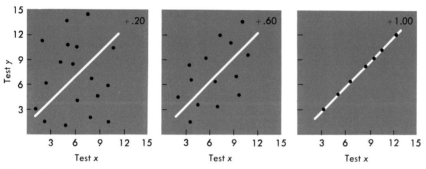

Figure B-2
Correlation Scattergram

When two sets of numbers are correlated, it means that as one set of numbers changes, the second set also changes in varying degrees. However, it does not mean that one of them caused the change in the other. Bad weather is positively correlated with an increased number of colds, but it doesn't mean that bad weather itself produces colds.

Sampling Statistics

Statistics are often based on samples taken from larger populations. A *sample* is a small part of the total population usually carefully and systematically selected. The *population* is the well-defined group to which we wish to generalize the results of the sample. For example, if we wished to know the average height of college freshmen, we would measure the heights of a carefully selected sample of students who are as representative as possible of all college freshmen. Sampling statistics would tell us how well the statistics from the sample apply to the population. Sampling statistics are also used to evaluate the results of scientific experiments. For example, if a scientific experiment results in the cure of 16 patients in a sample of 20 patients, should the same treatment be given to all patients who suffer from the same disease? The key question that would be answered by sampling statistics is the probability of getting the similar results when the treatment is repeated over and over again with different samples of patients.

The problem of how much faith to place on the results of one experiment is a very common one. We know that the results obtained from one experiment cannot be duplicated exactly in future repetitions. There will always be some degree of error as we make statements about a population on the basis of measurements from samples. Sampling statistics provide us with a statement of the probability of obtaining similar experimental results if the experiment were to be repeated over again many times. Psychologists as well as other scientists have agreed to consider results that could occur over again 95 per cent of the time or more statistically significant. That is, results of an experiment are statistically significant even if different results (wrong) are obtained 5 per cent of the times that the experiment is repeated. Thus, scientists speak of the 5 per cent level of statistical significance as the minimal level of acceptability of scientific findings.

The different tests of statistical significance are discussed in statistics books. Some of these are illustrated in the workbook prepared for use with this psychology textbook.

Recommended Further Readings

Paperback Books
Adler, I. *Probability and statistics for everyman* (rev. ed.). New York: New American Library, 1963.
Alexander, H. W., and Smith, R. F. *Descriptive statistics: a self-instruction program.* Boston: Heath, 1965.
Elzey, F. F. *Programmed introduction to statistics.* Belmont, Calif.: Brooks/Cole, 1966.
———. *First reader in statistics.* Belmont, Calif.: Brooks/Cole, 1967.
Franzblau, A. N. *Primer of statistics for non-statisticians.* New York: Harcourt, 1958.
Hays, W. L. *Basic statistics.* Belmont, Calif.: Brooks/Cole, 1967.

Hardcover Books
Edwards, A. L. *Experimental design in psychological research* (3rd ed.). New York: Holt, Rinehart and Winston, 1968.
Guilford, J. P. *Fundamental statistics in psychology and education* (4th ed.). New York: McGraw-Hill, 1965.
Kurtz, K. H. *Foundations of psychological research; statistics, methodology, and measurement.* Boston: Allyn and Bacon, 1965.
Schoer, L. A. *Introduction to statistics and measurement: a programmed book.* Boston: Allyn and Bacon, 1966.

Appendix C Selected References for Special-Interest Topics

Abnormal Sexual Problems

We have already discussed some of the more common forms of abnormal sexual problems (homosexuality, pedophilia, and exhibitionism) under the heading of Sexual Defenses (see Chapter 11). Although this is not a textbook in abnormal psychology, our students have often expressed a high interest in this area of human behavior; yet, they cannot find research or theoretical material written by persons with some degree of training or specialized knowledge. All that seem available are the more sensational case studies found in the back room of the local liquor store. This list of references is reflective of the current research and clinical interest in this area, which has been partially responsible for our changing views of certain sexual behaviors.

Selected References

Bergler, E. *Counterfeit-sex: homosexuality, impotence, frigidity*. New York: Macmillan, 1967.

Caprio, F. S. *Female homosexuality*. New York: Citadel Press, 1954.

———. *Variations in sexual behavior*. New York: Citadel Press, 1955.

Ellis, A., Brancale, R., and Doorbar, Ruth R. *The psychology of sex offenders*. Springfield, Ill.: Charles C Thomas, 1956.

Ellis, A. *The American sexual tragedy* (rev. ed). New York: Lyle Stuart, 1962.

Ellis, A., and Sagarin, E. *Nymphomania; a study of the oversexed woman*. New York: Gilbert Press, 1964.

Evans, Jean. *Three men*. New York: Grove Press, 1956.

Gagnon, J. H., and Simon, W. (eds.). *Sexual deviance*. New York: Harper, 1967.

Henry, G. W. *Society and the sex variant*. New York: Macmillan, 1965.

417

London, L. S., and Caprio, F. S. *Sexual deviations.* (2 vols.) New York: Award Books, 1968.

Stekel, W. *Impotence in the male.* (2 vols., rev. ed.) New York: Liveright, 1955.

———. *Sadism and masochism.* (2 vols.) New York: Grove Press, 1955.

———. *Sexual aberrations.* (2 vols.) New York: Grove Press, 1964.

———. *Sexual deviation.* Baltimore: Penguin Books, 1964.

Wahl, C. W. *Sexual problems.* New York: Macmillan, 1967.

Dreams

The process and meaning of dreams have up until recent years been highly controversial subjects among psychologists. Sigmund Freud was the first to develop a theory around the use and meaning of dreams for patients in psychoanalysis. Since that time dream content has been used primarily as a therapeutic tool for trying to better understand some of the unconscious conflicts within the individual. Recently (especially since the development of techniques for measuring whether a person is dreaming or not), however, physiological psychologists have become more concerned with studying the bodily and psychological effects of dreaming. Both the psychoanalytic and physiological orientations are reflected in the following list of references.

Selected References

Becker, R. de. *Understanding of dreams.* New York: Hawthorn, 1968.

Caligor, L., and May, R. *Dreams and symbols.* New York: Basic Books, 1968.

De Martino, M. F. *Dreams and personality dynamics.* Springfield, Ill.: Charles C Thomas, 1959.

Dement, W. C. An essay on dreams: the role of physiology in understanding their nature. In F. Barron, *et al., New directions in psychology II.* New York: Holt, Rinehart, and Winston, 1965, pp. 135–257.

Foulkes, D. *The psychology of sleep.* New York: Scribner's, 1966.

Garma, A. *Psychoanalysis of dreams.* New York: Dell, 1967.

Jastrow, J. *Freud: his dream and sex theories.* New York: Permabook, 1932.

Kelsey, M. T. *Dreams: the dark speech of the spirit.* Garden City, N.Y.: Doubleday, 1968.

Murray, E. J. *Sleep, dreams, and arousal.* New York: Appleton-Century-Crofts, 1966.

Sechrist, Elsie *Dreams, your magic mirror.* New York: Cowles, 1968.

Singer, J. L. *Daydreaming; an introduction to the experimental study of inner experience.* New York: Random House, 1966.

Stekel, W. *The interpretation of dreams.* New York: Washington Square Press, 1968.

Tauber, E. S., and Green, M. R. *Prelogical experience; an inquiry into dreams and other creative processes.* New York: Basic Books, 1959.

Von Grunebaum, G. E., and Caillois, R. (eds.). *Dream and human societies.* Berkeley: University of California Press, 1966.

Drugs

419
Appendix C
Selected
References
for Special
Interest Topics

The use of drugs for the treatment of the mentally ill has revolutionized mental hospital procedures:

Wards which before their introduction had bedlam-like overtones are now orderly and conducive to therapeutic approaches. Some patients, who in the past had to be placed under restraint, sedation, or in seclusion, are now amenable to treatment. The tranquilizer drugs help disturbed patients to function without the shattering effects of their anxieties, to live with disturbed thoughts without panic.

Conversely, the more recent development and use of the "psychic energizing" drugs for the depressed patient, is now working to help lift the patient out of his lethargy.

No pill, however, is likely to take the place of skillfully directed human relationships in restoring the mentally ill to health. The value of drug therapy lies in opening the way so that human help may get through. (California Department of Mental Hygiene. *Pattern of Progress.* Sacramento, Calif., 1965, p. 27)

The use of other drugs such as LSD have had tragic results:

A young man under the influence of LSD left a party and took a walk along a busy street. Suddenly he stepped into the path of an oncoming car, an arm upraised, and shouted, 'Halt!' Death was instantaneous. (California State Department of Education. *Drug Abuse,* Sacramento, Calif., 1967, p. 38)

And yet, many young people claim:

Drugs, generally, I see as a tool through which you can achieve greater understanding. LSD and grass are very much the same sort of thing, though grass is very, very inferior, if you want to look at it in those terms. (Carey, J. T. *The college drug scene,* Englewood Cliffs, N.J.: Prentice-Hall, 1968, p. 148)

You should find the following list of references helpful in attempting to study this highly interesting and misunderstood area of human behavior; from it you can reach your own conclusions.

Selected References

Ausubel, D. P. *Drug addiction: physiological, psychological, and sociological aspects.* New York: Random House, 1958.

Brown, T. *The enigma of drug addiction.* Springfield, Ill.: Charles C Thomas, 1961.

Carey, J. T. *The college drug scene.* Englewood Cliffs, N.J.: Prentice-Hall, 1968.

De Ropp, R. S. *Drugs and the mind.* New York: Evergreen Black Cat, 1961.

Ebin, D. (ed.). *The drug experience.* New York: Evergreen Black Cat, 1961.

Gordon, H. L. (ed.). *The new chemotherapy in mental illness.* New York: Philosophical Library, 1958.

Jarvik, M. E. The psychopharmacological revolution. *Psychology Today,* 1967, 1(1), 51–59.

Selected References

Berne, E. *A layman's guide to psychiatry and psychoanalysis.* New York: Grove Press, 1968.

Freeman, Lucy, and Small, M. *The story of psychoanalysis.* New York: Pocket Books, 1960.

Freud, S. *A general introduction to psychoanalysis.* New York: Permabooks, 1935.

———. *The question of lay analysis* (Strachey, trans. and ed.). Garden City, N.Y.: Anchor, 1964.

Hall, C. S. *A primer of Freudian psychology.* New York: World, 1954.

Harper, R. A. *Psychoanalysis and psychotherapy: 36 systems.* Englewood Cliffs, N.J.: Prentice-Hall, 1959.

Nuttin, J. *Psychoanalysis and personality.* New York: Mentor–Omega Book, 1962.

Sarason, I. G. *Science and theory in psychoanalysis.* Princeton, N.J.: Insight Book, 1965.

Stewart, W. A. *Psychoanalysis: the first ten years.* New York: Macmillan, 1967.

Suicide

The two most striking facts about suicide are: (1) its widespread and serious nature, and (2) its proverbial taboo position. Suicide ranks among the first ten of the list of adult killers in the United States. In some states of the U. S., it is as high as sixth. In certain age groups (15–25) and certain occupational groups (college students, peace-time soldiers) it is as high as the third cause of death. Further, each suicide often has serious personal consequences which affect the mental health of many individuals, and thus of the community itself. Considering its magnitude and seriousness as a public health problem, it becomes readily apparent how much work needs to be done to further the current understanding and prevention of suicide. (Suicide Prevention Center of Los Angeles. *Information Booklet*, Los Angeles: University of Southern California Press, 1965, p. 2).

This quote summarizes some of the tragic statistics on suicide in the United States. Since the establishment of the Los Angeles Suicide Prevention Center, other centers have opened in large cities throughout the United States. Their work has saved countless lives and much of the research used to establish these centers is found in the list of references below.

Selected Readings

Durkheim, E. *Suicide: a study in sociology.* New York: Free Press, 1966.

Farberow, N. L., and Shneidman, E. S. (eds.). *The cry for help.* New York: McGraw-Hill, 1961.

Feifel, H. (ed.) *The meaning of death.* New York: McGraw-Hill, 1959.

Hendrin, H. *Suicide and Scandinavia.* Garden City, N.Y.: Doubleday, 1964.

Henry, A. F., and Short, J. F. *Suicide and homicide.* New York: Free Press, 1964.

Litman, R. E. *Clues to suicide.* New York: McGraw-Hill, 1957.

Menninger, K. *Man against himself.* New York: Harvest Book, 1938.

Shneidman, E. S. Suicide: trauma and taboo. In N. L. Farberow (ed.). *Taboo topics.* New York: Atherton, 1963.

Stengel, E. *Suicide and attempted suicide.* Baltimore: Penguin Books, 1964.

423

**Appendix C
Selected
References
for Special
Interest Topics**

Glossary

acting out (Ch. 9)—Tension-reducing behavior in the form of direct verbal or physical expression.

adolescence (Ch. 4)—The period of middle childhood wherein significant changes occur such as development of brotherly love, self-concepts, sex roles, interpersonal techniques, effective thinking and problem solving, personal values, and ideas of future life.

alcoholic defense (Ch. 10)—Consumption of alcohol to the extent that it interferes seriously with daily living while serving to reduce tension. It is an attempt at coping with failure.

alienation (Ch. 1)—Feeling apart or separated from one's real self; lack of ability to feel.

ambivalence (Ch. 9)—Attitude of liking and disliking something at the same time.

anxiety (Ch. 2)—Generalized feelings of fear, usually unexplainable.

anxiety reaction (Ch. 10)—The simplest neurosis, because only the repression mechanism is involved; it is characterized by anxiety for which one cannot account.

asocial (Ch. 10)—Having no feeling of duty to social custom or sense of social values.

asthenic defense (Ch. 10)—Being selectively fatigued, both mentally and physically, but not from exertion. The fatigue is the result of prolonged emotional stress related to unresolved problems.

attitudes (Ch. 1)—How one feels and/or thinks about something.

authoritarian orientation (Ch. 10)—Character that demands subservience and unquestioning obedience from others, has low tolerance for anything vague or not clear, and deplores any indication of weakness.

autonomic nervous system (Append. A)—The nervous system that regulates smooth muscle processes that generally do not come under voluntary influence.

autonomous (Ch. 1)—Independent of thought or action.

axon (Append. A)—The fiber of a cell.

behavior (Ch. 1)—Any activity that can be directly or indirectly observed or measured.

behavior therapy (Ch. 11)—A form of therapy that uses learning principles to help a patient overcome certain problems (especially habits or fears).

brotherly love (Ch. 4)—Love of fellow human beings including oneself, which involves feelings of respect, concern, love, knowledge of oneself, and others, and of the unity of brotherhood of all human beings.

C

California Test of Personality (Ch. 11)—An objective personality test that attempts to measure personal and social adjustment.

catharsis (Ch. 6)—Release or unloading of emotions. In psychotherapy the release of anxieties and tensions through interaction.

central nervous system (Append. A)—A classification term of the nervous system meaning composed mainly of axons lying within the brain and spinal cord.

central tendency (Append. B)—A number that represents a group of numbers with some number above and below: the three common measures are the mean, medium, and mode.

central theories of hunger (Append. A)—States that mechanisms controlling food intake are located in the hypothalamus (an area of the brain deep at its base) or other brain areas.

character disorders (Ch. 10)—Types of behaviors that occur when defenses against emotional hurt break down, whose symptoms are far more disturbing to others, or antisocial.

character structure (Ch. 1)—A consistent way of behaving.

childhood schizophrenia (Ch. 10)—Abnormal behavior including disinterest or unrelatedness to other people or objects, being withdrawn and passive, disorganized thought processes; very low frustration tolerance; and unrestrained outbursts of uncontrollable behavior.

chromosomes (Ch. 8)—The gene-carrying bodies found in the nucleus of cells.

chronic (Ch. 9)—Mental disorders or diseases that start slowly and continue for a long period.

client-centered therapy (Ch. 1)—A form of therapy in which the therapist provides a relaxed, accepting atmosphere so that the patient can express his honest feelings without fear of rejection; the patient takes the active role.

clinical or counseling psychologist (Ch. 11)—A psychologist usually with a Ph.D degree who is involved in the diagnosis and treatment of emotional problems using psychological tests, psychotherapy, and research in mental illness. His practice may be private, as well as at public and private hospitals or clinics or in industry.

closure (Ch. 7)—The behavioral phenomenon of completing that which is not complete. A partial drawing of a familiar object tends to visually have its missing parts filled in.

cognitive processes (Ch. 3)—How we imagine, remember, perceive, reason, and judge.

compassion (Ch. 1)—Sympathetic feelings for others.

compulsive neurosis (Ch. 10)—Neurotic behavior that consists of doing things one does not want to do. Lack of engaging in the unwanted behavior would, however, mean being overcome with anxiety. Obsessive thoughts may precede compulsive acts.

conceptual development (Ch. 4)—Formulation of ideas especially related to the developmental period of childhood.

continuum (Ch. 1)—An unbroken line connecting representative points on a scale or graph.

conversion defense (Ch. 10)—Also known as a psychosomatic disorder, it consists of organic symptoms with or without underlying organic disease. It is produced primarily by emotional stress and tension.

correlation (Append. B)—A measure of the closeness of the relationship between two sets of numbers.

criminal defense (Ch. 10)—Consists of breaking the law as part of a neurotic attempt to solve problems. The crime typically does not make sense, nor is the person a habitual criminal. No excuse is given because the offender desires his punishment.

criteria (Ch. 1)—A set of standards used for making a decision.

culture (Ch. 1)—The ways of living of a group of people.

D

death instincts (Ch. 8)—Destructive and hostile impulses that Freud used as part of his definition of the unconscious (id).

decompensation (Ch. 10)—The point at which the person's problems exceed his total adjustive capacities and is considered to be mentally ill.

defense mechanism (Ch. 9)—Psychological defense against feelings of inadequacy and failure. The defenses occur at ranging levels of awareness including the unconscious. Extensive use of it can produce mental disorders.

delusion (Ch. 10)—A false belief that the patient defends despite all contrary evidence.

depressive defense (Ch. 10)—Admitting defeat and developing feelings of unworthiness and apathy. The behavior may serve as an excuse for not trying to accomplish something; if it becomes severe it may result in suicide.

deprivation (Ch. 9)—The subject has been blocked from attaining his goal or meeting his needs such as food, water, or sex.

descriptive statistics (Append. B)—Mathematical procedures for summarizing large groups of numbers.

diagnosis (Ch. 11)—Determination of the nature of a disease or abnormal behavior or classification of a person according to an abnormality.

directive therapy (Ch. 11)—A form of therapy in which the therapist actively prescribes solutions to the patient's problems.

discriminate (Ch. 2)—Being aware of the difference between things.

displacement (Ch. 9)—Release of feelings of anxiety or hostility caused by frustration by displacing it onto another person or object.

dissociative defenses (Ch. 10)—Repression of acutely unpleasant situations from which there seems no escape. Amnesia and multiple personality are examples.

dogmatic orientation (Ch. 10)—That orders must be accepted from authority solely as a matter of faith.

drug addiction defense (Ch. 10)—Use of drugs as a way of avoiding the realities of life. The person typically has a negative self-opinion and has little confidence in his abilities.

drug therapy (Ch. 11)—A form of therapy that uses various drugs (depressants and energizers) in order to help mental patients control their emotions so that they may better participate in other forms of therapy.

E

effectors (Append. A)—Include the muscles and glands that receive neural information and create observable action either directly or indirectly.

egocentric (Ch. 4)—Individualized, self-centered way of viewing the world.

ego defense mechanisms (Ch. 10)—More powerful psychological defenses than those reality-oriented types that take over when these fail to relieve stress and anxiety. Of primary significance is that the motives are unconscious, though the behavior is not.

electrodes (Ch. 11)—A small metal apparatus used to deliver current to tissue.

electroshock therapy (Ch. 11)—A method of therapy using electrical stimulation of the nervous system; used with extremely depressed patients.

emotional insulation (Ch. 9)—Remaining aloof and detached from others to prevent emotional hurt.

emotions (Ch. 2)—Those feelings that accompany thoughts and/or actions.

environment (Ch. 2)—People and objects in your experiences.

energizers (Ch. 11)—Drugs that are depression-reducing.

exhibitionism (Ch. 10)—Exposing one's genitals in public.

F

fantasy (Ch. 9)—Behavior that transcends all physical and personal limitations. It allows for solution, creation, and invention, but can be detrimental if used as a crutch for living or in place of working toward understanding or improving our situation or behavior.

fatalism (Ch. 5)—All of man's behavior is predetermined.

fatherly love (Ch. 4)—A conditional type of love that must be deserved by doing what is expected, such as meeting the father's expectations because duty and respect of affection for him.

fear (Ch. 2)—Feelings aroused by threat.

field dependent (Ch. 7)—Behavior that is more dependent on what is seen than what is felt in bodily sensation.

field independent (Ch. 7)—Behavior that relies more on bodily sensation than on what is seen in the environment.

figure and ground (Ch. 7)—The bases of experiences applied to perceptual organization wherein two influences are operating but one is predominant (the figure) for a particular perceptual experience and the other is supportive (ground) in providing a background for emphasis of the figure.

free association (Ch. 8)—The therapeutic method originated by Freud wherein the patient is allowed to say whatever thoughts that enter into his awareness at the time.

frustration (Ch. 9)—The resulting unpleasant emotional state of anxiety and tension when an organism is prevented from achieving its desired goal.

functional psychoses (Ch. 10)—Strongest defenses that humans have against the unbearable emotional hurts of unresolved conflicts and frustration; non-organic.

G

genes (Ch. 8)—The trait-carrying and -regulating elements of heredity.

genetic characteristics (Ch. 2)—That which happens as a result of, or concerning, genes, which regulate many characteristics of people and lower animals.

goal gradient (Ch. 9)—Visual representation of the amount of feeling expressed in approaching or retreating from an object toward which feelings (liking, mixed, or disliking) are expressed.

group therapy (Ch. 11)—A form of therapy used with a group of individuals with emotional problems.

H

habits (Ch. 2)—Behavior without thinking.

hallucinations (Ch. 7)—Perceptions that have no basis (of appropriate stimulation) in the external world.

heredity (Ch. 2)—Characteristics that are inherited biologically.

hierarchy (Ch. 1)—Arranged in order of importance.

holistic approach (Ch. 11)—Use of experts from different fields such as psychology, biology, and sociology to determine what is wrong with a person.

homosexuality (latent) (Ch. 10)—An unconscious desire to have sexual activity with a member of the same sex.

homosexuality (overt) (Ch. 10)—Achieving sexual orgasm with a member of the same sex.

hyperthyroidism (Ch. 10)—Excessive secretion by the thyroid gland involving greatly increased metabolism creating restlessness, increased activity, and feelings of apprehension.

hypochondriacal defense (Ch. 10)—Behavior of one who is utterly convinced that he is physically ill when there is nothing organically wrong.

hypothesis (Ch. 3)—A prediction of the outcome of the research.

I

ideal self (Ch. 3)—What a person would like to become; the part of one's self-concept based on the expectations of other important people.

identification (Ch. 9)—The process of imitating the behaviors and values of persons or groups we admire and respect.

impulses (Ch. 1)—Actions without thought.

incubation (Ch. 6)—Growth of an idea or feeling during a time of nonapparent or no activity during which a solution to an idea or, especially, a problem occurs.

input (Ch. 5)—Stimuli fed into man through his sense organs; e.g. eyes, ears, nose, mouth, and skin.

intelligence (Ch. 2)—Learning capacity.

intense love (Ch. 4)—Mother's love for her infant during the first three months of life characterized by much physical handling and caressing.

involutional defense (Ch. 10)—Depressed feelings accompanied by increased activity are characteristic of this defense, which typically occurs in later life especially among women after menopause. Miserable and unworthy feelings are accompanied by restlessness, insomnia, etc.

L

learn (Ch. 2)—Change in behavior as a result of experience.

learning set (Ch. 4)—Learning to learn is the basis of this concept. When presented with several problem-solving situations such as discrimination problems, the subject applies the ability he gains to solve a test problem or problems in one trial.

life instincts (Ch. 8)—The Freudian concept of desire to stay alive and reproduce oneself, which is essentially sexual in nature.

local theory of hunger (Append. A)—The idea of a stomach-regulated phenomena of hunger from stomach contractions or organ distension.

M

manic-depressive defenses (Ch. 10)—Either extreme elation and a high level of activity, or a depressive reaction of the opposite type, or an alternation between the two moods typifies this defensive behavior.

mean (Append. B)—The arithmetic average; the sum of all the numbers divided by their number.

measure of variation (Append. B)—A measure of the amount of spread of scores around the average in a group of numbers.

median (Append. B)—A measure of central tendency or average obtained by finding the number that divides a group of numbers into two equal parts when the cases are arranged in order of size.

Minnesota Multiphasic Personality Inventory (MMPI) (Ch. 11)—The most widely used objective personality test for evaluation of personality and mental illness. It is designed to measure some common symptoms of selected neuroses and psychoses.

mode (Append. B)—A measure of central tendency or average obtained by finding the most common number in a group of numbers.

motives (Ch. 2)—Anything within or outside the person that creates a desire.

motivation (Ch. 2)—Behavior put to action because of a desire or need.

multifactor theory of hunger (Append. A)—Suggests that food intake regulation is controlled by organ distensions in addition to brain areas.

N

neoanalysts (Ch. 4)—Those psychoanalysts who modified some of Freud's original views.

nerve cell (Append. A)—The basic functional unit for communication in animals and people.

nerves (Append. A)—Nerves are made up of neurons or nerve cells of various shapes and sizes.

neural impulse (Append. A)—The message or activity of an electrical nature that provide for bodily communication.

neurologist (Ch. 11)—A doctor who specializes in diseases of the nervous system and their cure.

neurosis (Ch. 10)—See psychoneurosis.

nondirective therapy (Ch. 11)—A form of therapy in which the therapist provides a relaxed, accepting atmosphere so that the patient may express his honest feelings without fear of rejection. The patient plays the active role.

normal distribution (Append. B)—The symmetrical bell-shaped curve that often results when numerical data is plotted on a graph. A requirement for using the standard deviation and sampling statistics.

O

object constancy (Ch. 7)—Objects do not seem to change in size, shape, and color as the distance between changes, even though the actual image on the retina changes in size.

objective (Ch. 10)—Outside the person; elements of one's external physical world.

objective personality tests (Ch. 11)—Tests designed to measure the complex ways of behaving, thinking, and feeling that determine personality as a whole. Responses are compared with those of other people, which have been judged as well-adjusted or poorly adjusted.

objective principles of learning (Ch. 2)—Related to external factors outside the person such as study techniques.

obsessive neurosis (Ch. 10)—The process wherein a person is forced to think about things that he does not want to think about. Guilt feelings and tension arise from these irrational thoughts because their constant flow keeps repressed problems from consciousness.

occupational therapy (Ch. 11)—A form of therapy used in mental hospitals to help patients learn and/or relearn certain occupations; it also helps the patient regain a sense of self-confidence and self-worth.

ophthamologist (Ch. 11)—A doctor who specializes in diseases of the eye and their cure.

organic psychosis (Ch. 10)—Severe mental disorder caused by injury to the nervous system.

ovum (Ch. 8)—Female sex cell.

paranoid defense (Ch. 10)—A defense consisting primarily of a logical and intricate delusional system. The personality may be quite normal and intact in all areas except that of the problem.

paranoid schizophrenia (Ch. 10)—The most common of schizophrenic defenses, it consists of trying to maintain feelings of self-esteem by projecting the blame for all failures onto others.

parasympathetic nervous system (Append. A)—The nerves of the system that come out of the brain and tail end of the spinal cord. The system serves a conservation function (e.g., decreasing heartbeat rate).

parental love (Ch. 4)—Caring for a child, desiring that which is best for him, but especially realizing that his life belongs to him. The love provided the child does not smother him but allows for skills on his part to finally achieve independence.

pathological (Ch. 10)—Extreme behavior that is considered abnormal.

peer group (Ch. 4)—People of similar ages or involvements.

penis (Ch. 11)—Male sex organ.

perceiving (Ch. 1)—Awareness of the world through the senses.

perception (Ch. 7)—The process of gathering information by means of the senses.

peripheral nervous system (Append. A)—The axons in areas outside the brain and spinal column.

personality (Ch. 8)—Consistent ways of behaving and thinking; all of the factors within a person that influence his characteristic ways of behaving, thinking, and feeling.

phi-phenomenon (Ch. 7)—Motion perceived as a function of the eyes providing a series of still shots that appear as continuous motion.

phobic neuroses (Ch. 10)—Symbolic, learned, and irrational fears of objects or situations that present no actual danger in the present situation.

physiological (Ch. 2)—Involving components and functions of organisms.

physiological psychologist (Append. A)—A psychologist who is typically involved in experimentation with animals, because his operations and procedures may damage the organism. His knowledge and interest relates to studying relationships between psychological events and their physiological (bodily function) counterparts.

play therapy (Ch. 11)—A method used with disturbed children to help them release emotions and to help the therapist derive clues as to areas of conflict.

population (Append. B)—A well-defined group that includes all the cases from which a sample is selected.

potentialities (Ch. 1)—What one is capable of doing or learning.

preschool learning (Ch. 4)—Learning, after the sensory-motor experience type until about age 2, that becomes more rapid and complex through language and thinking, until formal school training begins.

primates (Ch. 4)—The highest developed mammals, including among some members: man, apes, and monkeys.

problem solving (Ch. 3)—Methods or techniques used in solving a problem.

projection (Ch. 4)—The process of attributing to others what is true of ourselves and not true for others.

projection (Ch. 9)—Transferring or applying one's own emotions, behaviors, or wishes onto another person or persons. Oftentimes the desire is against our own or society's morals, so therefore use of this defense mechanism limits or prevents feelings of inadequacy.

projective personality tests (Ch. 11)—Tests composed of vague and unstructured stimuli (e.g., drawings) that are presented to a person for purposes of gaining his response.

Interpretation of these responses is based on the assumption that they were determined by inner feelings and ideas and allow insight into his inner world.

proximity (law of) (Ch. 7)—The process whereby objects join to form a new group because of closer spatial relationships.

psychiatric attendant (Ch. 11)—One who assists the patients in the various kinds of treatments.

psychiatric nurse (Ch. 11)—A registered nurse (RN) who specializes in working with mentally ill patients in clinics or hospitals.

psychiatric social worker (Ch. 11)—One who works with mental patients and their families in a clinic or hospital setting.

psychiatrist (Ch. 10)—A medical doctor who specializes in helping persons who are mentally ill to become better able to function in society.

psychoanalysis (Ch. 11)—A form of therapy in which the patient freely expresses feelings and thought (free association) as well as dreams in order to help the psychoanalyst determine some of the unconscious conflicts of the patient.

psychoanalyst (Ch. 11)—A medical doctor who is involved in the private practice of psychoanalysis, which is a special type of therapy based essentially on Freud's theory of personality.

psychodrama (Ch. 11)—A therapeutic practice wherein patients act out short scenes through playing different roles (e.g., their mothers, brothers, bosses, etc.) that may provide them insight into their particular problems as they relate to other people.

psychodynamics (Ch. 1)—Studying mental and developmental processes with concentration on the energy force behind them.

psychologist (Ch. 1)—One who applies the scientific method to describe and predict behavior.

psychoneurosis (Ch. 10)—A long-term process from unsuccessful problem solving to reality-oriented defenses and ego defenses resulting in mental disorders that usually do not require hospitalization.

psychopathic defense (Ch. 10)—Taking undue advantage of other people and engaging in antisocial and illegal activities without any feelings of guilt or concern.

psychopathology (Ch. 1)—Inadequate ways of relating to oneself, others, and the world in general.

psychosis (Ch. 10)—Extreme mental disorder with characteristics of emotional disturbance; disorganized thought processes; loss of person, time, and spatial orientation; and often hallucinations and delusions.

psychosomatic (Ch. 10)—See conversion defense.

psychotherapy (Ch. 5)—The psychological methods used in helping people with emotional problems.

psychotic defenses (Ch. 10)—Those defenses wherein the patients are maximally out of contact with their real world. Those defenses used in extreme mental disorder. (*See* psychosis)

R

range (Append. B)—A measure of variation obtained by subtracting the largest from the smallest number in a group of numbers.

rationalism (Ch. 5)—A philosophy that suggests man is in control of his behavior because he has the power to reason, think, and decide for himself.

rationalization (Ch. 9)—The process of attaching what we believe to be logical or socially acceptable reasons to our behavior instead of the real reasons.

real self (Ch. 4)—That part of the self-concept based on what the person feels or believes about himself.

receptors (Append. A)—Special types of nerve cells, including the senses, that are the mechanisms that take in energy charges and process them into information for nerves and neural transmission.

recreational therapy (Ch. 11)—A form of therapy used in mental hospitals to help patients develop self-confidence and self-worth through such activities as sports, crafts, dancing, drama, etc.

regression (Ch. 9)—The use of a form of behavior from an earlier age (e.g., pouting or temper tantrums).

remotivation (Ch. 11)—A technique used by psychiatric attendants as a technique for restimulating patients to have interest in their surroundings.

repression (Ch. 5)—The nonpurposeful or automatic act of forgetting some unpleasant feeling or thought that may cause a person to feel uncomfortable or guilty about the self-concept.

research (Ch. 1)—Use of the scientific method to study that which governs phenomena.

Rorschach Inkblot Test (Ch. 11)—A projective test in which the person is presented with a series of inkblots. Interpretation by the person of the forms provides the psychologist with information to analyze in determining the presence of mental problems or illness.

S

sample (Append. B)—A careful selection of representative members of a population who are studied in order to make inferences about the population.

sampling statistics (Append. B)—Mathematical procedures for making evaluative and predictive statements about a population from data based on samples.

schizophrenics (Ch. 10)—Those psychotics who are categorized by the general term *schizophrenia*, which includes a group of psychotic reactions characteristically involving unrealistic contact with the world, inappropriate emotions, delusions and hallucinations, and deterioration of personal habits.

self (Ch. 2)—General term for what one believes to be true about himself.

self-actualizing person (Ch. 1)—One who is in the process of developing all his abilities and potentials.

self-concept (Ch. 1)—How one characteristically feels and thinks about oneself.

self-realization (Ch. 4)—The fulfillment of one's potentialities (aptitudes and talents).

sensory-motor (Ch. 4)—Pertaining to processes involving interaction between the senses and physical movements.

sex roles (Ch. 4)—The ways of behavior prescribed by the society or culture that are appropriate to a male member or a female member.

sexual defenses (Ch. 10)—Exaggerated expressions of sexuality as a defense against feelings of inadequacy. Sexual outlets include pedophilia, exhibitionism, and others.

shape constancy (Ch. 7)—An object retains its shape when observed from many sides even though the angles at which it is seen change.

siblings (Ch. 8)—A term that refers to brothers or sisters without denoting sex.

similarity (Ch. 7)—Objects that look alike tend to be placed together more readily than disimilar objects when all of the objects are equally spaced.

simple schizophrenia (Ch. 10)—Indifferent, lacking interest or enthusiasm in any activity or topic; withdrawn, secluded, and asocial describe this defense. These people are borderline psychotics who seem content to live a simple, irresponsible existence.

situational transient neurosis (Ch. 10)—Abnormal behavior, usually not requiring hospitalization, caused by unusually severe crisis or by prolonged external stress. The symptoms typically disappear when the crisis ends, or shortly thereafter.

size constancy (Ch. 7)—Objects do not seem to change in size as the distance increases, regardless of the fact that the retinal image has changed size.

socialization (Ch. 4)—Learning social behavior.

social psychologist (Ch. 8)—A psychologist who focuses his study on those aspects of human behavior influenced by the presence of other persons. He is interested in behavior changes as a function of the social situation.

somatic (Ch. 10)—Referring to the body; bodily, as opposed to psychological origin.

somatic nervous system (Append. A)—That nervous system affecting skeletal control, and principally involving the body's voluntary processes.

specific hunger (Append. A)—Specialized type of hungers involving appetites for specific foods that contain dietary deficiencies.

sperm (Ch. 8)—Male sex cells.

standard deviation (Append. B)—The most common measure of variation of scores around the average. It provides a measure of the number of cases included in the range from the mean to different standard deviations on either side of the normal curve.

statistical significance (Append. B)—The minimal level of statistical probability required for acceptance of experimental results, usually the 5 per cent level.

statistics (Append. B)—Mathematical procedures for describing, analyzing, and evaluating numerical information.

stereotype (Ch. 8)—A very general way of grouping other people together on the basis of some preconceived and prejudiced idea of what they are like.

stimulus (Ch. 2)—Anything that produces thoughts and/or actions.

stress (Ch. 9)—Psychological strain produced by an occurrence or situation wherein a person experiences strong unpleasant emotional tensions.

subjective (Ch. 1)—Having to do with personal thoughts and feelings; within the person.

subjective principles of learning (Ch. 2)—Related to internal factors within the person, such as heredity or past experience.

subject (Ch. 1)—Persons or animals used in research studies.

supportive love (Ch. 4)—Realization by the parents that the child is developing into an individual with formation of his own self-concepts, will, and interests.

suppression (Ch. 9)—Purposeful forgetting or denial of situations, experiences, or feelings that were embarrassing to allow us to feel better about ourselves; the willful denial of emotions that are still felt.

symbols (Ch. 3)—A word or sign that represents an object or an idea.

sympathetic nervous system (Append. A)—Those nerves located in the central areas of the spinal cord that are excitatory and instigate action in incidences of emergency (e.g., increased heartbeat rate).

synapse (Append. A)—The area between nerve cells where the message or impulse jumps and is transferred to another neuron.

T

Thematic Apperception Test (TAT) (Ch. 11)—A projective test using a set of pictures that are not clearly drawn. In describing each picture the person is believed to be revealing how he feels about his own relationship to the world.

theories (Ch. 1)—Reasonable explanations.

therapeutic community (Ch. 11)—A form of group treatment used in mental hospitals to help the patient feel that he is part of the community. It will help him get better so that he can return to his real community in the outside world.

therapeutic helper (Ch. 10)—One who listens to and advises another person who may be undergoing a period of severe stress.

therapy (Ch. 11)—Treatment attempting to cure an abnormal psychological condition.

thinking (Ch. 3)—Attempts at solving a problem; usually referring to ideas that precede an action.

trait (Ch. 8)—A relatively stable personality characteristic revealed by consistency in the acts or behaviors of persons (honesty, emotionalism).

trait approach to personality (Ch. 8)—That approach to understanding personality based on the idea that all persons are different, and that the key to a person's personality consists of knowing his unique pattern of traits.

tranquilizers (Ch. 11)—Drugs that function as relaxers.

U

unconscious motives (Ch. 5)—Behavior that the person engages in without fully being able to explain all the reasons for it.

undoing (Ch. 9)—Involves reduction of emotional hurts such as guilt and anxiety by admitting the disapproved desire, idea, or behavior and apologizing for misdeeds or offering compensation for the damage done.

V

values (Ch. 4)—Ideas or goals that are learned by being rewarded as achievements. The person gradually learns to invest more desire and satisfaction in these acquired ideas or ways of relating to the world.

visual grouping (Ch. 7)—Visual experience established by arrangements of the stimuli to allow for forming collections.

W

Western civilization (Ch. 6)—History, culture and religions; usually associated with countries of Western Europe as opposed to Eastern Europe and Asia.

Author Index

Subject Index

441